Catholics BELIEVE

🌲 **BROWN-ROA**
A Division of Harcourt Brace & Company

REV. MICHAEL SAVELESKY

BROWN-ROA

A Division of Harcourt Brace & Company

O u r   M i s s i o n

The primary mission of BROWN-ROA is to provide the
Catholic and Christian educational markets with the
highest quality catechetical print and media resources.
The content of these resources reflects the best insights
of current theology, methodology, and pedagogical research.
The resources are practical and easy to use, designed to meet
expressed market needs, and written to reflect the
teachings of the Catholic Church.

CONTENTS

Introduction
HEARING *the* GOSPEL 2

The Acts of the Apostles **4**
  The experience of Paul 4
  Paul's message 7
Setting a pattern **8**

Chapter 1
IDENTITY *and* RESPONSIBILITY 14

Your faith response **16**
Physical responsibility **18**
  In the image of God *19*
Environmental responsibility **20**
Intellectual responsibility **23**
Personal responsibility **24**
Sexual responsibility **27**
Social responsibility **32**

Chapter 2
SALVATION *and* GRACE **36**

Have you been saved? **38**
Being saved **40**
  Grace *41*
Human needs **43**

Chapter 3
The NATURE *of* FAITH ... 50

Life questions **52**
Faith as trust **54**
  The Apostles' Creed *57*
Belonging to a Church **58**
Religion **58**
  Experienced religion 58
  Practiced religion 59
Faith **61**
  Searching faith 61
  Claimed faith 62
Stages of faith development **65**
  Pilgrim Church *66*
Prayer **67**

Chapter 4
GOD SPEAKS *Through* HISTORY **74**

Setting the stage on our religious history . . **76**
  Covenant 78
Sacred time **79**
The Israelites and time **82**
The history of Israel **83**
  The call of Abraham 83
  Joseph and his brothers 84
  Moses and the Exodus 85
  Wandering in the desert 87
  The Ten Commandments 88
  The conquest of the promised land 89

The period of the judges................ 89

The period of the kings 90

God's prophets..................... 92

Division and exile.................. 94

The return from exile and the reform 95

Greeks and Romans 97

The fall of Jerusalem 99

Modern Judaism **100**

Chapter 5
REVELATION and SCRIPTURE......... 106

Revelation: God's gift of himself **108**

The written word................... **112**

Authorship of Scripture: How the Bible came
to be.............................. 114

Inspiration **116**

The truth of Scripture...............**117**

Study tools **119**

The Old Testament..................**121**

Formation of the canon of Scripture ...**125**

Chapter 6
JEWISH RITES, RITUALS, and PEOPLE...128

The Jewish tradition **130**

Covenant relationship...............**130**

Worship **133**

Religious practices **135**

Important people...................**146**

Chapter 7
JESUS CHRIST 152

The Christian framework...........**154**

Claimed faith in Christ.............**159**

**God saves us through
the humanity of Jesus**...........**163**

Jesus was born 164

Jesus shared the human condition 164

Jesus lived...................... 166

The Beatitudes *166*

Jesus died...................... 169

Jesus was raised from the dead 170

Jesus is the Messiah of God **172**

Chapter 8
GOSPELS, LETTERS, and OTHER BOOKS...176

Discipleship **178**

The formation of Scripture..........**181**

The Letters **182**

The Gospels......................**186**

Types of literature in the Gospels **190**

The Acts of the Apostles............**196**

The Book of Revelation **198**

Chapter 9
A TRADITION of CHURCH, LITURGY, and SACRAMENTS 202

The Church **204**

The experience of Church **208**

Creed **212**

Fragmentation of Christ's Church.....**212**

Liturgy 216
Liturgical calendar 219
Sacraments 224
The seven sacraments of
   the Catholic Church 227
The role of the sacraments 228

Chapter 10
The SACRAMENTS of CHRISTIAN INITIATION . . . 232

Becoming a Christian 234
Christian initiation 239
The experience of initiation 239
Baptism 242
Confirmation 243
Eucharist 248
Parts of the Mass 252

Chapter 11
The SACRAMENTS of RECONCILIATION and HEALING 258

Awareness of sin 260
Naming sin 262
God's reconciling love made
   known in Jesus 266
The Church is a reconciling people 267
The Church's Sacrament of Penance . . . 270
Anointing of the Sick 276

Chapter 12
The SACRAMENTS of CHRISTIAN LIFE . . . 284

Christian life 286
Holy Orders 287
Single life choices 298
   Single life 299
   Consecrated life 301
   Consecrated community life 304
Matrimony 306

Chapter 13
DISCIPLESHIP 318

The call to discipleship 320
Call to sainthood 326
The perfect saint: Mary 331
Conclusion: Virtues 335

APPENDIX 338

GLOSSARY 342

INDEX 346

PHOTO CREDITS: Archive Photos—3, 235; Art Resource (La Scala)—85;Catholic News Service—39, 104, 241, 277, 290, 300, 303, 325; Nancy Anne Dawe—36-37; Editorial Development Associates—4, 5, 77, 78, 103, 131, 154, 238; Mimi Forsyth—91, 232-233, 269; FPG Internaitonal—101, 164, 206, 277 (inset); Robert Fried—81; Courtesy of GIA Publications—215; Richard Levine—133, 138, 144, 322; Gene Plaisted OSC/THE CROSIERS—2-3, 50-51, 53, 56, 89. 92, 122, 152-153, 159, 168, 179, 183, 193, 199, 205, 211, 217, 267; Frances Roberts—141, 143; Robert Roethig—46, 70-71; James L. Shaffer—9, 10, 11, 30, 69, 74-75, 87, 94, 109, 115, 128-129, 136, 144, 185, 209, 244, 258-259, 270, 272, 280, 287, 289, 295, 315, 320, 329; Skjold Photography—6, 20 bottom, 21 middle, 26, 29, 225, 264, 309, 324; Tony Stone—18 (Don Smetzer), 20 top (Andy Sacks), 64 (Mark PoKemper), 191 (Nick Gunderson), 284-285 (Claudia Kunin); Three Lions—134; D. Jeanene Tiner—176-177; Jim Whitmer—14-15, 21 top and bottom, 22, 24, 55, 67, 106-107, 118, 197, 236, 263, 298, 305, 311, 330; Bill and Peggy Wittman—16, 40, 63, 65, 83, 98, 111, 194, 202-203, 218, 228, 249, 251, 255, 305, 318-319, 334

HEARING *the* GOSPEL

The Word of the Lord

[Paul] began to proclaim Jesus in the synagogues, saying, "He is the Son of God."

FROM THE ACTS OF THE APOSTLES, SEE 9:10–20.

The material in this textbook isn't meant just to be read and given back on a test. This textbook presents an outline of the Christian faith. The basics will be presented, but you will have to do a great deal of reflecting and thinking along the way.

1702 Beginning of the Galilean Ministry

nto his barn, but
rn with unquench-

of Jesus.† 13 Then
Galilee to John at
e baptized by him.
prevent him, saying,
aptized by you, and
ning to me?" 15 Jesus
reply, "Allow it now,
fitting for us to fulfill
ness." Then he allowed
er Jesus was baptized,
from the water and be-
eavens were opened [for
the Spirit of God

the parapet of the temple, 6 and said
to him, "If you are the Son of God,
throw yourself down. For it is written:

'He will command his angels
concerning you'
and 'with their hands they will
support you,
lest you dash your foot against
a stone.'"

7 Jesus answered him, "Again it is
written, 'You shall not put the Lord,
your God, to the test.'" 8 Then the
devil took him up to a very high
mountain, and showed him all the
kingdoms of the world in their mag-

The Beatitudes

the way to the
Jordan,
Galilee of the
16 the people wh
have seen a
on those dwell
shadowe
light has ar

17† From that tim
to preach and sa
kingdom of heav
The Call of t
18 As he was w
Galilee, he saw
who is called P
Andrew, castin
they were fish
them, "Come
ake you fis

To you, O LORD, I lift up my soul.
O my God, in you I trust . . . .

Let Us Pray

Make me to know your ways, O LORD;
teach me your paths.
Lead me in your truth, and teach me,
for you are the God of my salvation;
for you I wait all day long.
Be mindful of your mercy, O LORD, and of your steadfast love,
for they have been from of old.
Do not remember the sins of my youth or my transgressions;
according to your steadfast love remember me,
for your goodness' sake, O LORD!
Good and upright is the LORD;
therefore he instructs sinners in the way.
He leads the humble in what is right,
and teaches the humble his way.
All the paths of the LORD are steadfast love and faithfulness,
for those who keep his covenant and his decrees. . . .

PSALM 25:1–2, 4–10

1703   MATTHEW

lem, and Judea, and from bey
the Jordan followed him.

kness

over-

CHAPTER 5

The Sermon on the M

1† When he saw the crowds,
up the mountain, and after
sat down, his disciples cam
2 He began to teach them

The Beatitudes

us began
t, for the
and."
isciples.†
the Sea of
rs, Simon
his brother
to the sea;
He said to
, and I will
en." 20† At
d followed

3† "Blessed are the po
for theirs is the
heaven.
4† Blessed are they
for they will be
5† Blessed are the r
for they will ir
6† Blessed are the

The town square in Athens

Aeropagus, Athens, site of Paul's preaching

THE ACTS OF THE APOSTLES

Acts of the Apostles
book in the New Testament which tells the story of the early Church

apostle
literally, one who is sent; one of twelve men chosen by Jesus to be his closest followers and, after Jesus' death and resurrection, responsible for preaching the gospel and unifying the Christian community

gospel
the good news of Jesus

Paul
a Christian convert after Jesus' resurrection who eventually became known as the *apostle to the Gentiles* (non-Jews)

missionary
one sent on a task, such as taking the good news of Jesus to others, especially those in another area

The opening reading for this chapter is from the **Acts of the Apostles** (often called *Acts*). Perhaps you are already familiar with this "book" since it's found in the New Testament of the Bible. Those who study Scripture don't know exactly why this particular book was written or why it was made part of Scripture by the Christian community. Nevertheless, it helps us understand the life of the first Christians.

Included in this book are speeches by some of the **apostles** and other early followers of Jesus. In their speeches, these Christians proclaimed the **gospel**, the good news of Jesus. Other sections of the Acts of the Apostles read like a diary which someone might have written about the events which shaped the early Church.

The Scripture reading at the beginning of this Introduction is about the conversion of St. **Paul**. Paul (also known as Saul) became a follower of Jesus some time after Jesus' resurrection. He eventually became known as an apostle, even though he was not one of the Twelve. Paul changed from a persecutor of the first Christians to their greatest **missionary**.

The experience of Paul

Paul set off to share the good news in many cities and towns along the Mediterranean coast from Palestine to Rome. In chapter 17 of Acts, we read about an experience Paul had while preaching the gospel in the ancient Greek city of Athens. This story offers some important tips for anyone who preaches, teaches, or studies religion.

A little background information may be helpful. In Paul's day there were no schools like the one you're attending. Education was not common. Only boys, and only those from wealthy families, had the luxury of learning. They were taught by a master hired by their parents. More often than not, these teachers were well trained in three basic subjects: reading, writing, and public speaking.

When Paul was about your age, he attended such a school. As a result Paul was an educated man who knew his way around the Greek-speaking world. He was very familiar with its way of thinking and he knew where to go to get attention: the town square!

In Paul's day Greek men used to gather in the town square to exchange gossip, do business, and share ideas—in much the same way you may spend time in the mall on a lazy Saturday afternoon. At their leisure the Greeks discussed such questions as: What is truth? Is there eternal life? What is social responsibility?

Very few of these conversations had any practical impact on their daily lives. These Greeks enjoyed gathering in this fashion, nonetheless, to share ideas and meet people. Occasionally a special speaker would come to the city and take a turn at the town square's speaking stand. A visitor like this would provide a break from the usual speakers and, for that reason, would attract some measure of attention. Quite often this special visitor would be what the Greeks called a *protagonist*, a person who made a living from promoting his ideas, such as his particular approach to religion. Paul's visit to Athens, then, was not entirely a surprise and was not unusual.

With this background, let's return now to chapter 17 of the Acts of the Apostles. Like others who wanted to attract the attention of people, Paul took his turn at the speaking stand. He announced the good news of what God had done for people everywhere through Jesus.

Paul began his presentation with a simple but careful observation: "I see how extremely religious you are in every way." Just from looking around the town square, he noticed that the Greeks had built temples to various gods and had made statues of many of them. Most likely, they had constructed a temple there for the god of war, another for the god of rivers, another for the god of love—and certainly several others, since, like us, the Greeks wanted to "cover all the bases"!

Talk about it

Pretend that you have just arrived in this country. Take time to look around and watch people. Make a list of the signs that tell you the people you meet are religious.

1. What are the obvious signs?

2. What are the less obvious and more subtle ones?

Write it down

Would you describe yourself as a religious person? Why?

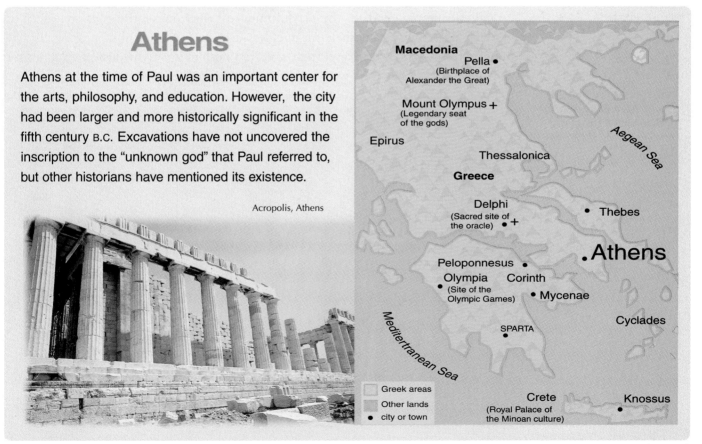

Athens

Athens at the time of Paul was an important center for the arts, philosophy, and education. However, the city had been larger and more historically significant in the fifth century B.C. Excavations have not uncovered the inscription to the "unknown god" that Paul referred to, but other historians have mentioned its existence.

Acropolis, Athens

Macedonia
Pella ●
(Birthplace of Alexander the Great)

Mount Olympus +
(Legendary seat of the gods)

Epirus

Aegean Sea

Thessalonica

Greece

Delphi
(Sacred site of the oracle) ● +

● Thebes

Peloponnesus ●

Olympia
(Site of the Olympic Games) ●

Corinth

● Mycenae

●Athens

Mediterranean Sea

SPARTA ●

Cyclades

Crete
(Royal Palace of the Minoan culture)

Knossus ●

Greek areas
Other lands
● city or town

The unknown god

Paul's attention was drawn to a temple dedicated "To an unknown god." Paul's sharp eye noticed something of great importance for his missionary effort. He noted that the people of Athens were trying to find happiness and fulfillment in their lives—but on a surface level.

Paul noticed that they were struggling to pay attention to something beyond their normal daily experience, something not even covered by their many gods. To Paul the fact that the Greeks in Athens had built a temple to an "unknown god" showed that they were unhappy with the other gods they worshiped. These Greeks were looking for something more, something to satisfy a deeper, inner yearning in their hearts.

After paying respect to the religious feelings of the people, Paul drew special attention to their unusual temple. "*This* is the God I have come to tell you about," he proudly announced. He then went on to tell them how this unknown God for whom the Greeks of Athens were searching was not unknown at all, but had entered human history in the person of Jesus of Nazareth—a real person, someone who had been born and had lived in a real time and a real place.

The God Paul wanted people to know wasn't a human-made god, a statue of "gold, or silver, or stone, an image formed by the art and imagination of mortals" (Acts 17:29). The God Paul wanted people to know was the Creator, the living God of Israel whose love was without measure, so much so that he sent his Son to live among us. Especially important for Paul to share was the fact that Jesus wasn't a made-up or imaginary god. Jesus didn't just appear and disappear like some fictitious Star Wars figure; he had a history; he was real.

The Greeks used to talk about how their gods could make sudden appearances on earth, sometimes even taking human form. They had no direct experience of these appearances, but they did have good imaginations! These brief appearances rarely brought about any good. In the playful minds of the Greeks, the gods were seen as carrying out their antics, their meaningless actions, and then disappearing. In the popular Greek way of thinking, these gods did nothing for individual people, nor for the human race. They truly were **myths** in the negative sense of that word.

Write it down

1. What do you believe about God?
2. When did you come to believe this?

Then do this

Read the daily newspaper for one week.

1. Identify four stories in which people seem to be "looking for God," but in which their search takes them to "all the wrong places and all the wrong faces."
2. Write a paragraph on each story, explaining how the people involved are allowing themselves to be misled.

myth
a traditional story that explains something about a worldview or a belief or practice; a story about the gods or God

The ruins of a temple in Athens

Paul's message

Although he was well-formed in the Jewish faith tradition, Paul didn't confuse his Greek audience with details about his Jewish faith. He cut to the heart of the matter. He spoke to them in ways they could understand. He talked about the things that concerned them. He spoke of the deep mysteries of human experience: life, death, and the desire for eternal life. Paul knew that a detailed background about Jewish history was not essential for understanding the truth of the message he'd come to announce, the good news he'd come to share.

So Paul briefly explained the gospel to his Greek audience in terms they could understand from their own experience. He wanted his listeners to accept the *known* God in such a way that their relationship with this God would lead them to the fullness of life that they obviously were seeking. He had something important to offer.

The religion Paul preached wasn't one of imaginary gods and merely human ideas. Paul taught about a God in whom "we live and move and have our being"; he told the people of Athens that everyone is a child of God, who has revealed or made himself known in Jesus.

The Jesus whom Paul preached had lived and loved and taught and died in a real place, Palestine (known as *Israel* before that time and again today), and had risen and is with us always. For Paul what God had done in Jesus was of extreme importance for people everywhere—including the people of Greece. Because of Jesus, all people could be assured of resurrection and eternal life with God.

Paul appealed to the people to freely accept the good news of God's love revealed in Jesus. He appealed to them to let go of their lifeless, human-made gods and to open their hearts to the living God of Israel who had made himself known in Jesus.

The response Paul received was interesting. Some people laughed at him and returned to their shallow lifestyles. Most likely, they continued to offer sacrifices to their marble and bronze gods. Others merely found Paul entertaining and wanted him to stay around for a longer discussion. His words hadn't touched their hearts. It was just that the other subjects brought to the town square were becoming boring.

A few—only a few—wished to explore more closely the news Paul brought. They invited him to their homes and opened their hearts to the news about Jesus. This was likely the beginning of a small Christian community at Athens. Paul had been able to move these listeners to greater self-awareness and honesty about the deeper needs in their lives. Paul preached, and the people of Athens heard the gospel, not just with their ears, but with their hearts. The good news took them beyond the daily pattern of their lives and the worship of human-made gods who couldn't give them true life.

Talk about it

1. If someone were to have a discussion with you about your personal belief in God, how would you want that person to treat you?

2. Why is it important not to condemn or make fun of the religious practices of others?

Talk about it

1. If Paul were speaking today, what might he say about the way people live?

2. How would you react to Paul's message?

Write it down

1. Who are the people who have most influenced your understanding of God?

2. How have they influenced you?

3. What difference will they make to the way you live your faith in the future?

We have spoken frankly to you . . . ; our heart is wide open to you.

There is no restriction in our affections, but only in yours.

In return—I speak as to children—open wide your hearts also.

2 Corinthians 6:11–12

Those who have welcomed Christ's call and have responded in freedom are urged on by the love of Christ to proclaim the good news to the whole world. This treasure, received from the apostles, has been faithfully guarded by their successors, the bishops. All the followers of Christ are called to pass on the faith to the next generation. They do this by professing the faith, living it lovingly, and celebrating that faith with liturgy and prayer.

See the *Catechism of the Catholic Church*, #3.

1. What good news does the world still need to hear?
2. What do you suppose Christ's call is?
3. What does it mean to "pass on the faith"?
4. How do ordinary people "pass on the faith" to those around them? How do parents do this? How do you do this?
5. How are bishops successors of the apostles? Why is this connection important?

SETTING A PATTERN

evangelization
the process of sharing the good news of Jesus and the reign of God

As we begin this course, let's look at Paul's method of **evangelization**, or method of sharing the good news about Jesus and the reign of God which he proclaimed.

Observant

faith
belief in someone or something and trust in a person or in God

First of all, **Paul was observant**. He didn't plow through the town square at Athens with a bulldozer, smashing the statues of the gods of the Greeks. Had he done so, he would have been one of the quickest human sacrifices Athens had seen in years! Rather, Paul was patiently observant. He began his task with the deep awareness that God had already been there ahead of him. He had **faith** that God moves in every human heart, including those of the intellectual Greeks. Their temple to the "unknown god" was convincing evidence.

Write it down

1. When have you felt the presence of God?
2. How did you feel when you felt God's presence?
3. Have you told anyone about this experience? Why or why not? If yes, how did the person react?

Your study this year will be a religious experience—but not the first religious experience of your life! You are already known and loved by God. God has already been at work in your life. You already have a sense in your heart of God's presence. Perhaps you have been practicing your religion for years in a Catholic parish or in some other Christian faith community.

The purpose of the chapters in this textbook is to open your eyes more consciously to the presence of God in your life. The message of Jesus and the practice of your faith are important parts of your teenage years. Like the hearts of the ancient Greeks, your own heart longs to be in touch with the living God.

Then do this

Pretend you are a Christian missionary speaking to a group of street kids. Write a brief talk about the importance of Jesus Christ in their lives. Explain what it means to be known and loved by God. Make sure your words of wisdom meet the young people at those points where *they* are searching.

Reverent

Second, **Paul was reverent**. You already realize that most people actually have a variety of what we could call "gods"—things, activities, and relationships that they turn to for happiness and fulfillment. These gods aren't the statues of the ancient Greek gods, like Zeus and Hermes. Today our "gods" are dollar bills, cars, grades, sports trophies, television sets, beautiful bodies, computer networks, and designer clothes. We don't often gather in town squares. Instead, we rush along freeways, stroll through malls, gather in clusters at fast-food restaurants, and chat on the Internet.

reverent
respectful, holding in awe

Some of the things we value are good; others aren't. Some are valued too much by some people; some are not valued enough. In all of the material things we hold up as "gods," we are searching for happiness and peace. This happiness and peace can be found only inside ourselves, where we meet the living and true God. When our lesser "gods" take over our lives, they choke our spirits and dull our hearts. It's important to not let this happen. It's important to live life with God in mind, to remember what really matters, to keep to the path God has set before us—to live reverently.

Paul paid respect to the genuine search for God that he found in the midst of the busy lifestyle of the Greeks in Athens. So, too, does this textbook. No one will bulldoze away the gods you have created and demand absolute attention to the things of God and religion. You are a free person created in the image of God; you are a child of God. So you are presented with a great challenge. If you live up to the challenge, you will in time freely set aside the created "gods" that hold you back from living in right relationship with God and others.

There should be no competition between genuine religion and life. Faith and religion are *part* of life. Religion is false and artificial if it's separate from life and born of false gods. Likewise, life that isn't guided by the light of faith is empty and without direction; life without faith is life without hope.

Therefore, this year you will touch on the basic truths of the Christian faith. If all goes well, you will be led to real living of that faith—the wholesome practice of your religion. Too often religion is seen as just another subject on which students are merely tested for information. This course, on the other hand, ought to help you open up and appreciate the gift of faith.

Write it down

1. When have you felt reverent?

2. When has someone treated you with reverence?

Then do this

Interview five adults who are Christians. Ask them why their relationship with Jesus is life-giving for them. Write up the results of your interviews and your conclusions.

Be subject to one another out of reverence for Christ.

Ephesians 5:21

Forthright

Paul was forthright. Like Paul's presentation in the busy town square at Athens, this textbook makes no excuses about concentrating on the significance of Jesus for your self-understanding as a human and your relationship with God. Nothing you find here will belittle the good found in other world religions.

At the same time, this book clearly affirms that God has revealed himself in a unique way in Jesus. It further affirms that what God has done in Jesus is offered as the gift of saving **grace** for all. It will save all who accept it and embrace it as a source of life and truth.

In that light you will reflect on what it means to follow Jesus from the viewpoint of the Catholic tradition. Several other Christian denominations give wholesome expression to many important aspects of the Christian tradition. The Catholic Church, however, considers itself fully to be historically the same community which Jesus founded. This doesn't make saints of the members of this Church, but it does recognize the long and valuable history of the Christian Church from the time of Jesus himself. As Catholics we believe that the Holy Spirit continues to guide the Church.

grace
God's life and love in us; God's help to do what is right

Talk about it
Have you ever had an opportunity to share your experience of God with someone of a different faith or a different Christian tradition? What did you say?

Then do this
Imagine that you are a youth minister and that your youth group is going to a village in another country to help build a water system. The villagers are not Christians. Write down the instructions you would give your youth group.

Changing methods

How to share the gospel? This question is always relevant. The methods of sharing the gospel vary with different circumstances: time, place, culture. The pastors of the Church are responsible for reshaping the gospel message for people today. They must do this boldly and with wisdom, and they must use suitable methods that communicate well.

See Pope Paul VI, *On Evangelization in the Modern World*, #40.

1. How are our times different from those of St. Paul? How are they the same?

2. What tools for handing on the gospel did Paul not have that you can use today?

Skillful teacher

Paul was a skillful teacher. Ages ago when Paul brought the good news of Jesus to the people of Athens, he spoke to them in language they could understand. He used their images and experiences to help them see beyond where they were to what could be for them. Paul opened the door to a new experience of God for these people.

Over time Paul became known as a great apostle of the Christians. He became the "apostle to the Gentiles." Paul traveled far and wide to Jewish communities from Palestine to Greece and eventually to Rome. Everywhere he preached the gospel, not just to the Jews but especially to non-Jews. He adapted his message to address the concerns of Jews who had a close connection with Israel, Jews who were culturally Greek or Roman, and non-Jews who were Greek or Roman. People in each group were touched and responded.

But Paul didn't leave people behind when he moved on. He left good and trusted people in charge of new Christian communities. He wrote to these leaders and these communities often. In his letters he praised and challenged, he corrected and explained. Always the teacher, he continued to be a major influence in the lives of those he had brought to the faith.

In every age the Church needs leaders and teachers like Paul. Today such leaders and teachers abound, from the pope to the catechist in a small parish to the parent of a small child. While some speak with more authority than others, all are called to be skillful teachers of the faith. You too are called to share the gifts with which God has blessed you to teach, lead, inspire, and walk with those who journey through life with you. You are not too young to take on this responsibility.

Talk about it

What do you look for in a good pastor or Church worker or religion teacher? Why?

Then do this

At church this weekend, listen carefully to the homily. In an essay describe how the homilist was or wasn't able to bring the good news of Jesus and of the kingdom of God to you at your level of understanding.

> For *this I was appointed a herald and an apostle*
> *(I am telling the truth, I am not lying),*
> *a teacher of the Gentiles in faith and truth.*
> **1 Timothy 2:7**

CONCLUSION

In our culture, where computers do so much of our "thinking," your task of reflecting on the basics of the Christian faith won't necessarily come easily. But that's all right. Studying takes work! By the end of this course, those who make the effort to study the good news and reflect on it will be more educated in the Christian faith. If you're willing to relate this study to your life, you will become a stronger, more committed believer.

Ultimately, you are responsible for what you learn. More importantly, you are responsible for the quality of life you have in relationship with Jesus Christ. This course will not involve you in empty talk, like that which was frequent in the town squares of the Greeks, where opinions were argued just for the sake of argument.

Rather, this course will help you hand on the good news about a God who still is unknown to many people (perhaps even in your own school), a God who seeks to reveal the saving love in Jesus. A major part of growing up is accepting responsibility for your life and embracing a community of faith in and through which you can grow. The goal of this course will be at least partially accomplished if you come to a deeper understanding and appreciation of your Christian faith and the Church which shares that faith with you.

Peace be to the whole community,
and love with faith,
from God the Father and the Lord Jesus Christ.
Grace be with all who have an undying love
for our Lord Jesus Christ.
Ephesians 6:23–24

Mission

The mission of the Church is carried out in obedience to Christ. It is motivated by the grace and love of the Holy Spirit. The Church is present to all people in order to lead them to the faith, freedom, and peace of Christ. It does this by its living example, its teaching, the sacraments, and other means of grace. Its aim is to provide the means for everyone to participate in the mystery of Christ.

See *The Documents of Vatican II*, "Decree on the Church's Missionary Activity," #5.

1. What is the purpose of the Church?
2. Why must the Church do more than just increase its membership?
3. What does the Church do for people?
4. How can you be part of the Church's mission?

Talk about it

1. Why do Christian Churches send missionaries to other countries?

2. Whom does God love more: the Christian who goes to church regularly, the holy person who is not Christian, or the **atheist**?

   • What is the challenge God presents to each of these types of people?

   • What should a Christian's attitude be toward people in these three groups?

atheist
someone who believes there is no God

Words you should know

Acts of the Apostles	**grace**
apostle	**missionary**
atheist	**myth**
evangelization	**Paul**
faith	**reverent**
gospel	

CHAPTER 1

IDENTITY *and* RESPONSIBILITY

CHAPTER OVERVIEW

- *Your faith response*
- *Physical responsibility*
- *Environmental responsibility*
- *Intellectual responsibility*
- *Personal responsibility*
- *Sexual responsibility*
- *Social responsibility*

The Word of the Lord

I am confident of this that the one who began a good work among you will bring it to completion by the day of Jesus Christ.

FROM THE LETTER TO THE PHILIPPIANS; SEE 1:3–6, 9–11.

Let Us Pray

Happy are those
who do not follow the advice of the wicked,
or take the path that sinners tread,
*   or sit in the seat of the scoffers;*
but their delight is in the law of the LORD,
*   and on his law they meditate day and night.*
They are like trees
*   planted by streams of water,*
* which yield their fruit in its season,*
*   and their leaves no not wither.*
In all that they do, they prosper.
The wicked are not so,
*   but are like chaff that the wind drives away.*
Therefore the wicked will not stand in the judgment,
*   nor sinners in the congregation of the righteous;*
for the LORD *watches over the way of the righteous,*
*   but the way of the wicked will perish.*

PSALM 1

YOUR FAITH RESPONSE

culture
the beliefs, social forms, and material traits of a group

responsibility
accountability, reliability, trustworthiness

In the Introduction of this book, you caught a glimpse of the early Christian apostle, Paul, who sought to bring the gospel to people of other lands and **cultures**. Paul didn't try to force his religion on his listeners. He spoke to them "where they lived," as they were—where they were searching for fullness of life. He also called upon them to take **responsibility** for their lives by asking honest questions about themselves and their culture, their usual ways of thinking about and doing things. He wanted them to be open to the good news he came to share, to let it speak to their hearts.

Although Paul respected their right to have their own opinions, he appealed to their sense of maturity. He asked them to be open to the good news of the gospel because it would lead them to the happiness they were seeking.

What is the good news? That God is love and that we are surrounded by love. Jesus was that love in-the-flesh, in human history. The call of his gospel is the call to live our lives in union with him and his way of loving and thereby make a difference in the lives of people we meet. This is a constant challenge.

Even if you were born into a Christian home, you yourself need to respond to the call of the gospel and take personal responsibility for that response. This is especially true as you grow older and develop a deeper sense of being your own person. Your faith response is always ongoing. It needs to be made continuously, right "where you live." That means as you are, where you're at, with your friends or your family . . . today, tomorrow, and every day.

Saying "yes" to the good news is different than buying a new poster to hang on your bedroom wall. It isn't an over-and-done task. The challenge of the gospel is the constant call to take a serious look at your life in light of what God has done for you in Jesus. It is a constant challenge to put it into practice in the way you live.

Write it down
What does the phrase *take personal responsibility* mean to you?

Then do this
A well-known magazine asked children and teenagers these two questions:

1. Who is God?
2. What would you ask God if you could?

The young people were told to respond with photos. Do the same:

1. Take a photo of something that, for you, answers one of the questions.
2. Share the photo with the class, and explain your reasons for choosing it.

Eusebio Francisco Kino
Missionary to the Americas

Since the time of Paul, thousands of people have become missionaries, bringing the good news to people all over the world. They responded to the challenge of the gospel wholeheartedly with the witness of their lives.

Eusebio Francisco Kino was an early missionary to the present-day United States. He was born in Italy in 1645. While a student, Kino met a Spaniard, now known as St. Francis Xavier, who was a missionary to the Far East. Kino joined the Jesuits when he was a young man, hoping also to do missionary work in Asia. However, in 1680 after becoming a priest, he was sent to Mexico. In addition to his work as a priest, Kino was the official map-maker for a colonizing expedition in lower California.

Eventually Fr. Kino established several missions in the present-day southwest of the United States. His maps and written reports provided valuable information on this new territory. Kino is credited with the beginnings of cattle ranching and the farming of many European fruits and grains in the southwest.

The most well-known mission established by Fr. Kino is located near Tucson, Arizona, and is named after his early acquaintance, San Xavier del Bac. Since the 1760s, Franciscans have served the Native Americans of the area. The present small, beautiful church was built in 1783 and is referred to as the "White Dove of the Desert."

Optional activities

1. Use the Internet or other sources to find out more about Eusebio Francisco Kino. What can you apply to your life from his life and experiences?

2. Do a presentation on the mission of San Xavier del Bac. Include some details of the work of the Franciscans at the mission today.

"RESPONSE-ABILITY"

By this time in your life, you may be tired of having people tell you to BE RESPONSIBLE. There may even be a chance that you aren't quite ready to accept the challenge. Perhaps you just would rather not have to grow up and deal with the world around you. Being responsible is one of the greatest challenges for maturing young men or women. We cannot escape it, because life itself calls us to respond to all that it offers.

It continues to be a great challenge for adults, too! Being responsible doesn't mean being without limitations and controls, those, for example, that parents, school, Church, and society place on you. Responsibility is the capacity to make *your own* response to life.

Literally, in fact, the word *responsibility* means "able to respond" to life, able to do what you're supposed to do. Responsible persons have the ability to make personal choices—choices that are reflected in the things they do and in the things they refuse to do. At this stage of your growth and development, you are "able to respond" in a variety of ways to the world around you.

Talk about it
What is *in*correct about this statement: "Teenagers are the Church of tomorrow"? What may be correct about it?

None of us is responsible for all the things that happen to us, but we are responsible for the way we act when they do happen.

PHYSICAL RESPONSIBILITY

Obviously the body you have is the one you'll have for life, give or take a few replaceable parts! Part of growing as a responsible person is learning to value your body, learning to appreciate the connection between your mind, your body, and the way you choose to be present and active in the world around you. You simply cannot be someone else's body—no matter how often television commercials and magazine ads may invite you to look like someone you're not.

As you've learned by now, the unique combination of your mother's egg and your father's sperm which became *you* was the beginning of a unique adventure in human history. *You* have never existed before and another *you* will never exist again. *You* are *you*—and wonderfully so!

How you feel about yourself, your personal identity, has a lot to do with how you feel about your own body. People tend to compare their bodies with other people's. When you look at someone else's body, you are looking into a kind of mirror of yourself and your own development. It's only natural that you would compare your development with that of others.

Then do this

Make a collage from newspaper and magazine ads which try to set standards of what the "beautiful" person should be. Explain the collage and your response to the class.

What isn't natural, and isn't good, is all the television and movie and magazine fuss about looking a certain way. We're not supposed to look a certain way just to make someone else happy or rich. Each person is different, and that's the real beauty of it!

When people aren't comfortable with their bodies, they sometimes develop a negative self-image or compare themselves wrongly to what another person looks like. Some people call this the "What If" game. What if you had prettier hair? What if you had bigger hands? What if you didn't have acne? This kind of self put-down leads nowhere except to isolation, senseless competition, and possible depression.

Negative comparisons breed resentment and deny the unique beauty which is yours as a son or daughter of God. Your body is your personal way of being present in the world. You might as well be proud of your body and make the best of it! There's not going to be another—no matter what advances in cloning the next one hundred years may bring. You are the person your body uniquely allows *you* to be.

The **genetic** combination which is *you* is absolutely awesome! As your body has grown, you have gradually come to realize what a marvelous tool and instrument of discovery it is. At the same time, you have come to realize that *you* are more than your body. You are your *self.* Gradually, you have come to learn how to use your bodily powers to carry your *self* into the world, as it were. You have learned how to make your presence heard and felt.

At this stage of your life, as your body matures and develops, you're able to do more with it. Perhaps that's why sports take on such importance in the lives of many adolescents. It's fun to develop muscle tone and the needed skills to shoot, hit, toss, kick, and chase balls of a whole variety of shapes and sizes. Music is another area in which young people expand on their talents and learn to perform with excellence. It's great to hear the cheers of others as they acknowledge your performance.

Many talents and skills are less physical and more mental. Often these aren't acknowledged by other young people, but they are very important to those who are developing the necessary skills. Examples are the talents for art, writing, speech-giving, acting, science, and learning other languages.

With this self-discovery comes more and more ability to respond. The more parents, teachers, and others give you the freedom to make your own way in the world around you, the more responsibility you have for what you do *to* and *with* your body. You are "able to respond" maturely as a physical self—you have physical responsibility.

genetic
relating to or determined by the origin or development of something; related to the traits carried in genes

Write it down
Make a list of ways other people learn about you.

REVIEW

1. What is the good news that Paul shared?
2. What does it mean to be responsible? To take responsibility for your life?
3. How does the way you feel about your body influence your personal identity?
4. What does it mean to say that your body is your personal way of being present in the world?
5. What does physical responsibility mean?

ENVIRONMENTAL RESPONSIBILITY

When you were little, you undoubtedly gained a great deal of attention by screaming, kicking, and storming around, or by just lying there smiling. You could make people change, even if the lasting effect was rather limited. You could influence—make changes in—your **environment**, the world around you.

At the same time, your surroundings had more effect on you than you had on them. The world, the people in your life, contributed to your self-image. In a sense, they made you who you are; in important ways they had a deep impact on the formation of your talents and skills, your hopes and dreams. These are important gifts in your life. Taking them seriously, appreciating how much they are true gifts, and using them are important parts of maturing as a young man or woman, of being a responsible person. Just think of the many important gifts in your life and their effect on you! Consider the following.

environment
the world around a person; where a person lives and the social, economic, and political atmosphere in the family, neighborhood, school, and Church

Write it down
If you could keep only five of your possessions, what would they be? Why?

Talk about it
What are the characteristics of a healthy home environment?

Talk about it
What kind of parenting skills are needed to help teenagers grow into young adulthood?

Write it down
What do you think are the qualities of an ideal family? Why is each quality important?

Home

The physical environment of your home was—and is—a gift that has shaped you profoundly. Just think of how much your surroundings have provided for your needs—the shelter, the warmth, the light, the places to be alone, the places to be together, the meals, the rest, the place to sleep and to wake; the room to grow. For you, this may include everything from carpeted floors, toys, and refrigerators to bicycles, pizza, and perhaps a computer. Everyone is affected by the elements of environment. But the important thing is not how many things you can collect; the important thing is how the things you have shape you.

Family

The members of your family have been an important part of your growing environment. This is true whether you're an only child or part of a small or large family. Scientists have made fascinating discoveries about the roles we adopt in the family and how much the interplay of all the members has on one another. Some people are so affected by their family surroundings that they even pick up certain family-identifying mannerisms. And without a doubt, all of us have picked up our basic value system from our families.

You have walked through life with your family and, in different ways, you always will. Together you learn, together you care, together you become better people. There is no greater influence than family—sometimes positive, sometimes negative. Communication in the family isn't always easy, but the responsibility to work at that communication brings its own reward. Your family gives you the opportunity to be understanding and patient, but most of all, it helps you experience love and learn to love in return.

Church

For many people, the connection with a community of faith, a Church, is an extremely important part of growing up and being responsible. This is true both in terms of going to church (and to Bible school, religious education classes, or Catholic schools) and in terms of how much just "going to church" has added to their lives. The regular practice of their religious tradition helps people form an identity and a value system that reaches very deep into their lives—much deeper than they may recognize.

This practice of your faith is an important part of your spiritual responsibility. As a human, you are called to grow in every way, including spiritually. Your Church community is there to assist you. Your faith environment is a gift in your life. Gratefully treasure and use it; the more you do, the more—like gold—it will shine.

Write it down

1. Write a letter to God. In your letter, explain how you experience him. Explain as well how you are spiritually growing at this time, and ask for God's grace to grow in an area that concerns you.

2. Write a letter from God to you explaining God's hopes and dreams for you twenty years from now.

Then do this

Interview a classmate or a friend. How is that person's Church community an important part of his or her personal growth?

Society

None of us can exist alone. Paraphrasing the poet John Donne, we can say that "No one is an island." We are all interconnected; by nature we are social animals. We need others in order to survive, we need others in order to grow, and we need others in order to be happy. It is through one another—a network of people and activities—that we learn to know ourselves and our place in the world.

Society helps you be conscious of yourself. It shapes the way you see the world around you, with all its challenges, surprises, and all its hopes. It's your responsibility, everyone's responsibility, to do everything possible to see that all people are free of suffering and are happy, and that all creation is cared for. Working together, this responsibility can be met.

Write it down

Write a brief personal biography.

1. Indentify the people, places, and events that have shaped you.

2. Identify how the way you've been raised has prepared you to be responsible for yourself and for your actions.

Action springs not from thought, but from a readiness for responsibility.
Dietrich Bonhoeffer

All the gifts

Talk about it

Sit down with a classmate or friend and give yourselves ten minutes to work independently to make a list of all the gifts in your life for which you are grateful. Call "Time!" and then compare lists.

By means of all these—home, family, Church, and society—you enter into this exciting stage of life with a marvelous package of gifts. The mature person is the one who deeply appreciates the gifts of life and who uses those gifts to help the world. The mature person gradually comes to realize that he or she is now responsible for the way he or she affects the world. You have been given so much! You are able now to take control, assume responsibility, use your gifts, create an environment in which you can grow. You too are called to become a gift yourself.

This is a rather powerful position to hold. Perhaps you already can see the effect you have on younger brothers or sisters at home, the effect your behavior has on your home environment. Perhaps you have already noticed the difference your participation in the Church youth group makes, or the power of peer pressure in your school. These are all experiences of moving from an environment you have been given to an environment you deliberately create, from what you have received to what you can give. You are now "able to respond."

REVIEW

1. What are the elements of an environment?

2. How does one's home influence a person's development? How does family? Church? Society as a whole?

3. How can a person's behavior express appreciation or lack of appreciation for the many gifts of life?

INTELLECTUAL RESPONSIBILITY

The human mind is absolutely awesome! From the tiny egg fertilized by an even tinier sperm, your physical body has developed. Its network of brain neurons controls a fabulous machine you know as your body. And you are conscious of the world around you. Your body knows the tug of gravity, for example, and the impact of an object hitting you. You shiver in the cold as much as many other animals do. You can even be conscious of relationships among things in much the same way a sunflower "knows" the position of the sun in the summer sky, physically tracing its path during the course of the day. Much like Gorbo, the neighborhood dog, you know—or are conscious of—the way home.

But there's so much more! Think of the inventions, the discoveries, the works of art, the symphonies, the books and the ideas which the choices and the decisions of so many people have produced. Think of knowing enough to build a space probe or to operate on someone's heart. Think of being able to make a computer or write music for a whole orchestra. Think of knowing enough to be unselfish. Think of knowing enough to know why to smile, when to wait, how to give. Think of knowing enough to be grateful, to pray, to care, to love.

And, unlike things, plants, and other animals, you can turn your consciousness back on yourself. You are a *self-reflecting* human. You are aware of being more than your body. You are aware of being a *self*, and you are aware of the world around you.

The more you grow in awareness of the world around you, the more you can relate to it. You have the intellectual ability to explore and to understand the world. Especially at this stage of your life, you have a thirst for knowledge. You want to know *what* makes things tick and *why* things are the way they are. With your mind you are able to explore the world and draw conclusions. You have entered into the stage of life where you can form your own opinions. Just remember to be open-minded.

As a young man or woman, you now stand at an exciting place of intellectual responsibility. Imagine what you'll learn about the world in the next few years. And think of how much you'll know—how much our society will come to know—in the years ahead! But the more you know, the more you are responsible—the more you are "able to respond," using what you know for the betterment of yourself and of the world.

Without a proper sense of your human dignity as a son or daughter of God, you also are able to use your knowledge for negative purposes. So take care to use your knowledge in good ways and for good reasons. Add wisdom to your knowledge, and all will be well!

Write it down

1. What does it mean to "get the most out of your education"?

2. Why should you?

3. How do you do that?

We become what we think of ourselves.
Abraham Joshua Heschel

PERSONAL RESPONSIBILITY

You are not just a functioning machine linked together like a set of computer parts. You are a very complex whole—a network of systems that work together at more than lightning speed as you make your way through life. You are a body–mind–soul unity. Even though you have a uniquely designed body which is formed and driven by a very unique genetic package, you are more than your body. You experience yourself as a self, a person.

You experience self-awareness. Isn't one of your deepest desires to be your *self*? You have a need to *be* the unique person that you are and to be *accepted* for who you are. You want to be yourself, and you want to express yourself in a unique way. The kind of clothes you wear and the way you decorate your bedroom are outward signs of your desire to be you in an important way.

Your sense of self puts you in touch with your dignity as a person. You are a child of God. You are not a handful of cosmic stardust or an impersonal machine. You have a soul, a self, or a personal center where you are intimately in touch with yourself in all your uniqueness. It is there that you experience yourself as created in the image and likeness of God. What does this mean? It means that you are a free person who is called to love unconditionally, as God does.

Personal **freedom** is often misunderstood. You say you are a free person. But doesn't your experience at home and in the world around you say the opposite? You experience many limitations! What teenager likes a curfew? True freedom, however, is not the ability to do whatever you want. In real life no one ever gets to do whatever he or she wants without any restrictions or limitations whatsoever. For example, you can't walk up the walls of your classroom and across the ceiling—no matter how much you may *want* to. You can't walk across the street whenever and wherever you like without risking your health and even your life. You can't be absolutely free in a physical sense.

freedom
liberation from restraint or the power of another, within reasonable bounds

Personal freedom.

Freedom is our power to act or not to act, to choose one action or another. We are free to do deliberate actions, and we are responsible for these deliberate actions. Our freedom is rooted in our ability to reason and to make choices. By using our free will, we shape our lives. Our freedom motivates us to grow and mature in truth and goodness. Freedom is most perfect when it is directed toward God, the source of our happiness.

See the *Catechism of the Catholic Church*, #1731.

1. What limits your freedom?
2. To love requires freedom. Why?
3. What does it mean to direct our freedom toward God?

The mature person recognizes and accepts the fact that life always has limitations. You are truly free if you get involved in your environment and take charge of the *kind* of person you become. True freedom is not found in the absence of physical restrictions or the absence of people who have authority over you. Freedom is found in your personal choices, choices that preserve and enhance your dignity. This is what lies at the heart and soul of personal responsibility—your ability to take charge of your life in a moral sense. Because you have the freedom that goes with personal responsibility, you have moral responsibility.

And what does this mean as you grow and mature? It means you use your ability to take charge of your life to do what is right and to not do what is wrong. You have the ability to shape and form the kind of person you will be. As you grow and mature, you have more freedom and less restrictions from home, Church, school, and society in general. As a result you also have more responsibility to be faithful to who you are as a person. True freedom is not the lack of limitations or the absence of responsibility. The person who is truly free cares enough to be responsible.

When parents and teachers and people at church talk about young people being responsible, listen to them. These people want your decisions to be well thought out, and they want you to be free of peer pressure and any other form of force. They want your decisions to be the kind that make you a good human with a loving heart, a son or daughter of God.

Listen to the word of God in Scripture:

> . . . *where the Spirit of the Lord is, there is freedom.*
>
> — *2 Corinthians 3:17*

> *As servants of God, live as free people, yet do not use your freedom as a pretext for evil. Honor everyone. Love the family of believers. Fear God. . . .*
>
> — *1 Peter 2:16–17*

Listen to the people who care about you. Receive their love. Use their wisdom. You will be a better person if you do. Your journey through life will be happier, and someday soon you too will be able to share your wisdom with those who come after you.

Talk about it

1. Do only adults have a role to play in creating a better world?

2. What unique gifts do teenagers bring to today's society?

Freedom is a package deal—with it comes responsibilities and consequences.

REVIEW

1. What does it mean to be intellectually responsible?

2. What does self-awareness mean?

3. How is personal responsibility practiced?

4. What is true freedom?

Covenant House
A home for homeless teens

Hundreds of thousands of teenagers live on the streets; many of these young people could be classified as society's "throwaways." They may come from abusive homes, families without physical homes, families that have fallen apart. They may have burned all their bridges with a family that has run out of options. They are often addicted to alcohol or other drugs. They are usually reduced to "selling their bodies" for food or shelter or drugs.

Certainly, these teenagers are easy prey for pimps and drug dealers. By the time many of these young people have come to regret the direction their lives have taken, they may feel that they are caught in a prison with no exits. They are powerless.

In several major cities in the United States, Canada, and Central America, there is a safe house or these teenagers—Covenant House. The first of these houses began in the early 1970s on the US East Coast. The houses provide free emergency shelter for street people under the age of 21. This is the mission statement of the people who work at these houses:

We who recognize God's providence and fidelity to his people are dedicated to living out his covenant among ourselves and those children we serve, with absolute respect and unconditional love. That commitment calls us to serve suffering children of the street, and to protect and safeguard all children. Just as Christ in his humanity is the visible sign of God's presence among his people, so our efforts together in the covenant community are a visible sign that effects the presence of God, working through the Holy Spirit among ourselves and our kids.

Typically, in addition to emergency shelter, Covenant House provides outreach programs, sanctuary, health care, counseling, education and career guidance, teen parenting classes, and child care. The staff will help a young person connect with his or her family or, if that isn't possible, with agencies that can assist the teen in beginning again. No matter how terrible the weeks or months or years have been for any one of these street kids, there is always hope when someone reaches out with unconditional love.

Optional activities

1. If there is a Covenant House in your city or a nearby city, visit it and find out how it helps street kids. Report to the class.

2. Research Covenant House on the Internet. Prepare a presentation on the organization as a whole or on a specific site.

3. Organize a fund-raiser for the Covenant House organization or for a specific Covenant House.

4. Research the reasons why teenagers end up living on the streets. Also find out what organizations in your area are addressing this problem and how they are doing so. Present your research in a paper or an oral report.

SEXUAL RESPONSIBILITY

In all areas of life there is an unbreakable connection between being free and being responsible. In your heart you know that true freedom means caring enough to be responsible. True freedom is seeing to it that what you do is good, is not harmful—not to anyone, not now, and not later on. Take, for example, the area of sex and responsibility. Nowhere is the battle between personal freedom and unavoidable limitations played out more intensely than in the realm of human sexuality.

At this time in your life, sexuality occupies more and more of your attention. You certainly notice the physical changes which have been taking place in your body. For some people this is a frightening time. For others it's a time of special joy. For others it's just a part of growing up. Whatever the case for you, the development of sexual responsibility is a critical part of your maturing as a person.

Let's look at some words and ideas related to this area of life.

Gender

Gender means what "sex" you are—male or female. In the world of plants, animals, and people, this classification is made on the basis of reproductive systems. Each of us falls into one gender or the other, depending upon the reproductive system with which we were born. Usually the first question we ask when someone gives birth to a baby is, "Is it a boy or a girl?"

Your gender is intimately tied up with your sense of self. From your earliest years your family and culture have reinforced your gender identity. Sometimes that reinforcement has been healthy; at other times it has not been so. This influence is healthy if it helps you appreciate your personal identity and take responsibility for it. It's unhealthy if it makes you think that one gender is more important or valuable than the other or leads you to abuse or take advantage of others because of their gender.

As you were growing up, you may have heard some stereotypical comments about one gender or the other, such as "Girls are silly," "Boys don't cry," "Girls can't play baseball well," and "Boys don't cook." Not one of these statements is true! Who are the good students in your class? The many girls among them are anything but silly. Science has shown that boys who don't cry become men who are prone to heart attacks. The young women who play softball in the Olympics are very good—and there are many others who weren't chosen for the team. Many great chefs are men.

gender
what "sex" a person is, male or female

The whole person

Sexuality affects the whole person, body and soul united. Most of all it affects people's ability to love and to create new humans. In a general way it affects how people relate to each other. Men and women have equal dignity; both genders reflect God's power and tenderness.

See the *Catechism of the Catholic Church*, #2332 and #2335.

1. Why does sexuality affect the whole person?

2. How does sexuality affect how people relate to each other?

3. How do people reflect the tenderness of God?

sexuality
one's way of relating to others as a male or a female person

Talk about it

1. How does the portrayal of men as "macho" influence how young men develop and how they relate to women?

2. How does the portrayal of women as "babes" influence how young women develop and how they relate to men?

genital
having to do with the sexual or reproductive organs

There is no certain way to "be a man" or to "be a woman." The important thing is to "be yourself." This means that your talents and interests are just as valid as those of anyone else. It also means that males are not more important than females. Each person is important and valuable. To truly understand gender means to respect each other and never take advantage of another person, never abuse another person.

Sex

The word *sex* usually refers to sexual activity, specifically, **genital** activity. As you grow physically, your body increasingly becomes capable of genital activity. That means that you can use your reproductive system; you are capable of mating and producing offspring. You have reached that stage of physical growth that is called *puberty*. Physically speaking, you can "have sex" and reproduce.

Your ability to use your reproductive organs is not in itself a sign of personal maturity. If all goes well, cows, chickens, and alligators reach a stage of growth where they can reproduce. The same is true for humans. The ability to reproduce, however, involves far more than the mere physical ability to engage in genital, or reproductive, activity.

This is where responsibility is most important. In its effort to reflect gospel values which lead to genuine life and happiness, the Catholic Church teaches that sexual intercourse is the right and privilege of married couples. *Married* means loving, committed, faithful, and united in a mutual bond. The Church believes there are two important reasons for marriage and sexual intercourse in marriage—(1) the expression of and building up of mutual love, and (2) the procreation of children.

The Catholic Church teaches that, for those who are not married, sexual intercourse is not justifiable behavior. In any situation outside marriage, sexual intercourse lacks at least one important element: mature and mutual love, commitment or the ability to make a lifelong commitment, faithfulness, openness to children and the ability to responsibly raise and educate them. The desire for pleasure alone is not enough to justify the use of our genital powers. Responsibility means not using one's genital capability in situations that lack the essential elements; it means using this capability as God intends it. Many broken hearts and shattered lives give witness to the wisdom of exercising the utmost responsibility when it comes to sexual activity.

All actual life is encounter.
Martin Buber

Human acts

The gift of freedom means that a person can make a moral choice. When we act with free will and conscious choice, we can be held accountable for our actions. A human act is one we choose freely after using our conscience to make a judgment about the act. Such an act can be morally good or morally evil.

See the *Catechism of the Catholic Church,* #1749.

1. What does it mean to be "held accountable"?
2. What does it mean to act with free will and conscious choice?
3. What does it mean to say that a free person is a responsible person?

Sexuality

For human beings, sex and sexuality are separate but connected realities. Sex refers to an ability achieved through physical maturity; it is related to specific body parts necessary for reproduction. *Sexuality* means relating to others as a male or a female person. When you think of yourself and sexuality, what do you think? Do you think of yourself as a man? Do you think of yourself as a woman? Who are you sexually? What is your sexual identity? Who attracts you sexually?

Sexuality deals with your orientation or direction, your attraction toward others. Most—but not all—men are sexually attracted to women. Most—but not all—women are sexually attracted to men. It isn't known exactly why some men are sexually attracted to other men and some women are sexually attracted to other women. The Catholic Church refers to this inclination toward persons of the same gender as "objectively disordered," that is, not the expression of sexuality that is in accord with the purpose of procreation. Homosexual orientation in itself, that is, the feeling of attraction, is not considered sinful. On the other hand, homosexual *activity*, just like premarital sexual intercourse, is morally wrong.

Your **sexual orientation** is important to your identity. Your sexual orientation is most probably influenced by your biological and genetic package, as well as your environment. Even though your sexual orientation may be "determined" by these influences, you are challenged to find a proper, moral sexual expression which preserves your human dignity and that of others.

Sexuality has everything to do with the relationship between people. For that reason, the way you use your sexual ability is radically important. The way you put your reproductive system to use is never a matter of mere physical activity. It's always an expression of your self. Sexual activity is a form of **intimacy** which calls for genuine responsibility. But simply making sure that a sex act is "safe" is not the answer. It fools no one, least of all yourself.

Write it down
Jot down your thoughts on some of the questions in the first paragraph of "Sexuality."

sexual orientation
a person's direction or sexual attraction toward others: toward members of the other gender or members of the same gender

intimacy
the state of being in a close, personal relationship

Your good reason tells you that sexual activity is best expressed in a mature, loving, faithful, and committed marriage relationship. This is why the Catholic moral reflection considers sexual activity outside of marriage to be morally wrong.

Abstinence, or the choice not to engage in intercourse outside of the situation intended by God, is a personal statement that sexuality (relationship) is of paramount value for you and that you are a responsible and mature person. Outside of marriage, intercourse is not the moral way to express your intimate love for another person.

Chastity is the virtue that helps you control your sexual powers and use them in proper and morally right ways. The person who is chaste respects him or herself and all other persons.

Because the expression of human sexuality requires such a degree of responsibility, parents and teachers seem full of caution regarding sexual matters at this time in your life. They don't want you to make the mistake of merely giving in to sexual urges. They want you to wait to engage in sexual activity until you are in a true loving and lasting relationship, sealed with the vows of marriage. This is not just for their personal comfort; it is for *your* lasting happiness.

The sex drive is a beautiful part of God's creation, but it's not a need for pleasure that automatically requires satisfaction. You will be happiest when your self-expression in an act of intercourse is within a permanent loving commitment. You will be unhappy if your sexual expression is selfish or abusive.

abstinence
the choice not to engage in intercourse outside of the situation intended by God, namely, marriage

chastity
the virtue that helps you control your sexual powers and use them in proper and morally right ways

Talk about it

1. What is "safe sex"? Is it safe?

2. Why does intimacy require responsibility?

3. What is abstinence a choice for?

4. What are the abusive ways in which the sex drive can be expressed?

Love alone is capable of uniting living beings in such a way
as to complete and fulfill them,
for it alone takes them and joins them by
what is deepest within themselves.

Pierre Teilhard de Chardin

The teenage years are a time when you really feel the need for acceptance and closeness with others. You experience strong emotions. But these needs and emotions, while normal, can be misleading. Take care, beware! Respect others, respect yourself. A mature person engages in sexual activity only in the context of a permanently committed and loving marriage. Only in that context is the act of intercourse a true statement—that is, the complete committed gift of your self to another person. Sexual intercourse is a statement of ongoing and lasting commitment.

Sexual matters are a concern for everyone, and not just because our society seems to be preoccupied with sex. It's a fact of life that we can't escape our sexuality. Taking responsibility for our sexual expression is a basic part of maturing. Being capable of having sex with another person is one thing; being mature sexually is another thing. The selfish person who is seeking only pleasure or false intimacy is not mature. The abusive person is not mature. The promiscuous person is not mature.

What makes the difference between an immature and a mature person is personal responsibility, being "able to respond" in an appropriate and moral way. At the root of this sense of personal responsibility is a true understanding of love. In the First Letter to the Corinthians, Paul summarized the qualities of love, all of which certainly apply to a relationship with a member of the other gender:

> *Love is patient; love is kind; love is not envious or boastful or arrogant or rude. It does not insist on its own way; it is not irritable or resentful; it does not rejoice in wrongdoing, but rejoices in the truth.*

> — *1 Corinthians 13:4–6*

Passions

Having strong feelings doesn't make you moral or holy. It's what you do with your feelings that matter, that make you a moral person. If your passions contribute to a good action, they are good in a moral sense. They are evil when they contribute to a bad action. Responsible persons direct their feelings, or passions, toward what is good for themselves and for others. Irresponsible persons let their feelings control their lives. This leads to the breakdown of personal integrity. If we use our emotions and feelings wisely, they will help us become virtuous people.

See the *Catechism of the Catholic Church*, #1768.

1. What are some of the things about which you have strong feelings?
2. Can you name any outstanding leaders who have been driven by deep passion for a cause?
3. What is the responsible way to use your feelings?
4. What happens when you let your feelings control you?
5. How can you be in charge of your feelings?

SOCIAL RESPONSIBILITY

Truly mature persons forget themselves and live for others. But this isn't easy to do. We have a selfish streak in us, and we live at a time when many in society proclaim themselves to be number one ("me first"). But don't be fooled—it isn't mature to live a "me first" life. A "me first" life doesn't bring happiness; it will eventually destroy a person and harm others. Our true value and dignity are to be found in relationships with other people, relationships that promote human dignity and personal growth.

You are a social being. You cannot escape this fact—you cannot run off to the hills to hide! When you look at another person, it's possible to have a perspective of a "whole" person. You can never see yourself this way because you are physically limited, due to the fact that you see with the two eyes on the front of your face. But your view of another person goes deeper than the external body. You are intimately linked with others.

And the world you help build will be a better place or a worse place because of you. Your decisions will be for the betterment or the detriment of your growth and the growth of those around you. Mature persons take seriously their role in society. Because society is a network of individual persons whose decisions affect one another's lives, the decisions each person makes—even now—make a difference. It's not only the rich and famous who are the movers and shakers in our society! It's *you*, too!

The mature person recognizes his or her responsibility for other people and for all creation. When you reach out to other persons to help them *in whatever manner*, you say something very important about yourself. You say that you are a loving and caring person. By valuing yourself in this way, you also help others appreciate their value as persons. This is what it means to be truly social. It isn't a privilege to be in society; it's a responsibility. When you are "able to respond" to your society, you are on the road to happiness.

Talk about it

1. Brainstorm a list of fifty "movers and shakers" (famous or not-so-famous) living today.

2. Choose five and discuss how they have influenced society.

Then do this

Who have been the four most influential people in your life?

1. Write a paragraph on each of them. Explain why each has been so important.

2. In small groups, share one paragraph.

> We were made for action,
> and for right action—for thought,
> and for true thought.
>
> **John Henry Newman**

REVIEW

1. Why is the development of sexual responsibility a critical part of maturing?

2. What does each of these terms mean: gender, sex, sexuality, sexual orientation, sex drive?

3. What does the Catholic Church believe are two important reasons for marriage and for sexual intercourse in marriage?

4. Why is being in society a responsibility and not a privilege?

St. Frances Xavier Cabrini
Missionary to immigrants

Like Eusebio Kino, Frances Xavier Cabrini was born in Italy and wanted to become a missionary to China. However, Frances, born in 1850, was not physically strong. After being turned down by two religious communities, she was asked to manage a poorly run orphanage. In time, Frances and several of the women she worked with formed a religious community, the Missionary Sisters of the Sacred Heart.

In 1889, Cabrini and several of her sisters set out for New York City to respond to the needs of Italian immigrants in the United States. This time there wasn't even an orphanage to begin with, and the students she was to educate had no school building. But again, Mother Cabrini met the challenge. Over the next twenty-three years, she established hospitals, orphanages, and schools from New York to Chicago to New Orleans to Seattle, not to mention Chile and Brazil.

The story is told that Frances found a loaf of fresh bread at the feet of the statue of Jesus when her first orphanage opened. She prayed:

> *Bread of Heaven,*
> *Bread of Love,*
> *Bread of Life*
> *shall never be lacking from God's little*
> *   orphaned children.*

Mother Cabrini died in Chicago in 1917 and was buried in New York City. But the little dynamo continued her fast-paced missionary work through her community of sisters. Frances was the first US citizen to be named a saint.

Optional activities

1. Use the Internet or other sources to find out more about Frances Xavier Cabrini. What can you apply to your life from her life and experiences?

2. Do a presentation on the history of Catholic hospitals in North America or in your area.

3. Research the life of St. Francis Xavier. Why was he named "Patron of the Foreign Missions"?

CONCLUSION

Between home and the church

There was once a proud woman who believed she was devout and religious and loved God. She went to church every day. But she never heard the beggars or the children who called out to her. She was praying and didn't even see them.

One day the woman walked to church in her usual way. She arrived just in time for the service. She pulled on the door handle, but the door was locked. She pulled harder, but to no avail.

Afraid she would miss the service for the first time in many years, she looked up. And there, right in front of her, was a note taped to the door. It said, "If you can't find God out there, you won't find him in here."

Optional activities

1. Choose a theme from this chapter, and write a parable about it.

2. Share this story with a group of children, and discuss its meaning.

3. Share this story with the adults in your family, and discuss its meaning.

This chapter offers but a brief description of your environment as a teenager. You know that scene well—it swirls around you each and every day. This is a time of great change in your life. It's also a time of opportunity and challenge. In the new freedoms you're discovering, you're growing toward personal responsibility.

The gospel is announced in your own day and age; hearing the message and responding to it brings new life. Often in our world lifeless gods compete with a loving God made known to us in Jesus. People spend much time, talent, and money pursuing happiness. In the midst of this search, you are asked to open your mind and your heart to God's love, a love which surrounds you. In the midst of the complexities and excitement of your adolescent years, you are "coming alive" as an adult. You are becoming your self. In your own quiet—and sometimes not-so-quiet—manner, you are searching for happiness and fulfillment.

If you are a responsible person, you recognize your limitations in this search for the fullness of life. There are certain things you can and should do for yourself. There are other things that are beyond your ability and your control. Your ultimate happiness in God is one of the things that is not totally within your ability and control. Fullness of life with God is a gift from God. Jesus promised all of us this fullness of life when he spoke to the Samaritan woman at Jacob's well:

"If you knew the gift of God, and who it is that is saying to you, 'Give me a drink,' you would have asked him, and he would have given you living water." The woman said to him, "Sir, you have no bucket, and the well is deep. Where do you get that living water? Are you greater than our ancestor Jacob, who gave us the well, and with his sons and his flocks drank from it?" Jesus said to her,

"Everyone who drinks of this water will be thirsty again, but those who drink of the water that I will give them will never be thirsty. The water that I will give will become in them a spring of water gushing up to eternal life."

— John 4:10–14

You are responsible for making important choices as you take moral charge of your life, as you respond to God's gift. It's a sign of maturity when you recognize and admit that you aren't the source of your own ultimate happiness. It's a sign of maturity to admit that you don't know, that you need help to find your way. It's okay at times to say "I can't" and to stand in need before God. God is there, always sharing with you all you need to be your true self, always offering you happiness, now and forever—living water "gushing up to eternal life."

Write it down
Look back over your life thus far. What influences have most shaped you during each stage of your growth? Have you become your own person? Why or why not?

Then do this
Create a poster which calls people to some form of responsibility.

Talk about it
What are the qualities of a mature person?

Words you should know

abstinence	**gender**
chastity	**genital**
culture	**intimacy**
environment	**responsibility**
freedom	**sexuality**
genetic	**sexual orientation**

CHAPTER 2

SALVATION
and GRACE

CHAPTER OVERVIEW

• *Have you been saved?*

• *Being saved*

• *Human needs*

The Word of the Lord

. . . since we are justified by faith, we have peace with God through our Lord Jesus Christ, through whom we have obtained access to this grace in which we stand; and we boast in our hope of sharing the glory of God. . . .

FROM THE LETTER TO THE ROMANS, SEE 5:1–2, 6–11.

Let Us Pray

O LORD, you have searched me and you know me.
You know when I sit down and when I rise up;

you discern my thoughts from far away.
You search out my path and my lying down,
 and are acquainted with all my ways.
Even before a word is on my tongue,
 O LORD, you know it completely. . . .
Where can I go from your spirit?
 Or where can I flee from your presence? . . .
If I take the wings of the morning
 and settle at the farthest limits of the sea,
even there your hand shall lead me,
 and your right hand shall hold me fast. . . .
For it was you who formed my inward parts;
 you knit me together in my mother's womb.
I praise you, for I am fearfully and wonderfully made.

PSALM 139:1–4, 7, 9–10, 13–14

HAVE YOU BEEN SAVED?

People often ask us embarrassing questions. In response we mumble an answer which we hope will send them on their way. Once in a while, however, someone hits us with a personal question that is not easily answered. One such question may be, "Have you been saved?" Did anyone ever ask you that?

This question may be presented to you at the strangest times—in the locker room, at the store, in the school cafeteria. The question may make you feel awkward. In our Catholic tradition, we don't usually talk about "being saved," so we don't always know how to respond.

Catholics certainly believe that Jesus Christ has saved us. We just don't seem to talk about it or ask people if *they* have been saved. The question itself seems to require a definite answer, and not a partial "Well, I think so." We're not sure about what to say, not sure how to answer the question ourselves. Maybe we think that answering this question means that we have made a serious faith commitment—and maybe we haven't. The question may embarrass us because we may not have thought in any serious way about salvation.

Actually all the **religions** of the world deal with this matter of "being saved." This is one of the central questions of the human heart, and it is the central question of the Christian faith. In one of the stories about Jesus in the Bible, a rich young man asks Jesus, "What must I do to have eternal life?"—meaning, "What must I do to be saved?"

When we raise the question about being saved, we're asking about happiness: What will make us happy now and in the hereafter? This question of happiness takes us to the beginning point of our relationship with God: Do *we* create our ultimate happiness—by means of the "gods" that we make for ourselves in life? Can these "gods"—our looks, our clothes, our friends—save us? Can they make us happy *forever*? Or is there something else? Do our hearts look for something more? It comes down to this: Do we create the "fullness," the completeness, of our life, or is it a gift?

Write it down

Have you been saved?

Then do this

1. Ask four people the question: Have you been saved?

2. Record their answers and write about your impressions from the interviews.

3. With a classmate who interviewed four other people, discuss the responses and your reactions.

religion

an organized group of worshipers who share beliefs, religious practices, and a moral code

Then do this

1. Interview several people; ask them where they find real happiness.

2. Compare the answers given, and then compare the answers to your own answer.

Gift and response

God freely gives himself to us. This gift requires a free response on our part. God has created us in his image and has made us free. God has given us the ability to know and to love him. Through the correct use of our freedom, we are united with God. Love must be freely given. God touches our hearts; God is at work in our heart of hearts. There we experience a longing for truth and goodness, a longing which only God can satisfy.

See the *Catechism of the Catholic Church*, #2002.

1. What kind of things are you naturally attracted to? Is this God touching your heart?

2. Can you truly love someone if your love is demanded or expected?

3. How does your love for others bring you closer to God?

Mary MacKillop
Australia's first native-born saint

Australia saw its first settlement by Europeans after the Revolutionary War which separated the United States from Britain. Britain's practice of shipping prisoners and military guards to the North American colonies then shifted to Australia. The first white settlement is now the city of Sydney. By the end of the eighteenth century, freed prisoners and military personnel had begun farming on government-granted lands.

Mary MacKillop was born in Australia in 1842, a time when the interior of the continent was just beginning to be explored. After working as a governess, a shop assistant, and a teacher in South Australia for some years, Mary met Father Julian Tenison Woods. Together they formed a new community of religious women, the Sisters of St. Joseph of the Sacred Heart (Josephites).

Mother Mary, who was well-educated, set out to establish schools for poor children. Her work didn't go smoothly, however, as she ran into opposition from several bishops. Eventually Mother Mary succeeded and won the admiration and financial support of many people because of her insistence that the dedicated members of the community live poorly, like those they served. She didn't want the sisters to own any property, even their headquarters.

By 1873 there were 127 sisters and thirty-four schools. In addition the community established hostels, homes of refuge, and orphanages throughout Australia and New Zealand. No one was turned away, and no one was pressured to become Catholic. The example of the sisters and their founder spoke the good news more strongly than many sermons. The work of the sisters extended beyond the white population to the aborigines. Mother Mary herself was also known for her care for the environment and for conservation (the eucalyptus is her emblem).

Mother Mary MacKillop once wrote: "Do not resist God, for your souls are very dear to him: Jesus Christ came into the world, suffered and died to save each one of us." She died in 1909, and in 1995 was beatified. She is honored as Australia's first native-born saint.

Optional activities

1. Research the religions found today in Australia. Write a paper or orally present your research to the class.

2. Research a religious community of women that works or has worked in your area. If possible interview a member of the community. Share your research with the class.

3. Rent a video of a story that takes place in Australia. Watch the video with a few classmates and discuss how you would practice your religion there.

BEING SAVED

When someone asks us if we have "been saved," they make us think. They force us to look at something that most people have tucked away beneath the surface of their lives. It's possible—even for regular church-goers—to have never thought about this question in a serious way. It's possible that we have let our busy schedules and our little "gods" keep this question at a safe distance. Or perhaps we just don't want to be reminded that we are in need of anything. Or maybe we're doing some things with our lives that aren't so good and we don't want to look at ourselves honestly.

In the dictionary the word *salvation* has several definitions. The most interesting definition says that **salvation** means "being made whole." Salvation is not making oneself whole; it is *being made* whole. That means we receive it as a gift!

Let's take a closer look at this question of salvation, starting with the experience of saving things. Saving is a common experience. Some people even carry it to an extreme. Do you save baseball cards, stamps, coins, bottle caps, insects, dolls, tea cups? Do you save your money? Do you ever try to save time? In all of these examples of saving, notice that you yourself are the one who does the saving. The question which opened this chapter, however, wasn't, "Do you save?" or "Have you saved yourself?" The question was, "Have you *been* saved?"

The religious question of salvation obviously deals with something you cannot do for yourself. The question touches a deep part of your experience where, if you are honest, you have to recognize that *you are not* the source of your ultimate happiness. The little "gods" we create cannot save us, cannot make us happy forever, and cannot make us deeply happy even now.

Indeed there is much that you can do for yourself—much that you should do. Your experience of life, however, teaches you that you are not complete in yourself. Your search for your own wholeness and completeness will bring you to the point where you will know there is some thing you cannot do for yourself. To be happy, you need others. You need others even to know who you are.

salvation
being made whole by God, made right with God; saved from the power of sin and everlasting death

Then do this
Using magazine pictures, make a collage of ways people unfortunately turn to things in the search for happiness.

ultimate source
that from which we come: God

Above all, you need God. Salvation deals with what you cannot do for yourself down at the deep level of your search for happiness and wholeness. Salvation deals with the **ultimate source** of your being, your goodness, and your true happiness. At the heart of faith is this truth: Only God ulti-mately can save us—only God can give us deep and lasting happiness.

Grace

All life and holiness comes from God. *Grace* is another word for God's life and holiness, which he shares with us. Grace is the free, unconditional, and undeserved help that God gives us. Grace helps us respond to the call to become children of God. We are "adopted" by God and welcomed into union with God forever.

Grace is not a thing. It is our participation in the life of God, which means that we share in the intimate union of God, Father, Son, and Holy Spirit—the Trinity. By Baptism we take part in the life of Christ. God "adopts" us through Christ. With Christ, we call God "Father." And through Christ, we receive the gift of the Holy Spirit who breathes love into us and who forms us into the Church.

See the *Catechism of the Catholic Church*, #s 1996–1997.

1. In your own words, what would you say grace is? What does it mean to "experience God's grace"?

2. Why do we say that God's grace is unconditional? What does that mean?

3. How can God as Father, Son, and Holy Spirit be seen as a family of grace and love? How is the Church a family of grace and love?

4. There's a well-known and much-loved hymn called "Amazing Grace." Why is grace amazing? Why do people like this hymn so much?

God our Savior . . . desires everyone to be saved and to come to the knowledge of the truth.

1 Timothy 2:3–4

Christians believe that Jesus has made known to us the gift of God's salvation. From Jesus we learn that God is personal and that God loves each of us and wants us to become the best persons we can be. The God who is greater than anything we can imagine is also in relationship with each of us, his precious creations. God is like a protective and loving father or mother. God wants to be in relationship with us forever.

In our heart of hearts, we know that God is the ultimate source of our happiness. Every day we carry on a dialogue with God, even though we often don't know it. We are always looking for the source of our salvation. We are always "talking with God." One of the saints (St. Augustine) put it this way: "O Lord, our hearts are restless until they rest in you." To some degree, we all spend our lives in this state of restlessness. In a variety of ways—some we're aware of and some we're not—we struggle with the question of our need for salvation, for the fullness of life. This yearning comes from God.

Everyone has a sense of being a person. Everyone is searching for happiness. Everyone, in different ways, is searching for some direction in life. All people want to be free from suffering and unhappiness; everyone wants to be happy forever. Believers and "non-believers," those who practice their religion intensely and prayerfully, as well as those who carelessly attend church, all grapple with the question of salvation. We are all looking for salvation, for that which will bring us happiness—deeply and for eternity.

Talk about it

1. What is your image of God?
2. How has this image changed since you were a little child?
3. What might influence a change in how you see God in the future?

Write it down

What does it mean to be a friend of God?

Talk about it

What does it mean when we say that God knows us?

Christians believe that the search for salvation comes from God. Since the very moment we were created, God has been a part of our lives. When we experience the need for deep and lasting happiness, we are "hearing" God call us to the fullness of life that can be found only in God. **We are created with a need for God.** Our lives are not truly fulfilled until there is communion with God who has created us.

As you will see as you work your way through this book, the good news offered to us in the gospel of Jesus is that God not only has made all humans with this longing for deep happiness, this need for salvation. God also is the one who saves, the one who brings us wholeness of life. As Christians we believe that we know God and become one with God through Jesus. In Jesus, God has made himself known in human history. Jesus is the way to ultimate happiness and fullness of life. We follow Jesus when we reject selfishness and sin. God blesses us with his own life, grace, the gift for which our hearts yearn. Followers of Jesus believe that

> *"There is salvation in no one else, for there is no other name under heaven given among mortals by which we must be saved."*
>
> *— Acts 4:12*

Sometimes we don't realize that we need God. Or we don't realize *how much* we need God, how much our hearts long for God's love. Sometimes our response to God's love is limited. There could be several reasons for this:

- Perhaps you simply haven't realized that you need God.
- Perhaps your family and faith community have not helped you recognize your need for God.
- Perhaps you have had some negative experiences of religion which have "turned you off."
- Perhaps you have been led by friends or other influences in the culture to believe that you don't need God.
- Perhaps you're a bit "spiritually lazy," ignoring the tug of God's Spirit on your heart.
- Or perhaps you reject the presence of God in your life. You think you can get by on your own.

Talk about it

Is addiction—to alcohol, other drugs, food, or other things—a disease of the body or a disease of the "heart" or both? Explain.

Then do this

1. Find out something about the twelve steps of Alcoholics Anonymous.

2. Talk about the steps, especially the first two steps.

God is more interested in the salvation of the human race than in the labor of philosophers.

Jacques Maritain

REVIEW

1. What is the relationship between being saved and happiness?

2. What does it mean to call God the "ultimate source"?

3. What is grace?

4. What do we mean when we say we are created with a need for God?

Catholic-Lutheran dialogue

In 1998, representatives of the Catholic Church and the Lutheran Church discussed the following statement which attempts to repair an important division in theology between the two Churches.

All people are called by God to salvation in Christ. Through Christ alone are we justified, when we receive this salvation in faith. Faith is itself God's gift through the Holy Spirit, who works through word and sacrament in the community of believers and who at the same time leads believers into that renewal of life which God will bring to completion in eternal life.

Catholic-Lutheran *Joint Declaration on the Doctrine of Justification*, **1998, #16.**

1. According to this statement, what is faith?
2. How are we justified?
3. What does this statement say about salvation?

HUMAN NEEDS

Let's look more closely at this matter of needing to find happiness and fulfillment. It's not easy to admit that you are needy, especially not when you are just now gaining a little independence from home and finding your place in the world around you, not just right when you're starting to concentrate on what you're going to do with your life.

The culture in the United States tends to speak against being needy. We're taught nearly from early childhood to stand alone and do for ourselves. We're encouraged to be tough individuals who don't need anyone or anything. This is part of the **frontier mentality** that has been such an influence since the founding of our nation. People like the early settlers were expected to "go it alone" and to "pull themselves up by their own bootstraps." To need other people or any thing came to be seen as a weakness. Unfortunately, most of us suffer from this error in one way or another.

Neediness, however, doesn't have to have a negative meaning. To admit that we're needy is simply to recognize—and tell—the truth. We *are needy*. If you are honest and mature, you will be able to admit that. To be needy is something that everyone experiences. In fact, the study of human growth and development makes it quite clear: We have been needy since the moment we were conceived. And we still will be needy when we die.

frontier mentality
rugged individualism; the expectation that we stand alone and do for ourselves

neediness
the state of being in want of something

> *Pure friendship is an image of the original and perfect friendship that belongs to the Trinity and is the very essence of God.*
>
> **Simone Weil**

Brothers

One day a father gave his two sons each a basket and sent them into the world with this advice: "The purpose of life is to become wealthy. Go out and make your fortune." On the way the one brother found some money, and put it into his basket. Once he had money he learned very quickly about all the wonderful things money could do and buy. Thus, he devoted his life to doing whatever he could to find money, get money and make money. His brother on the other hand went about putting into his basket just a little bit of this and maybe some of that.

In the end the one brother became an extremely rich man while the other brother had . . . only money.

John R. Aurelio, *Colors! Stories of the Kingdom* (New York: Crossroad, 1993).

Optional activities

1. Draw a comic strip based on this story.

2. Write a brief story in which the ending is unexpected and makes a point about living a good life.

3. Think of someone you know who is like the brother who collected "a little bit of this and maybe some of that." Tell the class about this person.

The shapes of neediness

Talk about it

1. Why should we be honest about our neediness?

2. How can we do that?

When you were an infant, your needs were many. Just ask a parent who heard you crying in the middle of the night. Those needs were quite basic: food and drink, warmth and shelter, air to breathe, a clean diaper, the touch of other people, and love. Without someone satisfying these needs for you, you would have died. There was no way you could have provided these sources of life for yourself. You needed to get them from someone else. Ever since conception, you have "been saved"!

As a growing child you still had many needs. As you grew, you experienced new needs—the need to establish a good self-image, the need for a sense of identity, the need for an ability to move around in the world. You still have many needs, and you are probably especially experiencing the need for wholesome relationships. That's why your parents might be picky at times about your friends. Your friends affect how you see yourself and the kind of person you become.

Ah, but a man's reach should exceed his grasp,

Or what's a heaven for?

Robert Browning

Among all these human needs, the experience of love has been your greatest need. You need to be accepted and valued for who you *are*. You need to be loved for just being *you*—not for what you *do*, but for who you *are*. This gift of unconditional love is always important. It's especially important now, during your adolescent years. You are developing a self-image. You are growing in your awareness of being a unique person with your own personality, talents, and abilities. You are probably very grateful for friends with whom you can be yourself. The gift of **friendship** is a real treasure.

Adolescence is a time for best friends, for friendships that satisfy your need for being made whole, alive, and active. Dare we call this experience in some way the "whisper" of your need to be saved? Is God speaking to your heart in the events and circumstances around you, especially through the people in your life who give you love and affirmation? Is this a time in your life when the search for God's love seems to be a powerful force? Certainly, adolescence is a time of searching. God is your close and special friend. You feel the presence of God. If this relationship with God doesn't develop, this time of your life can be lonely and depressing.

As you read earlier in this chapter, you can be sidetracked in satisfying your neediness. You can be looking for love "in all the wrong places." Whether it be a thing, a person, or a relationship, it is important to recognize that regardless of how satisfying these are at the moment, they are not God, the ultimate source of happiness. They are not the total answer. As you have matured, you have come to realize that things or possessions especially don't satisfy the deepest hungers of your heart. They cannot "save" you.

friendship
a relationship based on mutual acceptance and love

Write it down
Why is it more important that your friends and parents love you than that they give you presents?

The virtue of love

Love influences our practice of all the other virtues. Love binds all our practices of virtue together in perfect harmony. Love is the source and the goal of life, and certainly of the Christian way of life. Because of love, we know that God is present in our lives. Because of love, we are able to love. True love is a sign of God's love in us.

Therefore, God's love in us inspires us to live a good moral life. We experience the spiritual freedom of God's children because of the love God has given us in Christ. Christians are not slaves before God, obeying out of fear. Christians are children of a loving God. Christians don't love just to receive love back; we love because God has first loved us and set us free to love others unconditionally.

See the *Catechism of the Catholic Church*, #s 1827–1828.

1. Why is love the most important of all the virtues?

2. What have we learned from Jesus Christ about God's love?

3. Why is it easier to love others when we know we are loved by someone else? Why is it easier to love others—even our enemies—when we know that God loves us and them?

4. What is unconditional love? Is real love always unconditional?

Real love

Write it down

How do you search for God?

Talk about it

Why is genuine love so important for growth and development?

People, unlike things, can bring you to God. The heart cries out for a personal relationship, for the love of another. Let's look more closely at this need. Another person's love for you is truly "saving"—if it is really love. Real love respects you for who you *are* and not what you can *give*. Real love makes you free. It doesn't make you a thing or a love-object. You don't want to be used or abused because of the physical or emotional neediness of another. For love to be saving, or whole-making, it must be freely given. Likewise, it must leave you free to be yourself. For that to happen, genuine "saving" love must be given without conditions, no strings attached. It must be unconditional. The full blossoming of this kind of love can be found in very special friendships and in committed love.

In all of these experiences of love—and your searching for them—you are also reaching out for the heart of God. You are reaching out for a love relationship that makes you completely happy. There truly is a restlessness in your heart which only God can calm. Even when people have found that "someone special" in their lives—the one they truly love—the restlessness of the heart continues. The search for God continues. This doesn't take away from the incredible beauty and power of human love. It just says that people are not God and cannot satisfy the longing of the human heart for ultimate happiness.

The Divine Image

To Mercy, Pity, Peace, and Love
All pray in their distress;
And to these virtues of delight
Return their thankfulness.

    For Mercy, Pity, Peace, and Love
    Is God, our father dear,
    And Mercy, Pity, Peace, and Love
    Is Man, his child and care.

For Mercy has a human heart,
Pity, a human face,
And Love, the human form divine,
And Peace, the human dress.

    Then every man, of every clime,
    That prays in his distress,
    Prays to the human form divine,
    Love, Mercy, Pity, Peace.

And all must love the human form,
In heathen, Turk, or Jew;
Where Mercy, Love, and Pity dwell,
There God is dwelling too.

William Blake

Optional activities

1. Write a personal reflection on the poem by William Blake.
2. Find another poem that reflects your understanding of God's relationship with people. Share and discuss the poem with the class.
3. Write a poem on the topic: God and us.

God's love for us

It may seem at times that you will grow into a need for God only later in life. It may seem that you can do well without God for the time being. Nothing could be further from the truth. Catholics believe that from the very moment of conception—the split instant you became a person—you were created in the image and likeness of God. Obviously, we don't look like God physically, because God is pure spirit. God has no body. We "look like God" when we love like God, that is, unconditionally. Like God, we are self-aware and we are free. The more mature you become, the more you grow into the image and likeness of a son or daughter of God.

You are someone special who is called to the heart of God. Your life is **sacred** because it comes from God and returns to God. From the moment you were conceived, there has existed a love relationship between you and God. We could say that from the moment of your conception, God has offered you the gift of salvation, the gift of complete happiness—which is the purpose of your existence.

The call to wholeness is the same thing as the call to **holiness.** The more you grow toward your full dignity as a son or daughter of God, the more in the image of God you become. Likewise, the more you respond to God's loving presence in your life, the more truly human you become. To be holy means to become the whole person God has created you to be.

Some people define this holiness as "doing God's will." God's will is that you become fully human, that you grow to full stature in his love. You do this through those zillions of decisions you make during your lifetime. God has no secret plan, unknown to you, written down somewhere in heaven. Just as parents want their child to grow up and make free choices that are wholesome for their well-being and lead to real happiness, so it is with God. God wants you to blossom and flourish, to enjoy the good things of life, and to develop relationships that reflect his unconditional and freeing love. The author of the Letter to the Ephesians tells us:

> You were taught to put away your former way of life, your old self, . . . and to be renewed in the spirit of your minds, and to clothe yourselves with the new self, created according to the likeness of God in true righteousness and holiness.
>
> —Ephesians 4:22–24

sacred
holy, comes from God, set apart for God

holiness
the state of being the whole person God created one to be

Write it down
Who is the holiest person you have met? Why do you consider that person holy?

Then do this
Read through a newspaper and, from your reading, make a list of ways people are searching for meaning and purpose in life.

See what love the Father has given us, that we should be called children of God; for that is what we are.

1 John 3:1

REVIEW

1. What is the difference between the frontier mentality and neediness?

2. What do we mean when we say that adolescence is a time of searching?

3. What is genuine "saving" love?

4. What is holiness? What is wholeness?

CONCLUSION

Faith is the ability to know that God loves you. Like God's love, faith is a gift from God. Because faith is truly a gift, you are free to respond. Through faith God calls you to open your heart to his love. God calls you to open your heart to the people in your life, to people in need everywhere, to the world in which you live.

With faith you can be confident of God's love, no matter what. Faith gives you the strength to put up with whatever bad or disappointing things that come your way. With faith you have the confidence to believe that somehow everything fits into the goodness of God. So faith is an attitude of trust that God "speaks" to you in the events of your daily life, that God is right here with you, that God is guiding you.

Christians believe that faith is a trusting commitment to a relationship with Jesus Christ in whom God's love has been so clearly shown. Our relationship with Jesus—and a willingness to "be saved" by God alone—gives meaning and purpose to the practice of religion.

. . . when the goodness and loving kindness of God our Savior appeared, he saved us, not because of any works of righteousness that we have done, but according to his mercy, through the water of rebirth and renewal by the Holy Spirit. This Spirit he poured out on us richly through Jesus Christ our Savior, so that, having been justified by his grace, we might become heirs according to the hope of eternal life.

— Titus 3:4–7

The more you experience the saving power of God's grace, the more you will love and the happier you will be. One day, that grace—that loving presence of God—will indeed lead you to eternal happiness and eternal life. Until that great and happy day, the question remains: "Have you been saved?" How you answer this question—how you keep on struggling with this question—will make all the difference in your life.

> I *admire the serene assurance of those*
> *who have religious faith.*
> *It is wonderful to observe the calm confidence*
> *of a Christian with four aces.*
> **Mark Twain**

F. Scott Fitzgerald
Touched by faith

At the time of his death, F. Scott Fitzgerald, the author of *The Great Gatsby*, was no longer a practicing Catholic. As a result, his body was buried in the nondenominational cemetery across the street from the Catholic cemetery in which he had wanted to be buried. After the Second Vatican Council, his family requested that he be buried in the Catholic cemetery, and the request was honored. Cardinal Baum of Washington, DC, at the time, said this:

F. Scott Fitzgerald . . . was a man touched by the faith of the Catholic Church. There can be perceived in his work a Catholic consciousness of reality. He found in this faith an understanding of the human heart caught in the struggle between grace and death. His characters are involved in this great drama, seeking God and seeking love. As an artist he was able with lucidity and poetic imagination to portray this struggle. He also experienced in his own life the mystery of suffering and, we hope, the power of God's grace.

Optional activities

1. Discuss: What is "a Catholic consciousness of reality"? What does it mean to be "caught in the struggle between grace and death"?

2. Write a report on a novel you have read that gave you some insight into being a Catholic.

Words you should know

friendship	religion
frontier mentality	sacred
holiness	salvation
neediness	ultimate source

CHAPTER 3

The NATURE of FAITH

CHAPTER OVERVIEW

• *Life questions*

• *Faith as trust*

• *Belonging to a Church*

• *Religion*

• *Faith*

• *Stages of faith development*

• *Prayer*

The Word of the Lord

*Now faith is the assurance of things hoped for,
the conviction of things not seen.*

FROM THE LETTER TO THE HEBREWS, SEE 11:1–3 AND 12:1–2.

LORD, you have been our dwelling place
in all generations.

Let Us Pray

Before the mountains were brought forth,
or ever you had formed the earth and the world,
from everlasting to everlasting you are God. . . .
Satisfy us in the morning with your steadfast love,
so that we may rejoice and be glad all our days. . . .
Let your work be manifest to your servants,
and your glorious power to their children.
Let the favor of the LORD our God be upon us,
and prosper for us the work of our hands—
O prosper the work of our hands!

PSALM 90:1–2, 14, 16–17

LIFE QUESTIONS

In the last chapter we took a serious look at our human experience of neediness. (Remember, this neediness isn't a bad thing; it's part of life!) The main point of the last chapter was our need to reach out to a source beyond ourselves for our ultimate happiness and fulfillment. Because we are created with a need for God—because we are created in relation to God—we know that our wholeness of life (our salvation) is not found in ourselves. We cannot save ourselves. We cannot make ourselves completely whole.

This is a basic experience of life. You *know* that you are incomplete in yourself. Like all humans, you reach out in your neediness to other people, to things, to experiences. You reach out for a sense of salvation, for a sense of happiness and wholeness.

This search for ultimate happiness affects your entire life. It's as if your heart were crying out, "Is there anything—anyone—'out there' to help me? Is there anyone who loves me so much that they will save me?" Sometimes this question can take the form of life questions. These questions are different from everyday questions like "What should I wear to school today?" "What's for dinner?" or "What time is it?" **Life questions** are those that tug at your heart, those questions that go much deeper than everyday questions:

- Who am I?
- Where did I come from?
- What is the purpose of my life?
- Why am I selfish when I really don't want to be?
- Is there life beyond death?
- Who is God?

Now, let's be honest. You don't run around the football field or wander through the halls at school shouting out these questions. In fact, you even may be thinking right now that these questions aren't a part of your life at all. Perhaps, like many people, you're so excited about daily life and all the things you have to do that you aren't aware of these questions inside yourself. And, yes, it's possible that even if you have heard these questions "speaking" to your heart, you may be ignoring them or hiding from them.

These deep questions about life aren't easy to answer, and they won't go away. They're part of being human. They push you and tug at you to find answers. You may never ask these questions aloud or even directly. Sometimes these questions come at you like a quiet whisper: Is there "something more" to life? Why am I so restless? Why am I so bored—even when I'm doing things, and even with my friends?

life questions

questions that go much deeper than everyday questions, that tug at the heart

Write it down

1. Respond to the life questions listed here.

2. What other life questions do you have?

Talk about it

When does the search for a relationship with God end? Explain.

> *One may understand the cosmos, but never the ego;*
>
> *the self is more distant than any star.*
>
> G.K. Chesterton

Why does this happen? It happens because your heart is searching for meaning in what you do, searching for a purpose in life. Your heart is trying to answer a life question. Sometimes these life questions come to the surface of your consciousness when you are overwhelmed by tragedy or loneliness. They come to mind when you have lost the very things or people you trusted in to make you happy. In reality, life questions can come up at any time, and they do surface for everybody. If it seems as if you're the only person in the world—in the whole of human history—who has this kind of experience, don't worry—you're not.

Life questions tug at the heart of *every* human. And every religion in the world deals with them in one way or another. In fact, the purpose of religion—including Christianity—is to help us deal with these life questions so that we can experience fullness of life. The unique thing about our Christian faith is that we believe God has entered into the human condition in Jesus. He addresses these questions as one of us. We believe that through the life, death, and resurrection of Jesus, God has opened the way to our eternal happiness.

Happiness is the natural life of humans.

St. Thomas Aquinas

The whole character of the creation was determined by the fact that God was to become man and dwell in the midst of His own creation.

Thomas Merton

incarnation
the act of God becoming
a human in Jesus

Sharing the human condition

Christians use the word **incarnation** to describe the fact that God entered the human condition and fully revealed himself in the person of Jesus. God didn't just take on a human appearance, nor is Jesus part God and part man, a confused mixture of the divine and the human. The Church teaches that Jesus became truly human while remaining truly God. In other words, Jesus is true God and true man at the same time; he is the Son of God by nature, not adoption.

The Catholic Church teaches that Mary is the Mother of God—she is the mother of Jesus who is God become human. This doesn't mean that she created God! It means that her son, Jesus, was born "according to the flesh." This means that, through his conception in her, the Son of God took upon himself the fullness of our human condition. Jesus was born and grew in human consciousness.

See the *Catechism of the Catholic Church*, #s 464–466, 471.

1. What is the incarnation?

2. Why is it important that Jesus was born like us and grew like us, that he shared our human condition, rather than just appearing among us like a vision?

3. Make a list of the kinds of experiences Jesus certainly must have had since he was "truly human."

FAITH AS TRUST

Your experience tells you that life questions are indeed very real and very deep questions in your own heart. It's not just adults who face the important questions in life. Don't you experience the need for help in figuring out the meaning of life and the meaning of God in your life? Aren't you in need?

Faith is trusting that there are answers to your life questions. With faith, you trust God as the source of your ultimate happiness. With faith, you open your heart to express your willingness to be embraced by God. It is God who reaches out to save you; this is the foundation of Christian faith. You cannot save yourself; God has taken the first step to reach out and save you from your sense of being lost and without purpose. Faith is your trust that, yes, there is someone "out there" who cares and who wants you to know that *you are special* and that *you are loved*. To put it simply, faith is being open to being helped, *to being saved*.

So we are always courageous . . . for we walk by faith.

2 Corinthians 5:6–7

We think we know how to define *faith* and *love*. We use these words often and in many different ways. But, if we're asked to define faith, we stumble and get confused. It's important to know what words mean so that we know what we're talking about. A look at a dictionary shows that there are many different ways to understand the word **faith**:

faith

openness to salvation; trust in someone, especially God; a firm belief; an expression of loyalty; a system of beliefs; a set of principles; a belief in something real that can't be proved

Faith

- Faith can be a firm belief in a truth. For example, you may have faith that all people are basically good.
- Faith can be an act of trust in another person or in an object or thing. For example, you have faith that the chair you are about to use will hold your weight. You have faith that if he promised to do so, your brother will pick you up after school.
- Faith can be an expression of loyalty to a person or thing. For example, you have faith in your country. Your parents have faith in you to do your best in school; they loyally stand by you.
- Faith can be a system of beliefs. For example, the Creed used at Sunday Mass is a summary of what Christians believe. It's a statement of our faith.
- Faith can be a set of principles. For example, the Catholic Church believes that workers have a right to work, to just wages, and to a decent human working environment.
- Faith can be a belief in something that is very real but cannot be proved. For example, you have faith in God.

It's easy to see why people—and not just young people—are confused at times about faith. The word has so many different meanings. The last definition above is the one that we are talking about in this chapter. Some of the other definitions depend on this one. As we heard, the author of the Letter to the Hebrews put it this way:

> *Now faith is the assurance of things hoped for, the conviction of things not seen . . . By faith we understand that the worlds were prepared by the word of God, so that what is seen was made from things that are not visible.*
>
> — *Hebrews 11:1, 3*

Sometimes people don't understand something their Church teaches. When this happens, they may fear that they don't have faith. At times people may have difficulty accepting a truth taught them by their Church. Again, they are afraid that they have no faith. When certain religious ceremonies at their church change, some people feel that they can no longer believe or have faith. All these people confuse the different meanings of faith. In truth, if a ceremony or a thing becomes the measure of faith, there is the danger of making this thing more important than God. This is idolatry.

Talk about it

Share examples of each definition of faith given here.

idolatry

an act or attitude in which a person gives to a thing the power of salvation, the power to bring ultimate happiness and fulfillment

dogma

an official, essential teaching of a Church or other group

Idolatry is an act or attitude in which a person gives to a thing the power of salvation, the power to bring ultimate happiness and fulfillment. Idolatry happens whenever we pour our hearts into any thing or activity, expecting that it will bring us ultimate happiness. In that sense idolatry can be part of any human activity, not just Church matters. Religious ceremonies, things, and other man-made activities cannot save, however. Only God can bring us ultimate happiness and fulfillment of life.

The central focus of faith is not intellectual understanding. **Dogmas**, or official teachings of a Church, are not the same as faith. They are an attempt to *explain* faith. We can argue all day about *what* we believe. The point of this chapter is the fact *that* we believe. We are asked to open our hearts to the loving presence of God who searches us out to save us.

The Creed

We don't believe in rote word-formulas, but we believe in the realities they express. Faith is our way of touching the realities behind the words. Words about our faith help us express that faith and share it with others. Words help us celebrate our faith in a community and live it. The Creed is an important statement used by the Church generation after generation to hand on a statement of our beliefs. Think of a mother who teaches her children to speak and thus to understand and communicate. In a similar way the Church teaches us the language of faith to help us understand and live the faith.

See the *Catechism of the Catholic Church*, #s 170–171.

1. What do all Christians who proclaim the Nicene or Apostles' Creed believe?
2. Why is it important to remember that God is more than anything we can say?
3. Why is it important to have a community of faith?
4. Why do you think the Creed is nearly always a part of Sunday Mass?

Later in this textbook we'll explore aspects of our Christian faith more deeply. We'll study how God has entered human history for our happiness, for our wholeness of life, for our salvation. But all that will be just information, words, unless you are in touch with your need for God.

If you don't recognize this need, you'll find the good news announced by the Christian community strange and unrelated to your life. Then going to church or talking about religion will be boring for you. You may not be in touch with the deep longing in your life for ultimate happiness. If you think you can find happiness all by yourself, if you think you are the source of your happiness, then what the Christian community has to share with you—in church, the religion classroom, youth group activities, and times of **prayer**—may seem to be unimportant.

Write it down

1. What does it mean to believe?
2. What do you believe about God?

Going to church doesn't have to be boring. Just remember that God speaks to you in a special way during prayer and worship. It isn't phony to go to church, even if your faith is challenged by many questions. No one ever said that only perfect people should be seen in church. When you go to church, you are telling others that you believe that God alone saves and that you stand in need of God's help. Going to church is one important way to say you can't do it alone; you need others; you need God. People don't go to church to be entertained; they go to be saved.

prayer
turning the mind and heart to God

The Apostles' Creed

I believe in God, the Father almighty,
  creator of heaven and earth.
I believe in Jesus Christ, his only Son, our Lord.
He was conceived by the power of the Holy Spirit
  and born of the Virgin Mary.
He suffered under Pontius Pilate,
  was crucified, died, and was buried.
He descended to the dead.
On the third day he rose again.

He ascended into heaven,
  and is seated at the right hand of the Father.
He will come again to judge the living and the dead.
I believe in the Holy Spirit,
  the holy catholic Church,
  the communion of saints,
  the forgiveness of sins,
  the resurrection of the body,
  and life everlasting. Amen.

Optional activities

1. Most Christian Churches share the same Creed. Talk with someone of another denomination about this Creed. Discuss your understandings of each sentence or phrase. Write up your response to the discussion.

2. Research a non-Christian religion, and find out the essential beliefs, especially about God (the Internet may provide the necessary information). Prepare a presentation for the class in which you compare the beliefs of the religion with those of Christianity.

3. In small groups generate a list of other things Catholics believe (in addition to the Creed). Compare these lists, and compile a class list. Discuss as needed.

I know only scientifically determined truth, but I am going to believe what I wish to believe, what I cannot help but believe. . . .

Louis Pasteur

REVIEW

1. Why are some questions "life questions"?
2. What do Christians mean by the word *incarnation*?
3. What is faith?
4. How might idolatry be practiced today?
5. Why does a religion have dogmas?
6. Why do people go to church?

BELONGING TO A CHURCH

Then do this

Ask a friend or classmate from another Christian Church to share with you how his or her faith community prays together. How is this worship different from or like the worship of your faith community?

Talk about it

1. How does a believer stay connected with his or her faith community?
2. Is that important?

Earlier in this book we talked about an "environment" of family, Church, and society. Let's take a closer look at Church and at this business of "going to church." One of the struggles that may be going on in your life right now is about belonging to a faith community and going to church. Perhaps there is a battle over this between you and your parents—or perhaps a battle within yourself.

To help deal with this question, let's look at faith and religion—and the difference between them. They aren't the same thing. Faith is our openness to God. Religion is our attempt to respond to God. The interplay between faith and religion can be found in every culture on the face of the earth because God is present to everyone, working in every heart.

> *Every religion must . . . go back to the fundamental problem of optimism and pessimism, the problem of whether existence has a meaning and whether there is a world order which makes for the good.*
>
> **Leo Baeck**

RELIGION

Experienced religion

experienced religion

religion that is experienced through interaction with people who have faith and who practice (or don't practice) their religion

Let's look first at what we'll call **experienced religion**. When you were an infant and throughout your childhood, you "experienced religion." This experience of religion took place before you were even aware of what was happening around you. Experienced religion is religion that is experienced through your interaction with people who have faith and who practice (or don't practice) their religion. In other words, you grew up in a family, and perhaps in a Church, and you experienced religion long before you were aware of its influence on your life. To varying degrees religion as an expression of faith was part of your surroundings.

You experienced religion in the way people related to you. You experienced it in the way your parents and other family members talked to you about God. You experienced it when you imitated the religious behavior of others. You did what Mom, Dad, or your big brother or sister did. If they made the sign of the cross, you made the sign of the cross. When they bowed their heads to pray, you did too.

This experience of religion was necessary for your spiritual growth. You were already beginning to understand that a relationship with God was important. More was going on than the shaping of your behavior. Your parents and those around you were sharing their faith with you. You could pick up from their attitudes and behavior a sense of God's presence. In your own small and limited manner, you too were relating to God who has been with you since the moment of your conception.

Talk about it

Why do you go to church?

Practiced religion

As you have grown and matured, you have become more and more aware of being part of a family. This belonging to a family has been very important to you—for your security, your well-being, your self-image, your feeling of being loved, your personal development, your growing up. You needed to belong.

If your family went to church, you went to church too. And there too you felt a sense of belonging. Gradually, the religion you experienced through others turned into the religion you practiced—lived—yourself. That's what we mean by **practiced religion**. Being involved in a faith community nurtured your practice of religion. You identified with your community and were proud to be part of it. You *wanted* to be there!

Like experienced religion, practiced religion is deeply rooted in feelings of awe, wonder, and mystery. As you grew into and through this stage of your faith development, the religious ceremonies and activities of the Church community played a very important role in your life. They helped form your self-identity, and they gave you ways to respond to God's love. They motivated you to reach out to serve the needs of others.

Going to church gave you a family of faith, and your faith family helped you trust God even more. Your faith family helped you know that God was there for you and that God was trustworthy. It helped you realize that it was okay to respond to God in love and prayer.

Over time, every community of faith has developed its own special devotional practices, prayers, and **rituals**. People need these things to express their faith. People need to respond to God. In our response of prayer, signs, symbols, and gestures become very important.

Some important ways we respond with signs, symbols, and gestures are in the sacraments—for example, Baptism, the Eucharist, and Anointing the Sick—and our community worship. Through our families and our faith community, we have learned special prayers—such as the Lord's Prayer and the Hail Mary. We have also learned prayerful gestures—bowing, genuflecting, raising our hands, and making the sign of the cross. All of these are part of our worship. They help us live what we believe.

practiced religion
religion that a person lives with a certain degree of commitment

Then do this

1. Read Romans 12:4–21.

2. Discuss these questions: What was Paul saying to the early Christians about living as a Christian? To us?

ritual
action or actions repeated in a particular manner on similar occasions by a person or group

Then do this

The next time you're in church, watch people's body language. Identify five different postures. How does each posture reflect an attitude of prayer?

> The prayers of the Church are the age-long poetry of [hu]mankind,
> lifted above the perfection of poetry,
> for they are the prayer of Christ on earth.
> This is what ritual means, with its ordered movements,
> its wide encircling gesture of love, its kiss of peace,
> its extended arms of sacrifice.
>
> **Caryll Houselander**

1. Ask four people if they go to church on a regular basis. Then ask them why or why not.

2. Write down their responses and your reaction to the responses.

3. Without using their names, share the responses and your reactions with the class.

Practiced religion continues to play an important role in your life. This class itself helps nurture your practiced religion as you learn more about *what* we believe as Christians. The teachings of your community of faith are a basic part of your faith development. God doesn't depend on our teachings to love us. The teachings are for us, to help us know and love God. They help us show our love for God and for one another; they help us live what we believe.

Our response to God is important. Talking about our experience of God helps us express our understanding of how God is present to us. If we see ourselves as sons and daughters of God, we will more likely respond to God in wholesome ways that reflect God's goodness and our dignity.

Another important part of practiced religion is the way we've been taught right and wrong. All through your childhood, parents, teachers, and Church leaders have been telling you how to behave. You have learned which attitudes and actions are right and which are wrong. You have a sense of what's right and what isn't.

How often have you heard, for example, "Jesus wouldn't do that!" or "That's not a Christian way of acting!" or "What would Jesus do?" Statements like these have taught you that there is an expected way for Christians to behave. You have learned the connection between religion and faith, between belief and action—belief and life! God is present in your life—and in all our lives, indeed, in all creation. How we understand that makes a great difference in how we live.

Prayer

The Church offers its members a "language" for prayer: words, songs, actions, pictures, and images. During the history of the Church, the language of prayer has changed, shaped by historical, social, and cultural developments. Church authorities help us make sure that our prayer is faithful to Jesus. From pastors and others who teach religion, we can learn the meaning of our prayers in relationship to Jesus.

All Christian prayer is expressed through Christ. Whether our prayer is together or alone, spoken or silent, we pray to the Father "in the name" of Jesus. We do this because the life, death, and resurrection of Jesus give us the freedom to come before God in faith and childlike confidence.

See the *Catechism of the Catholic Church,* #s 2663–2664.

1. What is prayer?

2. Do you pray? Why?

3. Why would pictures and songs help people pray?

4. Why do Christians end their prayers with words like "through Christ our Lord" or "in Jesus' name"?

REVIEW

1. What is the difference between faith and religion?

2. What is experienced religion?

3. What is practiced religion?

4. Why do communities of faith develop special devotional practices, prayers, and rituals?

FAITH

Backing up our beliefs

The fields were parched and brown from lack of rain, and the crops lay wilting from thirst. People were anxious and irritable as they searched the sky for any sign of relief. Days turned into arid weeks. No rain came.

The ministers of the local churches called for an hour of prayer on the town square the following Saturday. They requested that everyone bring an object of faith for inspiration.

At high noon on the appointed Saturday the townspeople turned out en masse, filling the square with anxious faces and hopeful hearts. The ministers were touched to see the variety of objects clutched in prayerful hands—holy books, crosses, rosaries.

When the hour ended, as if on magical command, a soft rain began to fall. Cheers swept the crowd as they held their treasured objects high in gratitude and praise. From the middle of the crowd one faith symbol seemed to overshadow all the others: A small nine-year-old child had brought an umbrella.

Laverne W. Hall in Chicken Soup for the Christian Soul.

Optional activities

1. Read a section of one of the *Chicken Soup for the . . . Soul* books. Choose one of the stories to share with the class, and relate it to this course.

2. Write a chapter of your definitive autobiography. In the chapter describe the role faith and religion have played in your life. Use examples of people and events that have shaped you.

Searching faith

Most likely at this time of your life you find yourself somewhere between the practiced religion stage of faith development and the stage of **searching faith**. Moving into this new stage of faith development requires a sense of self and an ability to reflect, to think about things in a deeper than superficial way. At this stage of development, you are becoming aware that you're *not* a robot; you're not programmed for a certain way of acting and speaking. You are *you*.

You have the ability to step back and take a look at what you have learned and the religious practices which have been a part of your life. You may have some questions about these practices, and that's fine. You're searching and thinking. You're testing the community's attitudes, teachings, and practices. You're seeking your own ideas and trying to form your own convictions.

searching faith
the stage in which people seek their own ideas and try to form their own convictions regarding their understanding of God and of religion and the practice of religion

> Faith is to believe what we do not see,
> and the reward of faith is to see
> what we believe.
>
> **St. Augustine**

For you, searching faith may include the desire to experiment with different faith expressions, different religions and Churches. You want to know what other people believe, how they "practice their religion," what they do and say in church. And you take a close look at your own Church. What does your Church believe? Does it have meaning for you? How does it relate to your life? These are the questions all maturing people ask—at different times and in different ways. It's not because you don't want to believe. It's because you do!

Committing yourself to persons and causes, even if only for a short time and in rapid succession, is characteristic of this kind of searching faith. Searching faith often signals a movement from an unquestioning acceptance of your faith community's beliefs and practices to an acceptance which comes from your head *and* your heart. This movement isn't always smooth. It can be painful and awkward for you and for those around you. But it's very important.

You're growing up. You're looking for freedom. You want to be yourself. You want to be respected for who you are. That means you have to respect other people—and their beliefs, their teachings, and their religious services. To dismiss or ridicule other people and their beliefs and religious practices is hardly a sign of maturity. Like you, other people are on a faith search and are looking for happiness and freedom. This is the human condition.

Claimed faith

You have just studied how experienced religion leads to practiced religion, which in turn matures into searching faith. Now it is time to *claim* your faith. Let's review the process, the journey. Experienced religion is the religious beliefs and practices you learned from your parents and others. Practiced religion is the religion you practiced, were a part of, as you grew up. Searching faith is looking for your own place "in religion." And **claimed faith** is taking a stand in that place.

Your growth from experienced religion to claimed faith is commonly called *conversion*. At first you may think of people who change faith communities when you hear the word *conversion*. For example, your Aunt Jenny may have "converted" from Lutheranism to Catholicism. This is not really the best use of the word *conversion*, since Aunt Jenny is moving from one Christian denomination to another.

In other words, the word *conversion* refers more properly to a radical and significant change in one's religious outlook, a movement from one faith to another. For example, a person who changes from Buddhism or Judaism to Christianity is converting to Christianity, no matter what **denomination** the person joins. Likewise, a Methodist (or a member of any other Christian denomination) might convert from Christianity to Islam.

claimed faith
faith that has been made one's own through a process of conversion

denomination
a subset of a religion, a group within a major religion

The wonderful thing about saints is that they were human. They lost their tempers, got hungry, scolded God, were egotistical or testy or impatient in their turns, made mistakes and regretted them. Still they went on doggedly blundering toward heaven.

Phyllis McGinley

The word *conversion* means "turning with"; it especially means "turning from the way we're going and turning toward God, letting God lead us. **Conversion**, then, has another important meaning for us: It means deepening a relationship with God. This conversion is a lifelong process. In terms of everyone's personal faith, we all need to convert, to turn from wrong directions in life and toward God.

We all need to grow up spiritually, to move from "habits of religion" to a faith that is alive with love and service of others! In other words, we need to move from experienced and practiced religion to personally claimed faith, to live in union *with* the way of God in our life.

It's possible to get stuck at one of the early stages of faith development. Even an adult can merely keep on practicing religion without any question or examination of its role in life. Likewise, people can spin in the mud of an angry rejection of religion and religious practices.

Being willing to grow up depends on our sense of personal responsibility—our ability to respond to God's presence in our lives. Are we responsible enough for the journey toward claiming the faith? Ongoing conversion means turning from self-centeredness. It means paying attention to God in our lives, to the way our actions and behavior show—and don't show—our thankfulness and appreciation of God's presence. Conversion is a journey with God—letting God guide us to real happiness.

As you begin to claim your faith, you experience deeper personal conversion. You recognize that God is at work in your life. You experience a need for a faith community to nurture you and journey with you. You begin to live your faith with conviction. You show others what you believe by your words and actions. Your words are true and your actions kind. You mend the gap between belief and action by how you live. Your mind and heart are open to respond with faith and love to God's saving presence in your life.

conversion
(1) the lifelong process of developing a relationship with God; (2) the radical and significant change from one faith tradition to another

Talk about it
Why do some writers refer to life as a "journey of faith"?

> *F*aith is a kind of climbing instinct,
> which draws us upward and onward.
> **William Ralph Inge**

Joseph Cardinal Bernardin
A man of faith

Joseph Cardinal Bernardin was the spiritual leader of the Archdiocese of Chicago from 1982 until his death in 1996. Over 100,000 memorial cards were distributed to people who came to the cathedral to pay their last respects. Thousands of people lined the streets for twenty miles as his body was taken to the cemetery. Firefighters raised the ladders of their trucks, children held candles, many adults wept as the snow fell softly.

Why would so many people brave wintry days and nights in Chicago to say good-bye to a Catholic leader? The priest who gave the homily at the funeral Mass answered that question well. Msgr. Kenneth Velo built his homily around the cardinal's favorite prayer—"Lord, make me an instrument of your peace." After his reflections on each section of the prayer and on the life of the cardinal, the homilist asked: "Didn't he teach us? Didn't he show us the way?"

Cardinal Bernardin was a man of faith, a man of peace, reconciliation, and prayer. As priest and bishop he dedicated his life to building up the the Church, the body of Christ. Whenever he saw a problem or a need, he took action.

One of Cardinal Bernardin's last projects was the establishment of a forum called *Common Ground,* in which Church leaders—liberal, moderate, and conservative—could meet on "common ground" to discuss important issues facing the Church. His intent was to help the Church work as one and, therefore, be the sign of the unity Christ wants for his Church.

Some years earlier, Bernardin had been the guiding force behind an important pastoral letter by the US bishops, *The Challenge of Peace: God's Promise and Our Response.* With this statement the Catholic Church in the United States took a major step forward as a witness to peace among nations and peoples.

A short time after this letter was published, Cardinal Bernardin expressed the Catholic Church's pro-life stand as a *seamless garment,* referring to the Church's consistent ethic of life. In other words, the Catholic Church is pro-life in *all* life issues: abortion, the death penalty, war, euthanasia, and so on.

Cardinal Bernardin's greatest example of reconciliation was very personal. A young man dying of AIDS falsely accused the cardinal of sexually abusing him when the young man was a student years before. Cardinal Bernardin denied the charge, but he never spoke harshly of his accuser. In time the man admitted that he had lied about the cardinal to gain attention for his case against another teacher, and he asked for forgiveness. The cardinal went to see his former accuser and prayed with him.

Cardinal Bernardin was diagnosed with cancer in 1995. During his last illness, he ministered to hundreds of sick people. Wherever he went, people asked him to pray for friends and relatives who were also dying. Not only did the cardinal pray—he called, wrote, and visited as many of these people as he could. And, by his example, he taught hundreds of thousands of people how to die. In his death, as in the Prayer of St. Francis, he showed them how to live.

Optional activities

1. Do more research on the life of Joseph Cardinal Bernardin (check the Internet). Prepare a presentation for the class.
2. Read Cardinal Bernardin's book, *The Gift of Peace* (Chicago: Loyola Press), or at least one chapter of the book. Then write a reflection in response.
3. Locate more information on *Common Ground* or on the Catholic Church's consistent ethic of life. Find a creative way to present your findings: poetry, art, music, or another creative method.
4. Reflect on the Prayer of St. Francis (see the Appendix). Which verse is most significant to you? Write out your reflection.

STAGES OF FAITH DEVELOPMENT

Those people who study religious behavior have been able to identify the process of faith development. They have identified different stages. You should be able to recognize changes in yourself in how you respond to God. And you shouldn't be surprised to find people at different stages in their faith development. Obviously, a second grader will not have the faith of a ninth grader and certainly not that of an adult.

Interestingly, you have to grow *through* these different stages. You don't leap from one to the other or skip one. Your growth in faith is greatly influenced by the experiences of Church that you have had. It's also influenced by the freedom you have had along the way to think your own thoughts and come to your own conclusions. The right environment and opportunities help you progress through the stages of faith.

The stages of faith development require time. They aren't like rungs on a ladder that you climb to success or mature faith. Each stage is drawn into the next, incorporating the values or good points of one into the others. We should not give into the temptation to ignore one stage or another or think that it's not important.

That would contradict the way humans grow. We grow by integrating. Even people with a mature claimed faith need to experience simple, childlike trust in our loving God. Likewise, we all need a community of faith to establish our religious identity. We need a religious community that can give us direction and guidance, which we, in turn, must examine with a critical eye and make our own.

Every person is at some level of faith development. You might see yourself at the level of searching faith. If that's where you really are, great. But remember, in order to grow further, you must integrate what you have gained so far. Every once in a while, you may display attitudes and behaviors of a higher level. That's a welcome sign because it shows that you are open, moving, and growing. It's also possible to slip back to a less mature level of faith development, especially when you are stressed, personally or socially.

"Speak, LORD, for your servant is listening."

1 Samuel 3:9

The older you get, the less your stage of faith will be related to your age. As has been noted, it's possible to get stuck at one stage. Unfortunately, you can even be an adult who still is at the level of experienced religion. This might happen if you lack opportunities or the practice of faith in your home or with a faith community. People like this are sometimes called **unchurched**.

You can also get stuck at the level of practiced religion if you identify yourself only in terms of your current stage of understanding regarding your faith community and its practices. To the outsider an adult who remains at this stage may appear to be hung up on certain practices or ways of understanding certain religious concepts. The sad result is that some adults at this stage condemn or judge other people and faith communities.

You can also get stuck in a searching mode. Adults who do this often become angry or critical of other people of faith and of certain or all religious groups.

Finally, remember—you never reach a point in your life where you "graduate" from the school of faith development. There will never come a time when you have "arrived," neither needing nor expecting further growth. Because your relationship with God is ever-growing, like all relationships, you are never finished with your journey of faith.

unchurched
people who have no association with the practice of organized religion

Then do this

1. Read the story of the man born blind in John 9:1–41.
2. Discuss how the man's story may be similar to the story of some people today.

Write it down
Review each stage of faith and ask yourself which stage you think you are in. List examples to support your decision.

> "I am the way, and the truth, and the life.
> No one comes to the Father except through me.
> If you know me, you will know my Father also."
>
> **John 14:6–7**

Pilgrim Church

Neither the Church as a whole nor any one of its individual members have reached a stage of perfection. It's only in heaven that the Church and its members will be perfect, perfected in Christ. Meanwhile Christ, through the Spirit, is continually active in the world in order to lead all people to God. We believe that all things will be restored in Christ and that this has already begun. Our faith and the Church itself show marks of imperfection and "groans" while it awaits the time it is made perfect in the new creation.

See *The Documents of Vatican II*, "Dogmatic Constitution on the Church," #48.

1. What is perfection?
2. What are some signs that the Church is not perfect? That you are not perfect?
3. If God will eventually make all things perfect, what is our responsibility?
4. What do you think it will be like when all things are "perfected in Christ"?

REVIEW

1. What is searching faith?
2. What is claimed faith?
3. What does it mean to say that someone experienced a conversion?
4. Why does faith development take time?

PRAYER

The journey of faith requires prayer. People who are confused about the meaning of faith are often equally confused about prayer. What do you say when someone asks you if you pray? Your answer to that question will depend on how you understand prayer.

There's a difference between praying and saying prayers. Praying is turning your mind—and your heart—to God. In prayer you place yourself before God with a heart that is willing to be loved and accepted for who you are. You can go into church while your heart is angry and while your mind wanders some other place, but you can't pray like that. If you're going to pray, you have to be there with God, really be *there*.

Prayer and experienced religion

Have you ever noticed how easy it is for little children to pray? It's spontaneous; it just happens on its own. They talk to God as they would their closest friend. And they pray with great confidence! They relate to God—and rightfully so—as the one who knows and takes care of everything—the one who takes care of them. It's no wonder that Jesus often used this simple openness of children to describe the kingdom of God. In fact, one time Jesus said that unless we become like little children, we will not enter the kingdom of God. As you grow to adulthood, there's a powerful lesson for you here.

Prayer, or turning the mind and heart to God, is a most basic human experience of faith. Prayer is faith in action. It's opening our minds and hearts to God in whom we trust for our wholeness of life. Children find it easy to pray because the union between God and them has not been weakened by choices which separate them from God.

Talk about it

1. Do many people think of God in terms of what God can do for them or give them?

2. What causes this way of thinking about God?

3. How would you help someone see that God is asking for a response from us, a relationship of love?

Write it down

1. Are you ever alone and quiet—no music, TV, computer, and so on?

2. Do you like quiet when you pray?

3. Would more quiet time help you in any way? If so, how?

4. When you're upset or worried, does quiet time help you? Do you pray when you're upset or worried? How do you pray at such times?

Prayer and practiced religion

Some aspects of your prayer life have been learned from your contact with other believers, beginning with your parents and family. Those people who have taught you how to pray most likely have taught you how to fold your hands or bow your head. You have learned the *practice* of prayer.

Interestingly you have, in fact, learned the importance of praying with your entire body. Your very body is the vehicle through which you turn to God. Your body language is an important part of prayer. Do you bow your head when you pray? Why do people do that? Why do people sometimes look upward when they pray? Why do you sometimes fold your hands, or raise them up, or hold hands with others as you pray? Why do you sometimes kneel or make the sign of the cross or bless yourself with holy water? All these gestures are part of prayer.

You learned prayerful body postures and gestures from the groups with which you identified so far in your faith development. These postures and gestures have become connected with your comfort zone. Later in life you may feel uncomfortable when someone asks you to use a different body posture to pray or new gestures as part of your prayer. On the other hand, you may find yourself exploring new ways to express yourself in prayer as you grow older.

You also have been taught the formal prayers of your parish or faith community. Some Christian groups or denominations use more of these formal prayers than others. Catholics have a traditional set of prayers which includes the Lord's Prayer, the Hail Mary, the **Doxology** (Glory to the Father), and the Act of Contrition. The Mass itself is a prayer with a set form of celebration.

These formal Church prayers help you identify with the community and help the community unite in public prayer. Formal and familiar Church prayers give form and focus to your prayer, and, when used privately, they keep you connected with your faith community.

Prayer and searching faith

It may appear that no particular type of prayer is connected with the searching stage of faith development. Often the prayers learned in childhood are abandoned or the person seldom or never takes time for personal prayer. In this stage you may find the prayers of the Church lifeless and boring because the searching of your heart seems to be so intense. Church prayers often just don't help at such a time. If anything, perhaps prayer in this stage is more like an inner yearning for a fuller life and happiness. This deep longing is a form of prayer because it involves the turning of your mind and heart to God.

Because this is a time of searching in your life, you may find that your prayer often is expressed in terms of what you want to be given or what you want done for you. You want an "A" on a test or a trophy at the end of the basketball or volleyball season. In the searching stage, you try to find your own form of prayer; you feel a special closeness to God. Just "talking things out" with God while running or alone in the bedroom is a valuable form of prayer. Sometimes the right words may not come; sometimes no words come to mind at all. You just relax with God. This is a form of prayer all the same. It really is a turning of your mind and heart to God.

Talk about it

1. Respond to the questions in the second paragraph of "Prayer and practiced religion."

2. How can a change in body posture help you pray better?

doxology

prayer or hymn of praise to God, such as the "Glory to the Father"

Then do this

Write a prayer for your class to use.

Then do this

Interview 3 or 4 persons you admire who are good Christians. Ask each person to describe his or her prayer life. Think about the comments. Determine if any of those ways of praying would work for you.

Prayer and claimed faith

When you come to the point where you claim faith as your own, you begin to use all forms of prayer. You come (back) to a childlike simplicity and trust in God who is recognized and accepted as the ultimate source of life. The struggle of searching is far less intense or painful. You spend more time in listening prayer. And you share the prayers and traditions of your faith community because these help you develop a personal relationship with God. Instead of rejecting the community's prayers and traditions, you integrate and use them.

At this level of claimed faith, you value the opportunities for communal celebrations of faith because you know that the community is an important part of your identity. You also find time and place for personal private prayer. You have learned that the life of faith involves both a personal *and* a community response to the saving love of God.

With mature faith development, you feel drawn to serve others and care for the needs of the community, especially the needs of those who are poor and rejected in society. On your faith journey, you will have learned that loving God and loving your neighbor are two sides of the same coin. You cannot separate loving God from loving people, especially those who need you the most. Loving God is expressed in loving your neighbor. And if your love, your care for others, is God-like, then it must be unconditional.

Finally, the more you come to this level of claimed faith, the more you will be aware of your imperfections and personal weaknesses. But you will recognize that it's understandable not to be perfect: you are still on the way. Even though God's saving love has not yet become a full reality in your life, you stand before God, aware that God alone is the ultimate source of your happiness and fulfillment in life.

Write it down

1. Do you pray? Why?

2. Where do you pray best? Why?

Talk about it

Why is it important to develop some form of prayer on a daily basis and not just to pray at times of personal crisis?

Write it down

Make a list of the kind of things you most often pray about. Study this list. What does it tell you about your spiritual growth?

> *Surely we may with reverence say that, in a true and deep sense,*
> *God himself is the answer to prayer.*
>
> **Caroline Stephen**

Why we pray

See the *Catechism of the Catholic Church,* #2644.

To bless and adore God

We bless God because of all God's gifts to us:

Blessed are you, Lord, God of all creation.
Through your goodness we have this bread to
*   offer,*
which earth has given and human hands have
*   made.*
It will become for us the bread of life.
Blessed be God for ever.

Prayer at the Presentation of the Gifts
at the Eucharistic liturgy

We adore God by acknowledging God's greatness
and exalting him.

O Lord, my God, when I in awesome wonder
Consider all the worlds thy hands have made,
I see the stars, I hear the rolling thunder,
Thy pow'r throughout the universe displayed;
Then sings my soul, my Savior God to thee;
How great thou art! How great thou art!

Stuart W. Hine, "How Great Thou Art," hymn.

To petition God

For forgiveness

Have mercy on me, O God,
*   according to your steadfast love;*
according to your abundant mercy
*   blot out my transgressions.*
Wash me thoroughly from my iniquity,
*   and cleanse me from my sin.*

Psalm 51:1–2

For the fullness of the riegn of God

"When you pray, say:
Father, hallowed be your name.
Your kingdom come."

Luke 11:2

For the things we need

Vindicate me, O God, and defend my cause
*   against an ungodly people;*
from those who are deceitful and unjust
*   deliver me!*

Psalm 43:1

Write it down

1. What is your style of prayer? Give examples.

2. How does your style of prayer relate to your stage of faith?

Prayer to be fruitful must come from the heart and must be able to touch the heart of God.

Mother Teresa of Calcutta

To intercede for others

"I ask not only on behalf of these, but also on behalf of those who will believe in me through their word, that they may all be one. As you, Father, are in me and I am in you, may they also be in us, so that the world may believe that you have sent me."

John 17:20–21

To thank God

We give you thanks for all your gifts, almighty God, living and reigning now and for ever. Amen.

Thanksgiving After Meals

To praise God

*Praise the Lord!
Praise God in his sanctuary;
    praise him in his mighty firmament!
Praise him for his mighty deeds;
    praise him according to his surpassing
    greatness!*

Psalm 150:1–2

Optional activities

1. Write a prayer in each of the forms listed here. Begin a booklet of your prayers.

2. Write about times in your life when you have been moved to pray in each of the ways listed here. Describe the event and how you were feeling at the time.

3. Borrow a missalette and find in the Eucharistic liturgy an example of as many of the forms of prayer as you can. Share these in small groups.

4. Study a book of hymns and choose ten songs; decide which form of prayer is used in each. If possible, share a recording of one of the songs with the class.

REVIEW

1. What is the difference between praying and saying prayers?

2. What is typical of prayer in the stage of experienced religion?

3. What kind of prayer is common in the stage of practiced religion?

4. How does a person in the stage of searching faith pray?

5. What kinds of prayer experiences are common in the stage of claimed faith?

6. What are the usual forms of prayer (based on the reasons to pray)?

CONCLUSION

St. Francis of Assisi
A saint for today

Francis was born in 1182. Through his youth and as a young man, Francis was not a particularly religious person. Following in his father's footsteps, he became a buyer and seller of cloth. He loved popular songs and the stories of troubadours, and he loved to spend money. His spending habits made him a leader among other young people. On the other hand, he was often generous in giving to people who were poor.

Francis's town of Assisi went to war against Perugia, a neighboring town, when Francis was twenty. Naturally, Francis went to war, hoping for great adventures and acclaim. But Assisi lost the battle, and Francis became a prisoner of Perugia for a year. Soon after his release, he became seriously ill for another year.

Two such years can change a person. Although Francis set off to join the pope's army in southern Italy, he never completed the journey. After a dream in which he heard the message, "Follow the master rather than the man," Francis returned home and began to spend much of his time in prayer. This was his time of conversion, life-change. Soon he was visiting hospitals and leper houses and financially helping those who were ill.

While praying before a crucifix one day, Francis heard a voice say, "Francis, go and repair my church, which as you can see is in ruins." At first, Francis interpreted this literally and began to repair neglected churches in the area. When his father put a stop to the use of family money for this task, Francis began his life of poverty. In the streets he preached repentance, conversion, and a life of peace. Francis came to understand that the message he had received referred to the Church as an institution rather than to church buildings.

Many young men followed Francis in his life of prayer, poverty, and good works. Eventually they became a religious community, but one very different from the existing ones. They traveled around preaching the gospel, depending on others for their food and shelter. Nor did the brothers build monas-teries and large churches or seek places of honor in the Church. Considering himself unworthy, Francis never became a priest, although in time some of the brothers did. Francis's simple message appealed to many people who responded by trying to imitate his way of life in their day-to-day work.

At about the same time, Dominic was forming a similar type of religious community, with an emphasis on preaching the good news. The result of the efforts of Francis and Dominic was a grassroots reform of the Church. Thousands of people were drawn back to the gospel and to gospel living. Many new religious communities arose over the centuries after Francis and Dominic, and most of these were patterned after the way of life initiated by them. The journeys of faith made by Francis and Dominic continue today in the lives of Franciscans and Dominicans.

Francis died in 1226 at the age of 45. He is the patron saint of merchants and of those concerned with ecology. His feast day is October 4.

Optional activities

1. Interview five people on what they know about St. Francis of Assisi. Then read an account of his life (library or Internet) to see how accurate the interviewees were. Prepare a presentation on Francis for the class, and include something from your research that was not mentioned by those you interviewed.

2. What customs are associated with St. Francis? Research this and write a paper explaining the background on at least one custom.

3. Many children's books have been written about St. Francis. Find one or more of these and read it (them). Then write and illustrate a book of your own on St. Francis.

It takes time to grow through the stages of faith development. But you are not alone. God lives in your heart and continuously calls you to growth and fullness of life. Your path of conversion becomes exciting as you develop the freedom to search out and claim faith as your own way of living. Faith is a gift. Faith is your personal openness to God's loving and creative presence. You did not create your own openness. Your need for God—for a relationship with God—is the way God made you.

At the same time, God's creative love has made you free. It's up to you to claim your faith, to have your own heart-to-heart conversations with God. It's up to you to believe—to open your heart to the reality that God loves you unconditionally and is leading you to fullness of life and happiness. God continues to speak to your heart through all of creation and through your community of faith.

You are not alone, but the personal choice to believe is yours alone. No one can make you believe, that is, open your heart to God. Religion and religious practices can be learned and imitated, but there comes a point in your life when you must take responsibility for your own faith. This doesn't mean that you become your own Church. Personally claimed faith is not the same as claiming your own personal opinions.

Mature faith lets *God* speak. Mature faith is an openness of mind and heart to God and an awareness of how God has shown himself in human history. Mature faith is a response to what God has done for you. Ever since you were a child, the Christian community has shared the story of what God has done for us and for our salvation. The Church has offered you the good news of salvation so that your searching for true happiness and life will not have to take place in the dark.

The heart has reasons which reason cannot understand.
Blaise Pascal

Write it down

1. How can you develop a happier and more powerful life of faith?
2. How can you help those around you to do so?

Then do this

In a small group, plan a time of prayer for your class. Include Scripture, reflection, and intercessions (planned and spontaneous).

Words you should know

claimed faith	incarnation
conversion	life questions
denomination	practiced religion
dogma	prayer
doxology	ritual
experienced religion	searching faith
faith	unchurched
idolatry	

CHAPTER 4

GOD SPEAKS
Through HISTORY

The Word of the Lord

"I will judge the nation that they serve," said God, "and after that they shall come out and worship me in this place." Then he gave him the covenant.

FROM THE ACTS OF THE APOSTLES, SEE 7:2–8.

CHAPTER OVERVIEW

- *Setting the stage on our religious history*

- *Sacred time*

- *The Israelites and time*

- *The history of Israel*

- *Modern Judaism*

Not to us, O LORD, not to us, but to your name give glory,
for the sake of your steadfast love and your faithfulness.

Let Us Pray

Why should the nations say,
"Where is their God?"
Our God is in the heavens;
he does whatever he pleases.
Their idols are silver and gold,
the work of human hands.
They have mouths, but do not speak;
eyes, but do not see.
They have ears, but do not hear;
noses but do not smell.
They have hands, but do not feel;
feet, but do not walk;
they make no sound in their throats.
Those who make them are like them;
so are all who trust in them.
O Israel, trust in the LORD!
He is their help and their shield.

PSALM 115:1–9

SETTING THE STAGE ON OUR RELIGIOUS HISTORY

There's a certain security in infancy and childhood. People are aware of your needs and do things for you. It's a rather comfortable world. When you entered high school, however, your comfort zone may have shattered. High school is a time of great change and challenge, especially when it comes to faith and religion. You now must move beyond the old safe ways. Now you are asked to enter into a search for claimed faith—and a deeper, more personal relationship with God. This is your continuing journey of faith.

But you don't make the journey alone. Your peers share the same experience with you. Many others—including your parents—have been in your situation or are now there. As you respond to God's call to wholeness, you are supported by a community of faith and its tradition of faith. That tradition and the history of your faith community are very important guiding lights. You need to know that history—how God has been active in the history of the world and is active today.

As Christians we are blessed with a marvelous faith tradition. We are members of the **Judeo-Christian** (Jewish and Christian) tradition, we believe that the **Hebrews** (the ancestors of today's Jewish people) were the focal point of God's saving love in human history. We say that the Jewish people are God's chosen people. What does that mean? Are the Jews better than other people? Does God love them more than other people? No, that's not at all what it means. To answer the question, let's first look at the origins of these people.

Judaism is a minority religion in the United States—only a small percentage of the population practices Judaism. Depending on where you live, you may know only a few people who practice the Jewish faith. In some parts of our nation, there are very few members of the Jewish faith. In other parts of the country, however, those who belong to this faith tradition form a large and very important part of the social fabric.

The idea that Jews are God's chosen people is not rooted in something that the Jewish people have achieved on their own. It is their testimony to what God has done for them in their history.

> *For you are a people holy to the LORD your God; the LORD your God has chosen you out of all the peoples on earth to be his people, his treasured possession.*
>
> — *Deuteronomy 7:6*

The Hebrews, the ancestors of the Jews, originated in the ancient Middle East two or three thousand years before the time of Christ. They were a wandering people who moved back and forth across desert lands, looking for water and pasture for their flocks of sheep and goats.

Perhaps these ancient Hebrews were the **Apiru**, a people referred to in some ancient documents. In the original languages, the names are similar. Much like present-day gypsies, groups of the Apiru formed a loose association. At times the Apiru people were an important part of society. At other times they were outcasts, left to wander the barren hills of the ancient Middle East.

Judeo-Christian

the tradition based on the religious concepts and experiences of Jewish and Christian peoples

Hebrews

ancestors of today's Jewish people

Talk about it

1. Why is it important to know about important events of the past?

2. What is your favorite Old Testament story? Why is this story special to you?

Apiru

an ancient wandering class of people, possibly the ancestors of the Hebrew people

The actual details of the ancestors of the Jewish people are lost in the dust of history. They didn't pass on to us a clearly defined identity, and they certainly didn't have a national political structure. They were likely a humble people, an ordinary people, who lived on the rather barren land and survived as best they could.

Working through the circumstances and events of their history, God formed this wandering group into a nation, his chosen people—but, as we shall see, God had a purpose for them. They experienced being favored by God. Aware of the many useless gods which the people around them worshiped, they came to see their God as the real God—the one, true, and living God. This God was experienced as powerfully present. They came to know their God as the protective, mysterious one whose very name was so special that they dared not pronounce it.

This wandering Apiru (Hebrew) people did not choose God. God chose them and formed them little by little into a people close to his heart. When the Jews refer to themselves as "God's **chosen people**," they are not claiming superiority. Rather, they are being faithful to their history, a history understood as religious experience. Being singled out from among all the nations of the earth, including some very powerful nations, the Hebrew people came to recognize that God was doing something very special with them—and through them for the rest of the world.

Unlike the people around them whose many gods were feared, the Hebrew people came to believe in one God. This God was loving—so loving as to be jealous when they turned away. This God held these scattered and rejected people close. They came to express this relationship as a covenant.

chosen people
a people favored by God; the Hebrews or Jews

Write it down

1. How would you describe God?

2. Where did you get your information?

Then do this

Interview several adults. Ask them to describe for you some special moment when they had an experience of God. Write up your reactions to their stories.

> **H**appy is the nation whose God is the LORD,
> the people whom he has chosen as his heritage.
>
> **Psalm 33:12**

Covenant

covenant

a solemn, unconditional promise between two parties, such as between God and the Hebrew people

salvation history

the concept that history—the passage of time and events—is the very place where God makes himself known for our well-being

Talk about it

Why is it important to make a conscious effort to listen to the word of God with our hearts and not just with our ears?

A **covenant** is a promise, a deep promise. It's different from a contract or a "deal." A contract or a deal is an exchange: "If *you* do such-and-such, *then* I will do such-and-such." God's covenant, by contrast, is a solemn promise—an unconditional promise. God took the first step in making the covenant. God says: "I will be your God and you will be my people."

These few words don't seem to say much, but actually they say everything. Right in the middle of human history, God shows people who he is. God reveals himself as the loving, caring Creator of all things. God reveals himself as the all-powerful one who cares for humanity as his sons and daughters. God binds himself to them with a love that is unconditional, a love that will never let go. All humanity and all creation are bound to God with this strongest of ties.

The history of this covenant and the history of the Jewish people are one. This is why Christians and Jews talk about **salvation history**. Our loving God takes part in human history in order to save us. This is what the covenant—"I will be your God and you will be my people"—is all about. The self-revealing love of God at work in the history of the Jewish people is the foundation and root of our own Christian faith. We Christians believe that in Jesus there is a blossoming or coming to fruition of God's covenant— right in the middle of human history.

View from Mt. Sinai

REVIEW

1. What does the term *Judeo-Christian* mean?

2. Who were the ancestors of the Jews?

3. Why are the Jews the chosen people?

4. What is a covenant?

5. What do we mean by the term *salvation history*?

> *Time is our destiny. Time is our hope. Time is our despair.*
> *And time is the mirror in which we see eternity.*
>
> **Paul Tillich**

SACRED TIME

It is very important to note that God's self-revealing love and human history are the key ingredients of salvation history. When we talk about history, we're talking about time. And when we talk about time, we need to know what kind of time we're talking about. In salvation history, we're dealing with **sacred time**.

You may not usually relate to time as sacred, so let's take a moment to reflect on this experience of time. It's said that time is one of the most precious things we possess. Actually, it's not something we possess like a set of keys. Nor is time something we control. Rather, time embraces us with meaning—regardless of how we try to package it in minutes, days, eons, or whatever. All time is God's time; therefore, all time in the truest sense is sacred time. What happens in sacred time is not random nor coincidental; it is part and parcel of God's plan for our salvation.

Cyclic time

People don't always experience time as God's sacred time. Some people think of it as cyclic. *Cyclic time* refers to the experience of time passing in circles, with events merely repeating themselves. The same things happen over and over again. Haven't we all been bored at some time with what we might want to call the vicious circle of life?

Cyclic time is a reflection of people's experience of the seasons coming and going, day becoming night becoming day. In a similar way, events are repeated, not just remembered and celebrated (as we remember and celebrate our birth each year). In cyclic time, an event, such as a birth, seems to recur year after year. Its repetition is the only source of meaning. Life lived in such a fashion is awfully lonely.

The nations around Israel experienced time in this manner. They watched the regular movements of the stars, the changing of the seasons, and the rising and setting of the sun. They thought that Something must be controlling this regular cyclic movement; the same Something must also be controlling people. These nations saw meaning in their lives when they saw a relationship between the events of their lives and the cyclic repetitions of nature; they saw themselves as part of the circle.

These people gave expression to their beliefs in nature religions. **Nature religions** were filled with religious rituals that were faithfully repeated simply to keep order and meaning in the community. The village king, for example, was dethroned and then crowned again, year after year, in the same ritual. The problem with this view of time is that it often resulted in a sense of being controlled by forces beyond oneself or the community. Life can then become boring and without purpose. It can also be quite frightening.

sacred time
God's time

Talk about it

1. Can you think of any event today that is celebrated as if it were part of cyclic time?

2. How do you celebrate Christmas? Is there any cyclic feeling to how you celebrate? Why is our celebration not truly cyclic?

3. How do you feel when the pattern of celebrating Christmas or another yearly celebration has to change because of new circumstances?

cyclic time

the experience of time passing in circles, with events repeating themselves in some fashion

nature religions

religious expressions that see nature as a visible extension of the spirit world

The strange weed

A man went out to grow a garden. He tilled the ground, planted seeds, and watered the soil. Eventually, small buds began to emerge. Unknown to him a strange weed also took root and began to grow. . . . The weed grew quickly, sending out sprouts and shoots in every direction.

It was only when the weed had begun to choke the plants and itself blossom into foul-smelling flowers that the man decided to take action. He grabbed hold of the stem to uproot it, but it had thorns and they punctured his flesh. . . . Eventually, he took a pair of shears and went through the garden cutting away at the weed's many tentacles. He felt that he had finally rid himself of the pesty thing.

Unfortunately, as every good gardener also knows, a weed will continue to grow unless you kill it at the root. . . . The problem became too overwhelming for him to bear so he moved away.

At his new home, the man once again decided to grow a garden. He tilled the soil, planted seeds, and watered the ground. After a few weeks, tiny buds began to appear. So too did the strange weed. Without knowing it he had brought its seed with him.

John R. Aurelio, *Colors! Stories of the Kingdom* (New York: Crossroads, 1993).

Optional activities

1. Write an essay on a time when you brought your problem into a new situation. Explain what you could have done to change the direction things were going for you.

2. Using the concept "History repeats itself," prepare a report on examples of nations or groups repeating poor decisions rather than learning from past mistakes.

Linear time

linear time
the experience of time as progressing, moving forward

We can also experience time as **linear time**—time experienced not in a circle, but "in a line," progressing, moving forward. This is the experience of time with which we are most familiar in our culture. We live and plan our days within this kind of time. Think of a date book. Time moves forward—like a series of calendar boxes. There is a sense of progress from the past to the present to the future. A series of events leads somewhere.

There is a more natural meaning in this experience of time, but we're still the ones who give life its meaning. For example, we make the appointments, set the dates, schedule the events. We pack our calendars with "meaningful" events until the calendars are full: swimming lessons, piano lessons, football practice, dance rehearsal, golf games, visits to the dentist, Scouts, soccer meets, shopping, movies, vacations, family gatherings, graduation, and on and on. Time out!

This kind of time, like cyclic time, ultimately runs out of meaning. We feel empty, even when we have "filled our time" completely. We feel like we're always running somewhere, while our hearts cry out for "something more"—something more promising. Deep in our hearts we feel that the true meaning of time has escaped us.

We can control the date book, but we can't give time its meaning. The meaning of time is that it is a gift. If we converse with God, we will gradually come to understand how important and sacred time really is. We all have hopes and dreams for life, for "the future." But we also know that for each of us, time will end. There will come a point when we run out of time. Then what? Whether our number of years is great or small, we all want to know the purpose of our existence and the meaning of all that we do. This question is one of the life questions you studied in an earlier chapter.

Write it down

Make a timeline of your life thus far. Reflect on the things that will never be repeated in your life. Then complete the timeline as you hope your life will be. Take note of the things you have already done or are doing that will help the rest of your life go in the direction you envision.

Kairos time

Let's return now to the insight that history itself is God's sacred time. This experience of time is different from cyclic and linear time. St. Paul himself helps here; he would have referred to God's time as *kairos*. The ancient Greeks had two words for time—*chronos* and *kairos*. *Chronos*—or linear time—was measured time—seconds, minutes, hours, days, weeks, months, years. **Kairos time** referred to the meaningfulness of time. In *kairos* time the meaning of things is shown to us in the midst of human events.

We all know the experience of *kairos* time: We speak of it being "time" to begin or end a relationship, "time" to grow up, "time" to get a job, "time" to win the state championship, "time" to get serious about studying. You may know someone who has experienced a call to the priesthood, the sisterhood, the brotherhood, and felt it was "time" to respond to the call. Or you may sense that the right "time" has come to have a serious conversation with a friend or a parent.

kairos time
the experience of time as an invitation to respond; time where meaning and purpose are discovered

> *If you picture Time as a straight line along which we have to travel,*
> *then you must picture God as the whole page*
> *on which the line is drawn.*
>
> **C.S. Lewis**

All of these are experiences of *kairos* time—time(s) when we realize something about the meaning of life; we realize that "the time has come"—and that doesn't mean a specific date on a calendar or a certain placement of hands on the classroom clock. It refers to a sense we have of ourselves. We experience a call, as it were, and an invitation to respond.

In a religious sense then, we recognize that time is controlled and directed by God and that time is moving toward the fullness of God's kingdom, for which we pray, "Your kingdom come." Time truly is sacred, bound up with the experience of God, God at work in human history to save us. In a true sense, then, we could say that God "speaks" in and through time.

Each experience of time has a place in our lives. It's good that some things in our lives happen in a somewhat cyclic way. It's important for good order that we measure time with clocks, calendars, and date books. But most of all we need to relate to time as meaningful, because we want our existence to be full of meaning. We need to listen to the call of God in our lives as we experience the slow, sure passage of time. God gives our time ultimate meaning.

The Israelites and time

If we can see the differences between these ways of experiencing time, we'll understand Israel's sense of salvation history. There's no doubt that the Hebrews (Israelites) had routine things they did each day, each week, each month, each year, each decade. Theirs is a history that can be studied in the same manner as other people's history. Specific events and happenings molded and shaped their identity.

But to fully understand the experience of the people of Israel as God's chosen people, we need to see that there is more to their history than a mere series of events. In a very real sense, the history of Israel (the Jewish people) is not a record of what they did for themselves, but rather a testimony about *what God did* for, with, and through them. God spoke through human events. Because God's presence was made known through these events, they considered time itself as holy or sacred.

> *But as for me, my prayer is to you, O LORD.*
>
> *At an acceptable time, O God,*
>
> *in the abundance of your steadfast love, answer me.*
>
> **Psalm 69:13**

REVIEW

1. What is *sacred time*? How does it differ from our ordinary sense of time?
2. What is the difference between seeing time as cyclic and seeing it as linear?
3. What is *kairos* time? What is it in a religious sense?
4. How did Israel interpret history?

THE HISTORY OF ISRAEL

Whether or not you love history, as a responsible, educated young adult, you need to have a general grasp of the history of Israel. It anchors your Christian faith. This history of Israel—salvation history—is the history which Christians recognize as having prepared the world for the life, death, and resurrection of Jesus. Here are a few highlights of that history.

Talk about it

How does God speak to us through the events of history?

The call of Abraham (about 2000 B.C.)

Israel did not appear on the stage of world history as the nation it is today. The details of its origins are lost to the mysteries of time. We will begin with what we know. In much the same way that the history of the United States is often studied through its founding fathers, such as George Washington or Benjamin Franklin, so too the history of Israel begins with its **patriarchs.**

The first of the patriarchs of Israel was Abraham. His story is found in the first book of the Bible, the Book of Genesis. Abraham and his wife Sarah's clan or tribe lived a comfortable life in the countryside of what is now Iraq. God asked Abraham to take his family and to leave their comfortable life, to leave their security, and to make a journey of faith.

patriarch
founding father

God promised to make Abraham's descendants as numerous as the sands on the seashore or the stars in the sky. Abraham responded with complete confidence in God. He packed up his family and their belongings and set out, following God into a completely unknown future. He simply trusted God. Thereafter, Abraham has been seen as a model for anyone who seeks to listen for the will of God and who responds in faith.

Then do this

Read Genesis 22:1–18. Summarize the story and explain the message you see in it.

Abraham and Sarah had one child, a son called Isaac, born to them when they were already far along in age. One day, according to the story in the Bible, God asked Abraham to sacrifice his son. (It was the custom in those days to offer live sacrifices to the gods to please them. Sometimes, though rarely, these sacrifices were human sacrifices.) Abraham struggled with this challenge to his faith. He and Sarah loved their son deeply. And, since he was their only child, it seemed that the only way God could keep his promise to give them many descendants was through Isaac.

An obedient follower, Abraham nevertheless set out to sacrifice his son. Right at the very moment when Abraham was ready to make the final act of sacrifice, the knife in his hand, an angel of the Lord stopped him. Abraham's faith had been tested severely; his trust in God was clearly shown.

Perhaps this story was first told to condemn human sacrifice. The main point of the story, though, is faith. Abraham was faithful to God; he was completely open to God's will as it became known through the circumstances of his life.

Joseph and his brothers (1650? B.C.)

Few stories in the Old Testament are more full of feeling than the stories of Joseph, the shepherd boy with the coat of many colors. Joseph and his brothers were the sons of Jacob, who in turn was the son of Isaac—which means that Joseph and his brothers were great-grandsons of Abraham and Sarah.

As the story in the Bible goes, Joseph was his father Jacob's favorite son. Naturally, Joseph's brothers were jealous, nearly insanely so. In their blind envy, they got together and plotted to kill Joseph. But, conveniently (according to God's plan), a caravan was traveling through the area on its way to Egypt. Joseph's brothers sold him to the merchants and sent him off into slavery in Egypt.

Joseph found that he could interpret dreams (a skill highly favored among the Egyptians). Through the use of this skill, Joseph won his freedom and began a steady climb to important political positions. He eventually rose to power in the high courts of the land. By interpreting certain dreams correctly, Joseph was able to warn the rulers of Egypt to store up great quantities of food before a famine began.

Apparently, the famine spread throughout the Middle East, because in time Joseph's brothers came to Egypt looking for food. When they were brought before Joseph, he recognized them. They, however, certainly didn't recognize him. He was now an adult in a high position rather than the young shepherd boy sold into slavery. In time Joseph told his brothers who he was and encouraged them to bring his father as well as their families to live in Egypt. Imagine the tears at this family reunion!

These stories are important because they perhaps explain how the people we know as the Apiru (Hebrews) got from Ur in present-day Iraq, to present-day Israel, and then to Egypt. The story tells us why they made these moves. It would be common and natural for this nomadic people to travel south in search of food when a famine occurred. But remember, God works through "natural" events.

In the story of Joseph and his brothers, such events as famine and migration gain a human face. As religious history, the story tells us how God worked through human events to begin to mold and shape a people, a great nation, out of a small group of desert survivors. That great nation would be Israel.

Then do this

Read the story of Joseph and his brothers in Genesis 37, 39–46:7. Summarize the story and explain the message you see in it.

Then do this

If you have the opportunity, see the play "Joseph and the Amazing Technicolor Dreamcoat." If not, listen to the music. Choose five scenes from the play or songs from the recording and find the chapter and verses in the Book of Genesis that correspond to the scene or song.

Moses and the Exodus (1250 B.C.)

For a time, things went well for the Apiru or Hebrew people. They blended into Egyptian society—until something went seriously wrong. The pharaoh (the Egyptian ruler) turned against the Hebrews. They were put into slavery—as poor and helpless people often are.

A man named Moses, a Hebrew, was raised up by God to save the Hebrew people from being slaves to the Egyptians. As the story goes, the pharaoh decided to diminish the numbers of Hebrews by having all their newborn boys killed. Moses' mother put him into a basket and placed it in the reeds along the bank of the Nile where the pharaoh's daughter often came. Just as Moses' mother planned, the pharaoh's daughter found the baby and took him home. Moses was raised in the royal court.

As he grew up, Moses was sickened by the way the Egyptians treated the Hebrew people. Eventually he found out that he himself was a Hebrew. After killing an Egyptian who was brutally beating a Hebrew, Moses fled for his life into the desert.

In the desert Moses encountered God in the burning bush, where he learned God's name and that God is very present to his people. God sent Moses back to the pharaoh. The words he was to speak have echoed down through the centuries: "Let my people go!" Moses spoke those words, not for himself, but for the God of the Hebrew people. In God's eyes, these poor and rootless people were not slaves, but *God's* people, and God had great plans for them.

Famine and illness and all kinds of plagues came upon Egypt. Moses said they were signs from God. Still the pharaoh wouldn't let the Hebrew people go. Finally, when all the oldest sons of the Egyptians died, including the pharaoh's son, Moses was taken seriously. This last plague is recalled to this very day with the annual Jewish feast of **Passover:** The angel of death took the Egyptian sons, but passed over the houses of the Hebrews, leaving *their* sons alive.

Then do this

Read Exodus 3. Summarize this story of the burning bush and explain the message you see in it.

Passover

the Jewish celebration of the night the Hebrews in Egypt were spared the death of the firstborn sons and gained their freedom from slavery

This Passover night is the heart of Jewish history, Jewish religion, and Jewish identity. It is also the "anchoring point" of our Christian sense of liberation from sin and death in Jesus Christ. On Passover night the angel of death passed over the doors of the Hebrews because those doors were marked with the blood of a specially sacrificed lamb. This is the reason we call Jesus the "Lamb of God." It is he who "takes away the sin of the world," and who, through the sacrifice of his life, saved us from the power of sin and everlasting death.

The final defeat of the Egyptians came with the crossing of the Sea of Reeds (popularly referred to as the Red Sea). Movie makers have overly dramatized this scene, but what is clear is that this simple, defenseless people was saved from the mighty forces of the Egyptians by the miraculous hand of God.

If the Hebrews had been defeated by Egypt, their very existence would have been erased from the pages of history. But that didn't happen. God saved the Hebrews! From this moment on, the Hebrew people realized that they were nothing without God. God was truly their God and they were God's people!

This experience of freedom from slavery—the **Exodus**, or "going out from" Egypt—became the central point in the religious life of the people of Israel. In a dramatic and definite way God proved his covenant love.

Exodus
the Hebrews' escape from slavery in Egypt, through the Sea of Reeds, into the desert of the Sinai peninsula

Then do this
Read Exodus 11–14. Summarize the story and explain the message you see in it.

Go Down, Moses

When Israel was in Egypt's land:
Let my people go;
Oppress'd so hard they could not stand,
Let my people go.

Refrain: Go down, Moses,
Way down in Egypt land,
Tell ole Pharaoh,
Let my people go.

Thus saith the Lord, bold Moses said,
Let my people go;
If not I'll smite your firstborn dead,
Let my people go. *Refrain.*

The Lord told Moses what to do,
Let my people go;
To lead the children of Israel through,
Let my people go. *Refrain.*

O come along, Moses, you'll not get lost,
Let my people go;
Stretch out your rod and come across,
Let my people go. *Refrain.*

As Israel stood by the waterside,
Let my people go;
At the command of God it did divide,
Let my people go. *Refrain.*

When they had reached the other shore,
Let my people go;
They sang a song of triumph o'er.
Let my people go. *Refrain.*

We need not always weep and moan,
Let my people go;
And wear these slavery chains forlorn,
Let my people go. *Refrain.*

This world's a wilderness of woe,
Let my people go;
O, let us on to Canaan go,
Let my people go. *Refrain.*

What a beautiful morning that will be,
Let my people go;
When time breaks up in eternity,
Let my people go. *Refrain.*

Optional activities

1. Find a recording of this gospel spiritual and play it for the class (and teach it, if necessary).
2. Research the meaning of this spiritual and others like it in relation to the slavery experience of Africans brought to the United States.

Wandering in the desert (1250–1200 B.C.)

Once again the Hebrews found themselves on the run, without a home, without the security of a normal life. They came from a variety of backgrounds, this loose band of tribes. Now they were united by their common experience of freedom from slavery by the hand of a loving God.

This experience taught them something very important—that behind all the divine beings they had worshiped as their own tribal gods was the one, loving, and saving God. This awesome God could not be seen face-to-face and certainly could not be reduced to an image made by humans.

So the Hebrew tribes were bound together by two things: a common religious experience—their miraculous escape from the hands of the Egyptians by the hand of God, and the sense of responsibility this experience brought to them. They lived under the covenant, which, the story goes, God renewed with them on Mt. Sinai in the midst of their desert travel. And again God promised them a land of their own.

The Ten Commandments are a part of that covenant. God gave these commands to Moses to give to the people—to live by. If we search our consciences, we realize that the Ten Commandments are written on our hearts as well as on the tablets of stone given to Moses. They are the most basic of laws necessary for good order in society and for happiness in our relationships with God and others.

The laws of our religion, though no policeman enforces them, form an organic whole, a living pattern of behavior for a community and for each individual in it.

Herman Wouk

Then do this
Read Exodus 19–20:21.
Summarize the story and
explain the message you
see in it.

It takes time—and understanding—to learn to be faithful to God. So it was that the Hebrew people spent some forty years wandering in the desert of the Sinai peninsula. There God molded and shaped them for nearly two generations. Times were not easy, but when the people were hungry, God provided water and quail and a bread-like substance called *manna*.

At one place in particular, the people grumbled against God because things were not going their way. Even Moses doubted the faithfulness of God. This time of grumbling and hard-heartedness happened at a place called *Meribah*. It is remembered forever in Scripture:

> *For he is our God,*
>   *and we are the people of his pasture,*
>   *and the sheep of his hand.*
> *O that today you would listen to his voice!*
> *Do not harden your hearts, as at Meribah,*
>   *as on the day at Massah in the wilderness,*
> *when your ancestors tested me,*
>   *and put me to the proof, though they had seen my work.*
>   — *Psalm 95:7–9*

The Ten Commandments

Decalogue means "ten words." The Ten Commandments, we are told, were written by God, not by Moses. Above all, they are God's words. The Ten Commandments were given to us in a special context: the Exodus of the chosen people from Egypt. This event of liberation is the key event in the covenant God made with the Israelites. These Commandments provide a path of life.

See the *Catechism of the Catholic Church,* #s 2056–2057.

1. Why is it important that the Commandments are "God's words"?

2. What do you think of when you hear the word *liberation*? What does the word mean in this paragraph?

3. Why are the Ten Commandments an important part of the covenant between God and the Israelites?

REVIEW

1. According to Genesis, what did God promise Abraham?
2. What role did Joseph play in the story of the Hebrews?
3. Why is Moses so important to the Jews?
4. What is the Exodus?
5. What was the most significant event during the years the Hebrews wandered in the desert?

The conquest of the promised land (about 1200 B.C.)

The Hebrew people finally had a chance to return to their homeland, the land God promised them. Land was important to them: They needed a place to live, somewhere to *be*. And land was important to them because they knew God works in history, in people, in places, and in events. So God needs land too, a real place to work, to show his love. For the Hebrews, possessing the land meant not just stability and life, it meant having a place where God could act, where God could be with them and love them.

The Hebrew people most likely found parts of the promised land already occupied by distant relatives; in those areas they found it easy to resettle. Other occupants of the land put up resistance. Perhaps this is the historical setting behind the famous and exaggerated story of the Battle of Jericho, where amid blaring trumpets the walls came tumbling down!

The period of the judges (about 1100 B.C.)

The Hebrew people didn't come out of the exhausting experience of Egypt and the wandering in the desert as one united people. They remained a loose band of tribes, each of which had its own local leaders. Once settled in the promised land, these tribes moved into those same areas where their ancestors, the sons and grandsons of Jacob, had lived.

The Hebrew tribes settled in the land, each tribe going its own way—until there was trouble. And there seems to have been trouble quite often—perhaps in circumstances not unlike those of the Middle East in modern times. After all, the area known as "the promised land" formed the crossroads of the ancient Middle East. Lots of people wanted control of this piece of land! Time and time again there was crisis in the land. There were always threats from the non-Hebrew tribes who also lived there. When this happened, the Hebrew tribes joined forces to face the common threat.

God raised up special leaders to help the people through these times of crisis. These men and women came to be known as **judges**. These individuals weren't judges like the judges in our modern court system. They were men and women whom God inspired to lead the people through a time of crisis. Once the crisis was over, everyone went back to their homes, fields, and flocks.

Then do this

Read Joshua 6. Summarize the story and explain the message you see in it.

Then do this

Choose one:

1. Find a copy of the spiritual "Joshua Fit the Battle of Jericho." If you are familiar with the song, sing it. If not, try to find a recording of it to play to the class.

2. Locate another spiritual based on one of the events discussed so far in this chapter. Sing or play it.

judge
a charismatic leader raised up by God to unify the Hebrew tribes during times of crisis

Then do this

Read the story of Deborah in Judges 4–5. Summarize the story and explain the message you see in it.

The period of the kings (1000–587 B.C.)

The system of judges worked well for the defense of the tribes when they were fighting against someone their own size. But about a thousand years before the time of Christ, a huge military and political power arose on the coast of Palestine. This power threatened the very existence of Israel. This was a group of people called the *Philistines* or *Sea People*, and they possessed a highly organized political and military structure. They also had developed the use of iron for weapons. Israel and its loose band of tribes were used to fighting with sticks and stones, so the Philistines were indeed "the enemy."

Obviously something had to be done. Organization and military power were needed. **Israel** (the name of the twelve tribes together) sought to have a king who could lead them to battle in the name of God, a king who would make Israel a strong and mighty people.

However, there was one not-so-small problem: Israel's form of government was not a **monarchy**, where a single king (monarch) ruled. Israel was a **theocracy**, *God's* nation, and God alone was the sole "king" or law-giver. Would a change to a monarchy be a rejection of the loving and protective presence of God?

This was a moment of great crisis in the land of Israel, a change in the form of government! Can you imagine the United States switching from a democratic form of government to that of a dictatorship? Hardly! Well, imagine how much upset there must have been in the land of Israel one thousand years before Jesus!

In the end, because it was necessary, Israel chose a king—in fact, a series of kings. The first king, Saul, was followed by David. Some of the kings were good and some were not. Even King David, the most famous of them all, had his problems. Some of the kings, such as David's son Solomon, engaged in huge building campaigns, financed by heavily taxing the people.

Under the rule of some kings, the political power of Israel reached far beyond the territory covered by the contemporary nation of Israel. Under other kings Israel grew very wealthy and prosperous. But the true measure of a "good" king was determined by none of these measures of success. The true measure of a good king was faithfulness to God, to God's commandments and covenant love.

Israel
the twelve tribes, named for sons and grandsons of Jacob; eventually, the united kingdom, and later the northern kingdom

monarchy
rule by a single person

theocracy
rule by God

Then do this
Read the story of King Solomon in 1 Kings 3. Summarize the story and explain why King Solomon was known for his great wisdom.

King David was not allowed to build the Temple in Jerusalem because he had been a man of war; the privilege of constructing the Temple was reserved for his son, Solomon, whose very name is derived from shalom [peace].

Roland B. Gittelsohn

REVIEW

1. Why was possessing the promised land so important to the Hebrews?
2. What did the judges do?
3. What is a theocracy?
4. Who were the three kings of a united Israel?

King Solomon and the Ants

This poem is by John Greenleaf Whittier, an American poet who lived in the nineteenth century. The story on which this poem is based can be found in Islam's Qur'an.

Out from Jerusalem
　The king rode with his great
　War chiefs and lords of state,
And Sheba's queen with them.

Proud in the Syrian sun,
　In gold and purple sheen,
　The dusky Ethiop queen
Smiled on King Solomon.

Wisest of men, he knew
　The languages of all
　The creatures great or small
That trod the earth or flew.

Across an ant-hill led
　The king's path, and he heard
　Its small folk, and their word
He thus interpreted:

"Here comes the king men greet
　As wise and good and just,
　To crush us in the dust
Under his heedless feet."

The great king bowed his head,
　And saw the wide surprise
　Of the Queen of Sheba's eyes
As he told her what they said.

"O king!" she whispered sweet,
　"Too happy fate have they
　Who perish in thy way
Beneath thy gracious feet!

"Thou of the God-lent crown,
　Shall these vile creatures dare
　Murmur against thee where
The knees of kings kneel down?"

"Nay," Solomon replied,
　"The wise and strong should seek
　The welfare of the weak;"
And turned his horse aside.

His train, with quick alarm,
　Curved with their leader round
　The ant-hill's peopled mound,
And left it free from harm.

The jeweled head bent low;
　"O king!" she said, "henceforth
　The secret of thy worth
And wisdom well I know.

"Happy must be the State
　Whose ruler heedeth more
　The murmurs of the poor
Than the flatteries of the great."

Optional activities

1. Write another poem about King Solomon.

2. Research another king of Israel and present your findings to the class.

3. Find another poem based on an Old Testament person. Share the poem with the class.

God's prophets (about 1000–500 B.C.)

As we ourselves know, it's not easy to stay close to the ways of God. The chosen people of God, the people of Israel, knew this well. From its beginning, the monarchy of Israel was in a deep spiritual conflict between the ways of God and the ways of the king. In other words, it was easier for the people—or so they thought—to rely on their own cleverness and strength than to rely open-heartedly on God's inspiration and guidance.

Time and time again, in order to be safe, the Israelites made pacts with neighboring nations. Sometimes these deals meant that they accepted their neighbors' gods and, at times, their pleasure-seeking lifestyle. Often the kings of Israel surrounded themselves with well-wishers and official court priests and prophets who would support the king and his building projects and military campaigns.

In the midst of this struggle between the ways of God and the ways of the king and his followers, the people of God had some very unusual experiences. From time to time, individual people would raise their voices in protest against the godless plans of the king. They always spoke in the name of God against people who blindly followed ways that were not God's way, not in accord with the covenant of love.

These individuals who spoke for God condemned the injustices and maltreatment of the people who were poor. They called the people back to following the living God of Israel. These individuals came to be known as the **prophets**. Men like Isaiah, Jeremiah, Ezekiel, and Malachai made both kings and people shake in their shoes!

When we talk about prophets, we're not speaking about fortunetellers. Prophets didn't sit before a crystal ball, predicting future events. No smoke and mirrors or magic show for them. The prophets were deeply caring people who were very concerned about the direction in which things were going. The word they spoke was not their own personal opinion, but the word of God which demanded a response of faithfulness.

The prophets of Israel spoke of the experience of being called by God to help the community. Usually they did not attend a school for prophets or read books and manuals in preparation for their work. They knew the experience of God's Spirit moving in their hearts. They *had* to speak out in order to be faithful to themselves. In the name of God, they *had* to say "Stop!" to the injustices which they saw in their community. The prophets spoke to the conscience of Israel.

prophet

a person who speaks for God; one who speaks forth God's call to repentance and reform

The prophet Isaiah

> *The LORD rises to argue his case;*
>
> *he stands to judge the peoples.*
>
> **Isaiah 3:13**

Talk about it

Have you ever tried to discredit someone who called on you to change and improve? Why did you do this?

As we can see in the prophetic statements recorded in the Old Testament, the prophets did not speak in their own name. Standing bravely before kings, priests, and people alike, they spoke in the name of God: "Thus says the Lord God. . . ." The prophets spoke the word of God as forthrightly and sincerely as they "heard it" addressed to their hearts. The prophets' task was to be faithful in speaking that word. The prophets didn't need to worry about how people responded. That wasn't their responsibility. Often the people didn't respond and didn't return to the ways of God. And they paid for it! Respecting their freedom, God let them suffer the consequences of their choices.

Above all, the prophets constantly reminded the people of their unique and special vocation as the chosen people of God. Their God was a jealous lover who loved them too much to let them follow ways which would lead them away from life. Yet so very often the people of God would harden their hearts against the will of God. They experienced the same stubbornness of heart and will that the Hebrews experienced in their time of wandering in the desert. Time and again, the people rejected the prophets—and even killed them. We too can be as hard-hearted and stubborn. We too can "kill the messenger" when we don't want to change.

Then do this

Read the Book of Obadiah. Summarize the message of the prophet.

Isaiah

The most famous prophet in the Old Testament is Isaiah. In the book which bears his name, we find the prophecies of at least three different prophets and their disciples. The first Isaiah lived in Jerusalem and spoke his prophecies during the years 742 to 701 B.C.

The Gospels show Jesus quoting this book several times. Many other prophecies in this book have been interpreted by Christians to refer to Jesus, although they have another meaning for members of the Jewish faith.

Optional activities

1. Read the prophecies in Isaiah that are quoted in the Gospel according to Matthew. For each of the following verses in the Gospel according to Matthew, list the reference in Isaiah and tell who spoke the verses in the Gospel (some are written in by the evangelist as explanation). Then explain why the prophecy may have been included in the Gospel.

   - Matthew 3:3
   - Matthew 3:17
   - Matthew 4:15–16
   - Matthew 8:17
   - Matthew 11:23
   - Matthew 12:18–21
   - Matthew 13:14–15
   - Matthew 15:8–9
   - Matthew 21:5
   - Matthew 21:13
   - Matthew 24:29

2. Search one of the other Gospels for references to Isaiah. For each verse in the Gospel, list the reference in Isaiah and tell who spoke the verses in the Gospel. Then explain why the prophecy may have been included in the Gospel.

3. The Book of Isaiah includes references to a suffering servant. Read Isaiah 52:13–15, 53:1–12. In writing explain why Christians see Jesus in these verses.

4. Listen to the "Hallelujah Chorus" from Handel's *Messiah*. Compare the lyrics with Isaiah 9:1–6.

Our "gods"

From the comfortable distance of time, it is tempting to judge our ancestors in faith. Why would a people so blessed by God's guiding hand be so willing to trade it all for false gods and useless treaties. Why would God's chosen people worship pieces of metal and plaster (some of which can be seen today in museums), believing these things could offer them salvation? Why would they turn to deals and agreements with people whose ideas were not life-giving?

We may be puzzled by such actions, but if we were to honestly look at some of our own actions, we might be even more puzzled. At times we too follow some pretty strange-looking gods. We too engage in behavior that doesn't reflect our dignity as sons and daughters of God. There are prophets of God in our own times, but do we hear them?

1. What are our "gods"?

2. What kind of behavior "doesn't reflect our dignity as sons and daughters of God"?

3. Who are our prophets today?

Division and exile (722 B.C. and 587 B.C.)

The period of the kings was a "magnificent failure." This description seems strange, but it's a true one. The period of the kings was magnificent: building programs multiplied; the economy did very well; the government became organized and very powerful; places of worship were built; military power and influence expanded all over the Middle East. The "people of God" would have been the envy of any modern world power.

Yet all this was a failure because little or none of it brought the people closer to God. Quite the opposite! They thought they could save themselves. They often forgot the directives of the Ten Commandments. For many the practice of religion became merely a habit. What was worse, their mere external practice of religion covered up what was really going on—unkindness, selfishness, dishonesty, injustice, greed.

Even politically, the people paid the price for neglecting God. When the great and wise King Solomon died, his sons fought over who would be king, and God's people found themselves divided: the Kingdom of Israel in the north with its capital in Shechem (present-day Nablus) and the Kingdom of Judah in the south with its capital in Jerusalem.

The kingdom in the north had one king after another until it was overrun by the Assyrians in 722 B.C. The southern kingdom, where things stayed more even under the descendants of King David, did better for a time. But eventually the people's rejection of God's ways led them to their end. Their kingdom fell in the year 587 B.C. when the Babylonians destroyed the entire remaining Kingdom of Judah.

When the kingdoms fell, God's chosen people experienced great loss and exile. Many of the people, especially those in leadership positions and those who were strong, were sent into captivity and exile in the victor's country. Often the king and members of his court were quickly put to death, and anyone who could be a military threat faced torture and eventual death. Frequently the women were raped. Towns and villages were laid to waste. Only the poor were left to roam the hills to try to survive.

Interestingly, even in those days there were people who were willing to do anything to save their own necks. As God's people were carried off into slavery, some people collaborated with the occupying forces. These people, especially those who were from an area called Samaria (approximately in the middle of present-day Israel), joined forces with the occupiers in much the same way that some people in European nations collaborated with Adolph Hitler's reign of terror during World War II. In New Testament times, the Samaritans (as these people came to be known) were shunned and hated by the Jews.

Then do this
Read 2 Chronicles 36. Summarize the story and explain the message you see in it.

The return from exile and the reform (536 B.C.)

Obviously, during their time in exile the people of God yearned for the day they would be free to return home. Their exile reminded them of the time of their ancestors' slavery in Egypt. Without a place of worship (the **temple** in Jerusalem, which had been destroyed), the people of God were left with their memories. And indeed they had plenty of time to think about the misery they had brought on themselves.

temple
the central place of sacrifice and worship for the Jewish people, located in Jerusalem

> *By the rivers of Babylon—*
> *there we sat down and there we wept*
> *when we remembered Zion.*
> *On the willows there*
> *we hung up our harps.*
> *For there our captors*
> *asked us for songs,*
> *and our tormentors asked for mirth, saying,*
> *"Sing us one of the songs of Zion!"*
> *How could we sing the LORD's song*
> *in a foreign land?*
> *If I forget you, O Jerusalem,*
> *let my right hand wither!*
> —*Psalm 137:1–5*

Then do this
Read Ezra 6. Summarize the story and explain the message you see in it.

Religious faith is not a storm cellar to which men and women
can flee for refuge from the storms of life.
It is, instead, an inner spiritual strength which enables them
to face those storms with hope and serenity.
Sam J. Ervin Jr.

Torah

Torah
the Law, the first five books of the Bible: Genesis, Exodus, Leviticus, Numbers, and Deuteronomy; also called the *Pentateuch*

During this time of exile, three important developments took place.

The first five books of the Hebrew Scriptures (the **Torah**, or *Law*) were put into a final, edited form. The people of God needed something to pull them together and unify them. They found it, not in themselves, but in the word of God. Much of this word had come to the people in spoken or oral form. Even after it was written down, they continued to memorize much of it. As this collective memory of Israel took written shape, it reformed and reshaped the people. The written word of God—especially in the form of the Torah—became the measure for faithfulness to the way of God.

A group of people called scribes, who were responsible for the writing, editing, and preservation of the sacred texts, became prominent leaders during this time. Gradually the priests, in contrast, lost their influence because their sacrifices could be offered only in the temple in Jerusalem and not in the land of exile. The scribes filled the vacuum. They not only copied texts of the books of the Hebrew Scriptures (which are also the major part of the Old Testament for Christians), but also offered their ideas regarding the way the people should live their life of faith.

In the year 538 B.C., King Cyrus came to power in the Middle East. Having no reason to keep the Israelites under political suppression, he decreed that those in exile could return to their homeland and worship as they wished. The people returned with grateful and joyous hearts. They eagerly rebuilt the temple in Jerusalem so that the priests once again could offer sacrifices. As a result, the priests regained some of their leadership. The scribes and the priests worked together to guide the people and to develop their religious practices.

Synagogues

synagogue
Jewish house of prayer in which the Torah is read and where people pray and are instructed in their faith

With the passage of time, the rich tradition of the prophets faded. By around 450 B.C. the voice of the prophets was no longer heard. Despite this absence, the people continued to seek a close relationship with God. It's understandable that without the personal voice of God spoken through a prophet, the *written* word of God—or Sacred Scripture—took on central importance. When the people couldn't make it to Jerusalem to the temple, they would gather in local places of worship, called **synagogues**, to hear the Scriptures read and explained and to pray.

Messianic expectation

messiah
the anointed one who ushers in the time of salvation, the Christ

In this time of political and religious change, a deep hope grew in the hearts of many of the people that God would act in a final and complete way in their history and would bring salvation. Many people waited for the day when God would send his Spirit upon the prophet, the priest, the king—a specially anointed one—who would "usher in" God's final day of salvation. The Hebrew word for this "anointed one" is **messiah** (the Greek word is *cristos*, or "the Christ").

Then do this
Find a story in the Old Testament which gives you an insight into what God is like. Using magazine clippings, make a poster to portray this insight.

REVIEW

1. What was the role of the prophets?
2. Why did the kingdom split into the Kingdoms of Israel and Judah?
3. Why were many of the people sent into exile?
4. What three important developments took place during the exile?

Greeks and Romans (335–1 B.C.)

The history of Israel didn't end with the return from exile. The people didn't just sit around waiting for the messiah. The few people who returned from exile, the "holy remnant," continued to pass on the faith. So did their descendants.

This didn't mean that the people of God were immune from political troubles. The Jews were under the constant threat of domination and control, as the powerful nations of the world continued to fight for control of what we now refer to as the *Holy Land*. After all, it was the crossroads of the ancient Middle East and a key intersection in paths of trade and the exchange of goods, ideas, and culture.

About three hundred years before Jesus, a young Greek named Alexander set out to conquer the world. He met great success and his influence quickly spread around the Mediterranean Sea—and even farther east. As a result of his amazing conquests, he earned the title "Alexander the Great." And he was only in his late twenties!

Along with Alexander's victories came the influence of Greek culture with its philosophy ("love of learning"), its ideas about truth, justice, and the eternal life of the soul. These ideas became important even in tiny Israel where Greek became the dominant and "politically correct" language of the time. That's why the New Testament was written in Greek.

About a century and a half before the birth of Jesus, the Greeks brutally suppressed the Jewish people during a rebellion led by the Maccabee brothers. The temple in Jerusalem was desecrated and statues of Greek gods were set in the Jews' sacred places. To faithful Jews this was an abomination of abominations!

Write it down

When a nation is faced with a natural disaster or with the threat of war, large groups of people often turn to prayer.

1. Have you ever experienced this group need to pray? If so, when?

2. Why do people turn to prayer at such times?

An oppressive government is more to be feared than a tiger.

Confucius

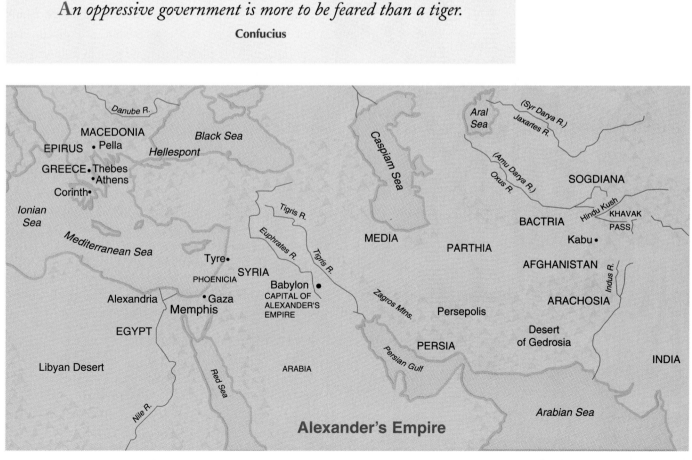

Alexander's Empire

But the rule of the Greeks didn't last forever. Domination by the Greeks was followed by that of the Romans. Like the Greeks, the Romans set out to establish an empire all over the known world. They extended their powerful influence deep into Africa, as far north as the present British Isles, and far into the Middle East, subjugating the many nations and peoples they conquered. Some of the people in these areas were able to become citizens of Rome, which brought them a certain degree of protection not available to non-citizens. Paul himself was one such citizen. He used this privilege to facilitate his missionary journey to Rome.

The conquered nations of the empire were left to the control of kings and governors who swore loyalty to Rome. Rome gave limited autonomy, or self-rule, to these mini-kingdoms, expecting only two things in return: no disturbance of the peace and the payment of tribute, or taxes, to Caesar (the Roman government). The Romans totally crushed any rebellion. Anyone suspected of rebelling against Caesar and Roman rule was put to death—often by crucifixion.

The Romans were the occupying force in Palestine at the time of Jesus. They made their presence known, especially in the city of Jerusalem, at the time of the high holy days. The Jewish people resisted the Roman system as much as they could. Unlike many peoples who simply bowed to the domination of the Greeks and then the Romans, the Jews continually pushed for their political and religious freedom. Many of their people

"Are you the king of the Jews?" Jesus said, "You say so."

—Matthew 27:11

were willing to sacrifice their lives for the cause of freedom from oppression. Because the Romans wanted peace (and money), they granted the Jewish people more freedom than they did other conquered nations.

The Jews themselves wanted nothing more than their final deliverance from their oppressors. Many of them longed for a deliverer, a messiah. It's understandable then that some people followed one or another charismatic person who claimed to be the "anointed of the Lord." For several of these messianic leaders, their causes either came to nothing or the leaders and their followers were crushed by the Romans.

Jesus was born into this complex world of political struggle and religious fervor. Many of Jesus' followers experienced him as the long-awaited, expected deliverer, the messiah. The life and ministry of Jesus need to be seen against this setting. Contrary to the political hopes of other "messiahs" of his day, Jesus proclaimed a kingdom that was not political. But the Romans made no distinction; they regarded Jesus as a rebel and an enemy of Rome. Some of the religious leaders in Jerusalem also regarded Jesus as an enemy of their way of life and peaceful coexistence with Rome. Between the two groups, Jesus was trapped—and crucified. The year was about A.D. 33.

The fall of Jerusalem (A.D. 70)

In the year A.D. 70 the rebellion of the Jewish people against the domination of the Romans reached a fever pitch. The Romans moved against the Jews. They attacked Jerusalem—as had so many nations in past times—and totally destroyed the city. They burned Jerusalem to the ground and, most significantly, destroyed the grand temple that stood brilliantly on a high hill in the middle of the city. To this day the temple has not been rebuilt. The Jews and the newly formed community of Christians had to flee Jerusalem at this time.

Jewish guerrilla fighters held out until the end on the top of a mountain called *Masada* on the shore of the Dead Sea. At the last moment the fighters committed suicide rather than surrender to the Romans. The final conquest of the Masada fortification signaled the end of the nation of Israel as it existed then. The fortification remains to this day an important place of pilgrimage.

The Jewish people were scattered to the ends of the earth. This movement out of Palestine actually had begun long before this, however, which explains why Paul found small pockets of Jews around the Mediterranean as he traveled and proclaimed the gospel. But with the fall of Jerusalem, the Jewish people were once again left without a land of their own—this time with a fate far worse than when they had gone into the Babylonian Exile. An earlier prophecy came to pass again; they could find little comfort in these words:

> *Judah has gone into exile with suffering*
>> *and hard servitude;*
> *she lives now among the nations,*
>> *and finds no resting place;*
> *her pursuers have all overtaken her*
>> *in the midst of her distress.*
>> — *Lamentations 1:3*

It is usually in the wake of frustration,

in moments of crisis and self-disillusionment, . . .

that radical reflection comes to pass.

Abraham Joshua Heschel

REVIEW

1. After the exile, what two major groups took control of the territory inhabited by the Jews?

2. What was the political situation of Palestine at the time of Jesus?

3. What happened to the surviving Jews and Christians in Palestine after the fall of Jerusalem?

MODERN JUDAISM

For Christians, the life, death, and resurrection of Jesus are the turning point of human history, so much so that we date historical events in relationship to the date of Jesus' birth. For centuries most of the world has used the designations "before Christ" (B.C.) and "after Christ" (A.D.—*anno Domini* (Latin) meaning "in the year of the Lord") to date events.

Although most Christians today are unaware of many of the details, the history of the Jews did not end with the death of the first followers of Jesus. The Jewish people have continued, and they have continued to write a rich history. From the perspective of faith, the Jewish people remain to this day the chosen people of God. They are the recipients of the promise God made to bring forth from them the salvation of the world. Christianity must see itself in this light.

The Holocaust and the State of Israel (1930s–1940s)

For the Jewish people, the time of wandering and exile lasted from the end of the first century to the middle of the twentieth century! Such a time of suffering and separation from the land of their heritage is hard to imagine. This time of exile became intimately linked with the relationship between Christians and Jews and even with the struggle for political and economic power.

Jesus was a Jew and practiced the Jewish religion (Judaism) throughout his life. His teachings are rooted in and intertwined with the Law. His first followers were Jews. The Church itself grew out of Judaism, and our worship today still parallels the worship of Judaism in many ways.

There is no justification whatsoever to condemn Jews for the death of Jesus. Unfortunately, Christians lost the truth of their relationship with Judaism and persecuted Jews for centuries. Christians have a truly terrible history of oppressing the Jews in many ages.

One name reminds the world of the suffering of the Jews. That name is Adolph Hitler. During World War II, Hitler took advantage of what he called the "Jewish problem" during his campaign to conquer the world and establish the "perfect race." He appealed to the anti-Jewish feeling that had evolved over the centuries, and he set out to exterminate the Jews from the face of the earth. This "final solution"—in which over six million Jews were murdered in the concentration camps and gas chambers of Europe—remains forever in the memory of the world as a lesson to be learned about hate. This was the **Holocaust**.

Holocaust
the systematic, bureaucratic annihilation of six million Jews by the Nazi regime and their collaborators during World War II

After the war, the United Nations, under the leadership of the United States and Great Britain, moved to re-establish the political state of Israel (1947). As a result, the small but powerful nation of Israel was born in 1948 in the same land the Hebrews called the promised land. The chosen people have returned home.

> *We cannot contemplate without terror the extent of the evil which man can do and endure.*
>
> **Simone Weil**

The death of Jesus

The story in the Gospels of Jesus' trial hints strongly at the complex historical situation. In God's eyes, there may have been personal sin on the part of some of the participants. But we cannot blame all the Jews in Jerusalem, and certainly not the Jews of other places and times for the death of Jesus. The Second Vatican Council taught that Scripture must not be used to reject or discriminate against the Jews. They are not guilty of any crime related to the death of Jesus.

See the *Catechism of the Catholic Church*, #597.

1. How did the complex historical situation in Jerusalem influence the decision to put Jesus to death?

2. Since that time, what have been some of the results of blaming the Jews for the death of Jesus?

3. Why is it wrong to blame the Jews for the death of Jesus?

Sister Antonia
Haunted by a photo

Mary Brenner was a forty-eight-year-old divorced mother of seven children. She worked in Beverly Hills. She had some kind of a carbon paper manufacturing company. She dealt with all the movie stars. She went to their parties. She hobnobbed with the celebrities, the kind of people whose faces leer at us out of People *magazine.*

What turned her around and made her see life differently? She came across a very famous photograph . . . The photograph was taken during the Holocaust and is of the people lined up; a little eight- or nine-year-old boy is standing with his hands up and a Nazi is pointing a rifle at the kid, whose little eyes show deep fear and bewilderment.

And she looked at that photograph and suddenly realized that life could never be the same for her. She felt an enormous compassion for all those who were victims of other people's brutality, for those who were the most marginal.

So she went to the bishop of San Diego and said, "I'd like to have some kind of a little religious order here, and I'd like to dedicate myself to those people nobody wants. Who are the most deprived?"

And she wound up being called Sister Antonia, and she works with the women in the Tijuana Prison, a women's prison in Mexico, certainly the most abject and forlorn and neglected segment in humanity. She's their friend, companion, sister, mother, grandmother, all wrapped in one.

William J. Bausch, *Telling Compelling Stories*.

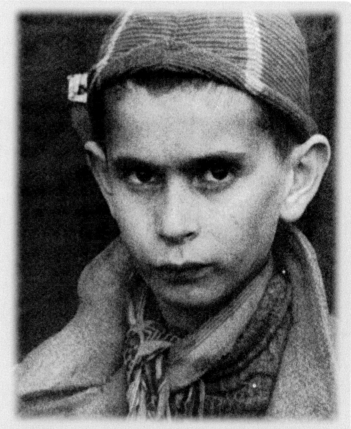

Optional activities

1. Read a book about the Holocaust. Share with the class the story of someone who was not Jewish whose life changed because of the Holocaust.

2. Visit the United States Holocaust Memorial Museum in Washington, DC—in person or through the Internet at http://www.ushmm.org. Write up a report or give a presentation to the class.

3. Find out something about other groups of "undesirables" targeted by the Nazis before and during World War II. Present your research to the class.

The Israelis and the Palestinians (1948 to the present)

The nation of Israel still exists. But its presence "on the land" contributes to an extremely explosive situation in the Middle East. When the Romans kicked the Jews out of Jerusalem in A.D. 70, this part of the world did not sit idly vacant like an empty abandoned car in a back parking lot. The Arab people of the area—who had been around for centuries themselves and who traced their heritage to the God of Abraham—quickly occupied the land. The central part of this geographical territory was settled by the semi-nomadic Palestinian people.

When the modern-day nation of Israel was formed, hundreds of thousands of Palestinians were forced from their land into what were supposed to be temporary refugee camps. At the time the Palestinians rejected a settlement, so the camps remain to this day—*generations* later. As a result we often see the anger and frustration played on in the nightly television news.

The Six Day War (June 1967)

The nations of the Middle East include Egypt, Syria, Lebanon, Jordan, Saudi Arabia, Iraq, and Iran; most of these nations are Arab. In June 1967 Syria, Egypt, Lebanon, and Jordan jointly waged war against Israel. Though Israel is a small nation, its military power has been tremendous. Its armies—like its armies of ages past—are well trained and advanced in technological abilities. The war was over in a very short time and now is referred to as the "Six Day War." As a result of this war, Israel took control of the Golan Heights (a very important segment of land overlooking the Valley of Israel) and the Gaza Strip between Israel and Egypt.

Of greatest significance in terms of the result of the war was the unification of the city of Jerusalem. When the political nation of Israel was created, a significant part of the city of Jerusalem was left in the hands of Jordan. This particular part included the golden-domed **mosque** (the Dome of the Rock), which is one of the three most sacred places on earth for the religion of Islam. It is believed by Muslims (those who practice Islam) that their prophet Muhammad was taken into heaven from the huge rock preserved under this dome.

The problem is that this same plot of land is also sacred to the Jews. It's situated on a few acres of land called the *Temple Mount*. This is a noticeably raised area in the old part of the City of Jerusalem. Located in the west side of this area is the Western Wall (also known as the Wailing Wall)—the remaining stones of the temple which King Solomon had built. These huge stones provide a place for Jews to come, even to this day, to pray for their people and for the restoration of the temple itself. On top of this temple mount, there once stood the Great Temple with its most sacred sanctuary, the Holy of Holies—that part of the Jewish temple which the high priests entered once a year to offer sacrifice for the atonement of the sins of Israel. Undoubtedly, Jesus had prayed in the last temple built here.

mosque
community place of prayer for Islamic men

Then do this
Research the Islamic religion: its founder, its beliefs, its practices.

Ascribe to the Lord the glory due his name;

bring an offering, and come before him....

1 Chronicles 16:29

Though no one knows the exact location of the Holy of Holies, obviously, this temple space is sacred to the Jewish people. Strictly conservative Jews today push for the rebuilding of the temple on this mount. In their eyes such a reconstruction would be not just a re-establishing of an ancient structure; it would also hasten the coming of God's kingdom.

Over the decades following the Six Day War, efforts continued to bring peace to this vital area in the Middle East. Because the situation is complex, peace plans are also complex. World opinion on rights to land differs somewhat from group to group. While the Arab nations as a whole tend to oppose the demands of Israel, there is some give-and-take when it comes to the specifics. It has never been easy for the Jews to hang on to this land, and for the foreseeable future there will probably be more struggles to balance the demands of Israelis and Palestinians.

Then do this
Work with a group of classmates to make a mural showing the highlights of the history of salvation.

Jerusalem today

REVIEW

1. Why are the Jewish people today still the chosen people of God?

2. What was the Holocaust?

3. When did Israel again become a nation?

4. What problems has Israel faced since becoming a nation again?

CONCLUSION

Edith Stein
Jew and Catholic saint

Edith Stein was born in 1891 in present-day Poland. She was the youngest child in a large Jewish family. A good student, Edith studied philosophy at the university in her hometown (Breslau, Germany, now Wroclaw, Poland) and two other universities.

During her university studies, Edith realized that she would eventually become a Christian. She became particularly interested in the Catholic faith when she read the life of St. Teresa of Avila, a famous Spanish Carmelite nun. On New Year's Day in 1922, Edith was baptized at the beautiful cathedral in Cologne, Germany. She then taught at a Dominican college for women until the Nazis forbade professional employment by Jews.

After her mother's death, Edith entered the Carmelite convent in Cologne. Her name in religious life was Sister Teresa Benedicta of the Cross. Because of the political situation in Germany, Teresa Benedicta moved to a Carmelite convent in Holland in 1938 in order to protect the other sisters of the community.

But in 1940 the Nazis conquered Holland. After a 1942 pastoral letter signed by the leaders of the Catholic Church and several Protestant Churches protesting the persecution of the Jews in Holland, many Catholics of Jewish descent were arrested. Among them were Teresa Benedicta and her sister Rose. Those arrested were sent to the concentration camp at Auschwitz, and there, just days later, Teresa Benedicta died in the gas chambers. She was fifty-one.

In 1987, Pope John Paul II beatified Sister Teresa Benedicta in the cathedral at Cologne. She was canonized in 1998. Despite the great evil of Hitler's campaign against the Jews, Edith Stein lived a life of dedication and prayer. She is remembered for her scholarship and her holiness—a faithful Jew and a faithful Catholic religious.

Optional activities

1. Find out more about Edith Stein and share the information with the class.
2. Research St. Teresa of Avila and write up a report.
3. Read *The Diary of Anne Frank*, another story from Holland during the Nazi occupation. Write a reflection.

The history of Israel continues. Faithful Jews still await the coming of a messianic age that will usher in the last days of God's kingdom. As Christians we believe that Jesus *is* the Messiah! We wait for God to bring all things together in his Son at that point in time we have come to call the second coming.

Christians believe that God has shown himself fully in Jesus; revelation is complete in him. Christians believe that the life, death, and resurrection of Jesus—the Paschal mystery—is a "hinge in time." Jesus is the special "lens" of God though whom Christians understand God's unfolding plan of salvation in the history of the chosen people. World history continues to unfold, but the meaning of salvation history is to be found in the Word of God made flesh in Jesus.

Every act leaves the world with a deeper
or a fainter impress of God.
Alfred North Whitehead

Words you should know

Apiru	**monarchy**
chosen people	**mosque**
covenant	**nature religions**
cyclic time	**patriarch**
Exodus	**prophet**
Hebrews	**Passover**
Holocaust	**sacred time**
Israel	**salvation history**
Judeo-Christian	**synagogue**
judge	**temple**
kairos time	**theocracy**
linear time	**Torah**
messiah	

REVELATION
and SCRIPTURE

The Word of the Lord

"I will judge the nation that they serve," said God, "and after that they shall come out and worship me in this place." Then he gave him the covenant.

FROM THE ACTS OF THE APOSTLES, SEE 7:2–8.

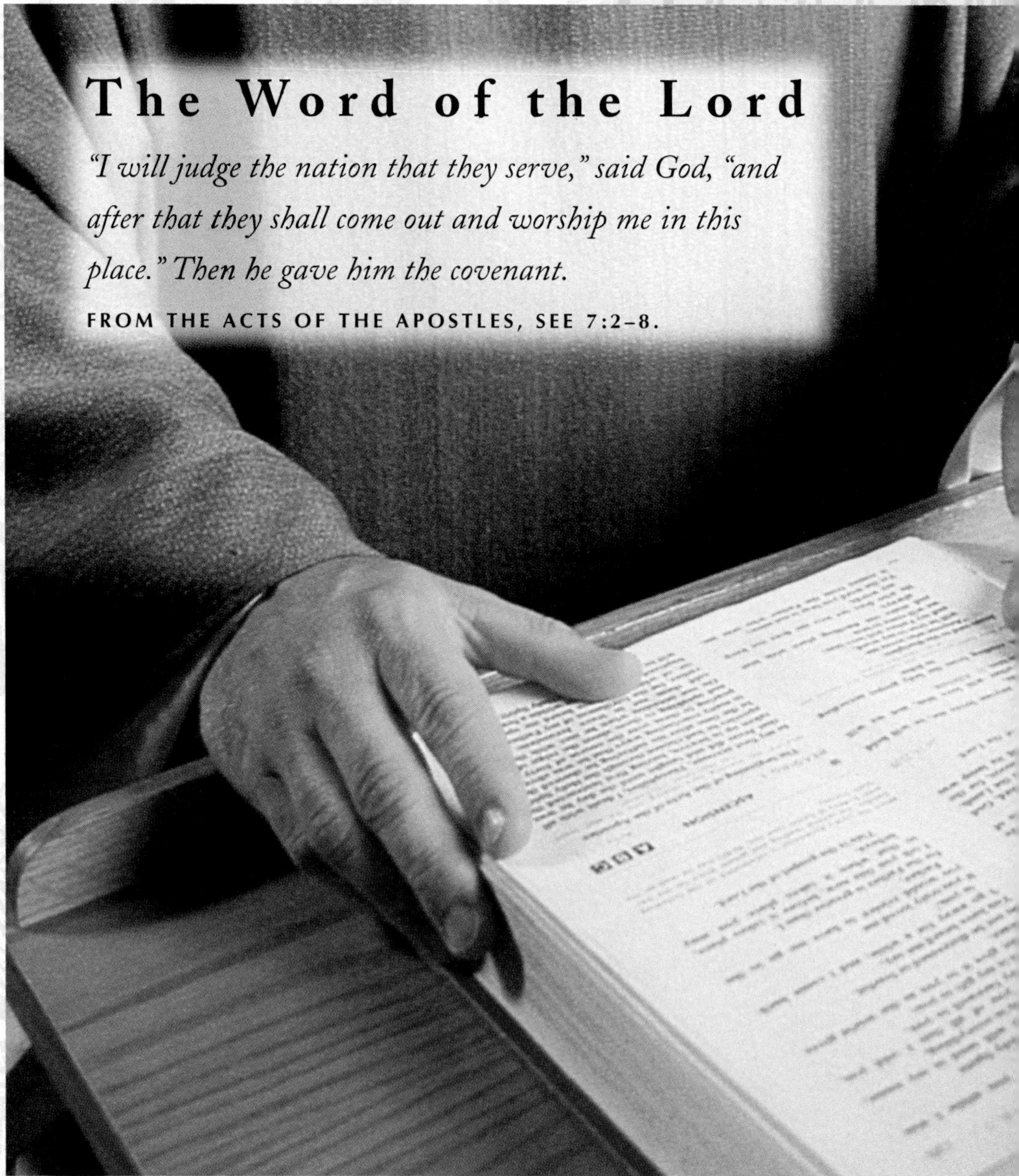

CHAPTER OVERVIEW

• *Revelation: God's gift of self*

• *The written word*

• *Inspiration*

• *The truth of Scripture*

• *Study tools*

• *The Old Testament*

• *Formation of the canon of Scripture*

O God, do not be far from me;
  O my God, make haste to help me!

Let Us Pray

. . . I will hope continually,
  and will praise you yet more and more.
My mouth will tell of your righteous acts,
  of your deeds of salvation all day long,
    though their number is past my knowledge.
I will come praising the mighty deeds of the Lord GOD,
  I will praise your righteousness, yours alone.
O God, from my youth you have taught me,
  and I still proclaim your wondrous deeds.

PSALM 71:12, 14–17

REVELATION: GOD'S GIFT OF HIMSELF

Each of us thinks about God. Each of us has an idea of what God is like. These ideas have much to do with how we look at life and how we act. Listen to someone talk about God. If you listen carefully, you'll learn how that person "sees" God. You may also learn about the person! You may understand the person's actions and ideas about life.

Our images of God are powerful—and they come from *some*where. We don't simply make them up. We don't sit down on a lazy Tuesday afternoon, for example, and dream up an image of God. We could, but that wouldn't be real. Our images of God come from our *experiences* of God—our own experiences and the experiences other people have had of God. Back and forth, all throughout history, people have shared their images and understanding of God. So we don't just make up images of God. Our images of God always come from a community—from people's experience of God.

As we grow, our God-images may change. We understand more. Our ideas change. Our relationships become stronger, and this includes our relationship with God. On the other hand, if we haven't worked at keeping an active and growing relationship with God, we'd probably just rely on the images other people have handed on to us. When that happens, our ideas about God seem as if they came from a book rather than from real life.

With book ideas about God only, people usually become more distant from, rather than closer to, God. Or at least book ideas about God make God so impersonal and far away that people give up any hope of relating to him! The ideas may even lead to an unhealthy fear of God.

We aren't the only ones who have struggled for a truer image of God. The people who lived around the ancient Hebrews (or Israelites) often pictured their (many) gods as distant and uninterested. To prod the gods to respond, a person had to gain their attention or wake them up first and then "bomb" them with requests (prayers) over and over to win their response.

This image of gods who were uninterested in people was very different from the Israelites' experience of God. During their long history, the Israelites came to an increasingly strong sense of God, not as far-away and uninterested, but as nearby and active in their world. They *experienced* God in their lives! They became aware of God's involvement with them. God cared! God freely and lovingly made himself known to people through the events of history—through sacred time, God's time.

Talk about it

1. What is the difference between book ideas about God and the experience of God?

2. Why might book ideas alone make a person fearful of God?

Write it down

When have you experienced God? How did you feel during these experiences?

> *God always was and always is and always will be;*
> *or rather, God always IS,*
> *for* was *and* will be *are fragments of our time*
> *and of our changeable nature.*
>
> **St. Gregory Nazianzen**

God is present in human life.

The Israelites' experience of God

The Israelites also came to realize that God could not be reduced to an image, an idol, or an idea. God was *active*. God was very much present in all of life, especially human experiences. In fact, it was through those experiences that God revealed himself, letting us know who God is and that God promises us fullness of life. We use the word **reveal** to express this relationship of love because it means to "uncover," to "make known as true" or to "bear upon one's heart."

The people of Israel began to understand not only that God is *present* in human life, but that God makes himself personally known in those very events! In other words, the Israelites experienced God as taking the first step in building a relationship of unconditional love with them. God took the first step in love and continued to love them no matter what, no strings attached. The Israelites experienced God as One who wants a relationship of love with his people and who works to make this happen. The covenant God made with the Israelites is a sign of this relationship of unconditional love.

reveal
to make known as true, to open, to establish a relationship based on trust

Talk about it
What does it mean to reveal yourself to another person?

> "O LORD, God of Israel, there is no God like you
> in heaven above or on earth beneath,
> keeping covenant and steadfast love for your servants
> who walk before you with all their heart. . . ."
> **1 Kings 8:23**

God speaks

In order to reveal himself to us as a free gift of love, God speaks to us in human words through Scripture. God does this in the same way we offer the gift of self in the use of human words. This is why we honor God's presence in Scripture just as we honor the Lord's true presence in the Eucharist. In Scripture we find nourishment and strength. We welcome Scripture as the word of God. In Scripture God meets us and talks with us!

See the *Catechism of the Catholic Church*, #s 101, 103–104.

1. What does it mean to give your word to someone?
2. What attitude is necessary in order to meet God in Scripture?
3. When do you meet God in Scripture?

revelation
God's sharing of himself with humanity

Then do this

1. Close your eyes. Have someone speak good, affirming words to you about yourself. How does that feel?
2. Now have that same person speak negative words about you. How does that feel?
3. Discuss: What makes words so powerful?

Revelation is a partnership of self-sharing. We believe that in the history, in the story of Israel, God reveals himself. (We also call the history of Israel the *history of salvation* because we believe that through the history of Israel, God shared himself with the world.)

What does God reveal? That we are surrounded by unconditional and life-giving love! God has taken the first step. God has entered into a special relationship with us so that we can experience salvation, our ultimate happiness and fullness of life. In the course of human events, God doesn't try just to make known hidden points of information. God seeks to give us life through the gift of his very self. God freely reveals himself and forms us into a people who look forward to full union with him for all eternity.

We don't always understand what God wants to give. God's offer of grace and unconditional love is a perfect gift. It is total and all-embracing. We are the ones who "limit" God. In fact, our response to God, both as individuals and a people, is always limited. First of all, given our limited understanding and insight, our awareness of God is incomplete. That's just the way it is! It's part of the human condition. Moreover, we always respond to God as we are and through the world in which we live—our bodies, the ideas in our mind, the things around us, the language of our community, and so on.

Our response to God is always limited because, as humans, we are limited. And part of that limitedness is that sometimes we just don't understand how much God loves us and how very important and necessary that love is to us. So we limit our relationship with the One who wants to make our lives whole and unlimited in terms of love and peace and happiness!

One of the reasons we do this is because our human condition is fragile and fragmentary. But there are more deliberate reasons, such as laziness, selfishness, and the choice to separate ourselves from God. We let our weakness or our sinfulness get in the way of our relationship with God who loves us always. We are free to reject God, but it's *we* who suffer the loss of life.

REVIEW

1. How do people experience God?
2. How did the Israelites experience God?
3. What is revelation?
4. What has God revealed about himself?

The woman and the kid in Lincoln Park

One Saturday morning I was in Chicago's Lincoln Park looking over toward the zoo. Ahead of me was a young woman about the age of thirty-five and a boy of eight or nine.

They were walking toward me down the walk. Grassy hills sloped up on both sides of them. As I'm watching them, the woman suddenly turns, grabs the boy's hand, and says something to him. I couldn't hear what she said, but whatever it was pushed his button. He took a swing at her—but it was one of those eight-year-old swings that by the time it gets there it has lost everything.

Besides that, the woman ducked under it like a skilled boxer, and as he swung she pulled him against her, his face into her stomach. The boy flailed away at her shoulder blades. Then he tried to kick her. When he tried to kick her he lost his footing and slid down a little bit. But the woman had a tight grip on him and pulled him up. Then she took his hair, pulled his head back, and looked down at him. . . . I could see he was crying.

Then she lost her grip. The boy spun away from her and ran. She began to run after him but he got away from her. The boy turned around and yelled, "I don't like you!"

It was only then that I was sure she was his mother.

What happened next was like a scene from an old cowboy movie. The son would come down the hill and get close to her. She'd go after him and he'd run away.

Finally, he got too close and, in the three fastest steps of her adult life, she tackled him. She threw him down on the ground, sat on his stomach, pinned his arms against the grass with her knees, and then gave him a nuggie on his head!

Exhausted, she rolled off him and lay there on the grass huffing and puffing.

The boy sat up and just did nothing for a minute.

Then suddenly he jumped on her and began to tickle and tickle and tickle and tickle and tickle and tickle her.

And she began to laugh and laugh and laugh and laugh and laugh and laugh. Then he began to laugh and laugh and laugh and laugh and laugh and laugh.

Finally there was only the sound of their laughter. . . .

John Shea, *The Legend of the Bells and Other Tales: Stories of the Human Spirit* (ACTA).

Optional activities

1. Write a reflection on what this story tells you about God.

2. Write a story of your own on some quality of God.

3. Share this story with your family and talk about its meaning.

THE WRITTEN WORD

As we understand God's great wish to share himself with us and to give us life to the fullest, we also understand the development of those unique and special books we refer as the *Sacred Writings, Holy Scripture*, or the *Bible*. The Bible didn't drop out of the heavens one day onto the desk of some publisher who was praying for a best seller. Nor did the Bible start out as a finished book. The writings in the Bible took shape and were put together into books over a long period of time. And still later, monks and rabbis of the Middle Ages divided the Scriptures into chapters and verses for the sake of convenient reference and study.

Bible
the written story of what God has done in human history and particularly over that span of several thousand years we call "salvation history"

The **Bible** is the written story of God's love—the love that creates life and keeps it going and makes it good. The Bible is the story of God's revelation of himself in human history and particularly over that span of several thousand years we call "salvation history." Christians believe that God's love is most clearly shown—and most fully given—through Jesus.

God's love was revealed among us in this way: God sent his only Son into the world so that we might live through him.

— 1 John 4:9

We Christians believe that Jesus is the Word of God, that in him God has become personally present in and part of human history. Jesus reveals God, tells us what God is like, shows us God's love. Jesus is the "fullness of revelation." All of our personal experience of God speaking to us must be measured beside the Word God has spoken in Jesus, the Son of God.

God is love, and those who abide in love abide in God,

and God abides in them.

1 John 4:16

Gift of self

God revealed himself in actions and words. These actions and words are linked in the history of salvation. Words describe actions. Words tell stories of what happens. Words and stories tell about what God is like. Words and stories about God tell what God did and does. The Word of God is Jesus the Christ. Jesus tells us what God is like. Jesus is God's Word about God! And what does Jesus tell us?—that God is love, that he speaks to us as friends, and that he lives among us.

See *The Documents of Vatican II*, "Divine Revelation," #2.

1. Identify five actions through which you share your *self* with others.

2. What does it mean to "keep your word"?

3. What does it mean to say that Jesus is the Word of God?

The word *bible* comes from the ancient Greek word *biblos*, which means "book." Certainly the Bible is a book—an obvious fact to anyone who owns one. On a library shelf, the printed book we refer to as the Bible looks basically like any other book. Yet, for believers, the Bible is not just a book. It is *the* book! It is *the* book to us because we believe that it puts us in touch with God!

Actually, we need to be careful in referring to the Bible as a book—even *the* book—because the Bible really is not a single book with one writer, one editor, and a publisher as with most other books. In reality, the Bible is a mini-library collected into a single binding. It puts together many different writings, each of which tells in its own way the truth of God's love.

The Christian community divides the Bible into the Old and the New Testaments. The Old Testament books are about the Hebrews, the Israelites, before the time of Jesus, and their relationship with God. The New Testament is about the life and teachings of Jesus and about his followers' experience of Jesus as the revelation of God's love. Although it has been the tradition of the Christian community to refer to Old and New Testaments, the Bible is *one* testimony, the unfolding story of God's love in history.

Therefore, as Christians, we need to recognize that the Old Testament, like the New Testament, is important to our faith. In fact, we cannot understand the significance of Jesus for the salvation of the world without the background of the Old Testament. The Old and the New Testaments together tell the story and show us the way to God.

Talk about it

1. How do words and deeds lead us to know another person?

2. How do words and deeds lead us to know God?

3. How does reading Scripture lead us to know God?

4. What do we mean when we say that God *is revealed* in Scripture?

Steps in creating the Book of Books
The formation of Scripture

1. God acts in human life (God's revelation of himself).

2. People talk about this experience (pass it on by word of mouth).

3. People preserve God's word (pass it on in writing).

4. Using the written story brings about more stories and more writing.

5. Additions, corrections, and deletions are made (**editing** phase).

6. Final preservation of the text is assured.

7. Finally, the decision is made about which books should be kept.

editing
the process of making additions, corrections, and deletions to a manuscript

Authorship of Scripture: How the Bible came to be

Who wrote the Bible? People did. Many people. They wrote, edited, and probably rewrote over time the various books of the Bible. But the authorship of these books must be seen differently from the way authorship is commonly seen. Usually we can identify the author of a book. We expect that what we read is the author's creation.

Scripture is God's word written by people. In that sense, God is the primary author of Scripture. This doesn't mean that God wrote or dictated the Bible. It does mean that Scripture is the written story of what God has done in human history. That is to say, God's action in human history is the truth behind the story. If God had not acted in human history, there would be nothing to write about. So, we believe that God inspired Scripture—God reveals himself and the truth he wants us to know through the words and stories of Scripture.

It's important to recognize that people talked about their experiences of God long before they wrote about them. That's what it means to give testimony: to tell your experience of something. To *testify* is to "speak truthfully." When this testimony about God's actions took on written form, it came to be called a **testament**.

We testify all the time. We tell about our experiences. We share our feelings about these experiences. We express our ideas, our opinions, our worries, our hopes. We seek to share the meaning of our life experiences, and we automatically use a variety of means to help us communicate the point: gestures, tone of voice, exaggeration, certain expressions. . . . Also, without knowing it, we adapt our testimony to those we're talking to so that they can "get inside" our experience.

Yes, human communication is extremely complex. It's a skill we use all the time without knowing how highly complicated we are and how much intelligence (awareness) is needed in order to share thoughts and ideas.

The formation of the Bible took place over many centuries. The various writings were put together over a long period of time. These writings didn't roll off the press one after another as books are speedily published nowadays. Until the sixteenth century after Jesus, word of mouth was the major source of information and communication. People got together to tell their experiences, to share their stories, to remember together their history. Scripture came from such stories.

Remember too that in those days a person's identity was found in relation to the community. Today we see ourselves as individuals with separate experiences. The people of the Bible were first and foremost a community with a common history.

In the midst of time, which we now call *salvation history*, these people developed a growing understanding of who God was and a growing sense of God's presence. They talked about God and about events that showed God's providence or guiding love. They shared the stories and passed them on, one generation to another.

What was this all about? People were passing on the faith! And it was against this background that later generations recognized God's actions in human history. They learned to be aware of God! They remembered the stories they had heard from the generation before. This was the period of the **spoken tradition**.

The **written tradition** came much later. Perhaps in order to guide people, leaders wrote down the religious laws. Perhaps some people wrote down the major stories of God's saving actions. Even the experts don't know for certain how the Bible came to be. They do know it took a long time.

testament
a statement of the truth about someone or something, especially concerning God's actions as written in Scripture

Talk about it

1. In what sense is God the author of Scripture?

2. In what sense are humans the authors?

3. What is the difference between knowing God from *thinking* and knowing God from *experience*?

4. How are thoughts and experience related?

spoken tradition
stories and teachings of a group passed on by word of mouth

written tradition
stories and teachings of a group passed on in written form

This is especially true of that part of the Bible we call *Torah*, the *Law* (the first five books of the Bible), which existed as spoken tradition centuries before it achieved its final form. Its final written form came about only six hundred years before the time of Jesus. Other parts of Scripture—for example, what we call the *Prophets* and the *Psalms*—were written down more quickly. Still others may have been the direct work of a single author, for example, the book called the *Song of Songs*.

Again, who wrote the Bible? Some of its books may have been written by individual authors. Other books were "authored" from the living memory or spoken tradition of the community and written down later by individuals or groups of individuals. As the years passed, these writings were edited: corrections and additions were made. And sometimes mistakes! And so the composition of Scripture comes out of this mixture of the spoken and written sharing of faith, faith in a God of love, the one God who is at work in our world and in our lives. That's what the Bible is about, and that's why it was written.

Write it down

1. Think about someone who is important to you, somebody you consider a good person. What has that person said and done that makes him or her seem good?

2. What has God said and done that helps you know that God loves you?

The writers of the Bible were . . . not cool historians but passionate prophets.
Herman Wouk

REVIEW

1. What is the Bible about?

2. What were the steps in the creating of the Bible?

3. Who wrote the Bible?

4. What is a testament?

5. What is the difference between a spoken tradition and a written tradition?

INSPIRATION

inspired, inspiration
God's influence in
Scripture, working through
human authors and their
powers and abilities to
reveal religious truth

We believe that Scripture is **inspired** by God. But that doesn't mean we should picture holy men or women locked in private rooms listening to the voice of God telling them what to write. To understand the development of the books of Scripture, all we need to do is to think about how we communicate.

But this doesn't reduce the Bible to just another book on our bookshelf. It's not just an ordinary book written by people. In fact it's an extraordinary book written by people who have put their faith into words. For that reason we say that Scripture writers were inspired. In other words God acts—"speaks"—breathes meaning into human life and experience. In that sense God inspired the writers of Scripture.

Because the Bible is identified as the word of God, we may be tempted at times to use it as a recipe book for living. We sometimes think we can turn to Scripture to find all the answers to life's questions. We must be careful with this approach to Scripture. The Bible certainly contains fundamental truth about God—that God is loving, merciful, patient, forgiving.

But this information doesn't solve all our problems, back up our opinions, or provide specific directions for every detail of our lives. We can't properly use the Bible just to support our personal prejudices and desires. And we can't use a verse or two of Scripture to "prove" something. Someone else can use another Scripture passage to "prove" the opposite view. We must look for the whole truth, the revelation about himself that God is sharing with us.

Each man marvels to find in the divine Scriptures truths

which he himself thought out.

St. Thomas Aquinas

Inspired by God

For the composition of Scripture, God chose human authors and worked through their powers and abilities. These human authors, while using their gifts for story-telling and teaching, wrote what God wanted and only what God wanted. They were inspired.

See *The Documents of Vatican II*, "Divine Revelation," #11.

. . . continue in what you have learned and firmly believed, knowing from whom you learned it, and how from childhood you have known the sacred writings that are able to instruct you for salvation through faith in Christ Jesus. All scripture is inspired by God and is useful for teaching, for reproof, for correction, and for training in righteousness, so that everyone who belongs to God may be proficient, equipped for every good work.

2 Timothy 3:14–17

1. Have you ever felt inspired? What does that mean?

2. What does it mean to say that the Bible is inspired?

3. What do you think God wanted to communicate through the books of the Bible?

THE TRUTH OF SCRIPTURE

We also cannot properly use the Bible as a recipe book or a proof text. The truth contained in the Bible is not a list of easy answers. Nor is the Bible a history book in the usual sense of the term. The Bible does contain some historical information, but the focus of the Bible is the relationship of God with humans and with all creation. Scripture is a written word which carries the reader into the presence of God. Scripture scholars, both Catholic and Protestant, talk about *literal truth* and *spiritual truth* in Scripture.

Talk about it
If Scripture isn't a "recipe book" for behavior, how is it a guide for behavior?

Literal truth

Literal truth is what the Scripture text says. To understand what the text says, Scripture scholars must study a great deal. They must pay close attention to several areas of concern:

- What is the most accurate text available? (There are no existing copies of the whole Bible which date back even to the time of Jesus. The oldest complete text of the Old Testament dates only from the sixteenth century.)
- What do the words mean in themselves?
- How did the time and the place of the writing influence the writing?

The uncovering of the literal meaning of a Scripture text is not just a matter of picking up the Bible and reading it. The work of determining as clearly as possible the exact origin and wording of a text is a strict science and requires disciplined study. Above all, the text must be allowed to speak for itself. The scholar must not allow personal prejudices to interfere. This calls for some self-discipline and honesty.

literal truth
what is said or written exactly as said or written

Talk about it
Can the use of Scripture be abused? If so, how? Give examples. If not, why not?

Spiritual truth

Spiritual truth is the meaning of the text in terms of our understanding and experience of God. Spiritual truth is the religious truth brought to us by means of the literal words. Spiritual truth changes people! Spiritual truth points us to Jesus who is the fullness of God's revelation. Errors can be found in the literal truth of Scripture. There is no error in the spiritual truth of Scripture.

spiritual truth
the religious meaning of a text in Scripture

When we use Scripture in public worship or for private prayer, we need to focus our attention on the Scripture's message for *us*. If we listen with our mind and with our heart, Scripture will lead us to an awareness of God and to a relationship with God. Since God speaks to us in Scripture in a human way, that is, through words and images, we need to be attentive to these words and images. What did the Scripture writers want to tell us about God? What is God saying to us through them?

When we read or listen to Scripture, we need to be aware of both the situation behind the particular Scripture passage *and* the Scripture's meaning for us. Because Scripture is God's word, we need to read it with listening hearts. It was God's Spirit of Love that inspired the writing of Scripture. That same Spirit of Love will inspire us as we read.

Write it down

Other than on Sunday in church, does Scripture really have anything to do with how you think and act and how you live your life? If it doesn't, why doesn't it? If it does, why and in what way?

This is another point to keep in mind about discovering the meaning of Scripture: Each separate passage of Scripture belongs to the *whole Scripture*. God speaks to us in the Scriptures, helping us be more loving, more caring, and more kind. Scripture is not a bundle of information packs that we break open like fortune cookies. Scripture is walking with God, and its truth must be considered in the context of the entire Bible.

Another point to keep in mind is that the Catholic Church teaches that Scripture must be understood in terms of Church tradition. In other words, when we read Scripture, we don't just say, "What does it mean to *me*? What do *I* think this means?" We also ask, "What has this Scripture meant to others over the years?" What do other people say about this Scripture passage? As Catholics, we ask: "What does our Church say about this passage of Scripture?" and "How can that help me with my Scripture study, my search to understand what God is saying?"

Scripture must be read as a whole, and individual passages must be understood in light of the whole of the Sacred Writings. Understood as a whole, what does the Bible say about God, and life, and us? Here are some of its important truths:

- There is one God who creates all things and makes himself known in human history.
- All creation is good and beautiful. There is an order in creation.
- Humans, created in the image of God, share in the life of God's Holy Spirit and are free—even to turn away from God.
- God forms a people and loves them unconditionally.
- The self-revealing love of God moves people toward promise and fulfillment.

Religion of the Word

Our Christian faith is not a "religion of the book." Rather, it is the religion of the "Word" of God. This Word is not silent now, nor merely written—it is alive and enfleshed! Scripture is not a meaningless text. Christ, who is the Word of God alive in human history, opens our minds and hearts through the Spirit to understand the Scriptures.

See the *Catechism of the Catholic Church*, #108.

1. What special kind of listening is necessary to "hear" God's Word?
2. At Mass or Sunday worship, why does a homily (sermon) follow the reading of the word of God?

REVIEW

1. What does inspiration mean?
2. What is literal truth?
3. What is spiritual truth?
4. Is the Bible true? Explain.
5. What are the important truths in Scripture?

STUDY TOOLS

God gave us intelligence, and we need to use our intelligence in approaching Scripture. The more Scripture scholars understand about a Scripture text, the better they can place it in the story of God's love for us. Here are some of the "tools" that Scripture scholars use.

Language studies

The first Scriptures were written in either Hebrew or Greek. Scholars need to know these languages as they consider why authors may have used certain words, phrases, and images. But the meaning of some words has changed over the centuries, so scholars must study the meaning of the words used in Scripture at the time the particular passage was written. One way this is done is to compare the word as it is used in Scripture with the way it was used in other manuscripts of the time. That's why new discoveries of ancient scrolls helps scholars do better translations of the Bible.

Then do this

1. Talk to someone who speaks another language in addition to English. Ask the person to identify some words or ideas the person finds difficult or impossible to translate directly from one language to another.

2. In class talk about how this exercise relates to the translation of the books of the Bible.

St. Jerome
Scripture scholar

Jerome was born about the year 347. As a young man he traveled to Rome where he was baptized. He then studied theology and lived as a monk and a hermit for some time. Jerome was not an easy man to like or get along with, as he frequently spoke and wrote without considering the effect his harsh words would have on others. But he was sincere in his studies and his attempts to live the monastic life. In time he founded monasteries for men and for women, including a monastery in Bethlehem. That is where he died in 420.

During his life, Jerome studied many languages, among them Hebrew and Greek, original languages of the Bible. While he wrote many important works, Jerome is best known for translating the Bible from its original languages into Latin or revising other Latin translations. His translation is known as the *Vulgate* and was used well into the twentieth century for interpreting the Bible and for translations into other languages. At the same time Jerome was translating, he also wrote commentaries on many books of the Bible.

Today no one person undertakes the formidable task of translating the entire Bible from its original languages. Rather, this is a project divided up among many biblical scholars who each generally specialize in one part of Scripture. New translations from the original languages continue to be made. One reason for this is that new discoveries of ancient manuscripts continually update scholars' understanding of the original meanings for many words. Another reason is that these manuscripts help scholars expand their knowledge of the real-life situation at the time the original texts were written. In addition, since our own languages and situations evolve, new translations are needed to help express the truths of the Bible to people today.

Optional activities

1. Imagine devoting forty years of your life to one project. What would that project be? Write an essay exploring the project and its effect on your life.

2. Compare two or three translations of a chapter of the Bible. Do you see any differences that you consider significant? Which translation do you like best? Why? Prepare a presentation for the class.

3. If possible, find out something about one translation of the Bible. When was it done? Is it a translation from the original languages? Who were the translators? How long did the translation take? Write up your findings.

Types of literature

Scripture scholars need to identify what type of literature they are studying. The meaning of words can change according to the kind of writing an author uses. For example, the phrase "Blood-thirsty Sharks kill unsuspecting Bostonians" means one thing on the sports page of a newspaper and quite another as the front-page headline. Scripture scholars must determine the kind of literature they are studying.

These are some of the **literary forms** you will find in the Bible:

- history
- epics (glorified history)
- imaginative history
- lists
- laws
- court records
- poetry
- songs
- myths
- folklore
- legends
- speeches
- proverbs
- parables
- satire
- letters
- prophesy
- short stories
- apocalyptic literature (symbolic and allegorical)

History of the book

People speak of their experiences long before they write about them. Most of the books in the Bible were written many years after the events they record. And many were rewritten over and over again to meet changing circumstances in the history of Israel. Sometimes a careful study of the vocabulary, the language patterns, and the content of passages can show evidence of this historical development.

As the various texts of Scripture were pieced together, they were rearranged or sometimes rewritten from a better understanding of God's saving love, God's plan for our salvation. In time the various pieces and books were compiled into the Old Testament (the **Hebrew Scriptures** and a few other books) and the New Testament (the **Christian Scriptures**).

Consideration of the culture

The passages in Scripture need to be understood in their cultural setting. Culture gives us images and expressions which help us understand things. Those images and expressions change as a culture changes. By studying the culture at the time the books of the Bible were written, we can better understand what the author is saying. This is an area that is greatly helped by studying other manuscripts from a certain time period.

REVIEW

1. What do language studies help Scripture scholars do?
2. Why was St. Jerome important to Scripture studies?
3. Why does the literary form of a Scripture passage matter?
4. What is the difference between the sacred books of the Jews and the sacred books of Christians?
5. How does the culture of the time help us understand a book of the Bible?

THE OLD TESTAMENT

As you know, the Bible used by Christian Churches has two major divisions, an Old Testament and a New Testament. Here we consider only the divisions and books of the Old Testament. We'll take a look at the books of the New Testament in a later chapter. Various Jewish and Christian groups arrange the books of the Bible in different ways. One common way is to arrange the books in four categories:

The Law (Torah)	The Prophets	The Historical Books	The Wisdom Books
Genesis	Isaiah	Joshua	Job
Exodus	Jeremiah	Judges	Psalms
Leviticus	Lamentations	Ruth	Proverbs
Numbers	Baruch	1 Samuel	Ecclesiastes
Deuteronomy	Ezekiel	2 Samuel	Song of Songs
	Daniel	1 Kings	Wisdom of Solomon
	Hosea	2 Kings	Sirach (Ecclesiasticus)
	Joel	1 Chronicles	
	Amos	2 Chronicles	
	Obadiah	Ezra	
	Jonah	Nehemiah	
	Micah	Tobit	
	Nahum	Judith	
	Habakkuk	Esther	
	Zephaniah	1 Maccabees	
	Haggai	2 Maccabees	
	Zechariah		
	Malachi		

Over the course of time, some of the books of what we now call the Old Testament were considered more important for the faith community than others. We can find in museums and libraries other pieces of literature which date back to the time when the Bible was written. And every once in a while we read in the newspaper that a piece of some very old writing has been discovered in the dry sands of the Middle East. These additional writings are important for Scripture scholars to study, but they are not part of the Bible.

The Bible . . . . Its light is like the body of heaven in its clearness;

its vastness like the bosom of the sea;

its variety like scenes of nature.

John Henry Newman

The Dead Sea Scrolls and the "Protestant Bible"

There are a few writings in the Catholic versions of the Old Testament that are not in the Jewish Bible. For example, the Jewish Bible doesn't include the Books of Tobit, Judith, Wisdom, Sirach, Baruch, and 1 and 2 Maccabees. It also doesn't include parts of a few other books. As Jewish Scripture was compiled into one, books (and parts of books) which had been written in Greek rather than in Hebrew were not included, although some were included by some Jews for a time. Eventually they were considered unimportant for the faith formation of the Jewish community. The Catholic Church, however, has recognized these Greek books and passages and included them in the Bible.

Sometimes you hear people talk about a "Catholic Bible" and a "Protestant Bible." The "Catholic Bible" includes the Greek books, while the "Protestant Bible" includes only those books the early Jewish community eventually accepted.

An important discovery made by a shepherd boy in 1947 has helped us find a solution to this that many accept. While looking for a lost sheep on the shores of the Dead Sea in Israel, the boy threw a rock into a cave. He heard a breaking noise and went to investigate. He didn't find his sheep, but he did discover several clay jars containing, among other things, several scrolls which included some of the books of the Old Testament.

Scripture scholars have determined that these manuscripts were used at the time of Jesus by a conservative Jewish community, the Essenes. These manuscripts have come to be called the *Dead Sea Scrolls*, and the site is known as *Qumran*. Thousands of fragments of scrolls have been found in eleven caves. They are very important for the study of the Bible.

Some of these manuscripts were copies of the Greek books the Catholic Church includes as part of the Bible. Since this discovery, many Scripture scholars agree with the Catholic position that these books do belong in the Bible. Many "Protestant Bibles" include the Greek books and passages in a section called the **Apocrypha**.

Qumran today

Optional activities

1. Using the Internet or books in the library, find out more about the Dead Sea Scrolls. Prepare a presentation for the class or write an essay on the topic.

2. Using the Internet or books in the library, find out more about Qumran and the Essenes. Prepare a presentation for the class or write an essay on the topic.

Apocrypha
books of the Old Testament that are part of Catholic Bibles, but not Protestant Bibles; all of these were written in Greek rather than Hebrew

Torah, Law

The first five books of the Bible are often called the *Torah*. *Torah* is a Hebrew word which means "the Law." This use of the word *law* is different from the way we use the word today. For us a law is a regulation given by someone in authority to control our behavior or give us permission to do something.

We need to understand how the Israelites used this word. For them the word *Law* meant God's revelation and a way of living the faith. That way could be discovered by studying these first five books—Genesis, Exodus, Leviticus, Numbers, and Deuteronomy—and learning how God revealed himself and how God loves. This study of the Law formed the basis of spiritual life for the Israelites of old. It still forms the basis of spiritual life for the Jewish community today. Perhaps the words *revelation, sacrament,* and *wisdom* give us some idea of what *Law* or *Torah* mean to many Jews. The Law is also a very essential part of our Christian heritage.

The first five books of the Bible also are often referred to as the *Pentateuch*. *Pentateuch* is a Greek word which literally means "five jars." In the ancient Middle East, important documents often were stored in large clay jars or urns. The first five books of the Bible are like five very important "jars" of God's truth. They are a way of life.

In Psalm 119 the psalmist praises God's law for 176 verses. He begins in this way:

> *Happy are those whose way is blameless,*
> *who walk in the law of the LORD.*
> *Happy are those who keep his decrees,*
> *who seek him with their whole heart,*
> *who also do no wrong,*
> *but walk in his ways.*
> *You have commanded your precepts*
> *to be kept diligently.*
> *O that my ways may be steadfast*
> *in keeping your statutes!*
>
> — *Psalm 119:1–5*

Then do this

1. Read Psalm 119. Then write a few verses of your own on the theme.

2. In a Bible, read the introduction to the Pentateuch or to one of the five books. Together discuss some of the points made in the introduction.

The Prophets

Next to the Torah in importance are the writings of the prophets. The prophets were people who felt called to speak out against the evils of their society and call people back to a correct relationship with God. The word *prophet* literally means to "speak on behalf of." The prophets spoke on behalf of God. They spoke in God's name, often using the phrase, "Thus says the Lord your God!"

We should not confuse these men and women with the kind of "prophets" of today who claim to have insight into future events. The prophets of old were not call-in psychics; they were men and women who were faithful to God's ways and whose hearts burned with the love of God. They repeatedly called people back to a faithful walk with God.

To this very day, readings from the Law and the Prophets are the focus of the proclamation of word of God in the Jewish community. If you are attentive, you also will hear readings from these books at Sunday Mass or Sunday worship.

Then do this

In a Bible, read the introduction to the Prophets or to one of the prophetic books. Together discuss some of the points made in the introduction.

Historical Books

The historical writings are not exactly a collection of history books like the ones you use in your history class. But they do contain stories about the historical events that shaped the people of God. Eventually the books of history made their way into what we now call the *Historical Books* of the Old Testament.

Remember from what we saw earlier in the chapter why history is very important for faith. God "speaks" through human history. God's presence can be seen in the unfolding of human events. Remembering these events became very important because a "pattern" of promise could be seen in them.

The Israelites saw God at work in their daily lives and remembered their history—where they also saw the hand of God. They retold that history, too, passing it on from one generation to another. They were very honest about the shortcomings of the people—and about God's continual love and forgiveness. For example, in recounting the fall of Jerusalem, it is written:

> *The LORD, the God of their ancestors, sent persistently to them by his messengers, because he had compassion on his people and on his dwelling place; but they kept mocking the messengers of God, despising his words, and scoffing at his prophets, until the wrath of the LORD against his people became so great that there was no remedy.*

> — *2 Chronicles 36:15–16*

And when the exiles returned from Babylon, it is written:

> *When the builders laid the foundation of the temple of the LORD, the priests in their vestments were stationed to praise the LORD with trumpets, and the Levites, the sons of Asaph, with cymbals, according to the directions of King David of Israel; and they sang responsively, praising and giving thanks to the LORD,*

> *"For he is good,*
> *for his steadfast love endures forever toward Israel."*

> *And all the people responded with a great shout when they praised the LORD, because the foundation of the house of the LORD was laid.*

> — *Ezra 3:10–11*

Then do this

In a Bible, read the introduction to the Historical Books or to one of the books in that category. Together discuss some of the points made in the introduction.

Write it down

Page through the Book of Psalms.

- Jot down some of the kinds of psalms you find there: praise, intercession, and so on.
- Choose one psalm and write a paraphrase of it.

Then do this

In a Bible, read the introduction to the Wisdom Books or to one of the books in that category. Together discuss some of the points made in the introduction.

Wisdom Books

The fourth category of books in the Bible is the Wisdom Books. This is a rather loose collection of literature. The books carry no common theme or purpose. Individually they each have their history of composition and their purpose. They are called *wisdom* books because they put us in touch with the mind and heart of God. They show us God's way of looking at our lives.

The most famous and frequently used of these books is the Book of Psalms. It is said that there is a psalm for every occasion and every emotion. Most likely King David wrote some of the psalms, but not most of them, as was once thought. The psalms were used in worship and were sung. Appropriately, many modern hymns are based on one or another of the psalms.

FORMATION OF THE CANON OF SCRIPTURE

As we have seen earlier in this chapter, the books of the Bible didn't come off a production line as books do today. Each book had its history of development (often long), as well as its purpose for being passed on orally, in many cases, and eventually written down. The books of the Bible didn't become a collection until the first century after Christ. And the Church's final definition of this collection came even later.

This final collection of books is called the **canon**. (The word *canon* here has nothing to do with the cannons which armies use in warfare!) The word *canon* comes from an ancient word which literally means "reed." Because they were rigid, some types of reeds made excellent measuring instruments. In time the word *canon* took on an abstract meaning: "a measure or norm." In terms of the Bible, over the course of time certain books were kept by the community as canonical, or **normative**, for the faith development of the people of God. These books reflected the people's understanding of God and God's participation in their history.

canon
books of the Bible kept by the community as normative for the faith development of the people of God

normative
the standard for something, canonical

God answers

A man who had been lost in a high forest later described his adventure to his friends. He told them how he had nearly despaired before he knelt down to pray. He asked God to rescue him.

"So, did God answer your prayer?" his friends asked.

"No, he didn't! Before God could rescue me, a forest ranger found me and took me to his station."

Optional activities

1. Discuss: How does this story relate to inspiration and the way the Bible was written? How does it relate to how you see God?

2. Choose a truth you have learned while studying this book. Write a joke or draw a cartoon to illustrate that concept. Share the results with the class.

REVIEW

1. What are the four categories of the Old Testament?
2. What is the *Apocrypha*?
3. What are two other names for the Torah?
4. After the Torah, what is the next most important set of books in Scripture for the Jews?
5. What category of books in the Old Testament shows God's presence in the unfolding of human events?
6. What is the most frequently used Wisdom book in Scripture?
7. What is the *canon* of Scripture?

CONCLUSION

The Bible, the word of God, is very important to the Christian community. We continually "sit" before this word to be addressed by God as sons and daughters. This word of God anchors us in our faith and challenges us to open our hearts and lives to God's salvation, that is, to God's promise of full happiness and fulfillment.

Sacred Scripture, God's word, is not simply a history of events. It is not simply the story of people's faith. It is the presence of God. We need a special kind of listening for that—we need to listen with our hearts. Remember that at Sunday Mass or worship service, the reading of Scripture always has a prominent place. Also, whenever we celebrate one of the sacraments, we proclaim the Scriptures. The reading of Scripture should form a part of your daily prayer life as well. It's very important to open our hearts to hear God's word and to meet God in the relationship of love.

> Let sleep find you holding your Bible,
> and when your head nods
> let it be resting on the sacred page.
>
> **St. Jerome**

Talk about it

Why is the Bible so important to the Christian community?

Write it down

1. We say that we meet God in the Scriptures. Where else do we meet God?

2. Where is your Bible? When did you last read from it? How often do you pray with it?

Reading about our life

[One day] a man picked up the morning paper and, to his horror, read his own obituary! The newspaper had reported the death of the wrong man. Like most of us, he relished the idea of finding out what people would say about him after he died. He read past the bold caption which read, "Dynamite king dies," to the text itself. He read along until he was taken aback by the description of him as a "merchant of death." He was the inventor of dynamite and he had amassed a great fortune from the manufacture of weapons of destruction. But he was moved by this description. Did he really want to be known as a "merchant of death"? It was at that moment that a healing power greater than the destructive force of dynamite came over him. It was his hour of conversion. From that point on, he devoted his energy and money to works of peace and human betterment. Today, of course, he is best remembered, not as a "merchant of death," but as the founder of the Nobel Peace Prize—Alfred Nobel.

William J. Bausch, *Storytelling: Imagination and Faith*.

Optional activities

1. Discuss these questions:

   • Has a story ever changed you?

   • What stories in the Bible have motivated you to change?

   • What stories in the Bible have helped you change?

2. Write your own obituary—up to the present day. What have you accomplished? If too much of what you want your life to be about is in the future, what can you do to change that?

Words you should know

Apocrypha	**literary form**
Bible	**normative**
canon	**reveal**
Christian Scriptures	**revelation**
editing	**spiritual truth**
Hebrew Scriptures	**spoken tradition**
inspired, inspiration	**testament**
literal truth	**written tradition**

CHAPTER 6

JEWISH RITES, RITUALS, *and* PEOPLE

CHAPTER OVERVIEW

- *The Jewish tradition*
- *Covenant relationship*
- *Worship*
- *Religious practices*
- *Important people*

The Word of the Lord

When the time came for their purification according to the law of Moses, they brought him up to Jerusalem to present him to the Lord . . . and they offered a sacrifice according to what is stated in the law of the Lord. . . .

FROM THE GOSPEL ACCORDING TO LUKE, SEE 2:22–24, 39–40.

I waited patiently for the LORD;
 he inclined to me and heard my cry.

Let Us Pray

He drew me up from the desolate pit,
 out of the miry bog,
and set my feet upon a rock,
 making my steps secure.
He put a new song in my mouth,
 a song of praise to our God.
Many will see and fear,
 and put their trust in the LORD.
Happy are those who make
 the LORD their trust,
who do not turn to the proud,
 to those who go astray after false gods.
You have multiplied, O LORD my God,
 your wondrous deeds and your thoughts toward us;
 none can compare with you.
Were I to proclaim and tell of them,
 they would be more than can be counted.
Sacrifice and offering you do not desire,
 but you have given me an open ear.
Burnt offering and sin offering
 your have not required.
Then I said, "Here I am;
 in the scroll of the book it is written of me.
I delight to do your will, O my God;
 your law is within my heart."

PSALM 40:1–8

THE JEWISH TRADITION

In the last chapter, we investigated the formation of Scripture as the way the Israelites of old responded to God's action in their lives and in their history. If God had not acted, there would not have been anything to write about!

Scripture is the written testimony about what God did for people. This written testimony cannot be separated from the events that really happened, even if the written word is an interpretation of these events. Scripture was written from *within* the events of the history of the Israelites and of the early Church. It isn't about abstract ideas unrelated to people's lives. God doesn't reveal himself in abstract ways.

Sacred Scripture came from people who responded to the experience of God at work in their history. But Scripture is not the only way people responded. This chapter looks at some of the other ways people of faith, especially the Israelites, expressed their response to God. We give this people special consideration because we Christians find in them and in their response to God our own roots. By studying them and their religious practices, we can better understand and appreciate the way we pray and worship.

It's most important to remember that Christianity is not just another world religion founded by a man whose name happened to be Jesus. Jesus was a *Jew*. Jewish religious practices and ways of seeing the world helped form his self-image—and even gave him the vocabulary for his later ministry. Jesus, like other Jews, believed that God, whom he experienced as Father, is involved in the lives of all of us—relating, helping, caring, guiding, loving, saving.

How God has brought about the salvation of the world in Jesus can be understood only against this background of the Jewish faith tradition. In many instances, Jewish religious practices are the historical background for understanding the Christian faith and Christian worship.

COVENANT RELATIONSHIP

The word which describes the relationship between the Israelites and God is covenant. A *covenant* is different from a contract or an agreement. When people enter into a contract to buy a house, for example, they enter into a legal arrangement which is binding on both parties, both sides. The *language* of the contract or agreement measures levels of responsibility. You can own this particular house, for instance, *if* you pay to get the roof fixed and give the mortgage lender an additional $95,000 in monthly payments made over a thirty-year period. Contracts usually identify an exchange of rights.

A covenant is different. A **covenant** is the commitment of individual persons *to one other*. Marriage, for example, is—or should be—a "covenant of love." By law the married couple may have to purchase a marriage license to get married, but really marriage is a covenant, a giving relationship between two people.

In the history of the Jewish people, the sense of being in a covenant relationship with God developed over time. The people *grew* in their awareness of God's bond of unconditional love. The covenant was not their own construction. *God* had taken the initiative, the first step, to establish it. And God promised to always be faithful to it.

Then do this
Invite a rabbi or a member of a Jewish congregation to talk with your class about Judaism.

Talk about it

1. Have you ever made a contract with anyone? What were its terms?

2. What is a covenant? How does it differ from a contract or business agreement?

3. What is God's covenant with you?

covenant
a commitment of individual persons or groups to one another; a solemn agreement between God and people

Judaism does not lead man out of his everyday world,
but relates him to God within it.

Leo Baeck

God's covenant of love

At all times and in every place, every person who lived rightly was acceptable to God. God wanted, however, to make us holy and to save us—not as individuals without any bond between us but rather as a people who can recognize God in truth and serve him in holiness.

To do this, God chose the Israelites and established a covenant with them. God gradually instructed them through the events of their history. This initiative on God's part prepared the world for the new and perfect covenant established in Christ, the Word of God made flesh.

See *The Documents of Vatican II*, "Dogmatic Constitution on the Church," #9.

1. Why does love need to be expressed personally? Why can't we just "love at a distance"? Does our need to show love teach us anything about God's love?

2. Why do Christians believe that Jesus is the fullest expression of God's covenant love?

The covenant with Israel

The covenant between God and Israel could be expressed as follows: "I shall be your God and you shall be my people." Notice that this covenant relationship doesn't have any contract language. There's no use of the word *if.* God doesn't say, "*If* you love me back," or "*If* you obey my rules and commandments, *then* I will love you." No! God's love for us is unconditional, no conditions, no "ifs," no strings attached. God's gift of himself is precisely that, a gift. God loves his people no matter what.

During their long history, the Israelites came to see more and more clearly that God had established a life-giving love relationship with them. When the prophets challenged the people to be faithful to this relationship, the prophets often spoke in language that reflected a marriage relationship.

When the prophets called the people back to faithfulness to God, they didn't demand blind or fearful obedience to rules and regulations. Rather, they reminded God's people of the need to respond to God's saving presence, the need to respond to God's love. They reminded the people to remember what God had done for them.

Love asks for a response, a way of living which shows that you recognize and appreciate that love. Love is the reason for obedience to a generous God. This is the moral demand of the covenant—to love because God loves us.

Then do this
Interview a married couple and ask them to describe what it's like to live a covenant of marriage. Write a short paper comparing what they say with how the Israelites felt about their covenant relationship with God.

The people of Israel knew that God did not want just lip service from his people, just words and the external practice of their religion. God wanted the *heart* of his people. God wanted them to have fullness of life, the happiness of love. God's love sets us free to be our *true* selves. God's love does not enslave us, nor does it make us afraid.

Let's think about that as we look at the Ten Commandments. These commandments actually reflect the things people of good conscience abide by; they can be found in some form in all religions of the world. They are the fundamental basis for judging right and wrong.

The Ten Commandments are found in two places in the Old Testament: in the Book of Exodus and in the Book of Deuteronomy. These commandments come from the response God's people make to a God who is involved in their history, a God who cares. For the Israelites, the Ten Commandments arose out of their covenant relationship with the God of their salvation.

In the story in the Book of Exodus, Moses led the people from slavery in Egypt to a new life in the promised land. Along the way, the people lost their direction toward God; they forgot about God. In the Bible story Moses went up Mt. Sinai to ask God what to do. He came back with the Ten Commandments—God's answer.

The scene on Mount Sinai doesn't need to be read in a literal sense. The essential thing is that the story communicates a very important message: God's love relationship is one which calls people to proper human living. God wants people to act rightly. What does this mean? What are the Ten Commandments about?

The Ten Commandments aren't primarily about rules and regulations. They're about respect—for God and for people (including oneself) and for all creation. When respect is there, in our hearts, we choose to do what is right, we act rightly. This is what God wants us to do. Then we will live life to the fullest.

Then do this

You have already read the story of the Ten Commandments in Exodus. Now read Deuteronomy 5–6:9. Then discuss:

1. Was there anything in the phrasing of the Ten Commandments that was new to you? If so, what is the message?

2. Why were the people to obey the Ten Commandments?

3. What does Deuteronomy 6:1–9 add to your understanding of the Ten Commandments?

> *Some religions do not regard our sojourn on earth as true life . . . .*
> *Judaism, on the contrary, teaches that what a man does*
> *now and here with holy intent*
> *is no less important, no less true . . .*
> *than life in the world to come.*
>
> **Martin Buber**

REVIEW

1. Why do Christians study the Jewish faith tradition and religious practices?

2. What is the difference between a covenant and a contract?

3. What is the covenant between God and Israel?

4. What is the relationship between the covenant and the Ten Commandments?

WORSHIP

Our free and loving response to God is at the heart of what we call *worship*. **Worship** is the response we humans make to God, who has taken the first step to love us. God is involved in human history. God cares. The Israelites talked about the "mighty deeds of the living God." They responded with gratitude and praise. They really knew that they were nobodies without God.

"Thank you!" "Praise you!" they said. The people responded with frequent words of grateful prayer to the saving hand of God in their midst. They stood with open arms lifted upward to express their heartfelt gratitude for what God had done. This prayer stance also expressed their openness to receive even more from God. This gesture of open hands continues today in many places of worship. You have seen it in the prayer posture of the priest at Mass.

An interesting thing happens when people do you a favor, especially an unexpected one. If you are grateful, you not only *recognize* what someone has done for you, you also want to *show your gratitude*. You want to say "Thank you," and you need to show your gratitude by the way you relate to the person or trust the gift the person has given you. It's an automatic response.

It's understandable that the Israelites wanted to show their gratitude for the saving deeds of God. The most important way they expressed their gratitude was through the way they treated each other, especially in how they treated those who were poor. The behavior of the people of God needed to reflect how God treated them, how he loved them. Because God had taken the initiative to favor a group of nobodies (the Apiru, the Hebrews), the Israelites needed to favor those who were poor.

The covenant relationship with God brought with it a demand for **social justice**, that is, right relationships among people and the preservation of human dignity. When God's people became self-centered and especially when they neglected and abused those in their midst who were poor, God used the prophets to call them back to right living. The prophets recalled the people's responsibility—their "ability to respond"—to God's covenant love!

God didn't want just words! God wanted people to live right—to care and to take care of each other. True worship is found in the union between religious practices and love of neighbor. To begin with, then, the Israelites were concerned with love of neighbor.

worship
the response of adoration and praise we humans make to God, who has taken the first step to love us

Talk about it
What should be the attitude of your heart in order to properly share in religious ceremonies?

social justice
right relationships among people and the preservation of human dignity

Talk about it
1. Together make a list of the people in today's society who are God's poor people.
2. Discuss how these groups are treated by
   - the government
   - the Churches
   - the people in your school

Abraham and the old man

Abraham of old sat resting at the entrance to his tent. He was waiting to see if any strangers would pass by looking for lodging for the night. Finally a very old man came by. Abraham saw that the man was tired from his travels, so he invited him in. When talking to him, Abraham discovered that the man was one hundred years old.

Abraham helped the old man wash up and then led him to the place of honor at the table. He served the man a delicious meal, but the man ate in silence and didn't even offer a prayer before eating.

Curious, Abraham asked the old man if he worshiped God. The man responded that he did not, that he worshiped fire. Angry with the response, Abraham threw the man out into the night.

Then God came to Abraham and asked, "Where is the old man who came into your tent?"

Abraham replied, "I threw him out because he didn't worship you."

And God said, "I have put up with that man for a hundred years, even though he doesn't worship me. And you couldn't even put up with him for one night, despite the fact that he didn't cause you any harm."

Ashamed, Abraham went out and found the old man. Humbly he brought him back into his tent and gave him a place to sleep for the night.

A parable attributed to Jeremy Taylor (1613–1667).

Optional activities

1. Discuss: In what ways are we more strict and unforgiving than God is?

2. Write a parable about one of the Ten Commandments.

3. Find another story about right living. Suggested resources: *The Book of Virtues, The Moral Compass* (both compiled by William J. Bennett), *Chicken Soup for the . . . Soul*. Share the story with the class and discuss it.

Every act leaves the world with a deeper or fainter impress of God.
Alfred North Whitehead

RELIGIOUS PRACTICES

Another way the Israelites responded to God's covenant love was through the use of religious **rites and rituals**, special ways of praying and of expressing our faith. These involve the whole person and all our hopes and needs, our words, our physical senses, and our body language in the form of dance, gestures, and other physical movement. In religious rites and rituals, people express—and share—their faith. They do this directly in words, and they do this symbolically through signs.

Signs and symbols occupy an important place in human life. As social beings we need signs and symbols to communicate with others; we use language, gestures, and actions. The same holds true for our relationship with God. God speaks to us through creation. Through creation we can read traces of God, our Creator. A British poet said it very well:

> Glory be to God for dappled things—
>> For skies of couple-color as a brinded cow;
>>> For rose-moles all in stipple upon trout that swim;
> Fresh-firecoal chestnut-falls; finches' wings;
>> Landscape plotted and pieced—fold, fallow, and plough;
>>> And all trades, their gear and tackle and trim.
> All things counter, original, spare, strange;
>> Whatever is fickle, freckled (who knows how?)
>>> With swift, slow; sweet, sour; adazzle, dim;
> He fathers-forth whose beauty is past change:
>>>> Praise him.
>>> — Gerard Manley Hopkins, "Pied Beauty."

Things like light and darkness, wind and fire, water and earth speak to us of God and become symbols of God's greatness and nearness. These things can become means of God's gift of himself. At the same time, they can become the things we humans use to worship God. The same is true of signs and symbols taken from our social life. Actions like washing, blessing, **anointing**, and sharing food can express the loving and saving presence of God as well as our grateful response to God.

The Israelites used religious rituals primarily to express their gratitude to God. Many of these rituals took place on the top of high hills or mountains. The Israelites referred to these pinnacles as their **high places**. Very often sacred altars were set up on these high places, and the places became permanent sites for the worship of God. There is evidence in the history of Israel that there were several of these places.

The most important of these "high places" was Mount Zion, on which now stand parts of the city of Jerusalem. On that site the Israelites built the great temple where the priests could present sacrificial offerings to God. Gradually, this became the most significant high place for the Israelites. Jerusalem itself became the center of their religious practice and the place of their hope. Many believed that it was there that the messiah was to come, appearing in the temple, to usher in the final days of God's reign.

rites and rituals
special ways of praying and of expressing faith, directly in words, and symbolically through signs

Then do this
Ask someone who has been to the Holy Land to come to talk with your class. Ask the person to bring his or her slides, photos, or video.

Talk about it
1. Make a list of the religious practices that are special and unique to your particular Christian denomination.
2. Why is it important for parents to introduce their children to the religious practices of the parents' faith?

anointing
the pouring of oil over a person to signify a special role or identity

high places
places of worship situated on hill tops or mountain tops

Religious symbols and practices

We know from the great religions of the world that religious rituals have universal and symbolic meaning. The rites, or **liturgy** of the Catholic Church use things from creation and culture and makes them holy, giving them the dignity of signs of God's presence. The chosen people, the Jews, used special signs and symbols in their worship of God. These signs and symbols were signs of the covenant, symbols of God at work for his people.

Among these signs in the old covenant times are **circumcision**, anointing and **consecration** of kings and priests, the **laying on of hands**, sacrifices, and, especially, the Passover meal. For the Church, these signs prefigure the sacraments of the new covenant.

See the *Catechism of the Catholic Church,* #s 1149–1150.

1. What are some natural symbols? Why is it important to use natural symbols in religious services?

2. Can humans communicate without the use of symbols? What does it mean to "talk with your hands"?

3. Why do people who are in love show their love through signs and symbols? What is the best symbol that they use? Why?

4. Can a religious ceremony use too many symbols at one time? How?

liturgy
the structured rites or ceremonies of worship

circumcision
Jewish rite of inclusion for males, involving the cutting of the foreskin on the penis

consecration
act of making or declaring someone or something holy or sacred

laying on of hands
action of conferring God's blessing on someone chosen for a special task or identity

REVIEW

1. Why do people worship God?

2. What is social justice?

3. What are some examples of religious rites and rituals?

4. What is the purpose of a religious ritual?

Many of the rules and regulations which governed the daily lives of the Israelites came from their sacred rites and rituals. These rules and regulations were practical ways in which the people expressed their gratitude to God. Let's look briefly at some of the major Jewish religious practices.

Law

Observing Torah—keeping the Law—was and is the most important thing in the Jewish religion. But this involves more than obedience to rules and regulations. When you "follow the law" today, perhaps you think mostly of the restrictions placed on you by city government, the police, school authorities, or your parents. Perhaps for you a law is something to keep or to break (and pay the consequences).

To understand the role of law in the life of the Israelites, however, we have to think differently! For the Israelites the word *law* didn't refer primarily to rules and regulations, but to the living relationship between God and themselves. To "follow the Law" meant to be faithful to the covenant relationship which God had established with them.

In order to "follow" that covenant relationship, the Israelites studied the testimony of God's love found in the first five books of the Old Testament (Genesis, Exodus, Leviticus, Numbers, and Deuteronomy). They called this collection of books *Torah*, the *Law*. These books contained many rules and regulations governing religious practices, but more importantly, they spoke of a living relationship of faith. Obedience to these regulations was seen not as slavery to regulations but as an opportunity to give practical expression to one's faith.

Write it down

1. To me law is . . . .
2. I see a relationship between covenant and law because . . . .
3. Obedience means . . . .

Sacrifices

Many of the rules and regulations found in the Old Testament Torah, or Law, told how to offer sacrifices to God. The word **sacrifice** literally means "to make holy" or "to set aside." The Israelites recognized God as the source of all life and holiness, and they believed that God was actually with them. So they set aside for God a part of what they had—grain, cattle, lambs, doves, and pigeons. They sacrificed these things on special altars.

In a sacrifice an offering or an animal was usually consumed by fire. Through the ritual of sacrifice, the people gave their hearts to God or expressed to God some need. In giving things up through sacrifice, they were giving of themselves. The real gift in any sacrifice is the *gift of self*.

When the Israelites thought they could manipulate God through their sacrifices, the prophets stearnly reminded them what a sacrifice should be. A sacrifice made without a sincere, worshiping heart is **blasphemy** and **hypocrisy**. It is not worthy of God.

sacrifice
an offering of something, usually to God, to be made holy

blasphemy
the act of showing contempt or grave irreverence toward God

hypocrisy
the act of pretending to be what one is not or to believe what one doesn't really believe

> *No man can break any of the Ten Commandments.*
> *He can only break himself against them.*
>
> **G.K. Chesterton**

Sabbath

Sabbath or **Shabbat**

the Jewish day of rest, prayer, reflection, and study (sunset on Friday to sunset on Saturday)

Recognizing that God was the source not only of salvation, but also of all creation, the Israelites developed the tradition of observing a day of rest from work in order to honor God. This day was **Sabbath** or **Shabbat**; the Hebrew word means "rest." Even to this day the Jewish Sabbath begins with sunset on Friday (when the Sabbath meal is celebrated) and ends at sunset the following evening. During this twenty-four hour period, no unnecessary work is done. But more than an absence of work, this day provides the opportunity to recognize that God is the source of life and holiness.

The Sabbath was—and is—a day of reflection and prayer to help God's people keep in mind the true source of their identity and fullness of life. Prayer and the reading of Scripture in the home and often in the synagogue are part of the day.

The need to rest and appreciate the gift of life was considered by the Israelites to be an act of worship which came from the very depths of creation. According to the first creation story in the Book of Genesis, in six days God created the earth and the heavens and all that is in them. Then, on the seventh day, God rested, having seen that all creation was good.

"I will indeed bless you, and I will make your offspring as numerous as the stars of heaven and as the sand that is on the seashore."

Genesis 22:17

> *Remember the sabbath day, and keep it holy. Six days you shall labor and do all your work. But the seventh day is a sabbath to the LORD your God; you shall not do any work—you, your son or your daughter, your male or female slave, your livestock, or the alien resident in your towns. For in six days the LORD made heaven and earth, the sea, and all that is in them, but rested the seventh day; therefore the LORD blessed the sabbath day and consecrated it.*

— Exodus 20:8–11

Sabbath rest

The first creation story in the Book of Genesis speaks of God finishing the work of creation on the seventh day. After finishing the heavens and the earth (that is, everything) God rested, and thus made this day holy. This part of the creation story teaches us:

1. In creation itself God laid the foundation and gave lasting laws, on which we can be confident.

2. These laws are "written into nature" and are the sign of God's faithfulness and covenant.

3. We must respect these laws.

4. Creation included a day of rest. So must we.

5. We must keep the Sabbath holy, set aside for worship and adoration of God.

6. Worship is in the very order of creation.

7. The Sabbath is at the heart of Israel's law.

Christians believe that a new day has dawned: the day of Christ's resurrection. The first creation was completed on the seventh day, and the new creation begins on the eighth day. The work of creation reaches its peak in our redemption. The first creation finds its meaning in the new creation in Christ.

See the *Catechism of the Catholic Church*, #s 345–349.

1. What is the Sabbath? Why do Jews observe the Sabbath?

2. Why do most Christians honor Sunday as their holy day?

3. How do you "keep holy the Lord's day"?

4. Why do Christians think of Christ as bringing about the "new creation"?

5. What are some natural laws which can be learned from creation?

6. Why does observing the Sabbath require more than just the absence of work?

The Other

To the Hebrew people, and later to the Israelites and then the Jews—all one people—the God who is present is also the Holy One. God is with the people, but God is God. It was believed, at the time of the Hebrews that if you knew a god's name, you would be able to get the god to do what you wanted—you would have power over the god.

So Moses wanted to know God's name. According to the story, God answered, "YHWH," meaning "I AM" as in "I AM HERE" or "I AM WHO I AM." God is the fullness of existence and power. God could not be controlled, could not even be known—unless by God's own choice! God is absolutely and forever "other"—beyond control and manipulation. God is the Wholly Other who assures his people that he will always be present to them.

That's why taking God's name in vain is so offensive and is one of the prohibitions in the Ten Commandments. To take God's name in vain is to ask God to do something against his covenant love (for example, to "damn" someone). To this day, Jews do not speak God's "name." Instead they say *Adonai*, meaning "the Lord."

YHWH
the Hebrew "name" (vowels were not written) for God; "I AM" as in "I AM HERE" or "I AM WHO I AM."

Then do this
Find five different examples of how God is addressed in the psalms. In small groups, share these and discuss how and why they differ.

To be a Jew is a destiny.
Vicki Baum

Temple worship

The Israelites came to realize that their God was one, not many. Other people around the Israelites believed in many gods, but Israel had faith in one God whose covenant love formed a single people by means of a single plan of salvation. Eventually Israel came to have only one temple where the priests could offer sacrifice. That temple was in Jerusalem.

Temple worship was an important part of the religion of Israel. There the people brought the offerings for God—the grain, the foods, the animals. And there, the priests offered these things in sacrifice. Selected from the tribe of Levi (the descendants of one of Jacob's sons), the priests acted as mediators between the people and God.

Sacrifices were offered to show gratitude, to ask God's forgiveness for sins, or to obtain special favor. Most importantly, sacrifices were offered as a gift of self back to God. Through these sacrifices, the people sought to give themselves back to God, to have union with the God who saved them.

To the extent that these sacrifices became self-serving though, or attempts to manipulate God, they became empty religious practices. They were hypocritical. That is, the visible religious rituals seemed to express faith, but true faith and trust in God did not exist in the heart of these people.

Those who possessed true faith in God needed to express that faith in their loving and caring relationships with one another. Remember, God also wanted from the people, as a reflection of covenant love, the proper treatment of one another, especially those who were poor and rejected. For this reason God often used the prophets in Old Testament times to condemn empty religious practices.

> *Guard your steps when you go to the house of God; to draw near to listen is better than the sacrifice offered by fools; for they do not know how to keep from doing evil.*
>
> — *Ecclesiastes 5:1*

Then do this

Research the temple in Jerusalem. What did it look like? What purpose did each section serve? Present your findings to the class.

Write it down

When do you worship God with true faith and trust? When do you not?

> *Great is the Lord and greatly to be praised in the city of our God.*
>
> *His holy mountain . . .*
>
> *is the joy of all the earth,*
>
> *Mount Zion . . . the city of the great King.*
>
> **Psalm 48:1–2**

REVIEW

1. What do we mean when we say that for Jews the Law involves more than obedience to rules and regulations?

2. How do Jews "keep holy the Lord's day"? How do Christians?

3. Why did the Israelites not use God's name?

4. How was God worshiped in the temple?

Ritual cleanliness

The Israelites developed the custom of keeping themselves ritually pure, that is, ready to participate in their religious rituals. Certain diseases could make people ritually impure. Certain actions, especially those which involved contact with blood, made someone ritually impure.

> *When any one of you touches any unclean thing—human uncleanness or an*
> *unclean animal or any unclean creature—and then eats flesh from the LORD's*
> *sacrifice of well-being, you shall be cut off from your kin.*
>
> — *Leviticus 7:21*

After contamination by something or someone unclean, worshipers needed to go through a special ceremonial washing and a time of waiting before they could once again take part in the rituals. The people were careful to keep themselves clean of sin and impurities so that they could participate in worship. They said special prayers before synagogue service and washed their hands before meals.

Finally, the proper (**kosher**) preparation of food for meals became an important way of maintaining cleanliness before God. This preparation followed specific instructions —from the manner in which animals were killed to the pans and dishes used for different foods. Jewish law also prohibits the mixing of meat and dairy products in the same meal: "You shall not boil a kid in its mother's milk" (Deuteronomy 14:21).

Related to kosher is the complete avoidance of the eating of pork by the Israelites and contemporary practicing Jews. It may be that this prohibition against pork began because disease was easily spread through eating undercooked pork. It may also be that pigs were a domesticated animal for many of the non-believing peoples who lived next to the ancient Israelites. Shunning their food was a way of shunning them and their beliefs.

A rich spirituality underlies these practices, as the people tried to find practical, daily ways to express their identity as God's chosen people and to respond to God's covenant love.

kosher
ritually proper food or the preparation of food according to Jewish law

A kosher food exhibit

Grateful prayer

The main focus of Jewish spirituality at the time of the Israelites—and even now for both Jews and Christians—is gratitude. This deep gratitude came from centuries of realizing how deeply God shares himself with people and promises them fullness of life.

A faithful Israelite frequently thanked God for all the wonder of his saving love. *Everything* was seen as a gift which revealed God's presence and love. For that reason a thanksgiving prayer could be said for anything and everything. These prayers were brief and to the point. For example:

> *Blessed are you, Lord, God of all creation, for the air I breathe. You are the One who breathes life into all things. Praise you, Lord our God!*

An attentive Israelite found many opportunities during the day to pray like this. To "bless" something with this form of prayer was not to ask God to make "something" holy, but simply to recognize that God's holiness was already there. All things (except sin) reveal God's presence and holiness!

Write it down
Who taught you to pray? Write a letter to thank the person who did the most to teach you to pray.

The Israelites found many opportunities throughout the day to express gratitude for God's presence and saving love. They had both private and public prayers. The public prayers followed a certain form: first thanking God for creation, then for the deeds of salvation history, and then for his covenant love. This public prayer always ended by thanking God for the not-yet-accomplished but promised fulfillment of his plan of salvation for his people in the coming of the messiah.

A specific Thanksgiving Prayer was developed and used both at the evening meal and at the synagogue service. The evening meal—or supper—played a very significant role in the Jewish household, especially on high holy days like Passover. The evening meal was always an opportunity to celebrate their faith.

Women lighting the Shabbat candles

Prayer

Prayer comes from the whole person who prays, whether that prayer is in words or gestures. In the Bible, we may read that the soul or spirit of a person is the source of prayer, but more than a thousand times the Bible speaks of the heart as the source of prayer: it is the heart that prays. If our heart is far away from God, our prayer means nothing.

We speak of the heart as the place where we are, where we live. The heart is the hidden center of a person. Only God's Spirit can understand the full depths of the human heart. In our hearts we make our decisions. In our hearts we find truth; we choose life or death; we meet God. It is the place of our covenant relationship with God.

See the *Catechism of the Catholic Church*, #s 2562–2563.

1. What does it mean when people say they "prayed their heart out"? Have you ever done this?

2. What is the relationship between true prayer of the heart and religious words and gestures?

3. It is said that prayer may be very private, but "its fruit" shows. What does that mean? Can you tell if someone is a prayerful person?

4. What do you do to listen to your heart when you have an important decision to make? What are you listening for?

Then do this

First decide on a special feast in the Christian tradition. Then choose one of the following.

1. Look up the feast's origin (beginning), and share the information with the class.

2. Make a poster inviting people to celebrate the feast.

Feasts

Several very important days of festivity and celebration are found in the Jewish calendar. These include:

Passover

Passover

the eight-day Jewish festival commemorating the Exodus

The **Passover** feast (Pesah) commemorates the Exodus (departure) of the Hebrew people from Egypt sometime around 1250 B.C. According to the epic story, on the night of the Exodus, the angel of death passed over the houses of the Hebrews which had been marked by lamb's blood. The Hebrew families were safe—and free to leave Egypt after years of being in slavery there.

Passover celebrates God's saving love in this event. On the first two nights of this eight-day celebration, there is a special meal, or seder: The lamb recalls the sacrificed lamb whose blood marked the doors of the Hebrews in Egypt. Unleavened bread (bread made without yeast that would make it rise), called *matzo*, recalls the bread made in haste as the people prepared to flee. Bitter herbs and other foods remind the Jewish people of their ancestors' slavery and suffering in Egypt. Traditionally, the youngest participant asks the oldest, "Why are we doing this?" and the story of salvation is retold yet another time.

For the Israelites, the Exodus was a sign and the defining moment in the history of salvation. They knew that without the saving hand of God, they would have been reduced to nothing. And so, the feast of Passover is for Jews a celebration of God's love and their identity as God's chosen people.

If it were possible, Jews would travel to Jerusalem for the celebration of Passover, hoping for the day God would reveal his final plan of salvation. To this day, the Passover meal is shared in the home, not just as a family event, but also as a religious celebration of faith. The celebration of this special meal united the Israelites as a people and renewed their commitment to God. It still does to this day.

As Israel's history developed, some groups expected that the messiah, the anointed of the Lord, would come at Passover time to usher in the last days of God's salvation. Many people in these groups expected the messiah to make his appearance at the temple in Jerusalem.

Talk about it

1. Have you ever attended a seder? What was it like?

2. What Christian celebration reminds you of Passover and the Passover seder?

Pentecost

Pentecost

the Jewish spring harvest feast commemorating the gift of the Torah

The feast of **Pentecost** (Shavu'ot), or the feast of the spring harvest, concludes the Passover season. It's sometimes referred to as the *Feast of Weeks*. The date for this feast falls fifty days after Passover. It's a time to celebrate the gift of the Torah on Mt. Sinai and is considered the birthday of the Jewish religion.

Feast of Tabernacles

Feast of Tabernacles
the Jewish fall harvest celebration commemorating the time of travel in the wilderness between Egypt and the promised land

The **Feast of Tabernacles** or **Booths** (Sukkot) is a fall harvest celebration. It commemorates the time of travel in the wilderness between Egypt and the promised land. Special tents, or booths (tabernacles) were set up in the area of the temple in Jerusalem for this feast, bringing to mind the temporary dwellings in the desert. At the time of Jesus, the people set up three special booths in the temple area: one for Moses, one for Elijah, and one for the expected messiah. Today such booths are often erected on balconies or in yards and are decorated with fall harvest reminders.

Day of Atonement

Day of Atonement, Yom Kippur
the Jewish day of fasting and corporate confession of sins

Another major feast day is the **Day of Atonement** (**Yom Kippur**). On this special day the high priest would enter the holy of holies in the temple at Jerusalem to offer sacrifice for his own sins and then for the sins of the people. Only the high priests were ever allowed in this part of the temple. The people recognized how self-centeredness and sin destroyed their covenant relationship with God, and they sought to reestablish the union lost through sin. Today fasting, purifying rituals, prayer, and the corporate confession of sins mark the day.

Hanakkah

Hanakkah
the Jewish feast commemorating the rededication of the temple in 164 B.C.

Write it down
What is your favorite religious holiday? Why?

Another feast, **Hanakkah**, has become very popular in recent Jewish history. These eight days of celebration commemorate the rededication of the temple after the departure of the Greeks from Jerusalem in 164 B.C. Other names for this feast are the *Feast of Dedication* and the *Festival of Lights*. The menorah, an eight-branched candelabra, is used to mark the days because, at the time of the rededication, the only oil (one day's worth) lasted eight days.

> *God desires our independence—which we attain when, ceasing to strive for it ourselves, we "fall" back into God.*
>
> Dag Hammarskjöld

Then do this
Choose one:

1. Talk to someone from a different culture about the group's holidays and customs. Write a short paper about what you discover.

2. Research one of the Jewish feasts listed here. Write a short paper about what you discover.

REVIEW

1. To what does the word *kosher* refer?

2. What is the main focus of Jewish and Christian spirituality?

3. What does Passover celebrate? How is it celebrated?

4. What other major religious feasts are part of Judaism?

IMPORTANT PEOPLE

The Israelites responded to the saving hand of God in their lives. As we have seen, they responded in Sacred Scripture and in their religious practices. We have taken a brief look at these two major ways the chosen people saw themselves in relationship to God and to each other. We'll now look at the important groups of people in Judaism. This background is certainly important for us Christians, since we share this heritage.

Anawim

anawim
people who were completely without resources or social status

Anawim is a Hebrew word used in the Old Testament to describe people who are totally without resources or help. They are the poorest of the poor. Among the Jews in pre-Christian times the **anawim** were those people who were completely rejected by society. They had no economic, social, religious or cultural status. Many people of Jesus' day were anawim, "nobodies." They were extremely poor and lived in the countryside, scratching out a living under the domination of a few rich landlords.

The Israelites identified with these people because the Israelites came from a rejected people (the Apiru) and knew well the experience of being poor and outcast. For the Israelites, one of the sure signs that God was present was that the people who were poor, the "nobodies," his anawim, were being taken care of. This is still true today.

Another anawim

Behold, my brothers, the spring has come; the earth has received the embraces of the sun and we shall soon see the results of that love!

Every seed is awakened and so has all animal life. It is through this mysterious power that we too have our being and we therefore yield to our neighbors, even our animal neighbors, the same right as ourselves, to inhabit this land.

Yet, hear me, people, we have now to deal with another race—small and feeble when our fathers first met them but now great and overbearing. Strangely enough they have a mind to till the soil and the love of possession is a disease with them. These people have made many rules that the rich may break but the poor may not. They take tithes from the poor and weak to support the rich who rule. They claim this mother of ours, the earth, for their own and fence their neighbors away; they deface her with their buildings and their refuse. That nation is like a spring freshet that overruns its banks and destroys all who are in its path.

Tatanka Yotanka (Sitting Bull)

Optional activities

1. Research one Native American nation, especially the group's fate after the "discovery" and settlement of the continent by Europeans. Write a report or give a presentation to the class.

2. Research some of the religious views of one or more Native American nation. In an essay or a class presentation, compare the views with those of Christians.

3. In small groups make a list of present-day anawim. Share the lists and discuss those named.

Pharisees

About one hundred years before the time of Jesus, a movement developed among laymen in Israel to find more faithful ways to live a practical life of faith. These laymen sought to follow all the instructions they could find in the Law (the first five books of the Old Testament) and the spoken traditions of the elders.

Their intent was to put their faith into practice in their daily lives. Their exact observance of the Law was seen as a "fence around the Law," that is, the Law would be more faithfully kept when all the lesser laws that safeguarded it were kept.

These men came to be known as the **Pharisees**, or those who were "separators" or "distinguishers" of the Law. Some among them tended to see themselves as more faithful to the Law of God than were the common people.

Pharisees
Jewish laymen who practiced exact observance of the Law

The Pharisees were very influential at the time of Jesus, and some of their beliefs may have influenced his own comments about angels and spirits, resurrection, and judgment. Some of the Pharisees actively resisted Jesus, who often ignored ritual laws (by healing on the Sabbath, picking grain on the Sabbath, not washing before eating). On the other hand, other Pharisees, most notably Paul, became Jesus' dedicated followers. When Jerusalem and the second temple were finally destroyed in the year A.D. 70, the Pharisees preserved the essence of Judaism as the people fled out of Palestine.

Sadducees

Like the Pharisees, the **Sadducees** came from a kind of spiritual revival which occurred in Israel about a hundred years before the time of Jesus. The group included the priests and their families and supporters, among them many landowners and merchants. These people too wanted to draw close to God by studying and obeying the Law.

Sadducees
a group of priests and their followers in Judaism known for their reliance on the Pentateuch alone

While the Pharisees concerned themselves with behavior like work and religious ritual, the Sadducees were concerned with the accuracy of religious instruction. They became the "religious police" of their day, judging their own members and others as well in terms of the correct teaching of the Law. They believed that only the five books of the Pentateuch were authoritative. This group of men held a position of power and influence at the time of Jesus. When the last temple was destroyed and the priesthood ended, this group disappeared.

Pharisees among Jesus' followers

During Jesus' time on earth, his followers included two important Pharisees. These were Nicodemus and Joseph of Arimathea. In the stories of Pentecost and the council at Jerusalem, recorded in the Acts of the Apostles, we learn that there were other believers who were Pharisees. In time, Paul told the apostle James, "You see, brother, how many thousands of believers there are among the Jews, and they are all zealous for the law" (see Acts 21:2).

See the *Catechism of the Catholic Church*, #595.

1. What do you know about Nicodemus? Joseph of Arimathea?
2. What does it mean to be "zealous for the law"?
3. What did the Pharisees bring to Christianity?

Scribes and rabbis

Ever since the time of the great exiles which followed the destruction of both the northern Kingdom of Israel (721 B.C.) and the southern Kingdom of Judah (587 B.C.), the role of the scribe had been important. The **scribes**, as the name indicates, were the holders of the pen and paper, as it were; they kept the records. They were the recording secretaries of salvation history.

The scribes put in writing the story of God's salvation as experienced by the Israelites. They wrote, copied, and cared for the Sacred Scriptures. And so, they had both political and religious power. People recognized that the scribes really knew the Scriptures and could offer instruction about how to apply the Scriptures to daily life. Many scribes at the time of Jesus were Pharisees.

During the time of the exiles, the Jews came to rely more heavily on the Scriptures for their identity and for their spiritual lives. At this time, the temple in Jerusalem had been destroyed. Those who knew the Scriptures well soon came to be respected members of society. Their explanation of God's word came to be powerful.

Since there was no temple in Jerusalem, the people gathered in prayer houses, synagogues, to hear readings from the Scriptures and to be instructed in how to live the teachings. The one who explained the Scripture was called the **rabbi**, or *teacher*. Many of the rabbis at the time of Jesus were scribes.

Priests and Levites

The nation of Israel came from twelve tribes. According to tradition, one of these tribes, the tribe of Levi, had no land holdings like the other tribes. Instead, some men of this tribe were the **priests** who served as mediators between God and the people. They offered sacrifices in the temple and performed other religious rites.

When the first temple was destroyed, the priests' role diminished until the temple was rebuilt after the exile in Babylon. With the destruction of the second temple and Jerusalem in A.D. 70, physical sacrifice, the temple, and priests were no longer part of Judaism. That was because only priests could offer sacrifice, and only in the temple and only in Jerusalem.

The distinction between priests and Levites is not always clear, and at times in Scripture the term *Levite* refers to a priest. Levites who were not priests could not offer sacrifice in the temple, but they did assist the priests and performed some non-priestly ceremonies and provided music for the sacred rituals. They were also charged with the work of maintaining order in the temple, protecting the buildings, collecting the offerings, and caring for the needs of the many pilgrims who came there to pray and offer sacrifice.

scribes
the recorders of Scripture, often called on to instruct others in applying Scripture to daily life

Talk about it
What is the role of the rabbi in a Jewish congregation today? The priest in a Catholic parish? The minister in a Protestant congregation?

rabbi
in Judaism, a teacher; at the time of Jesus, especially from among the scribes

priests
in Judaism, men who offered sacrifices in the temple and performed other religious rites

Levites
usually non-priests who assisted at the temple

> *The full impact of the words of Jesus is not grasped unless we hear his words against the background of the history and the prophecy, the wisdom and the poetry of his own people.*
>
> **John L. McKenzie**

Gentiles

The chosen people, the Israelites, had a very deep awareness of being favored by God. Unlike the gods of the people around them, their God was one of promise and action. They knew that the people from the nations around them didn't speak of their gods in the same way or have the same expectations of them. To the mind of the Israelites, anyone outside their group was god-less. These other nations and tribes might have god statues sitting on their fireplace hearths or in their temples, but the Israelites saw these gods and their statues as powerless to save.

The Israelites lumped all of these people together. They were not Israelites, not Jews. They were *goyim*, **Gentiles**. As Israel matured in faith, the people came to realize that God also lived in the hearts of many of their Gentile friends and neighbors. Seeing that these friends and neighbors were trying the best they could to live a decent life, the Israelites referred to them as "God-fearing" people.

Gentiles, on the other hand, were those who did not have the light of true faith! In the Acts of the Apostles and the letters of the New Testament, we find the early Jewish Christians faced with the challenge to accept into their group Gentiles who may not have been considered "God-fearing" by other Jewish people.

Gentiles
non-Jews, *goyim*; those without the light of true faith

Tax collectors

Through its long history the nation of Israel knew what it was like to be oppressed, to be ruled by others—and to have to pay taxes to their oppressors. Even worse, some of the tax collectors were Jews, working for the enemy! Is it any wonder that tax collectors were very much disliked? In fact, they were considered public sinners. No good Jew was to have anything to do with them.

Also, for the Jews, the use of foreign coins was a particular problem, because on these coins was stamped the image of the foreign king—and that king frequently considered himself a god. The Jews worshiped the one true God and were never to "have strange gods before them." No images appeared in the temple or in the homes or workplaces of Jews. So the use of these coins was considered by many to be an act of **idolatry**, or the worship of false gods.

At the time of Jesus, the Jews had pressured the occupying Roman forces to allow them to take these idolatrous coins to the temple and exchange them for Jewish coins which could be used to buy offerings and give **alms** to those who were poor.

idolatry
the worship of false gods or of images

alms
donations for those who are poor

REVIEW

1. Who are the anawim?
2. Which group of laymen sought to follow all the instructions they could find in the Law and the spoken traditions of the elders?
3. How did the Sadducees differ from the Pharisees?
4. What was the work of a scribe?
5. Why was Jesus referred to as a rabbi?
6. What did priests and Levites do?
7. What was the difference between a Gentile and a non-Jew who was God-fearing?
8. Why were tax collectors not respected by most Jews?

Then do this
Scan one of the Gospels and make a list of the different groups of people you find there. Then name at least one person who belonged to each group.

CONCLUSION

This, then, was the world of God's chosen people—the Apiru, the Hebrews, the Israelites, the Jews. Salvation history is the story of real people in real time and in real places. God's unfolding plan of salvation created a people with an identity and with their own unique religious practices and ways of worship and daily life. This chapter has offered just a brief description of God's people, but sufficient to understand how wonderfully God has worked in this people to save them.

The chosen people believed in one God, and they believed that God takes action. This God saves. This God cares for people and, in return, wants people to care for each other, especially for those who are poor, the "nobodies." All through the history of the Jews, no one has cared more than they—and no one has suffered more.

Christians are blessed to follow in the footsteps of the Jewish people. They have given us a rich heritage and a challenge to be open to God who continues to save us. Our rituals and our prayers of worship and our feasts echo the work of God among us— Jews and Christians.

Talk about it

Why do you think the Jews have suffered so much?

Has not God chosen the poor in the world to be rich in faith and to be heirs of the kingdom that he has promised to those who love him?

James 2:5

Aquila and Prisca
Partners with Paul

After this Paul left Athens and went to Corinth. There he found a Jew named Aquila, a native of Pontus, who had recently come from Italy with his wife Priscilla, because Claudius had ordered all Jews to leave Rome. Paul went to see them, and, because he was of the same trade, he stayed with them, and they worked together—by trade they were tentmakers.

Acts 18:1–3

After being expelled from Rome, Aquila and Prisca (Priscilla in Acts) moved to Corinth where there were already a good number of Jews. There they met Paul, who stayed with them. Paul may have converted them to Christianity, or they may already have been Christians when he met them. They traveled with Paul to Ephesus and worked with him to establish a house church there. In Ephesus, Aquila and Prisca instructed Apollos in the Christian faith.

Now there came to Ephesus a Jew named Apollos, a native of Alexandria. He was an eloquent man, well-versed in the scriptures. He had been instructed in the Way of the Lord; and he spoke with burning enthusiasm and taught accurately the things concerning Jesus, though he knew only the baptism of John. He began to speak boldly in the synagogue; but when Priscilla and Aquila heard him, they took him aside and explained the Way of God to him more accurately.

Acts 18:24–26

Apollos eventually became a very successful preacher of Christianity back in Corinth. In the meantime Aquila and Prisca remained in Ephesus to work with the new Christians there and to bring others—Jews and Gentiles—the good news of Jesus. Periodically in his letters, Paul mentioned Aquila and Prisca, acknowledging their continual work for the Lord. To the church in Corinth, he wrote:

The churches of Asia send greetings. Aquila and Prisca, together with the church in their house, greet you warmly in the Lord.

1 Corinthians 16:19

In Romans, we find Paul in Corinth and Aquila and Prisca once again in Rome. In his Letter to the Romans, Paul writes about an interesting event which is mentioned nowhere else in the New Testament:

Greet Prisca and Aquila, who work with me in Christ Jesus, and who risked their necks for my life, to whom not only I give thanks, but also all the churches of the Gentiles. Greet also the church in their house.

Romans 16:3–5

It may be that this faithful couple eventually returned to Asia Minor to work with or near Timothy, another co-worker of Paul. They are mentioned in the closing of the Second Letter to Timothy. Some scholars have even suggested that either Aquila or Prisca was the author of the Letter to the Hebrews.

Over the years Aquila and Prisca worked together to preach Jesus and to establish and lead several house churches for the early Christians. With Paul, they brought the great wealth of the Jewish tradition into their work with new Christians. And with Paul, Aquila and Prisca helped facilitate the transition of Christianity from a sect of Judaism to a movement that embraces all peoples.

Optional activities

1. Scan the Acts of the Apostles and some of Paul's letters to find the names of other co-workers. List the names and give Bible references.
2. Talk to a person who practices Judaism about similarities and differences between Judaism and Christianity. Write a report.
3. Draw maps of Paul's missionary journeys (see the maps in some Bibles). Write the names of co-workers at some of the places to which Paul traveled.

Words you should know

alms	high places	priests
anawim	hypocrisy	rabbi
anointing	idolatry	rites and rituals
blasphemy	kosher	Sabbath or Shabbat
circumcision	laying on of hands	sacrifice
consecration	Levites	Sadducees
covenant	liturgy	scribes
Day of Atonement, Yom Kippur	Passover	social justice
Feast of Tabernacles	Pentecost	worship
Gentiles	Pharisees	YHWH
Hanakkah		

CHAPTER 7

JESUS CHRIST

The Word of the Lord

*This Jesus God raised up, and of that all of us are witnesses.
Being therefore exalted at the right hand of God, and having
received from the Father the promise of the Holy Spirit, he
has poured out this that you both see and hear.*

FROM THE ACTS OF THE APOSTLES; SEE 2:22–24, 32–33, 36–41.

CHAPTER OVERVIEW

- *The Christian framework*

- *Claimed faith in Christ*

- *God saves us through the
  humanity of Jesus*

- *Jesus is the Messiah of God*

Let Us Pray

*I give you thanks, O L*ORD*, with my whole heart;*
  before the gods I sing your praise;

I bow down toward your holy temple
  and give thanks to your name for your steadfast love
    and your faithfulness;
  for you have exalted your name and your word
  above everything.
On the day I called, you answered me,
  you increased my strength of soul.
*All the kings of the earth shall praise you, O L*ORD*,*
  for they have heard the words of your mouth.
*They shall sing of the ways of the L*ORD*,*
  *for great is the glory of the L*ORD*. . . .*
*The L*ORD *will fulfill his purpose for me;*
  *your steadfast love, O L*ORD*, endures forever.*
  Do not forsake the work of your hands.

PSALM 138:1–5, 8

THE CHRISTIAN FRAMEWORK

Talk about it

1. Why is Jesus the *Savior of the world* and not just a *great man*?

2. What does it mean to be saved in Christ?

faith tradition

the beliefs and practices of a particular religion

Living in this country, possibly you have grown up in a culture filled with Christian values. If so, the culture in which you live reflects the values found in the Gospels. You have probably heard about Jesus since you were old enough to remember, even if your family has not been particularly religious. And if you have grown up practicing your Christian faith, it's hard for you to imagine yourself as anything other than Christian. You tend to see and judge everything from the viewpoint of Christianity.

In previous chapters of this book, you have explored faith and the roots of the Christian faith. Those roots are in the faith of the Hebrews, the Israelites, the Jews. Remember, Jesus was a Jew by birth, and throughout his life Jesus practiced his Jewish faith. He saw himself as belonging to those who recognized well the saving hand of God at work in their history.

Without an understanding of the Jewish **faith tradition**, we cannot understand the full meaning of being followers of this Son of God and son of Mary we acclaim as our Savior. As Christians, we receive our faith perspective from our past—from the heritage of the Jews, the chosen people of God.

The gospel presents Jesus as the turning point of human history. What God has done in him has been done once and for all time and for all people. The Church announces this news as the gospel, the good news of salvation, the good news of God's love for all humanity.

> *The gospel is neither a discussion or a debate.*
> *It is an announcement.*
>
> **Paul S. Rees**

Good news

In the Introduction of this book, we met Paul as he announced the gospel to the Greeks in the ancient city of Athens. He had something important to share with them. He didn't go there to present his own ideas, but to offer testimony to what God had done for humanity in the person of Jesus. Paul had good news! In the reading at the beginning of this chapter, you heard Peter announce this same good news.

Now there's news, and there's *good* news. (And there's *bad* news, too, unfortunately.) What is news? What makes news good or bad? The answer is no farther away than your TV. When you watch the evening news, what are you experiencing? News is the telling of a version of the facts, or a narration of events. The examples are many:

Twelve people died last night in a bus crash on the freeway.

The president of the United States will visit China in February.

Company X has won the contract to build a new supermarket.

Tomorrow's weather forecast is for rain.

All of these events—and thousands of other possibilities—contain information. In themselves, these news items are "just the facts." They are impersonal.

What makes a piece of news good or bad is its significance for your life—if it makes any difference to you. The more personally the news affects your life, the more powerfully good or bad it is. For example, it probably doesn't matter to you that Company X has won the contract to build a new supermarket. It's just regular news. However, if you are the *president* of Company X, it's good news! Of course, if you're the president of a competing company, it's probably bad news for you!

It's important for us to understand what makes news good or bad, since the news about Jesus is announced in Scripture as *good* news. In fact, that's what the word *gospel* means. The Greek word for gospel is *euangelion*, which means "good announcement." This is where we get our word **evangelist**: one who tells the good news.

Talk about it
What's the difference between *news* and the *good news*?

Then do this
Watch the evening news. Make a list of the various news items. For whom is this news good news? For whom is it bad news?

evangelist
one who tells the good news; a Gospel writer

Restored humanity

In Jesus we see the invisible God. He is the perfect human who has restored our likeness to God, which has been disfigured by sin from the beginning of the human race onward. By becoming one of us—by becoming human—God's Son has raised our human nature to a dignity beyond compare, to the dignity of God. By the incarnation of the Son of God, each person has been united with him. The Son of God used human hands and a human mind. He acted with a human will and loved with a human heart. Born of Mary, the Son of God has indeed become one of us, like us in all but sin.

See *The Documents of Vatican II,* "Pastoral Constitution on the Church in the Modern World," #22.

1. What difference does it make that Jesus was really human?

2. What do you imagine Jesus' teenage years were like?

3. What does it mean that Jesus was "the perfect human"?

In the times of the Greeks like those men and women whom Paul met in the city of Athens, the word *euangelion* had a very special meaning. The *euangelion* ("good announcement" or "good news") was the report a runner made after he rushed back to the city from a big battle. If the battle had ended in victory, the runner stood in the town square and announced the *euangelion*, the "good news" of victory. The news was good because the city was safe. Had the troops not been victorious, their city likely would have been taken over by the enemy. That would have been *bad* news!

Paul saw himself as a type of runner. He had experienced the call to be an **apostle**. *Apostle* is another Greek word, and it means "one who is sent." In his personal conversion story, the story of how his life changed, Paul told how the risen Lord Jesus called him—sent him—to spread the good news to all the world.

As Christ's apostle, Paul saw himself sent to tell people about the victory God had achieved through Jesus. Paul didn't go around selling a book of ideas about Christianity; he preached Jesus. Paul was convinced that what God had done in Jesus was not just news, but good news!

Then do this
Listen carefully to the homily or sermon on Sunday. Write a brief report on the good news that was announced and on how well that good news came across to you.

Our presumption

There's a big presumption here! A *presumption* is a feeling that something will probably happen or is probably true. It's a kind of expectation. Your parents, for example, prepare dinner with the presumption, the expectation, that someone will be at the table to eat it. You could also say that they presume you will be hungry!

What was Paul's presumption about the people in Athens? What is the presumption of any preacher of the gospel—including the one at church on Sunday—about what's happening in the hearts of listeners? Remember, those who preach the gospel believe they have good news to offer. What the preacher has to offer and what the listener needs to hear must meet at some point!

Those who preach the gospel, who bring the good news, presume that their listeners are serious about their lives and honest about their limitations. The "big presumption" is that the listeners *realize* that they cannot bring about their own deep happiness and that they stand in need of salvation. The presumption is that their hearts are searching for the fullness of life that no amount of things, people, and daily life experiences are able to satisfy.

The announcement of the gospel is at the heart of all Christian worship. The announcement of the good news is the main reason for sharing the word of God—whether at Mass in a Catholic church, or in a Protestant worship service, or in Bible reading on television, or in Scripture study in a religious education class. In all of these, there is the conviction that what is said about the life, death, and resurrection of Jesus is far more than just news.

True, there's a "newsy" part about the life of Jesus that can be shared. He was a real human who lived in a certain time and place and did certain things and was executed by the Romans. That's news. If anything, this would have been bad news—first, because a good man was killed senselessly, and second, because there had been hope that Jesus would change the situation of the people. At least some of the people hoped that Jesus had something to do with the coming of God's kingdom. So Jesus was news—to many, the good—news!

The gospel announces more than just bits of news about Jesus. As Paul announced, the "rest of the story" needs to be told. The gospel announces *who Jesus is*! The **disciples** of Jesus experienced his life and his death—and they also experienced him as alive again and still with them! They knew that only God can raise people from the dead. Since Jesus had been raised from the dead and was with them, they knew that the reign of God had come.

In the life, death, and resurrection of Jesus, we see the clearest expression of God in human history. God had shown all people the way to fullness of life. The saving love of God, known in Jesus, could be trusted—because Jesus lives! He who was dead, lives! And lives eternally, to die no more!

This is *super* good news for us humans who yearn for the fullness of life with all our hearts. This is wonderful news for us humans whose very lives and meaning are threatened by the sureness of death. In Jesus there is hope and the promise of eternal life! There is something to live for! There is something to die for—because united with Jesus, our dying leads to eternal life!

This isn't an idea dreamed up by the early disciples who just couldn't let the memory of Jesus fade from their hearts. The resurrection of Jesus is part of his historical life. After his death and resurrection, he was seen, not as a ghost or figment of their imagination, but as a living and real person. They *knew* he was there with them.

This good news was just too good for the disciples of Jesus to keep to themselves. It wasn't just good news for the Jewish community who were comfortable with God acting in human history; it was good news for the Gentiles as well. The first disciples realized that Jesus, the Christ, was not only the fulfillment of the promise God made to the chosen people; he was a gift to the whole world. Thus, filled with the news of God's victory over the power of sin and everlasting death, the believers felt moved to set off to the ends of the world to share the good news—and they have been doing so ever since.

disciple
one who learns from and follows another

Talk about it

1. How do you feel about dying?

2. Does it matter to you that there is eternal life to look forward to? Explain why.

Christianity is in its very essence a resurrection religion.
The concept of resurrection lies at its heart.
John R.W. Stott

REVIEW

1. What does it mean to say that Jesus is the turning point of human history?

2. Why is the news about Jesus good news?

3. What is an evangelist? An apostle? A disciple?

God meets our need

The Church doesn't just decide on its own to preach the gospel. The Church preaches the gospel in every age because of what the gospel is—the good news of God's love. God wants everyone to be saved and to know the truth. In this gospel, we find the fullness of life, or salvation. All who listen to the Spirit are on the way to salvation. Entrusted with the treasure of the gospel, the Church must go to all people, since all are longing for salvation, and bring them to the truth, who is Jesus. Believing in God's plan that all be saved, the Church must be missionary—must share the good news.

See the *Catechism of the Catholic Church,* #851.

1. What does it mean to say that Jesus is God's truth?
2. Why must the Church not keep the good news to itself?
3. Is there room for the gospel in today's world? Why? A need for the gospel? Why?

Jesus and a Pharisee

Another time
a Pharisee, Simon by name,
whose fingernails were the white of ivory
and whose mind was a scroll of law
invited Jesus to a meal.
While they were at table
the storm of Magdelene,
all tears and hair and perfume,
broke upon the feet of Jesus.
Simon unrolled the parchment in his head.
   "If he was a prophet,
   he would know
   who this woman was
   who touched him."

Jesus did know
but not what Simon knew.
   "I have something to say to you, Simon."
  "Speak, Teacher."
   "Two men owed money to a lender.
   One 500 coins, the other 50.
   The lender wrote off both debts.
   Of the debtors
   who was the most grateful?"
With Jesus
it always ended that way.
A hook in the heart
in the guise of a question.

John Shea, *Stories of Faith.*

Optional activities

1. Choose a story about Jesus or a story Jesus told and rewrite it in the style of this story.
2. Search the Gospels and make a list of the questions Jesus asked, questions that were hooks in the heart. In writing respond to some of these questions.
3. Find or write another story that teaches a lesson. Tell the story to the class and lead a discussion on it.

. . . in him was life, and the life was the light of all people.

John 1:4

CLAIMED FAITH IN CHRIST

Where and when did the Church's missionary effort catch up with you? Your family and your faith community are a part of the continuing effort of Christ's disciples to share the gospel with the world. Ever since you were a child you have heard the news about Jesus. Is it just news or is it *good* news?

Like all humans, you are looking for fulfillment and happiness. You want to know who you are and what your destiny is. You want to know if God cares about you, cares enough to save you, to bring you to fullness of life. The Scriptures and the Church say, "Absolutely!" In Jesus, God has entered your world—where you live—and offers you fullness of life. You can't save yourself, but in Christ God can and does save you.

The gift of faith in Christ has been offered to you since you were a child. You have the opportunity weekly—if not more often—to hear the good news of your salvation in Christ. The big presumption is that you are honest about your life, that you let your heart do some serious seeking.

Ever since the days of the first apostles, the good news has been told, but not everyone who has heard has accepted it. Some people have been too busy to give it serious consideration. Some are caught up in their own efforts to achieve ultimate happiness. Some are busy being "Number One"; they don't need anybody else.

All the same, it's a fact of human nature that the search goes on within our hearts; everyone is looking for happiness and fullness of life. If fullness of life is not to be found in Jesus, then where is it found? Who or what else in the world can be the source of salvation? A bank account? A new car? Political power? Good looks? Fame? If not in Jesus, then in what or in whom? The question of ultimate happiness and salvation won't go away. It demands an answer. Those who refuse to deal with the question are only fooling themselves.

Write it down

How do you relate to people who tell you that they have seen the Lord?

Talk about it

1. What keeps people from hearing the good news?

2. Would Jesus find greater acceptance today than he did in his time of earth? Who would listen to him? Who wouldn't?

He utterly destroyed the power death had against mankind, as fire consumes chaff, by means of the body he had taken and the grace of the resurrection.

St. Athanasius

In a sentence

Have you ever been to a ball game and seen a man or woman carrying a big poster saying "John 3:16"? Perhaps you've seen people on television who stand behind the newscaster or appear in the crowd and bounce a sign like this up and down to get the viewers' attention. You may find this a bit rude. What are these people doing? Really, they are presenting the gospel. In the Gospel according to John, chapter 3, verse 16, you will find these words:

> *For God so loved the world that he gave his only Son, so that everyone who believes in him may not perish but may have eternal life.*

This is the good news in a single sentence. These words obviously don't say everything that can be said about Jesus, but they do speak the truth of the Christian gospel. Let us reflect on the significance of this single sentence.

Talk about it

What would you say to people at a ball game who carry placards reading "John 3:16"? Why?

God so loved . . .

In the whole of creation God becomes known as one who loves and who saves. The God of creation is the same as the God of salvation. In fact, in the goodness of creation, you can experience the gift of God himself. Creation is not just an enormous box of toys created by God for the pleasure of humans. Everything is an expression of God.

No one realized this more intimately than the chosen people, the Israelites, whom God singled out in love and with whom he established a covenant. God saved these people and gave them their greatness. God's covenant with the people contained a promise: "I will bless you, and through you I will bless the world."

Write it down

How does friendship reflect the saving power of God in your life?

. . . the world . . .

God's love is not just an idea. God's love is real. We can see this love of God in creation and in history. God's love meets you in the world where you live. That world is limited, and that world is broken by sinfulness. Yet, that is precisely where God becomes known.

. . . that he gave his only Son . . .

When we think of someone being a son or a daughter, we think of the relationship between that person and the ones who gave him or her life, namely, the person's father and mother. In a very real way, a child is the continuation of the life of the mother and the father. This is true in a special way since a child is usually born from love. The child is a communication of love.

Certainly this is true of Jesus. In Jesus we experience the full reflection of God's love communicated to us. When we speak of God giving us "his only Son," we understand that God is shared with us completely and fully in Jesus. God has left nothing unsaid, no love not communicated. There is no part of God that has not been shared. And God has done this as gift! God has acted freely and with unconditional love—"no strings attached."

Talk about it

1. Where do you see God's love in creation?

2. Where do you see God's love in history?

. . . so that everyone who believes in him . . .

Jesus is the fulfillment of God's covenant love-promise to the Jewish people. And although this promise was made to the Jewish people, the undeserved gift of God's saving love in Jesus is for all people. Jesus is the Savior, the one in whom all people can find salvation and fullness of life.

Yet because we are created in the image and likeness of God, we are free to open up—or not open up—this gift. The gift of salvation in Christ is a free gift to all those who give of their hearts to Christ, all who believe in him.

To believe in Christ, however, requires more than an emotional moment of personal commitment. *Claimed faith*, the free, personal decision to make Jesus the center of one's life, is a lifelong journey of conversion. Even in the end—even when we die—we still stand in need of being saved. Even in death the Christian trusts in God's gift of Jesus.

Write it down
How does your life reflect your belief in Jesus or your struggle to believe?

. . . may not perish . . .

Every human experiences the yearning for fullness of life. Our lives are a mystery to us. We are a question to ourselves, and we spend our entire lives trying to answer the question. We cannot find complete happiness on our own. Sometimes in our searching, we get very lost. We try to find love "in all the wrong faces and all the wrong places."

We can become so lost that we do things to ourselves and to others which deny our God-given goodness and dignity as God's sons and daughters; we sin. We kill the beauty of ourselves through our self-centered search for pleasure or power or money. This isn't God's plan for us. God's plan is happiness forever. So God, loving us unconditionally, comes to save us, to find us in the dark and lift us to the light.

> *Let the same mind be in you that was in Christ Jesus,*
> *who, though he was in the form of God,*
> *did not regard equality with God*
> *as something to be exploited,*
> *but emptied himself,*
> *taking the form of a slave,*
> *being born in human likeness.*
>
> **Philippians 2:5–7**

. . . but may have eternal life.

It's clear from God's action in the history of the chosen people—and certainly in the gift of his Son, Jesus—that God wants us to live—and live forever with him. Someone has said that when God creates human life, it is forever. We are created in the image and likeness of God. But because of humanity's original sin and our personal sins, we have been separated and can still choose to be separated from God.

Through Jesus, God restored us to grace. In Jesus, we are assured that our destiny is to be with God for all eternity. Forever! God's plan is that we never be separated from him, neither now, nor through death, nor after death. We are created to know, love, and serve God in this world and to be with him in the next.

From the resurrection of Jesus, we know that death is not the end of life. Death is a natural moment through which we will all pass. Death is not the end; it is a change. Through the work of the Holy Spirit, death is the path to union with the risen Christ, forever one with his Father.

Talk about it

What is your idea of eternal life?

Open doors

By his death and resurrection Jesus "opened" heaven. Those in heaven experience the fullness and perfection of all that Christ accomplished by saving us. Those who believed in him and were faithful to him are made partners with Jesus, the Christ. In heaven, they are part of the blessed community united with Christ.

See the *Catechism of the Catholic Church*, #1026.

1. What is your idea of heaven? Who gets to be in heaven? How do they get there?

2. Why can't we get to heaven by ourselves?

Christ has turned all our sunsets into dawns.

St. Clement of Alexandria

REVIEW

1. What do all humans seek?

2. What is John 3:16? Why is it important?

3. Name three ways in which we see God and come to know his love.

4. Who or what is the full reflection of God's love?

5. What is God's plan for us?

GOD SAVES US THROUGH THE HUMANITY OF JESUS

The single verse of Scripture, John 3:16, does indeed contain the good news. In fact, it says everything. God saves us through his Son, who, through the power of the Holy Spirit, has become one of us. What God has done for us in Jesus speaks to the human heart, where we hear the Holy Spirit of God's love. Remember, you cannot be separated from that Spirit. You can turn away from God (by your personal choice to sin), but God will never turn away from you.

Did you know that the name *Jesus* means "God saves"? And in the historical life of Jesus—a life which could be seen and heard, a life which could be touched and experienced—God entered into the human condition to bring us to the fullness of life; in Jesus, God saves. Let's think about how God has saved us in Jesus, the one born of Mary. It's through Jesus' humanity that God saves us. What does that mean? And why is it important?

Imagine yourself in that town square in Athens when Paul went to the speakers' stand and announced that God had saved us, that the "Unknown God" had made himself known. How would have you reacted if Paul had announced: "Hey, I've got great news for you. You won't have to search for your Unknown God anymore. Here's how you get in touch with God. If you make a huge stack of rocks, then this God will speak to your hearts, and your hunger for God will be satisfied." Perhaps you would have reacted by saying, "Great idea, Paul, but it doesn't float my boat! I can stack rocks as high as a mountain or until the day I die, but stacking rocks has nothing to do with my life!"

Or what if Paul had said, "Hey, I've got great news for you religious people. I know you are searching for God. It's obvious. Look at your temple to the Unknown God. Well, guess what? That Unknown God loves you so much that he became a garden slug over in Thailand!" Perhaps you'd find the idea a bit curious, but wouldn't you respond (with a disappointed heart), "Sorry, Paul, but I'm not a garden slug! I need someone who understands me and lives in the same world I do!"

These are obviously silly examples, but they make an important point. Stacking rocks and garden slugs may be news to someone, but for those who search for the fullness of life, they aren't good news. The good news we need to hear has to come to us in a way that "speaks" to our humanity and to our real human condition.

Having gone through this little mental exercise, perhaps we can focus a bit better on the importance of what we're saying: God has come to us in Jesus. Jesus is not the creation of someone's imagination. He lived a human life in a real time and in a real place. Like us!

Talk about it

What does it mean to "hunger for God"?

The Son of God became man in weakness, to help us to be fully human, giving us the power to become children of God.

Pope John Paul II

Jesus was born

It's very important to us that Jesus was born. He didn't "beam down" to planet Earth on a galactic starburst. He didn't just appear as the Greek gods were believed to have appeared. *You* didn't beam down to Earth, did you? *You* didn't just appear, did you? You were born. So was Jesus. He was conceived in the womb of a woman. His mother's name was Mary; his maternal grandparents were Joachim and Anna.

The conception of Jesus was unique, one of a kind. Natural conception requires the sexual union of a father and a mother. Jesus was conceived in Mary's womb by the miraculous work of the Holy Spirit. Nothing is impossible for God. Jesus' conception, however, should not be seen as just an awesome change from the normal process of conception. The conception of Jesus by the Spirit of God should be seen as God entering into human history—not from without, but from within.

This Jesus was the Son of God—God giving himself. He was also the son of Mary. Jesus had both a human nature and a divine nature. He had arms, legs, a nose, a mouth, fingers, and lungs—just like every human. With great love and generosity, God became one of us in Jesus.

Jesus shared the human condition

To be human, however, means more than just to have the body of a human. To be human also means to be born at a specific time and in a specific place. And so it was with Jesus. The Bible says that Jesus was born of the "house" or lineage of King David, the great king of the Israelites. Jesus was born to the family of King David.

To understand who Jesus was, we need to study and understand his family. We need to understand how life was then—what people were like, what they did, how they felt about things, what they believed. That's why we need to understand salvation history—God acting in history to save us. Jesus lived in that history and was the one who saves.

To say that Jesus shared in the human condition also means that he had the same life questions that you have. Who am I? Where did I come from? Where am I going? What is the purpose of my life? Like all other humans, you have to live with these questions.

Write it down

When I think about the Son of God becoming one of us, I feel . . . because . . . .

Write it down

Respond to the questions in the paragraph, "To say that Jesus shared . . . ."

Jesus shared the same search for meaning that you experience. He went through his "terrible twos," exploring every corner of the house. He went through the helpful sixes and sevens, and, as he grew, he helped out in the family and in the neighborhood. Jesus also experienced the lonely searching of adolescents as he struggled to find his true freedom and his true self. He experienced the ongoing mystery of adult life where the heart searches for ultimate happiness in God. He needed to pray, and he took time to pray—by himself and with his people.

A study of Jesus' religious upbringing would reflect his passage from experienced religion to practiced religion to searching faith and to claimed faith. He grew up in a Jewish household where, without a doubt, his mother Mary and his foster-father Joseph taught him his prayers. He joined the family for its religious ceremonies at the meal table, at the synagogue in Nazareth, and at the temple in Jerusalem. He joined the family, relatives, and townsfolk for prayer. He undoubtedly went with Joseph to the synagogue for prayer—even when he was tempted to stay home in bed!

Jesus experienced the struggles of adolescence as he grew and matured. All the while, his heart sought to do the will of his heavenly Father. In all the ways that you know human life—its joys and its pains—Jesus too knew life. He was fully human. What Jesus did *not* know was the experience of sin. He was without sin. He never said "no" to his Father. He always said "yes."

Then do this

1. Interview two members of your family, two other adults, and two other children:
   - When did you learn to pray?
   - Who taught you your first prayer?
   - What were you told about why we pray?
2. Write an essay on your interviews, summarizing your findings.

Take Jesus out of the perfumed cloisters of pious sentiment, and let him walk the streets of the city.

Peter Marshall

Time of temptation

In the Gospels we read that Jesus went to the desert after he was baptized by John the Baptist. Led by the Spirit, he went out to the desert to be alone. There he fasted for forty days. After the forty days, Jesus was tempted three times by Satan, who asked him to turn away from God the Father, to trust in other things instead. Jesus turned aside these temptations, which were the same temptations the first humans faced and the temptations of Israel in the desert.

The Gospel writers suggest the meaning of this event: Jesus is the new Adam, the one who remained faithful in the face of the very temptations the first Adam gave in to. Jesus is the perfect fulfillment of Israel's vocation. Christ reveals himself as the servant of God, completely obedient. His victory against the

tempter in the desert is a preview of the victory his suffering and death would bring. His passion is the supreme loving act of obedience to his heavenly Father.

See the *Catechism of the Catholic Church*, #s 538–539.

1. What do you think the real-life temptations of Jesus were? What are the temptations of teenagers today?

2. How does Jesus show you how to avoid evil?

3. Why is it important to know that Jesus was tempted? That he did not give in to sin?

Jesus lived

Jesus had a life. He grew from the diaper stage of infancy, through childhood and adolescence, to adulthood. Like all humans, Jesus showed who he was by what he did and how he did it. That's how we come to know anyone: by watching what they do and listening to what they say. Our actions and our words show people who we are.

No one can make contact with each and every person on the face of the earth—no matter how highly developed modern technology becomes. Jesus didn't even meet everyone who lived in his day and age. Those whom he did meet, though, described him as a person of unconditional love.

This love was especially evident in the way Jesus treated sinners and those who were rejected by society (the anawim). He assured these people of God's love and forgiveness. He told them that they were loved and forgiven *here* and *now*! God was with them.

Jesus spoke with authority, but that authority wasn't based on books or the religious experts of his day. He spoke with the authority of God—just like the prophets of old! Through wise sayings and especially through special stories with a twist (parables), Jesus taught people that God was not distant, nor to be feared. God was very present and loving.

Write it down

What do you understand the kingdom of God to be?

Choosing an image from his Jewish ancestry, Jesus called this presence of God the *kingdom*. He pleaded with people to let God be God in their lives, to open their hearts to the unconditional love of God who sought not to condemn but to save. He directed people back to grace, to the dignity of sons and daughters of God, their heavenly Father.

The primary commandment Jesus gave his followers was to imitate the unconditional love of God which they experienced in him. Everything else would fall into its proper place if they lived with love. The challenge was great, however, because it required self-denial for the sake of the welfare of others.

> *"I give you a new commandment, that you love one another. Just as I have loved you, you also should love one another. By this everyone will know that you are my disciples, if you have love for one another."*
>
> — *John 13:34–35*

The Beatitudes

"Blessed are the poor in spirit, for theirs is the kingdom of heaven.

"Blessed are those who mourn, for they will be comforted.

"Blessed are the meek, for they will inherit the earth.

"Blessed are those who hunger and thirst for righteousness, for they will be filled.

"Blessed are the merciful, for they will receive mercy.

"Blessed are the pure in heart, for they will see God.

"Blessed are the peacemakers, for they will be called children of God.

"Blessed are those who are persecuted for righteousness' sake, for theirs is the kingdom of heaven."

Matthew 5:3–10

1. What does each of these statements mean?

2. Do you think Jesus' listeners were surprised by these statements? Explain.

3. Considering Jesus' teachings, what Beatitudes could be added to these?

Jesus didn't condemn the religious practices of his Jewish faith, but he did place them in perspective. He rejected any practice or teaching that controlled people and kept them from an encounter with the saving love of God. And those whose practice of religion was only "lip service," he called *hypocrites*.

People who opened their hearts and lives to Jesus experienced the very presence of God in their midst! The words of Jesus freed them from self-doubt and sinful actions. His presence made them feel whole and accepted and loved without condition.

In the **miracles** of Jesus, people saw the love of God who wanted to make all things whole. They realized that more was happening in their presence than the good deeds of a good man. They realized that, in the person Jesus, *God* was touching lives!

Undoubtedly, the Jesus people met didn't float through the streets of the cities of Israel with a glowing light around him. The many movies that have been made about the life and times of Jesus actually may distract us from his humanness—a humanness through which God saves us. If Jesus is presented as other-worldly, with great powers and few human qualities, we may see him as divine alone.

The more lifelike and real the movies make Jesus, the more filmmakers capture the truth of the gospel. Many people passed by Jesus and saw no more than another man on the street. Those who truly met him encountered a person of immense, transforming, unconditional love—the kind of love that only God is capable of giving.

Many people followed Jesus and tried to live according to the demands of the kingdom he preached. They realized that if they were going to find true happiness, they needed something more in their lives. They needed God. And they were willing to learn from Jesus how to find God.

Jesus called these people around him and formed a community which continues today. We call this community **Church**—people who have heard the good news, believe it, and seek to follow it. Since the very beginning, Jesus entrusted this community with the partnership of announcing God's reign to the world.

From among his followers, or disciples (learners), Jesus selected twelve men to be his close friends. We call these special disciples his *apostles*. Among them were Peter and Andrew, John the Beloved, James, and Judas Iscariot (who, in the end, betrayed Jesus). These men, accompanied by other disciples, carried the good news of Jesus to the ends of the known earth—from Palestine to Greece and Rome.

Jesus' followers have continued this ministry to this very day. It is said that in selecting the Twelve, Jesus saw himself establishing the New Israel. Just as the Old Israel was founded on twelve tribes, now the New Israel would be founded on Jesus' twelve apostles.

miracle

an event that can't be explained naturally; a marvel that shows God at work

Talk about it

1. What miracles did Jesus perform?

2. What were the results of these miracles?

3. Have you ever experienced a miracle?

Church

the community of Jesus' followers who have heard the good news, believe it, and seek to follow it

Then do this

Ask four Christians where they meet Jesus, the risen Lord. Compare the responses you receive with those a classmate received. Are there any common experiences?

REVIEW

1. What does the name *Jesus* mean?

2. Why was it important that the Son of God became a human and not another creature?

3. How did Jesus teach? What literary form did he often use?

4. What did the miracles of Jesus tell people?

5. What is the Church?

St. Peter
Courageous leader

Peter was clearly the leader of the apostles. Much of his story is told in the Gospels and the Acts of the Apostles. While it would seem logical for Peter to stay in Jerusalem as head of the Church there, that isn't what happened. James took on this task, and Peter periodically returned to Jerusalem from his missionary travels. There he first faced prison for his preaching about Jesus.

Tradition tells us that Peter founded the Church in Antioch. He probably also spent time in Corinth, as did Paul. At some time Peter traveled to Rome, as 1 Peter indicates. It's not really known how long Peter preached in Rome, although he and Paul have long been honored as the founders of the Church there.

Although there is no written record, it has always been held by the Church that Peter was imprisoned and executed during the time of Nero's rule (A.D. 54–68). Tradition tells us that Peter was crucified head down, at his request, because he felt unworthy to die exactly like Jesus did.

When the predecessor of the Basilica of St. Peter was built, what was thought to be Peter's body was brought from the catacombs and buried at the site. In the late twentieth century, excavations did indeed uncover what some think is the grave of St. Peter, and what is possibly his remains now rest in the crypt directly below the main altar.

Optional activities

1. Work in small groups to make a list of everything you know about St. Peter from the Gospels and the Acts of the Apostles.
2. Write and illustrate a book for children on the life of St. Peter.
3. Research another of the apostles. Write an essay or prepare a report to present to the class.
4. Research St. Peter's Basilica in Vatican City. Write an essay or prepare a report to present to the class on your findings.

Jesus died

Jesus taught that God's unconditional love could enter people's lives here and now. This kind of faith was different from the ideas of many religious leaders of Jesus' time.

Many scribes didn't like Jesus because he disagreed with their uses of the Law and their interpretation of the Law and its role. Some of the Pharisees grew to hate Jesus because he shattered the control they had over God's people. They said that religious practices determined rightness with God. Jesus said rightness with God is God's gift, the work of grace. Many Sadducees joined forces with the Pharisees to condemn Jesus for not speaking according to *their* interpretation of God's Law. In particular, there were disagreements over the role of God's generous grace and the universal nature of God's offer.

Some of the elders of the people found that they were losing their control over the population and that their political status was threatened. The high priests of the temple sensed the growing danger. Jesus preached and taught and lived God's love—love which is without conditions, love which sets people free. Some religious leaders didn't like that. They wanted control over the people. They wanted power, just as they always had.

It all came down to this: Jesus had to go. The plots to weaken his authority quickly became acts which betrayed him. In the end, the Romans were asked to end the crisis. The conspiracy against Jesus took advantage of the Romans' desire for peace *and* thirst for power. Jesus was presented as a threat to the peace and a threat to the authority of Caesar in Rome.

The occupying government knew their orders well: Keep the peace and defend Caesar's power. Eliminate Jesus? Why not? They had seen other self-proclaimed messiahs come and go. For the sake of their peace and power, they agreed to the execution of Jesus. The sign that the Roman procurator, Pontius Pilate, ordered to be placed above Jesus' head said it all: "Jesus, the Nazorean, King of the Jews" (traditionally represented on crucifixes by the letters for the Latin words, INRI). Believers knew the truth, but for the Romans Jesus was just another pest. And to those who plotted his end, Jesus was a disrupting, opposing power.

Jesus *died* on the cross. This hour had haunted Jesus throughout his ministry. Undoubtedly he came to know that his mission would cost him his life. Since the Jews were authorized to execute people by beheading them, perhaps he saw this as his end. However, the twist of events during his last days led him to a horrible crucifixion at the hands of the Romans. Usually Roman criminals who were crucified hung on their tortuous crosses for days. Beaten and driven to physical exhaustion, Jesus died much sooner.

In the eyes of the world, Jesus was a failure. Even his own followers had fled. The only ones left at the cross were a few women—noncitizens and nobodies in Jesus' time.

But Jesus did die. He shared in the human condition to the end. There was no escape back into the glories of heaven at the last minute for this God-made-man. He died and his body was buried like that of any other human. This is really important to us—because all of us will face death. All of us will die.

If Jesus saves us through his human life—a life fully like ours in all things but sin—then death had to be a part of his experience. God so loved us that he gave his Son, who died to save us from the power of sin and everlasting death. Jesus redeemed us.

Then do this

1. Skim through one of the Gospels.
   - Make a list of types of people who opposed Jesus (remembering that there were no whole groups who did so).
   - Make another list of types of people who accepted Jesus (again remembering not to generalize; even the apostles had one member who did not accept Jesus in the end).
2. Now think about modern society. What types of people fit into these two lists today?

Then do this

1. Make a poster that portrays how people without faith deal with the reality of death.
2. Make another poster showing how Christians understand death.

Write it down

Jesus responded with love to those who sought his death. What practical things can you do to respond with love to those who wish you harm?

Jesus was raised from the dead

The conspiracy of opposition, the plotting of those who were against Jesus, succeeded—for a while. Death and human power had their day of victory over Jesus. Imagine the broken-heartedness! Many people had come to believe that God really was at work in Jesus. Jesus had been with them a while, and from what he did and said and from how much he cared, it did look like God's reign had finally come. But then there was disappointment—death by execution. It seemed as if sin and selfishness, abusive power, and evil had won.

The crucifixion of Jesus was a statement of people's thirst for absolute control. It was a statement of people's rejection of the ways of God. The crucifixion of Jesus was the sin of all sins—an absolute denial of the truth of God's kingdom. If you were God the Father, how would you have responded? What kind of response do we humans deserve when we do something like that?

What was God's response? Did God condemn those people and destroy them? No! God the Father raised Jesus from the dead! God the Father did not save Jesus from the human experience of death, but he didn't allow death to be the final truth about our lives. Through his suffering, death, and resurrection, Jesus lives forever! And, with him, so will we. That is the response of God the Father to the crucifixion.

Jesus' followers experienced his death. And then he was alive! Now they knew, they really understood! And they started talking about it everywhere. They were no longer afraid. They told everybody how Jesus came to them in powerful and unexpected ways: sometimes when they were eating together, sometimes when they were sharing the Scriptures, sometimes when they were praying alone.

Jesus was no longer with them as he had been during his life and ministry, but he was truly and really present among them. Only God could make this happen! They knew that, and it changed them forever.

Then do this

Write a poem about the resurrection of Jesus. Use any style of poetry. Share your poems in small groups.

Write it down

The resurrection of Jesus is important to me because . . . .

Glorified body

The risen Jesus directly contacted his disciples after his resurrection. He let them know that he was not a ghost and that his risen body was the same body that had suffered and died on the cross. His body was still marked with the signs of his suffering. However, this body had new qualities: it was "glorified."

Thus the humanity of Christ was no longer limited to Earth, by time and space. He belonged to the heavenly Father's kingdom. The risen Christ didn't return to his previous earthly life as did those he raised from the dead during his ministry—they died again later. At his resurrection, Christ's body was filled with the power of the Holy Spirit. In his glorified body, he shares fully in God's life.

See the *Catechism of the Catholic Church,* #s 645–646.

1. What is the difference between resuscitation and resurrection?

2. What did Jesus look like after the resurrection?

3. Why did the risen Lord still show the signs of his crucifixion? Why was this important to his followers?

4. After his resurrection, why didn't Jesus just go on living with his friends?

5. What does it mean that Jesus now has a glorified body?

Where did Jesus go? The resurrection of Jesus is the assurance that he has returned to his Father. Union with God was his beginning and it was his destiny. In union with Jesus, it is the destiny of his disciples too. Where he has gone, we hope to go.

The resurrection of Jesus from the dead is God's final word. The disciples of Jesus reported the fact that this was an event and not just an idea. It happened! They experienced it and were willing to trust their lives to its truth.

Although there were hints in Jesus' life and ministry that God was very close to him, it was not completely clear how totally God was present in Jesus. But the resurrection made it clear! The reign of God had come into human history in Jesus. The time had come for the fullness of the Spirit as promised in the Old Testament! The plan of God for our salvation was made known fully.

The disciples realized that God had acted in a most unique way in Jesus. Through Jesus, God had given himself completely; God had spoken the word of promise and life. And what God had done could not be undone. It would not be taken back. God has showed his hand, as it were. The statement of God's love stands for all eternity.

If we have not died with Christ,

we cannot possibly live with him.

Karl Barth

The ascension

After his resurrection, Christ returned to his heavenly Father, which is the destiny of all God's people. With the ascension, the one who came from God the Father and is God returned to the Father.

And what about us? Left to ourselves, we don't have access to God's life and happiness. But Christ makes it possible for us, his disciples, to some day follow him to the Father's house. Christ has entered into heaven and is seated at the right hand of the Father. There he intercedes for us and calls all of us into communion with God. When we say that he "is seated at the right hand of the Father," we mean that the Son of God who had become incarnate and whose human body was glorified, reigns in glory. The Messiah's kingdom has begun. This reign of God will never end.

See the *Catechism of the Catholic Church,* #s 660–664.

1. The Scriptures and the Church teach that Jesus returned to his heavenly Father. Why is this an important part of Christian faith? What does this belief say about our destiny?
2. What did Jesus mean when he said that he was the way to God the Father?
3. Why do Christians pray to God the Father in the "name" of Jesus?

REVIEW

1. What factors contributed to the decision to put Jesus to death?
2. What did Jesus accomplish with his death?
3. What do we learn from Jesus' resurrection?
4. What is the ascension?

JESUS IS THE MESSIAH OF GOD

The early Christian community had this understanding of God's final plan of salvation: Salvation was through Jesus. And that's why they called the risen Jesus by the title, the *Christ*.

Remember, the Jewish concept of time included everything from the day of creation to the day of God's final saving action in history. This great final day would be ushered in by a person anointed by God, a messiah, one who was especially filled with the Spirit of God.

During its history, Israel had experienced messiahs in the general sense of anointed ones, who spoke for God and led God's people back to faithfulness to the covenant. In Jesus the people of God experienced much more than just another holy man of God. It was obvious to them that God had acted in a definitive way in Jesus. They realized that Jesus was *the one* who had ushered in the final day of God's salvation. He was not just a messiah, an anointed one in the general sense, but *the Messiah* of God, *the Anointed*, *the Savior*.

As the good news about Jesus spread throughout the Greek world, Jesus was described as the *Cristos*, the Christ. *Cristos* is the Greek translation of the Hebrew word *messiah*. It wasn't long before Jesus and his title became one: "Jesus, the Christ," became a single name for the savior, "Jesus Christ." (Remember, though—*Christ* is Jesus' title, not his last name.)

Write it down

Imagine that you were one of Jesus' apostles. Write the sermon you would preach about Jesus.

Jesus was experienced as God's anointed one. The disciples of Jesus were astonished by the incredible generosity and unconditional love of God. God had not only provided for the salvation of humankind from the darkness of selfishness and sin; the Son of God had made this possible by becoming one of us and one with us! God saves us in Jesus by becoming completely one with us—completely human—and by Jesus' redeeming death and resurrected life.

So the early Christian community quickly came to realize that the meaning and destiny of all things can be understood only in light of what God had done in Jesus. The Christians proclaimed Jesus as the head of his Church, his community—and even the head of all human history. Jesus was seen as the way to the Father, as the fullness of God's truth in human history, and as the fullness of life.

Transforming effect

The news of Jesus' death probably didn't make page one of whatever would have been the equivalent of the newspapers of his day. But, at first glance, his death was good news for those who opposed him. The threat to Jerusalem had been eliminated.

The disciples, on the other hand, experienced Jesus as no longer dead but alive—and alive in an astonishingly full and transformed way. This was not just good news, but GOOD NEWS, with large capital letters! But *only the disciples* claimed this truth about Jesus. Interestingly, no one who had opposed Jesus reported experiencing him risen from the dead. Only the disciples—only the ones who were willing to place everything into the hands of Jesus—experienced him.

Jesus didn't return from the dead like a ghost to haunt his persecutors. He didn't come back to prove God's existence to non-believers. Jesus didn't return to scare his torturers or those who didn't care. Their choices simply left them in the darkness of their self-centered world.

Jesus, the risen Lord, appeared only to his disciples. He made himself known only to those who had entrusted everything to him. Jesus appeared to believers whose hearts were hungry and ready to receive the salvation of God. These were the ones who experienced Jesus as alive. These were the ones who experienced the community of God's love. They felt united in a bond of God's love.

The disciples couldn't prove that the resurrection had happened. The experience of Jesus risen was pure grace, pure gift of God. The disciples hadn't made the resurrection happen. All they could do, all they needed to do was be open to let Jesus show himself to them.

The disciples needed to give up trying to save themselves; they needed to admit that they needed to be saved. They knew that when they stood empty before God, God could fill them with the Spirit of the risen Lord—the Spirit Jesus promised. The day of Pentecost—the day of God's salvation, the day of harvest—had come. The Spirit was poured out on them!

Write it down

1. Write about a time you chose to act unselfishly.

2. What was your reason for choosing to act in this way?

3. What happened as a result of your choice?

4. What did this experience teach you about yourself?

Christianity . . . is Christ himself, living in those whom he has united to himself. . . .

Thomas Merton

Spirit of the risen Lord

In the Church the mission of Christ and the Holy Spirit is being to brought to completion. The Church is the body of Christ and the temple of the Holy Spirit. The mission of Christ and the Holy Spirit is to bring Jesus' followers into communion with the Father.

The Holy Spirit works in the hearts of all people, filling them with grace and drawing them to Christ. Through the Spirit, the risen Lord is manifested to the Christian faithful. The Spirit helps them recall Jesus' words and understand his death and resurrection. By the power of the Holy Spirit, Christ, the risen Lord, becomes present to the community of believers, especially in the Eucharist. The Spirit urges the faithful to respond with good works.

See the *Catechism of the Catholic Church*, #737.

1. How does the Holy Spirit draw people to Christ? Does this include non-Christians?

2. How is the Holy Spirit present in your life? In the life of other believers?

REVIEW

1. Why do Christians believe that Jesus is the promised Messiah?

2. What does the word *Christ* mean?

3. What final gift did Jesus promise his disciples before he returned to his Father?

4. How did Jesus' disciples change after Pentecost?

CONCLUSION

The first Christians had to learn; they had to grow. Once they experienced the unconditional love of God in Jesus, they had to free themselves from trying to control God, from trying to make new rules for God. It took some time for them to realize that God's community of love was open to everyone. Even though the Jews were God's chosen people, the ones who received God's promise of salvation, God didn't stop there.

These chosen people became the way in which God reached out to all people. Because of Jesus, the Christ, everyone could be saved. There were to be no divisions of circumcised or uncircumcised, Gentile or Jew, male or female in the community of Jesus' followers. All were equal. The forgiving love of God and the sacrifice of Christ on the cross brought all believers together in a new unity.

Because of Jesus, the reign of God began. Jesus became the "door," the mediator between God and humans. Jesus was the "high priest" whose sacrificial death on the cross atoned, or made up for, the sins of humankind. All people were restored to grace as God's sons and daughters. All people were now God's people.

They were the Church of Jesus Christ, these people who had heard the good news of God's saving love in Jesus. They gave their hearts to him and sought to follow in the way he opened to them. It was the way to eternal life . . . dying and rising in union with their Savior, Jesus, the Christ.

> The essential fact of Christianity is that God thought all [people] worth the sacrifice of his Son.
> **William Barclay**

Spreading the good news

Now many signs and wonders were done among the people through the apostles. And they were all together in Solomon's Portico. None of the rest dared to join them, but the people held them in high esteem. Yet more than ever believers were added to the Lord, great numbers of both men and women, so that they even carried out the sick into the streets, and laid them on cots and mats, in order that Peter's shadow might fall on some of them as he came by. A great number of people would also gather from the towns around Jerusalem, bringing the sick and those tormented by unclean spirits, and they were all cured.

Then the high priest took action; he and all who were with him (that is, the sect of the Sadducees), being filled with jealousy, arrested the apostles and put them in the public prison. But during the night an angel of the Lord opened the prison doors, brought them out, and said, "Go, stand in the temple and tell the people the whole message about this life." When they heard this, they entered the temple at daybreak and went on with their teaching.

Acts 5:12–21

Optional activities

1. Draw a mural of the events recounted in this selection.

2. Read a chapter or two of the Acts of the Apostles. In writing retell the story or stories you read.

The apostolic Church

The Church is apostolic because it is founded on the apostles.

1. The apostles were eyewitnesses to Jesus and were chosen by him, and it is he who sent them on mission.
2. The Church to this day is built on the teachings of the apostles.
3. With the guidance of the Spirit, the Church faithfully passes on the teachings of the apostles.

The Church's bishops, the successors of the apostles, in union with the pope and with the assistance of priests and deacons, teach and guide the Church.

See the *Catechism of the Catholic Church*, #857.

1. What do we mean when we say the Church is "apostolic"?

2. Why do we say that the Church "hands on the good news"?

3. Who guides the Church? How?

4. What did Jesus tell his followers to do?

Words you should know

Church
disciple
evangelist
faith tradition
miracle

CHAPTER 8

GOSPELS, LETTERS, and OTHER BOOKS

CHAPTER OVERVIEW

• *Discipleship*

• *The formation of Scripture*

• *The Letters*

• *The Gospels*

• *Types of literature in the Gospels*

• *The Acts of the Apostles*

• *The Book of Revelation*

The Word of the Lord

. . . many have undertaken to set down an orderly account of the events that have been fulfilled among us, just as they were handed on to us by those who from the beginning were eyewitnesses and servants of the word. . . .

FROM THE GOSPEL ACCORDING TO LUKE; SEE 1:1–4.

How beautiful upon the mountains
  are the feet of the messenger who announces peace,

Let Us Pray

who brings good news,
  who announces salvation,
  who says to Zion, "Your God reigns."
Listen! Your sentinels lift up their voices,
  together they sing for joy;
for in plain sight they see
  the return of the LORD to Zion.
Break forth together into singing,
  you ruins of Jerusalem;
for the LORD has comforted his people,
  he has redeemed Jerusalem.
The LORD has bared his holy arm
  before the eyes of all the nations;
and all the ends of the earth shall see
  the salvation of our God.

ISAIAH 52:7–10

DISCIPLESHIP

Talk about it

What motivated the early disciples to share the gospel?

Then do this

Search the resurrection stories at the end of the Gospels.

1. To whom did the risen Lord appear?

2. With which of these stories were you already familiar? Which were new to you?

From the first days of the early Church, the disciples of Jesus were touched very deeply with the Spirit he had given them as the risen Lord. This Spirit broke through all their fears. Experiencing the risen Christ was life-changing. The disciples knew themselves to be the new people God had promised. With the outpouring of the Holy Spirit, the last days of God's kingdom had arrived! The disciples felt compelled to go to the ends of the earth to get everyone ready for this last final act in the drama of salvation. The *disciples* ("learners") became *apostles* ("those who are sent").

The message the apostles carried was more than just abstract ideas about the meaning of Jesus. These apostles were not teachers; they were *believers*. They shared their experience of Jesus, telling others how God had entered into history in Jesus and through him had established the kingdom of God. They were eyewitnesses to this. They had good news to share—and off they went.

Eyewitnesses

The apostles were involved in everything that happened during the suffering, death, and resurrection of Jesus. This was true especially of Peter. These witnesses of the risen Jesus become the Church's foundation stones. The early followers' faith rested on these men who were known to them and lived among them.

Peter and the other apostles were the most important witnesses to Christ's resurrection, but there were many others to whom Jesus appeared. Because of the reports of these witnesses, many people came to believe that Jesus really had been raised from the dead. The resurrection truly was an historical fact.

Clearly, the disciples' faith was severely tested by Jesus' suffering and death. These events were so shocking that at least some disciples were unable to believe in the resurrection when they first heard the news. Far from being a rejoicing community at this point, the disciples were demoralized and scared. They didn't believe the women who had gone to the tomb and found it empty.

Even when the risen Lord appeared to the apostles, many of them still doubted. They thought they were seeing a ghost. But they weren't! In the end, the apostles' faith in the resurrection came from their experience of the risen Christ and the grace of God. The gospel which the apostles preached is rooted not on memories and wish-fulfillment, but on what they themselves had experienced.

See the *Catechism of the Catholic Church*, #s 642–644.

1. Why is the word of an eyewitness so important? Why is it important for understanding the good news about Jesus?

2. What does it mean to say that the apostles are the foundation stones of the Church?

3. How does Jesus, the risen Lord, appear to people today?

Destiny waits in the hand of God.

T.S. Eliot

Paul

Perhaps the most well-known of the early apostles is Paul. You will recall that Paul was a Pharisee and a religious leader among the Jews. He was well trained in the practice of the Jewish faith. One day he very unexpectedly encountered the risen Lord Jesus. Deeply moved by the Holy Spirit, Paul was convinced that he needed to share what he had experienced—the fullness of life made possible by Jesus. Experiencing himself as sent, he called himself "an apostle of Christ Jesus." Along with the other disciples, Paul announced the victory of God over sin, selfishness, and even death.

The proclamation of the gospel by these disciples of Jesus was not just a sharing of their private experiences. The disciples and most of the first followers of Jesus were Jews. They belonged to a community of faith. It was against the background of this faith tradition that they experienced the risen Lord.

In other words, they didn't just "get religion" with Jesus. God already had been present in their lives and history. The Spirit of God had been active in their own hearts, in the hearts of all potential listeners, and in the history of the chosen people.

So, when they proclaimed the gospel, they weren't proclaiming brand new news—their news was that God had fulfilled his promise. Their proclamation of the gospel brought together what God had promised to do and what God had done.

Write it down

1. When was the last time you shared good news with someone? What was the news?

2. How did the person receive the news?

3. How did you feel?

In their preaching, the early Christians often talked about the faith of the Jewish people. Those beliefs can be found in the Jewish Scriptures, which we include in our Old Testament. God's plan, God's promise of salvation, had come true in Jesus the Christ. In Jesus God was known in a clear and definitive way! In him the full dignity of humans and the full picture of their destiny was made clear! Good news indeed!

For we are the temple of the living God. . . .
2 Corinthians 6:16

St. Stephen
The first Christian martyr

The story of St. Stephen is told in chapters 6 and 7 of the Acts of the Apostles. It's in his story that we first meet Paul (Saul)—before his conversion and just as he was preparing to persecute the Christians.

Stephen was a Greek-speaking Jew who became a Christian, most likely after the time of Jesus' life on earth. At the time of the story in Acts, Stephen was living in Jerusalem. Apparently there was some difficulty between the Greek-speaking Jewish Christians and the Hebrew Christians. The Greek-speaking Christians complained to the apostles that their widows and other poor people were not being taken care of to the same extent as those in need among the Hebrew Christians.

The apostles told the Greek-speaking Christians to choose seven good men to do the necessary works of charity—these possibly were the first deacons. This would leave the apostles free to preach the good news. Stephen was among those chosen; the apostles prayed over them and laid hands on them.

Interestingly, Stephen is known for his preaching rather than his works of charity. His sermon recorded in Acts 7 traces the history of the Jewish people from the time of Abraham. Stephen recalled the time of slavery in Egypt and the Exodus under the leadership of Moses. David and Solomon and the temple were highlighted as well. Stephen's message to the council of Jewish leaders was clear and challenging:

"You stiff-necked people, uncircumcised in heart and ears, you are forever opposing the Holy Spirit, just as your ancestors used to do. Which of the prophets did your ancestors not persecute? They killed those who foretold the coming of the Righteous One, and now you have become his betrayers and murderers. You are the ones that received the law as ordained by angels, and yet you have not kept it."

Acts 7:51–53

This sermon wasn't well received, especially when Stephen continued, "I see the heavens opened and the Son of Man standing at the right hand of God!" (Acts 7:56). Stephen was dragged outside the city gates and stoned to death. His last words echoed words of Jesus on the cross: "Lord, do not hold this sin against them" (Acts 7:60). Those who stoned Stephen had left their coats with Saul, who stood by and approved. Stephen became the first Christian martyr.

Optional activities

1. Read another sermon recorded in the Acts of the Apostles and in writing compare it to the speech of Stephen in Acts 7:2–53.

2. Read about the conversion of Paul in Acts 9. In small groups write a short dialogue on this event and perform the skit for the class.

3. Look through a book of the lives of the saints for the story of another martyr of the early Church. In your own words, share the story with the class. Prepare a few discussion questions to follow the story and lead the discussion.

REVIEW

1. What does it mean to say the *disciples* became *apostles*?

2. Why was Paul an apostle?

3. What did the apostles preach?

4. Who was St. Stephen?

THE FORMATION OF SCRIPTURE

The Christian community lived its faith in Jesus, the risen Lord, and proclaimed the gospel long before the formation of what we now call the New Testament. Remember what we learned in an earlier chapter about the formation of the Old Testament. The same pattern applies to the formation of the New Testament.

- People experienced God at work in their history.
- The people shared their experience verbally—the spoken tradition.
- The people wrote down their story, their tradition—written tradition.
- Some editing of the testimony took place to make the writing more accurate or clear.
- All this resulted in a final written text.

Over time, the Christian community reached agreement about which writings were closest to what they had experienced in their encounters with Jesus. They established the canon of New Testament Scripture. Other writings from the time of Christ and the early Church may have told about the life and times of Christ, but these writings were not considered normative, or canonical, by the Church. Recall the purpose of setting up a canon of Scripture: to remember, to preserve the truth of the testimony, to anchor the faith, and to have an instrument for teaching or handing on the faith.

By around the fourth century, an unofficial canon existed in the Church. Still, there were disagreements about which writings were "true to the faith" and which weren't. The final canon or official list of books for the Christian community was set up in the sixteenth century, although, in a sense, the canon had long before been "set" in the living tradition of the Christian community. Over the centuries, some books, letters, and writings were accepted readily, and their authorship was unquestioned. Not so for a few others!

Talk about it

Why were the Gospels and other books of the New Testament written?

The canon

In the sixteenth century when the Church made an official list of its canon of the New Testament, there were no major surprises. The following collection of twenty-seven "books" was established as normative for Christians:

The Gospels	**The Acts of the Apostles**
The Gospel according to Matthew	**The Book of Revelation**
The Gospel according to Mark	
The Gospel according to Luke	
The Gospel according to John	

The Letters

Romans	Colossians	Titus	2 Peter
1 Corinthians	1 Thessalonians	Philemon	1 John
2 Corinthians	2 Thessalonians	Hebrews	2 John
Galatians	1 Timothy	James	3 John
Ephesians	2 Timothy	1 Peter	Jude
Philippians			

THE LETTERS

When you open to the first pages of the New Testament, the first books you find are the four Gospels. This leaves the reader with the impression that the Gospels were the first books to be written. But this isn't the case. Some of the various letters came first! These letters are sometimes called **epistles**.

epistle
a New Testament letter

The first Christians probably didn't see themselves as followers of a new world religion started by Jesus. Even after the resurrection and ascension of Jesus, his followers continued to go to the synagogue to hear the Scriptures and to learn from the rabbi. Likely it was there—in the synagogue—that the good news of Jesus was first shared, as the disciples told the story about what God had done in Jesus.

This led to obvious conflict with those who didn't believe their testimony, and the followers of Jesus were eventually no longer welcomed in the synagogues. Even though these early Christians could no longer attend the synagogue services, they continued the tradition of listening to Scripture and receiving instruction from their religious leaders. They often gathered in homes for this purpose.

At these gatherings, the Christians listened to readings from the Jewish Scriptures. Of course, now that God had fulfilled his promise of salvation in Christ, they had a different understanding of many of these readings. Already at these gatherings, the oral sharing of the gospel was happening as people told and retold stories about Jesus and his ministry. This was also the original setting for the sharing of letters from the apostles.

Talk about it
Tell a story about someone you admire. Include in the story what it is that you admire.

These early Christians believed that Jesus would return very soon in glory for the final end of all human history. This awaited event was called the **parousia**. Yes, another Greek word! It means "triumphal arrival" and was the word used in the Greek world to describe a military leader's victory march through the city after a battle was won. The early Christians used this image to describe the Lord's triumphant return at the end of time—a time which they firmly believed was right around the corner.

parousia
the return of Jesus in glory at the end of time

These first communities of Christians were far from perfect. They had their problems and challenges, just as all Christian communities have ever since. But they were known for their generous care for one another and for those who were poor and in need. Like all Christian communities, they had their saints, as well as their sinners.

Talk about it
How do you imagine the endtime?

The apostles and their helpers were very involved in starting and supporting these small Christian communities throughout the Mediterranean area. The gospel started taking root! Because they felt responsible that these communities know the correct gospel and live it, these early apostles often wrote letters to them.

These letters weren't usually private pieces of correspondence; they were letters to the community—words of encouragement, suggestion, explanation, and correction. The communities of early Christians circulated these letters among themselves and kept them. The letters taught them who Jesus was and how, as his followers, they should live.

The letters usually dealt with problems that seemed to be common. So, gradually, the letters came to be used for instruction in the Christian way of life. And even though each of the letters in the New Testament was written for particular reasons to a particular group of Christians, all of the letters are much read and much loved by Christians of all times and places. They remain a source of inspiration and instruction in the Christian way of life.

Most people are bothered by those passages in Scripture which they cannot understand; but as for me, I always noticed that the passages in Scripture which trouble me most are those that I do understand.

Mark Twain

Write it down
Pretend you are Paul and write a letter to your parish or school community. Try to imitate Paul's style of writing. What would you say about living the gospel?

On the way to perfection

Jesus Christ was sinless; he didn't sin. He came to make reparation for *our* sins and to free us from them. The Church gathers sinners within it as it continually does penance and seeks to renew itself. All members of the Church must realize and admit their sinfulness.

In the Church, sinners, already saved by Christ, are still moving toward holiness. Although the Church is made up of those who sin, it is holy because of God's grace. If the members of the Church live in God's love, they are made holy. If they turn away from that love, they fall into sin and thus interfere with the spread of the Church's holiness in Christ.

See the *Catechism of the Catholic Church*, #827.

1. Why can the Church be described as "a gathering of God's saved sinners"?

2. What does it mean to say someone is holy? How is the Church holy?

3. What kinds of actions keep the Church from reflecting God's holiness?

I write these things to you who believe in the name of the Son of God, so that you may know that you have eternal life.

1 John 5:16

The letters which have been preserved

Not all of the letters written to early Christians made their way into the New Testament. Several important ones did, however. Most of these were written by Paul or by others, perhaps his own disciples, using his name in order to claim his authority for their teachings.

This form of "ghost writing" may bother us today, but the practice was acceptable and common in the days of the apostles. People were more interested in what was said than they were in who wrote the letters, even though putting an important name on a writing added to the authority of the writing. The letters that were kept were the ones that best expressed the Christian faith and helped people live that faith.

The letters in the New Testament follow the usual style of letters written in Greek or Roman times. These letters were not just written and mailed. Writing materials like parchment (a type of paper made from sheepskin) were expensive and not easily made. Ink had to be specially prepared. Writing was slow and difficult because it had to be done with a quill. Often the letter writer dictated to scribes who frequently made their own interpretations of what the speaker said.

A typical Greek or Roman letter of the first century after Christ opened with the identification of the receiver and sometimes also the sender. Then came a paragraph or two of greeting. The main part of the letter followed and dealt with the concerns of the writer. Finally, the conclusion included personal greetings and instructions. Some letters were more formal than others. This difference can be seen in the New Testament. The Letter to the Romans is a good example of a formal letter. The Letters to Titus and Philemon clearly are more personal.

These letters were written before the Gospels were. Sometimes the letters talk about "preaching the gospel," but they don't refer to a *written* form of the gospel (which we now know as the Gospels according to Matthew, Mark, Luke, and John).

The authors of the letters didn't think of the gospel as just a story of the events in Jesus' life or as a statement of beliefs about Jesus. In the New Testament letters, not much is said about the actual life of Jesus. The gospel was something that had to be realized in people's own lives. (Besides, the Gospels were being developed for these purposes, and the writing by Paul could not focus in the same way on Jesus' life or Church beliefs because Paul didn't know Jesus before Jesus' death.)

This is the message of salvation—salvation is available to all people through faith in Jesus Christ, the risen Lord of history!

Write it down

Read 1 Corinthians, chapters 12 and 13.

1. What can you do to help the Spirit work in your life?

2. What signs do other people see in you that show the Spirit is at work in your life?

3. How do you know when you are called to use the gifts of the Spirit?

4. What talents do you have that can be used to help the community?

5. What kind of love is at work in your life?

REVIEW

1. What were the steps in the development of the New Testament?

2. What are the two main categories of New Testament books? What are the other two books?

3. What did the early Christians do at their religious gatherings?

4. Which category of New Testament books was written first?

5. What is the typical format of a New Testament letter?

Keeping in touch

Letter-writing is a lost art today (even though E-mail and the Internet may be reviving it to a degree). But that doesn't mean there aren't other important ways to keep in touch with people. In fact, like letters, other forms of communication can be life-giving and life-saving. Consider this anonymous story that was reprinted in *Chicken Soup for the Teenage Soul.*

Angela knew that Charlotte, her best friend, was having a rough time. Charlotte was moody and depressed. She was withdrawn around everyone except for Angela. She instigated arguments with her mom and had violent confrontations with her sister. Most of all, Charlotte's bleak and desperate poetry worried Angela.

No one was on particularly good speaking terms with Charlotte that summer. . . Angela was the only one who could reach her. Although she would have liked to be outside, Angela spent most of her time inside with her troubled friend. Then a day came when Angela had to move. She was going just across town, but Charlotte would no longer be her neighbor, and they would be spending far less time together.

The first day in her new neighborhood . . . Angela wondered how Charlotte was doing. When she got home . . . her mother told her Charlotte had called.

Angela went to the phone to return the call. No answer. She left a message on Charlotte's machine. "Hi, Charlotte, it's Angela. Call me back."

About half an hour later Charlotte called. "Angela, I have to tell you something. When you called, I was in the basement. I had a gun to my head. I was about to kill myself, but then I heard your voice on the machine upstairs. . . When I heard your voice I realized someone loves me. . . . I'm going to get help. . . ."

Optional projects

1. Review the ways, other than face-to-face speaking, people have communicated with you over the last week: phone, letter, E-mail, and so on. Write an essay on your communications for the week and their meaning in your life.

2. Interview several older people about how they communicated with other people at a distance when they were young. Then ask them how they communicate today. Write a reflection on their responses.

3. Read one of the letters in the New Testament. (A long letter can be divided up among several students, each of whom can read part of the letter.) Prepare a presentation for the class on the letter: author, audience, problems addressed, message, and so on.

THE GOSPELS

Recall—the gospel was experienced, proclaimed, and lived long before it was written down. The early Christians struggled to open their lives and hearts to the salvation announced to them. They experienced the risen Lord in their midst, they continued with their lives of prayer, and they talked about the good news of Jesus. The verbal sharing of the gospel shaped their lives, constantly calling them to a deeper conversion of heart and behavior. This sharing of the good news centered on the person of Jesus and what God had done through him.

Then do this

Research what was happening in the world around the year A.D. 70. Write a report which includes your thinking on why the first Gospel may have been written at about this time.

Because the good news centered on Jesus, the story of his life was really important. People began to tell that story. And as they told the story—perhaps even during the brief lifetime of Jesus himself—people started collecting the memories. They remembered the significant things he said. They collected the stories about events in his life which changed people: his encounters with sinners, the healings, the confrontation with his enemies, the miracles. Because Jesus was really human, as well as the Son of God, the people started piecing together his origins.

It was only after Christianity was rather well established and the early Church started spreading around the shores of the Mediterranean Sea that the written form of the gospel began to take definitive shape. Scripture scholars suggest that the final form of the stories about the life and ministry of Jesus were written about the year A.D. 70. They were written in Greek, the "politically correct" language of the day and the common language of business in the Middle East at the time.

Actually, there is only *one* gospel, that is, only *one* good news of the salvation of humankind by the loving and saving hand of God. That gospel is Jesus. He is the good news of God in the flesh! In handing on this good news, however, the Christian community produced four reports or versions about this one act of divine love. That's why at church you hear the reading of the gospel introduced by a phrase like, "A reading from the holy Gospel according to Matthew"—the good news about Jesus, according to Matthew. Jesus himself is the good news. The gospel is the life-giving person, Jesus.

The Old and the New

When Christians read the Old Testament, they do so from the perspective of the life, death, and resurrection of Jesus Christ. However, the Old Testament has great value in its own right, for it is truly God's revealed word. The Old Testament is the light by which Christians read the New Testament. In the early Church, the Old Testament was constantly used by those who taught others the good news. "The New Testament lies hidden in the Old and the Old Testament is unveiled in the New" (St. Augustine).

See the *Catechism of the Catholic Church*, #129.

1. Why can't Christians understand who Jesus is without understanding the meaning of the Old Testament?

2. Why do Christian Churches still use readings from the Old Testament as part of their worship services?

3. What does it mean to say "The New Testament lies hidden in the Old and the Old Testament is unveiled in the New"?

During our brief study in an earlier chapter of the formation of the Old Testament, we recognized that Scripture is the word of God written by people. The same thing can be said of the Gospels. The Gospels are the Word of God (Jesus) communicated in the form of human writings. The Gospels, like the rest of the New Testament, can be studied as pieces of literature. Scripture scholars have the tools to do this.

The tools used to study the Gospels (and other parts of the New Testament, too) are the same tools as those used to study the books of the Old Testament. Those tools include language studies, understanding the various literary forms, understanding the history of the book, and consideration of the culture in which the book was written. Along with faith, these tools help Scripture scholars better understand the literal truth of the text and reach the real goal—to understand the spiritual truth of the writing: what God is saying.

When the tools of Scripture study are applied, it becomes clear that all four Gospels are testimonies about the life and ministry of Jesus and that each was written for a particular group. That's understandable, because whenever you talk about your experiences, you adapt the way you tell the story so that the listener can understand what you are saying.

Each of the four Gospels was written in this manner, although all four have the same purpose: to bring people to faith in Jesus, the Christ, Savior of the world. The Gospels are not history books and they're not biographies. The Gospels were written by people who believed and who wanted the whole world to believe. They are accounts written from the viewpoint of faith to bring people to faith, faith in a loving and saving God. There are four versions of the gospel, and the four writers are called the *evangelists*, "messengers of good news."

The Gospel according to Mark

Scholars tell us that the Gospel according to Mark was the first to be written. It's the shortest of the four Gospels, and its narrative is more to the point and rather simple. Mark has no stories about the birth of Jesus. In this Gospel, Jesus begins his ministry in Galilee and heads toward Jerusalem. Along the way, Jesus announces the kingdom of God. His teachings explain the kingdom, and his miracles and exorcisms show that it is real. Jesus appeals to his disciples to open their lives to God's forgiving love, to let the kingdom come.

It becomes increasingly clear that in Jesus the long-awaited Messiah *has* come. Eventually opposing forces are responsible for Jesus' death. But God raises him from the dead. Before returning to his heavenly Father, Jesus empowers his disciples to spread the good news to the ends of the earth.

The Gospel according to Matthew

Matthew's purpose is to show that Jesus is the fulfillment of the promise of salvation to the chosen people of Israel. The Gospel according to Matthew is packed with references to the Old Testament and shows a rich awareness of the Jewish teaching tradition and Jewish religious practices.

The writer follows the basic outline of Mark's Gospel, but he adds his own material as well as material from another available source to show that Jesus is the fulfillment of God's plan. He goes to great pains to show that even the birth of Jesus reflects the fulfillment of God's promise.

Talk about it

1. Why is the gospel of Jesus best communicated through stories, images, and parables rather than through objective history?

2. What is the power of story or image, especially concerning Jesus and his message?

Then do this

Scan the Introduction to each of the Gospels. For whom was each Gospel written?

Then do this

Find outlines of the Gospels of Mark, Matthew, and Luke, and compare the three.

1. What are the similarities?

2. How are they different?

The Gospel according to Luke

Scripture scholars note Luke's interest in historical detail and the work of the Holy Spirit. This leads to the conclusion that the Gospel according to Luke was probably written more for a Gentile audience than a Jewish one. Luke wanted to show that the Old Testament promise of the coming of the Holy Spirit was a promise that was kept—in the life and ministry of Jesus. That Spirit was present in Jesus' life from the moment of his conception and led him through opposition and death to the glory of resurrection.

Scholars point out that Luke used Mark's Gospel (his basic framework) and some material used by Matthew, adding his own material to show how Jesus was Savior for the Gentile world, too. Scholars also note that the New Testament book of the Acts of the Apostles is a continuation of Luke's Gospel as the account of the good news of salvation spread over the known world.

Write it down

Read one of the miracle stories in one of the Gospels.

1. What does Jesus do—for the body, for the spirit?

2. Why does he perform this miracle?

3. What does the miracle tell you about Jesus? About God, his Father?

Synoptic Gospels

the three most similar Gospels: Matthew, Mark, and Luke

Synoptic Gospels

While studying the Gospels of Matthew, Mark, and Luke, Scripture scholars readily note that Mark's Gospel appears to be the backbone for the other two. Much of the Gospel of Mark is "borrowed" by Matthew and Luke. At the same time Matthew and Luke have made their own additions to help them show their particular readers the importance of Jesus for their lives.

Finally, in addition to using Mark's Gospel, they used a source which Scripture scholars call "Q" (from the German word *quelle*, or "source"). No copy of "Q" itself has been found.

If you lay out Matthew, Mark, and Luke side by side, it's easy to see the similarities among all three and the additional similarities in Matthew and Luke ("Q"). Because of this, scholars call Matthew, Mark, and Luke the **Synoptic Gospels**—from the Greek word *synopsis* (meaning "seen together").

The similarities point to a single proclaimed gospel. The differences suggest that the writers had different audiences, some different sources, and different interests. All three Gospels, though, point to Jesus as Savior, as the Messiah through whom God leads the people to the fullness of life and eternal happiness.

Miracles are God's signature, appended to his masterpiece of creation.

Ronald Knox

All this took place to fulfill what had been spoken by the Lord through the prophet....

Matthew 1:22

Matthew	Mark	Luke
20:26–27 It will not be so among you; but whoever wishes to be great among you must be your servant, and whoever wishes to be first among you must be your slave. . . .	**10:43–44** But it is not so among you; but whoever wishes to become great among you must be your servant, and whoever wishes to be first among you must be slave of all.	**22:26** But not so with you; rather the greatest among you must become like the youngest, and the leader like one who serves.
23:11 The greatest among you will be your servant.		
23:12 All who exalt themselves will be humbled, and all who humble themselves will be exalted.		**14:11** For all who exalt themselves will be humbled, and those who humble themselves will be exalted.
		18:14b . . . for all who exalt themselves will be humbled, but all who humble themselves will be exalted.

The Gospel according to John

John's Gospel is different from the other three. It's more complex, more artistic, and more involved with the mystery of the Christian life. John loves to play with images and the different meanings hidden in the words and events of Jesus' ministry.

Scholars point out that this Gospel was written much later than the others. Matthew, Mark, and Luke were written sometime after the year A.D. 70, the year the Romans destroyed Jerusalem. John was written sometime around the year A.D. 95. By that time, the Christian community, although few in number, was well established.

The audience for whom John wrote knew the story of Jesus. They believed in Jesus as the Christ, the Promised One, the Savior. John wanted them to understand their Christian experience and embrace the mystery of their life in Christ. He wanted them to *get inside* the experience of their Baptism, their sharing in the Eucharist, and their openness to the Spirit.

Then do this

1. Find another verse or two that is written in a similar way in all three Synoptic Gospels.

2. Share your findings in small groups

Then do this

From the Gospels, pick your favorite scene from the life and ministry of Jesus. Share the scene with the class or with a friend. Why did you pick this particular scene?

> *"I am the light of the world. Whoever follows me will never walk in darkness but will have the light of life."*
>
> John 8:12

REVIEW

1. What is the gospel? What is a Gospel?

2. What are the names of the Gospels?

3. Which are the Synoptic Gospels? Why are they called that?

4. How does the Gospel according to John differ from the other Gospels?

TYPES OF LITERATURE IN THE GOSPELS

In order to tell the story of Jesus and to bring people to faith in him, the authors of the Gospels used a variety of literary forms. Here's a list of some of those literary forms and a brief explanation of how the reader should use them to understand the message the author communicates to help you, the reader, grow in faith.

Death narrative

Each Gospel goes into great detail about the death of Jesus. Each author struggles with this tragic moment in the story of Jesus. Death is a "defining moment" in a human's life. It "defines" that person: What was the person's life about? The Gospel writers go to great lengths to share their insights into the last few days of Jesus' earthly ministry, especially his last hours, which led to death on the cross. The death narrative (the Passion) is a "mini-Gospel": Who is Jesus? What was his life about?

Each Gospel writer offers details about Jesus' death, but each narrative needs to be read within the context of that Gospel. For that reason, it's neither proper nor useful to lump together all the details of all four Gospels in hopes of obtaining a complete picture. It won't work! Each narrative is complete in itself for its audience.

On Palm/Passion Sunday of each year, the Passion account from one of the Synoptic Gospels is read in Catholic churches. On Good Friday, the Passion account from John is read. So, each year, Catholics are twice immersed in the death narrative which is the centerpiece of the Gospels. This is the story of our salvation—the apparent tragedy that became the means of redemption for all people.

History narrative

Jesus was a real person who lived in a real time and in a real place. The heart and soul of the gospel is about what God has done for humankind in the real person, Jesus of Nazareth. God's salvation happened in Jesus! The historical fact of God's unfolding love is the "golden thread" which runs through each of the four Gospels. But the Gospel writers were not writing history, nor were they writing **biography**.

As a result, many of the details of Jesus' life have been lost in the sands of time. We don't know the color of Jesus' hair, whether or not he had a beard, how tall he was, what kind of food he ate for dinner. We don't know with absolute certainty whether or not he said this or that in exactly the way it's recorded in Scripture. There were no cameras and tape recorders to capture these details.

But this kind of literal truth is not the purpose of the Gospel writers. Their purpose is to tell the world who Jesus is and how, through Jesus, God has come to bring salvation and fullness of life to all people. With this in mind, the evangelists used and rearranged their material to bring people to faith in Jesus. Thus, they put people in touch with God's saving love.

Then do this

Read the death narrative in Mark's Gospel—14:26 to 15:41. In small groups share your reactions to the reading.

Talk about it

How do the Passion accounts differ from obituaries?

biography
an historical account of a person's life

Then do this

Present a TV talk show in which Jesus is interviewed. Before the interview, work in small groups to generate a list of interview questions.

> *To know Jesus and him crucified is my philosophy,*
> *and there is none higher.*
> **St. Bernard of Clairvaux**

Hagiography

The story of Jesus is certainly the most important story for Christians. But holy men and women over the centuries have served as inspiration to others on how to live the way Jesus did. The word *hagiography* refers to stories about the lives of the saints—biographies of saints. The word comes from two Greek words, *hagios* and *graphe*, meaning "holy" and "writing." The first known hagiography (except that of Stephen in Acts) is the *Martyrdom of Polycarp*, written by an eyewitness to the bishop's death in about A.D.156.

The first lives of the saints were stories of martyrs, those who died for the faith. After the persecutions ended, monks became a common topic. Often a comparison was made between the life or death of the saint and the life or death of Jesus. In time a great deal of emphasis was given to miraculous events in the lives of holy people. These stories were an important part of the popular Christian culture.

In earlier centuries accounts of the lives of the saints made theology real and accessible to a largely unlettered public. Travelers went on pilgrimages to shrines in distant places and brought back new treasures and new stories of martyrdom and reputed miracles. Relics were eagerly sought after to give a focus for devotion in a new church or cathedral. At a popular level stories of saints from their homeland were recounted round the campfire by soldiers on campaigns; on the roads by merchants, pilgrims, and travelers; and on deck at night by seafarers slowly making their way round the Mediterranean. Oral tradition has played a considerable part in preserving and spreading knowledge of those whom the Church has come to honor.

Butler's Lives of the Saints, Preface.

Given the nature of oral storytelling and the generally low level of education, many stories of saints developed more along the lines of legends and folk tales than true history. The hand copying of manuscripts also contributed to many errors and questionable additions in the stories that were written down. By the middle of the nineteenth century, standards were being set for determining truth from error in these stories, and most hagiographies thereafter had a firmer basis in fact. Following the

Second Vatican Council, there was renewed interest in accuracy regarding the lives of the saints.

The most famous compilation of hagiography is *Butler's Lives of the Saints*. The first edition of this work was published in England between 1756 and 1759. A revised four-volume edition was published between 1926 and 1938. The years it took for the four books to go to press give us some idea of the time it took to research the stories of holy people who lived over a span of 1900 years. Other editions and revisions and corrections and additions took place over the rest of the twentieth century.

Beginning in 1995, Liturgical Press began publishing a twelve-volume edition of *Butler's Lives of the Saints*, one for each month—the saints whose feasts are celebrated in a given month. Each volume contains information on two hundred or so saints, and each book has about ten consulting editors.

Optional activities

1. Obtain a copy of *Butler's Lives of the Saints*. Read the stories of five to ten saints, and share one of the stories with the class.

2. Write and illustrate a children's book on the life of a saint.

3. Interview five adults on the stories of saints that they remember. Ask them how these stories influenced them. Write a report on your findings.

Sayings

Jesus said many things during the course of his ministry. While no one followed him with a tape recorder, people did remember. In many cases they probably memorized what Jesus had said. His "words of wisdom" reflect a deep knowledge of the Jewish faith tradition, but there is no way to tell with absolute certainty if the words recorded in Scripture are the exact words that Jesus spoke. In the Synoptic Gospels, we often see differences in how the same saying of Jesus is expressed.

It's clear, however, that the words he speaks in the Gospels do reflect the person of Jesus and his message of God's forgiving love. The Gospel writers used a great deal of freedom in taking the remembered and sometimes memorized words of Jesus and placing them at those special points in the Gospel where they would best help readers understand who Jesus is.

Talk about it

It cannot be proved absolutely that Jesus actually said every single thing that is recorded in the Gospels as his words.

1. How do you feel about that?

2. Have you ever somewhat quoted another person? Did you get the person's idea across without using the exact words?

3. What effect does this observation have on your faith?

Healing miracles

Today when we read the miracle stories in the Gospels, we tend to apply contemporary understandings to these scenes. We think of a miracle as a suspension of the natural law by God. At the time of Jesus, miracle stories were understood differently. But there is no doubt that Jesus "worked miracles"; even Roman and Jewish historians of his time described him as one who did miraculous deeds.

The stories of Jesus' miracles were used by the Gospel writers not to prove that he was God, but to show that God was at work in him. The miracles are signs of God's kingdom becoming real here and now. Usually the miracle stories begin by showing the difficulty of the situation which faced Jesus. He responds by acting with authority and command of the situation. He heals, casts out demons, restores to health, and sometimes even restores to life. The crowd reacts with awe, wonder, and praise of God.

The Gospel writers show that God is at work in the miracles of Jesus. They don't portray his miracles as dazzling displays of divine power, but rather as moments or events in which people come face to face with the wonder of God's saving presence. In such an encounter, the writers have to make a decision: *Is this event caused by the saving love of God made present in Jesus?* (The miracle itself doesn't force an answer—it "proves" nothing—but raises the question of faith. Do you believe or not? Do you trust in God's salvation or in your own efforts to save yourself?)

Talk about it

Identify five healing stories in the Gospels.

1. What do these stories have in common?

2. How did each of these healing miracles affect those who witnessed the miracle?

> *"Do not judge, and you will not be judged;*
>
> *do not condemn, and you will not be condemned.*
>
> *Forgive, and you will be forgiven; give, and it will be given to you.*
>
> *A good measure, pressed down, shaken together, running over,*
>
> *will be put into your lap;*
>
> *for the measure you give will be the measure you get back."*
>
> **Luke 6:37–38**

How the italicized question in the last paragraph on page 192 is answered makes all the difference in understanding who Jesus is. Jesus is not "defined" as a miracle worker. In themselves, the miracles are events which raise an important question: Is God here or not? What happens to the believer, the one who answers "yes" to that question, is far more important than the event itself.

The miracles of Jesus

The Israelites of ancient times recognized the hand of God at work in human history. They saw God's "mighty deeds" in the events around them. Likewise, Jesus' words were accompanied by mighty deeds and wond-rous signs. These signs gave witness to his claim that the kingdom of God had come into the world through him. These signs and wonders show that he is the promised Messiah.

These signs and wonders of Jesus strengthen his claim that God the Father had sent him. They invite us to believe in him. The miracles helped Jesus' followers believe that he did his Father's work and that he was indeed the Son of God. His miracles weren't for people who were curious or looking for magic. Even with his miracles, some people rejected Jesus and others believed his power came from demons.

Jesus performed messianic signs, signs of God's kingdom, when he freed certain people from hunger, injustice, sickness, and even death. But Jesus didn't come to do away with all evil on earth. Sin interferes with people's vocation as children of God and brings with it all kinds of slavery. Jesus came to free people from the power of sin.

See the *Catechism of the Catholic Church*, #s 547–549.

1. Do the miracles of Jesus in themselves prove anything? Why is faith necessary to understand them?

2. Are miracles possible today? Why?

3. Was the ministry of Jesus to heal people or to save sinners? How are these two different? How are they the same?

4. Which is a greater miracle of God's love: a healed relationship or a healed body?

REVIEW

1. What are some of the literary forms found in the Gospels?
2. What is the longest section of each Gospel?
3. How is a Gospel different from history or biography?
4. What is important about the sayings of Jesus?
5. The miracles of Jesus are signs of what?

Parables

A few Gospel passages refer to Jesus as the "son of Joseph, the carpenter." Perhaps at some point in his life Jesus too was a carpenter by trade. Still, as an adult, Jesus was a teacher. Not once in the Gospels is Jesus mentioned doing carpentry; he is portrayed more as a Jewish rabbi, a man who shared God's word with the people and helped them apply it to their lives. He is building God's kingdom.

Jesus concentrated on announcing and realizing the kingdom of God. He insisted that this kingdom, God's saving and forgiving love, is right here in our midst. Everything that Jesus said and did was focused on bringing people to awareness of God's kingdom, God's saving love. His miracles were signs of the saving presence of God. His forgiveness of sins reflected God's saving love. His teachings also were about the kingdom.

People everywhere still love a story with a twist or a play on words that makes a point. This form of teaching was very popular at the time of Jesus, and he used it to the full. Jesus was a masterful teacher. In his teaching, he used parables as a form of instruction more often than he used other forms of wise sayings.

Parables are stories which force the listener to address questions of faith. They don't just teach a lesson or end with a "moral of the story." They have a unique way of leading people to the decision to believe. Jesus used parables to announce the presence of God's kingdom.

parable
a story which teaches a lesson

> "To what should I compare the kingdom of God?
> It is like yeast that a woman took and mixed in with
> three measures of flour until all of it was leavened."
> **Luke 13:20–21**

Infancy narratives

The origins of important people are of great interest. (That's why the places where famous people were born are often preserved as museums. This helps us understand that these were real people!) While Mark's Gospel opens with Jesus already active in his ministry, the later Gospels try to offer a more complete picture of Jesus. The Gospels according to Matthew and Luke each contain a beginning portion which Scripture scholars call an **infancy narrative**. In these Gospels, the infancy narrative is a story which explains the divine origin and greatness of Jesus, even from the moment of his conception and birth.

Both Matthew and Luke tell the story of Jesus' origins from their own perspective. Most likely just Mary and Joseph were present at Jesus' birth! There were no family photo albums and videos either of his birth or of his early years. The historical facts are not the primary focus of the infancy narratives.

The infancy narratives in Matthew and Luke are similar to writings used at the time of Jesus when the birth of an important person was told. Matthew and Luke used this type of writing to help their readers understand that Jesus was a real person, but one whose origin is in God. In the years after Jesus' death and resurrection, Christians developed in their understanding of Jesus as both God and human. The infancy narratives helped people see this more clearly.

In his infancy narrative, Luke emphasized the work of the Holy Spirit and Mary as the first disciple. Matthew, following his usual style of writing, showed how Jesus is the fulfillment of Old Testament messianic hopes—for the whole world. When reading these narratives, remember, they were not written as literal, scientific, or biographical truth. They were written to communicate important spiritual truths about Jesus.

infancy narrative
a story which explains the divine origin and greatness of Jesus, even from the moment of his conception and birth

Then do this
Interview ten people of various ages about what the Christmas story means to them. Present your findings to the class, along with your response to the interviews.

Geographical images

All four Gospel writers made use of geographical images. That is, they used locations and travels to certain places to make a statement about what God was doing. We do the same thing when, for example, we speak of someone taking their problems "straight to Washington," meaning to the government.

In similar fashion, the Gospel writers used Jerusalem as the heart of Jewish faith. Jesus goes to Jerusalem: God's unfolding plan will be fulfilled in Jerusalem, the city of final glory. Or, Jesus is in the temple in Jerusalem, the place where God's saving love will be shown. Whether or not Jesus stood in each one of these places or did exactly what is written is not the point. The Gospel writers want us to understand who Jesus is!

Then do this
Scan one of the Gospels to find a travel reference. Is the place or the trip itself important? If so, why? What point is made?

REVIEW

1. What is a parable?
2. What is an infancy narrative? Which Gospels have one?
3. Why did the Gospel writers use geographical images?

THE ACTS OF THE APOSTLES

A rather unique book, the Acts of the Apostles, continues the story Luke began in his Gospel. The story started with Jesus' birth, continued through his death and resurrection, and kept on going—because God's plan required that the gospel be spread to all the nations.

People sometimes think that Acts is a history of early Christianity. It isn't really. Luke wasn't trying to record *all* the events that happened after Christ's resurrection. He simply wanted to show how God's plan of salvation continued to work itself out.

In Acts, after Paul begins his mission to the Gentiles in earnest, Luke drops the story of Peter. And by the end of Acts, even Paul disappears from the scene.

Clearly, Acts is not intended to be a literal history. Since the book continues the story of the gospel, however, it may well be called "biblical history." This special kind of narrative shows us how God's plan of salvation continued.

God's plan continued

How do we know what God's plan is? As we read through Acts, we see that even the disciples didn't know fully what God intended. Jesus had told them that a new stage in God's plan was about to unfold and that they would be an essential part of it. Luke makes it very clear, however, that the disciples didn't really understand God's plan. What was important was that they were open to the promptings and leading of the Holy Spirit—that they let God be in charge of the Church and its mission. This is why some say that Acts is really the "acts of the Holy Spirit." The Spirit still prompts and leads the Church today.

Simply put, Acts is the story of God intervening through the Holy Spirit in the spreading of the gospel. The Church is not alone; it is guided by God's Spirit.

Write it down

1. How have you experienced Jesus?

2. What difference has that experience made in your life?

Talk about it

1. With what images of the Trinity are you familiar?

2. Has your understanding of the Trinity changed this year? If so, how?

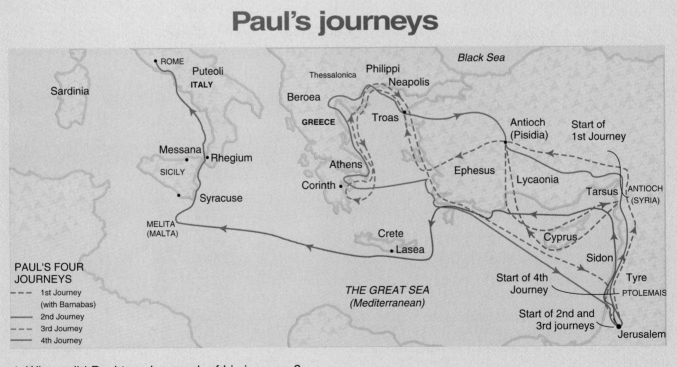

Paul's journeys

1. Where did Paul travel on each of his journeys?

2. To which of these sites did Paul write a letter that is now in the New Testament?

Though God's guidance is very important to salvation history, humans must learn to live right. As recorded in the Acts of the Apostles, the disciples had to figure out the meaning of their experiences. They asked for God's help and guidance. They also discussed events that had happened, as they prepared to make new efforts to preach the gospel.

The disciples weren't always in agreement with one another. The community was limited in its response to God. But their ability to look back on their experiences of God's presence helped the followers of Jesus understand what God was doing.

The Acts of the Apostles is the story of the preaching of the gospel. This story begins where the ministry of Jesus had ended, in Jerusalem. From there, the good news spreads until it embraces the whole circle of the Mediterranean Sea and Paul, the apostle to the Gentiles, arrives in Rome itself, the center of the Roman Empire.

By the end of Acts, it's clear that Christianity was no small matter; it was a force at work in the world. Christian communities dotted the empire. Many of these were communities to which Paul and the other apostles wrote letters. In fact, many were communities which Paul, "an ambassador for Jesus Christ," had started.

Talk about it

1. What signs might you see in someone's life that suggest that the person has heard and accepted the gospel?

2. What signs might you see that suggest the person has not accepted the gospel?

Sent on mission

The Church is God's sign of salvation for all people. Christ sent his disciples to preach the good news:

"Go therefore and make disciples of all nations, baptizing them in the name of the Father and of the Son and of the Holy Spirit, and teaching them to obey everything that I have commanded you. And remember, I am with you always, to the end of the age."

Matthew 28:19–20

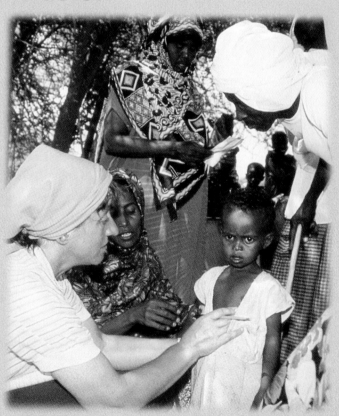

The Church is missionary. The reason for the Church's mission is to draw all people into the community of love that exists between the Father and the Son in the Spirit who is love. So the missionary command of Jesus is rooted in the love of the Trinity.

Because God loves *all* people, the Church always has an obligation to carry out its mission, and it has the inspiration to do so: We are urged on by the love of Christ.

See the *Catechism of the Catholic Church*, #s 849–851.

1. What did Jesus tell his disciples to do?

2. Who are Jesus' disciples today?

3. How could we do a better job of showing others God's saving love?

4. How can all the Churches do a better job of showing God's love?

Jewish and Gentile Christians

As you read through Acts, you will notice another feature of the mission of Jesus' disciples. They preached first to the Jews and then to the Gentiles, faithful to God's plan of salvation. Israel had first place in that plan. As the disciples preached the gospel, Israel received the first call to see the hand of God at work in Jesus.

But many Gentiles also responded to that call. The successful mission to the Gentiles makes us aware that Acts marks a turning point in salvation history. From then on, the story of salvation involved God's dealings with *all* the people of the world.

In summary, the Acts of the Apostles presents us with an outline of some key elements in our understanding of God's plan of salvation: The Christian faith must be viewed in relationship to Judaism. Through the Jewish people, God seeks the salvation of all people. In Jesus, born into the Jewish faith Tradition, God calls everyone to ongoing conversion under the guidance of the Holy Spirit. Like Jesus, Christians should expect opposition. In Christ, despite obstacles, God's kingdom will come in its fullness.

THE BOOK OF REVELATION

The last book in the New Testament is the Book of Revelation. At first, this book seems to be about a vision experienced by a man named John. On second look, it becomes more obvious that the book doesn't offer a word-by-word description of a vision. Rather, it reflects a type of writing which was popular in the first century after Christ. This type of writing is called *apocalyptic*, meaning *revelation*. **Apocalyptic** writing is about a great conflict between good and evil, ending in the destruction of evil and the victory of good. Writing of this type:

- uses a vision to communicate secret, divine knowledge—and to only a few persons
- uses numbers, signs, symbols, and images which carry hidden meanings and messages
- tells of a confrontation between good and evil, light and darkness
- sees all historical events in terms of victory and defeat
- deals with the end of time, the end of the world

The Book of Revelation is clearly this kind of literature. What's not so clear is its meaning. The early Christians struggled with accepting this book as part of the New Testament. They knew that the gospel of Jesus Christ was not a hidden secret available only to a few. The gospel is the full disclosure of God's love to all people.

We should observe that the Book of Revelation is not totally obscure. It clearly portrays Jesus Christ as the focal point of history. He is the one who is victorious over his enemies and is Lord of all. Beyond this basic framework, however, the Book of Revelation is difficult for us. It isn't possible to tell clearly what each of the images, symbols, and numbers means.

Talk about it

1. What attitude of mind and heart is necessary to read the New Testament?

2. What does it mean to read the Scriptures "with faith"?

---

apocalyptic

highly imaginative writing about a great conflict between good and evil, revealing hidden insights into the meaning of events by means of symbols and images

Since this book reflects the mentality of first-century Christians, we can't know for sure what some of the passages mean. Of course, that doesn't keep people from trying! Unfortunately, people over the centuries have used the symbols, numbers, and images in Revelation to prove just about anything. This is an abuse of Scripture.

The best approach to take in reading the Book of Revelation is to respect it for what it is: a mysterious type of literature whose full meaning we don't understand. We must rely on solid biblical research to tell us more.

Talk about it

1. Make a list of words, signs, and symbols that young people use to communicate—but which are not easily understood by adults.

2. What would adults have to do to understand the words, signs, and symbols?

3. How is this like reading the Book of Revelation?

Then do this

Scan the Book of Revelation for an interesting image. Refer to the footnotes for information on what the image may mean. Then draw a picture of the image and include the meaning in the drawing.

And the one who was seated on the throne said, ". . . I am the Alpha and the Omega, the beginning and the end."

Revelation 21:5–6

The one who testifies to these things says, "Surely I am coming soon."
Amen. Come, Lord Jesus!

Revelation 22:20

REVIEW

1. Who wrote the Acts of the Apostles? What is it about?

2. Where do we learn about the gospel being preached to the Gentiles?

3. What kind of literature is the Book of Revelation?

4. Why is the Book of Revelation difficult to understand?

CONCLUSION

Come, Lord Jesus!

Several of the hymns we sing in church and elsewhere use imagery from the Book of Revelation. Take for example "The Battle Hymn of the Republic":

1. Mine eyes have seen the glory of the coming of the Lord;

   He is trampling out the vintage where the grapes of wrath are stored;

   He hath loosed the fateful lightning of his terrible swift sword;

   His truth is marching on.

Refrain: Glory! Glory! Hallelujah!

   Glory! Glory! Hallelujah!

   Glory! Glory! Hallelujah!

   His truth is marching on.

3. He has sounded forth the trumpet that shall never call retreat;

   He is sifting out all human hearts before his judgment seat;

   O be swift, my soul, to answer him; be jubilant, my feet!

   Our God is marching on. *Refrain.*

And consider this spiritual:

   My Lord! what a morning,

   My Lord! what a morning,

   My Lord! what a morning

   when the stars begin to fall.

   You'll hear the trumpet sound

   to wake the nations underground

   looking to my God's right hand

   When the stars begin to fall.

Optional activities

1. Look through your parish hymnal and choose three hymns that are based on Scripture. If the Scripture reference is given, look up the verses. If the reference isn't given, try to find the verses. Is the hymn accurate in how it uses the Scripture? Write a brief response.

2. Choose a verse or two from one of the Gospels and write a poem or hymn using the verse(s) as your basis.

3. Teach the class a hymn that refers to the endtime or Christ's return in glory.

Liturgy and the New Testament

Since the days of the Old Testament, people have read and listened to the word of God to hear God's loving plan of salvation and to find their own lives reflected in it. Hungry hearts have sought to apply the word of God to their daily lives. This tradition continued in the lives of the early Christians.

The Jewish tradition of gathering in the local prayer house or synagogue was normal practice at the time of Christ. The first Christians continued this practice, but their belief in Jesus as Messiah often created conflict. As a result, Christians were sometimes expelled from synagogues.

Christians then gathered in their homes. It was there that they listened to the letters of Paul and other leaders. There they were taught how to live in a way that showed their union with Christ and his community of believers. As these home-churches became more organized and as Christians grew in numbers throughout the Roman Empire, church buildings were erected for common worship. The reading of Scripture and the breaking of the Bread (the Eucharist) became the central celebrations in these places.

A formal liturgy, or public form of worship, gradually took shape around these two basic practices. Catholics have maintained the unity of the two and celebrate the Liturgy of the Word before sharing in any of the sacraments of the Church, especially the Eucharist. The passage of time has seen changes and shifts of emphasis in this sharing of the Word and the Eucharist, but these remain the two basic parts of Christian worship.

The fullest expression of this union of word and sacrament is seen at Sunday Mass. After a time of prayerful preparation, the assembly listens to three readings. The first reading is usually taken from the Old Testament. The people respond with a psalm from the Old Testament. The second reading follows, and is usually selected from one of the letters in the New Testament. The focal point of the Liturgy of the Word is the third reading, the gospel, which announces anew God's saving salvation in Christ as the fulfillment of promise.

Then, since the word of God is alive in our daily lives, a **homily** is preached. Some people call this the "breaking open" of the word of God, others, a sermon. Technically, a homily is a reflection based on the Scripture readings; a sermon is a reflection on a scriptural or religious theme (for example, justice, fellowship, honesty). Most often at Mass, you will hear a homily on how God's action proclaimed in God's word continues to be a living force in us.

The way back to God is the way of worship.

Gerald Vann OP

homily
a reflection rooted in one or more Scripture readings proclaimed at a given liturgy

Talk about it

Why do Christian Churches read from the New Testament as part of worship?

Words you should know

apocalyptic	**infancy narrative**
biography	**parable**
epistle	**parousia**
homily	**Synoptic Gospels**

CHAPTER 9

A TRADITION *of* CHURCH, LITURGY, *and* SACRAMENTS

The Word of the Lord

. . . as often as you eat this bread and drink this cup, you proclaim the Lord's death until he comes.

FROM THE FIRST LETTER TO THE CORINTHIANS, SEE 11:23–28.

CHAPTER OVERVIEW

• *The Church*

• *The experience of Church*

• *Creed*

• *Fragmentation of Christ's Church*

• *Liturgy*

• *Liturgical calendar*

• *Sacraments*

• *The seven sacraments of the Catholic Church*

• *The role of the sacraments*

Let Us Pray

The LORD is my shepherd, I shall not want.
He makes me lie down in green pastures;

he leads me beside still waters;
he restores my soul.
He leads me in right paths
for his name's sake.
Even though I walk through the darkest valley,
I fear no evil;
for you are with me;
your rod and your staff—
they comfort me.
You prepare a table for me
in the presence of my enemies;
you anoint my head with oil;
my cup overflows.
Surely goodness and mercy shall follow me
all the days of my life,
and I shall dwell in the house of the LORD
my whole life long.

PSALM 23

THE CHURCH

In the last chapter we explored the formation of the New Testament. The New Testament came about because of God's saving action in history in Jesus. Without the experience of the life, death, and resurrection of Jesus, there would be no testimony to give. There would be no New Testament.

It's important to remember that before the writing of the various books and letters of the New Testament the Church was already a living and growing reality. It was a community of people who believed. Many years before the New Testament was written, the gospel was handed on by word of mouth. Those who had encountered Jesus, the risen Lord, were touching hearts and changing lives through the good news they announced.

In fact, the Church's tradition—the "handing on" of the gospel in word and deed—continues to this day! This religion class is a part of that tradition. The Catholic Church believes that in order to live the faith, we need both Scripture and Tradition.

Now, don't confuse this word *Tradition* with the word *traditions*. Our *traditions* (with a lower-case "t" and an "s") are those things that people do to practice their faith—like making the sign of the cross and saying special prayers. These practices change over time as people change and as times change.

Tradition
the truth that people have discovered as the result of the revelation of God

Tradition, however, is the truth that people have discovered as the result of the revelation of God. This Tradition matures as people understand more or understand better, but it doesn't just change with the times or for the sake of change.

For that reason the Church sometimes may appear to you to be slow or "behind the times." But it's important for the Church to keep the Tradition, to stick with and see that it is followed. The Church has to make sure that practices and teachings remain faithful to God. Just because someone has a new idea doesn't mean that the long-standing Tradition of the Church must change.

Believers must protect the core truth of the gospel. This sometimes produces tension, but tension doesn't have to be a bad experience. Tension can cause us to seek deeper wisdom and understanding. Faithfulness to the Tradition calls people to open dialogue and demands much patience.

Talk about it
Is it important for the Church to maintain its Tradition? Why?

The development of Christian Tradition must be seen as a further development, or fulfillment, of the Jewish faith Tradition. Jesus belonged to a religion that already existed—Judaism, and we can't really understand Jesus and his ministry unless we understand that background.

God's assembly

To help understand our Christian Tradition, it is helpful to understand how we see ourselves as a Church. Have you ever wondered where the word *church* comes from? One root is the Greek word *ecclesia*, which literally means "that which is called from" or an "assembly of people." Members of the early Church found this word very helpful in understanding what God was doing through them.

In a typical Greek city, the *ecclesia*, or "assembly," was a special body of citizens who were called together to make decisions which would benefit all the people. Selected by the people, the members of this group were known for their wisdom and good character. They were trusted members of society.

The work of this group, this *ecclesia*, affected the whole of society. The *ecclesia* was not about power, but about service. The members made decisions to help all the people. They also were supposed to set an example for others. It was a real privilege to be selected as a member of this *ecclesia* or "assembly."

The early Christian community saw themselves as God's *ecclesia*, God's assembly, God's Church! They knew that they themselves did not create this assembly. Since time began, God had been calling people together, to be a "place" where God's saving love could be seen and known.

How this "assembly of the Lord" lived in response to God's saving love made a difference for the rest of the world. That's why the prophets of old continuously called the Israelites back to faithfulness to the covenant, back to the privileged position of being used by God in the work of salvation.

The early Christian community saw themselves, then, not as a new religion, but as a new assembly. They were the continuation as well as the fulfillment of what God had prepared the way for in the chosen people of Israel. What was shocking—and exciting—for them to realize was that Christ's assembly, his Church, was open not just to the privileged few but to anyone who accepted salvation in Jesus, the Christ, the risen Lord! God's promise made to the chosen people of Israel had been fulfilled. God was revealed fully, once and for all time, in Jesus.

Write it down

1. To what assemblies do you belong?

2. For which of these do you consider membership a privilege? Why?

Characteristics of the Church

In the Creed, we say that the Church is "one, holy, catholic, and apostolic." These four marks of the Church are characteristics linked completely with each other. These essential elements describe the Church's work. Christ, through the Holy Spirit, makes the Church one, holy, catholic, and apostolic. Christ continuously challenges all members of the Church to live these qualities.

Our perspective of faith helps us understand that the Church possesses these characteristics. At the same time, the history of the Church helps us see that the Church does indeed possess these qualities. These marks make the Church a more credible witness to the mission it has received from God. See the *Catechism of the Catholic Church* #s 811–812.

1. What does it mean that the Church is one?

2. What does it mean that the Church is holy?

3. What does it mean that the Church is catholic?

4. What does it mean that the Church is apostolic?

5. When we read "the Church" here, what do we mean? Do we mean just the Catholic Church, or do we mean the Christian Church in all its different forms?

John XXIII and Vatican II
Church renewal

Angelo Giuseppe Roncalli was born in northern Italy in 1881. Already as an adolescent, Angelo became involved in the Catholic Action movement, an involvement that influenced many of his later decisions. He studied for the priesthood and was ordained in 1905. Study continued, and Father Roncalli eventually became a professor of Church history in his home diocese.

During World War I, Father Roncalli served as a hospital orderly and then as a chaplain. He came away from the experience believing that war was the greatest evil. Following the war he was appointed the Vatican's apostolic visitor to Bulgaria in 1925 and ordained an archbishop. In 1935 Roncalli was named the apostolic delegate to Turkey and Greece. In all he was to spend a total of thirty years as a diplomat.

World War II brought new challenges to Archbishop Roncalli who assisted thousands of Jews in escaping the terrors of the Nazis by helping them gain passage to Palestine. Still during the war, Roncalli was sent to Paris as papal nuncio. A decade later he was named a cardinal and sent to the important diocese of Venice in Italy.

In 1958 Roncalli was elected pope—at nearly 77 years of age. He chose the name *John* and became Pope John XXIII. In his diocese of Rome, he visited parishes, the prison, and hospitals. Within a short time he became known as "Good Pope John" and was beloved of people of many religions.

John XXIII had long been interested in Christian unity, and in late 1961, he convoked an ecumenical council. The Second Vatican Council (Vatican II) took place during the years 1962 to 1965. Bishops from around the world attended and welcomed observers from many other Christian Churches and diplomats from nearly ninety countries.

Pope John wanted the council to produce a new Pentecost, and it did. Sixteen documents were written to direct the revitalization of the Church and to help the Catholic Church begin to move toward a reunion of Christian Churches. Many other Christian Churches followed with renewals of their own. Ecumenical dialogues extended to non-Christian religions.

But Pope John XXIII didn't live to see all this; in fact, he died in 1963, after only one session of the council. Before his death from cancer, he said, "At the day of judgment we won't be asked whether we realized unity, but whether we prayed, worked, and suffered for it."

John's tomb in the crypt of St. Peter's is still frequently visited, but, more importantly, his vision for the Church continues. Catholics still disagree on how best to renew the Church; Christians still struggle to reunite—but no one forgets the kind, elderly man who felt called by the Spirit to stir up the hearts and minds of millions of people.

Optional activities

1. Research what topics were addressed by the Second Vatican Council; see the book of *Documents of Vatican II* or find the documents on the Internet. Share your findings with the class.

2. Research the Second Vatican Council and write a report. In the report respond to this question: What would the Church be like today if the Second Vatican Council had not been held?

3. Interview two or three adults who are old enough to remember the Church before the Second Vatican Council. Use questions such as these:

   • What was your parish like before the Second Vatican Council?

   • What was Sunday Mass like?

   • How did you feel when many things in the Catholic Church changed during and after the Second Vatican Council? Why did you feel this way?

The Church today

Throughout the centuries since the time of Jesus, those who believe he is the Christ have seen themselves as *ecclesia*, the assembly of Christians, the Church. The Holy Spirit continues to form the community of the Church. The Church is to be an instrument of God's saving love, to be a "place" of love, a community in which God continues to call people from the darkness of sin and blind searching for happiness to experience him "face to face."

It is a privilege and a responsibility to belong to this assembly of people united in Christ! Certainly, the members of the Church are not automatically perfect people or better than others just because they belong to the Church. Rather, they have a special call to participate in the work or mission of the Church and thus to respond to the gift of their salvation.

How do *you* experience being Church, a part of God's assembly? In the next chapter you will study the Sacraments of Christian Initiation (Baptism, Confirmation, and Eucharist), through which you became a member of God's assembly, the Church. When you were presented for Baptism, nothing magic happened. You were not poured into a mold, as it were.

Just as your physical life is a free gift from your parents, your life as God's child and a member of his assembly has been offered to you as a free gift. You were presented for Baptism and the other two Sacraments of Christian Initiation in a context of faith. Your parents are believers and wanted you to share their experience of Church from the earliest years of your life. Just as they want you to grow toward adulthood, they want you to personally choose to be a follower of Christ.

The Church is a symbol of eternity in the midst of the self-sufficient world.
Rudolf Bultmann

REVIEW

1. What is the difference between *Tradition* and *traditions*?
2. What kind of assembly did the people of the early Church see themselves as being?
3. What are the four marks or characteristics of the Church?
4. Of what is the Church an instrument?

THE EXPERIENCE OF CHURCH

You can experience Church at many levels. In the Sacraments of Christian Initiation, you entered on a path of belonging to the Church. Hopefully, in your infancy and early childhood, you experienced in your family what it means to live in Christ. Some writers even call the family a "little Church" or the "domestic Church."

As you grew, you recognized that your family is not all there is to Church. You experienced life in a parish or perhaps another community of faith. As you grow further in your awareness of the world around you, you will more fully realize that the Church is more than your parish.

A Catholic parish is part of a diocese. A **diocese** is a portion of the body of Christ which is entrusted for pastoral care to a bishop. The fullness of the Catholic Church exists in a diocese. It's not just a part of a bigger institution. Under the leadership of the bishop, however, a diocese is united to all the other dioceses in the universal worldwide Church. In the Catholic Tradition, the bishop of the diocese of Rome—the **pope**—is also the head of the entire Catholic Church. He is the first among equals.

Many volumes could be written about the meaning of the Church. And many volumes have been written! After all, how do you capture everything that could be said about the Church and put it into books? It's impossible. But the books do help us understand who we are as Church. Perhaps the following brief definition can help keep things in focus: **The Church is those people who have heard about Jesus (the good news), believe in him, share the good news of Jesus, and seek to follow it (him) in service of others**.

Those people . . .

Church is people. It isn't a building. It isn't an abstract idea. It isn't just an organization. The Church does have an institutional element, and it does construct buildings in which to gather and worship, but the Church is first of all a people whom God has called. So the word *Church* is usually used for that group of people who have responded to God's saving love made known in Jesus.

. . . who have heard . . .

The Church is people who have heard the good news of Jesus. But we know that we can hear and not *really* hear. We can use our ears to pick up sounds, but to really hear is to care what those sounds mean. People "who have heard" are people who care about what they hear. They have heard not just with their ears but also with their hearts.

The words you hear about God at church, in your home, and at school do touch your ears, but, unless they touch your heart, they literally "go in one ear and out the other." What makes the difference is that you freely choose to listen, not just with your ears but also with your heart. No one can make you listen in this way. Parents and people in authority can make you attend church services where you may physically hear the good news about Christ proclaimed, but only *you* can open your heart to that news.

diocese

a group of parishes headed by a bishop

pope

the bishop of the diocese of Rome and the head of the entire Catholic Church

Talk about it

1. Why is the family the "domestic Church"?

2. What is the name of your (arch)diocese? Who is your (arch)bishop?

3. What impact does the pope have on the world as a whole? Give examples.

Write it down

My heart is open to . . . because . . . .
My heart is not open to . . . because . . . .

. . . the good news . . .

The Church is those people who have heard the good news that the Church hands on. This good news isn't just information about a man who lived at one time in history. The good news isn't just religious information. It's not just a body of knowledge which your mind tries to understand (or ignore). The good news of God's love is Jesus, the Christ. The Church hands on its continuing witness to the life, death, and resurrection of Jesus, God's fulfilled promise of salvation for all humankind.

. . . believe it . . .

The Church is the people who have heard about Jesus and have believed. Only you personally can move from experienced and practiced faith to claimed faith. Only you can believe; only you can let God touch your heart, where you hunger for healing and wholeness, for fullness of life. To believe in Jesus is to open your heart to God's saving love. You cannot save yourself. But only you can let God save you.

Write it down
I believe in Jesus because . . . .

. . . share the good news . . .

Those who follow Jesus shouldn't be shy about it. This is good news! Why hold back? Why not share the good news of Jesus with all the energy you bring to those things you love best, those events you enjoy most, those talents at which you excel? If just once every day, every Christian shouted the good news, the world would change for the better within a week. To paraphrase the Prayer of St. Francis:

*Where once there was
  hatred,
    there would be love.
Where once there was
  injury,
    there would be pardon.
Where once there was doubt,
    there would be faith.
Where once there was
  despair, hope.
Where once there was
  darkness, light.
Where once there was
  sadness, joy.*

. . . seek to follow Jesus . . .

Those who believe in Jesus try to follow him. They seek to follow his way of love. Christian discipleship means ongoing conversion, or change of heart. Some people tell of life-changing moments when they realized how deeply God loves them and that they are saved in Christ. They often can identify the date and place of their conversion to Christ.

Then do this

Ask several people if they have experienced a conversion. For those who answer yes, ask them to tell you how the conversion made a difference in their lives. Share the results of your interviews (without using names) with the class.

For these people, and for all Christians, however, discipleship is a lifelong process. Those who have decided to believe, to open their hearts to God's saving love in Jesus, embark on a lifelong journey. Moments of religious experience do not transform people into living saints. Until the day we die, each and every Christian is still on the way. We are Christians, but not fully. We seek to follow.

Through its instructions and teachings, the community of Christ, the Church, helps us grow in the way of discipleship. That's why Catholic school education, religious education classes, parish retreats, and youth groups are all important for growth in the Christian life. Discipleship isn't a private matter. We must remain faithful to the Tradition of the community, to the core truth of the gospel. Otherwise, we end up thinking we individually are the Church, the whole community of Christ, and that our opinions are the only measure of truth.

. . . in the service of others.

We seek to follow Jesus' way. The way of Jesus isn't about power; it's about service. The Church exists not for itself, but for God and for people. The Church exists to be that place of God's saving love for all people.

Talk about it

Does the Church shape the world or the world shape the Church? Or does it work both ways? Explain.

The greatest service the followers of Jesus give the world is the witness of their lives. The more like Jesus we become, the more God's love can reach people. God continues to save through the Church—through *us!*

So we have work to do. We have a mission! Just like the disciples, we are sent! Every single place we go—school, home, the sports field, work, play—can become a place of God's love. Everything we do becomes the "place" where believing Christians can transform the world into a place of God's goodness and love.

The heart of religion lies in its personal pronouns.
Martin Luther

*The Church . . . is a new life
with Christ and in Christ,
guided by the Holy Spirit.*
Sergius Bulgakov

Common ministry as priest, prophet, and king

God the Father anointed Jesus with the Holy Spirit and set him apart as priest, prophet, and king. Through faith and Baptism, Jesus' followers share with him in these three ministries of priest, prophet, and king. All God's people are responsible for the mission and service which come from these roles or offices.

All the baptized share in the priesthood of Christ. Likewise we share in Christ's prophetic witness to the world when we cling to our faith. We also share in the reign of Christ the King, especially when we serve those who are poor.

See the *Catechism of the Catholic Church,* #s 783–786.

1. As followers of Jesus and members of the Church, how do we share in the ministry of priest, prophet, and king?

2. What kind of king was Jesus? How is that different from the way we usually think of kings?

3. Why is it not right or possible to expect priests and other ordained ministers to do all the work of the Church?

4. In what way is Christ's work our work?

God never intended his Church to be a refrigerator

in which to preserve perishable piety.

He intended it to be an incubator

in which to hatch converts.

F. Lincicome

REVIEW

1. What is a diocese?

2. Who is the pope (not the name of the present pope, but his position)?

3. *Who* are the Church?

CREED

The essence of Church is people. But this people has characteristics and does things that are important and necessary. Believing in God and opening your heart to God's saving love in Christ is the beginning point. The encounter between God and you is not all there is. God becomes known from within a community, from within a Tradition of faith. How that community has come to put its Tradition into words has always been important to the Church.

Words of testimony (whether written or spoken) are an important part of discipleship. In other words, *what* we believe about God helps us enter into the mystery of his saving love. There is a "content" to our Christian faith. Just as the Scriptures are a written testimony to what God has done for us in history, so too is our common statement of faith.

Our common statement of faith is the **Creed**. The Creed is a statement of the main things we believe about God and God's relationship to us. In the Tradition of the Church, this Creed has been expressed in two main ways; these versions of the Creed continue to be used by many Christian Churches. One form is the *Apostles' Creed*, and another is the *Nicene Creed*. The texts of these Creeds are in the Appendix of this book.

These Creeds are brief statements of our faith. In the Catholic Church, the Creed is spoken by the assembly as part of the regular Sunday liturgy. Its use is a constant reminder that we are not Church individually, but as a community. The faith of the Church is not a matter of personal opinion, but of shared belief. It is the faith of the Church that we share.

creed
a statement of the main things we believe about God and God's relationship to us

Write it down
Write a letter to Jesus about what you, as a member of your Church, believe. Also write about how you feel regarding those beliefs.

> *The proper question to be asked about any creed is not,*
> *"Is it pleasant?" but, "Is it true?"*
> **Dorothy L. Sayers**

FRAGMENTATION OF CHRIST'S CHURCH

The Church is a wonderful work of God. It's a great piece of handiwork. In one of his letters, Paul describes the Church as the living stones of God's grace. God uses each of us to build a living temple for the Holy Spirit, given to us by the risen Lord.

Jesus is our cornerstone, the stone that holds together the entire structure. This is a beautiful image for the Church. We are to be the sign for all people of the saving love of God in Christ. We have a common work to do: We are to proclaim God's saving love to a world searching for happiness and the fullness of life.

As we have seen in the letters and the Acts of the Apostles in the New Testament, the Church has never been a perfect community. People sin. Arguments and misunderstandings arise over many issues. Unfortunately, this can lead to division in the Church—and it has.

In the eleventh century, there was a great disagreement in the Church, resulting in a split, a division—the Catholic or Western Church (centered in Rome) and the Orthodox Church or Eastern Church (centered in Constantinople). Although Pope John Paul II worked hard to bring these two great Churches closer together, the scars of division still exist.

In the sixteenth century, there was more conflict and division in the Church in the West. The times were complex. There was a great deal of confusion and corruption in the Church. All it took was a spark of protest to ignite a movement led by those who sought their idea of greater faithfulness to Scripture as the true Tradition of the Church.

This movement began within the Church itself. Martin Luther, a Catholic priest and monk, became the leader of this reform movement—later known as the **Reformation**. The times were ripe for change. But tempers flared, and actions were taken which changed the shape of Christianity from then on.

Most of the reforming groups split from Rome because of a combination of differing theology and national politics. Luther's disagreement with the Church in Rome was over theology, but the princes of Germany who supported him were also anxious to cut their ties with the Holy Roman Empire. So began Lutheranism.

In England, King Henry VIII had political difficulties with the pope, who wouldn't declare void his marriage to Catherine of Aragon. Henry wanted to remarry and produce a male heir to the British throne. The king eventually declared himself head of the Church of England. This was the beginning of Anglicanism (Episcopalianism in the United States).

Out of the reform movement, in time, came many different Churches, many different expressions of the Christian faith: Presbyterian, Baptist, Congregationalist, Methodist, and so on. Altogether these pathways of faith are called *Protestant* from the word *protest*, though each of these groups has its own unique history.

This is true of later Protestant groups as well—the Quakers, the Disciples of Christ, the Adventists, the Jehovah's Witnesses, the Christian Scientists, the United Church of Christ, and so on. Sadly, the Christian Church is still very fragmented. Today in the United States there are many smaller denominational groups in addition to the mainline Protestant Churches. Some Churches are a single congregation with no ties to a larger group.

In recent years, most Christian Churches—most Christian denominations—have come to hear the Spirit's call for unity among Christians and the need for openness and tolerance toward all religions. There's plenty of responsibility and guilt for the fragmentation of Christianity to pass around. But many Christian Churches have begun a very serious effort to reestablish unity.

This coming together of Churches is known as the *ecumenical movement*. The purpose of this movement is not to produce a mega-Christian Church, but a community of faith which is unified in its understanding of faith, sacramental celebration, and exercise of authority. There are many ways in which this kind of unity can be experienced and lived. The task is not easy and it's far from over. But because of real listening to one another's positions, Christian denominations are drawing closer together and doing more good.

Reformation
the sixteenth century religious protest movement that resulted in a split in the Catholic Church in the West and the formation of several Protestant Churches

Then do this
Interview five people who belong to a different Christian denomination than you do. Ask these questions, and summarize the responses in an essay, adding your own responses and reaction to the interviews.

1. To what Christian denomination do you belong?

2. What is the history of your denomination?

3. Would you like to see all Christian denominations united? Why?

Unity of Christians

As has been noted, one of the major issues addressed by the Second Vatican Council was the restoration of unity among all Christians. Christ founded one Church, and this one Church is unique. However, many Christian denominations consider themselves to be the true inheritors of Jesus Christ. All indeed profess to be followers of Jesus, but they differ in what they believe and they go their different ways. Certainly, such division is not in line with what Jesus preached. The division of the Christian Church often scandalizes people, and it interferes with the preaching of the gospel.

Yet God is patient and wisely brings about all he has planned. In our day, God has generously led divided Christians to repent their divisions and long for unity.

In these days, people are responding more and more to God's Spirit of love bringing Christians together. Christians who take part in this ecumenical movement believe in the Trinity and proclaim Jesus as Lord and Savior. They do this as individuals and as members of different Churches. Most Christians long for one Church, a Church that gives honor and glory to God and draws all people to the gospel.

See *The Documents of Vatican II*, "Decree on Ecumenism," #1.

1. Why is the gospel best proclaimed when Christians are united?
2. What can you do to help build unity among Christians? What can your parish or faith community do?
3. What gets in the way of unity among Christians today? Among people in general?
4. Can the Church be one and yet have many expressions? Why?

When men are animated by the love of Christ,
they feel united, and the needs, sufferings, and joys of
others are felt as their own.

Pope John XXIII

REVIEW

1. What is a creed?
2. What Church division took place during the eleventh century?
3. What is the Reformation?
4. To what does the term *ecumenical movement* refer?

Taizé
Ecumenism lived

In a small village in eastern France, a hundred or so men live together in community. They have come from every continent and over twenty-five countries. But what's really unique about the community is that it is ecumenical—the brothers come from many different Christian Churches. This is Taizé.

The community of Taizé began in the 1940s as a monastic community devoted to prayer, work, and hospitality. The brothers and their guests gather three times a day for community prayer in the Church of Reconciliation. In fact, a distinctive type of meditative prayer and music has developed in the community. The songs often repeat a key phrase or sentence over and over again, making it easier for people of many languages to pray together.

The members of the community work to support themselves. They also offer refuge to victims of war and injustice. Starting in 1962, some of the brothers began to spend time in Eastern Europe to help the people there who were oppressed. Since 1989, many Eastern Europeans have in turn visited the monastery in France.

Today the community is well known as a place of retreat for young people (and many adults) of all religions. Visitors usually come for a week to spend time in private prayer, to pray and work with the brothers, and to share with people of other places and religions. The brothers ask for only enough money to cover the cost of food and lodging for each visitor. The visitors return home renewed and often ready to be more involved in their own Church families.

The brothers aren't sure what draws young people to Taizé. Perhaps it is the vision of what a reunited Christian Church may be like. Surely it is the Spirit.

Optional activities

1. Find out more about the history of Taizé. Write an essay or present your findings to the class.

2. Search through your parish hymnal for music from Taizé. Teach one of the songs to the class and use it for class prayer.

3. Visit a monastery for the community's prayer.

LITURGY

People's gratitude for God's self-revelation in history led to the formation of Scripture and creeds. It also led to the development of the Church's liturgy. What's liturgy? Let's take a look.

Many young people like to hang out on the streets, day or night, just to see what's happening. If they watch, they might see a truck that says "City Water Works." What does that mean? The dictionary tells us that *work* is "labor" or "an area of responsibility." The City Water Works is an area of responsibility. "Works" are things that are done—in this case, for the city, for the people, and, in a way, in the name of the people.

If you were hanging out in the streets of modern-day Athens, you might see a city truck with the Greek word *liturgia* on the side panel. The truck might be from the city water works. The word *liturgia* ("the work of the people") is where we get our word *liturgy*.

Liturgy means the Church in worship (such as sacramental celebrations); worship is the "work" of the community of faith. You have heard of the "Liturgy of the Eucharist," the "Liturgy of Baptism," the "Liturgy of the Word." All of these are forms of the Church's worship, its *liturgy*, the Church's "work."

Liturgy is the Church doing its "work" as the Church. Liturgy is the people of God "working" or being in worship. They are doing the work of the Church, that for which the Church is responsible—worshiping God. Somewhat like the city water works people, those who engage in liturgy are doing something that is very public. It's not secretive. They're also doing in a responsible manner what the people of God are entrusted to be doing. Liturgy is the Church giving expression to its self. It's the Church itself in action.

Talk about it

1. How is going to church similar to going to a sports event? How is it different?

2. How do you feel when you're at an event that's unfamiliar to you—a sports event or a celebration of another culture? How does this experience relate to being at an unfamiliar worship service?

3. What is your role in liturgical celebrations?

Liturgy is encounter

In every liturgical action of the Church, especially in the celebration of the Eucharist and the other sacraments, the Church encounters Christ. The unity of the liturgical assembly is the work of God's Holy Spirit, who gathers us into the one body of Christ. This assembly goes beyond racial, cultural, or social divisions—and all human connections.

The assembly must prepare itself to meet Christ in liturgy by having the right attitude. Together the Holy Spirit and the people of God, especially the ministers, prepare the hearts of those assembled. In the liturgy of the Church, the Holy Spirit works to awaken our faith, convert our hearts, and open us to doing God's will. If the worship of the Church is to help us receive God's grace and have its effects on our lives, we must have this kind of disposition.

See the *Catechism of the Catholic Church, #s 1097–1098.*

1. Is God present to the worshiping community even when its members aren't open to God?
2. Why is the right disposition of heart necessary for worship?
3. What are some things you can do to have the proper attitude and openness of heart when going to church?
4. What is an encounter? Why do we say that liturgy is encounter?

Liturgy pursues excellence

Liturgy is not about doing your own thing. Nor does the shape of the ritual depend solely on the one who leads the group. Good liturgy follows the "principle of excellence." That means that our public worship should be the truest and fullest expression of what we are celebrating. The words, gestures, environment, and so on should all work together to communicate the total experience.

The Catholic Church establishes rules and regulations that encourage that excellence while allowing for creativity and flexibility. Most people experience the creativity and flexibility of liturgy in their parish setting. There the people of a parish do their best to worship and pray together in union with the broader, universal Church. There liturgy is adapted to particular circumstances.

Flexibility and creativity in liturgy are often best seen by looking at various parishes with a strong ethnic character. While a certain style of liturgy may work in one parish, that style may be completely ineffective for another parish. No one parish is the norm for all other parishes. The principle of excellence is expressed in different ways in different parishes.

Since the liturgy is the work of the Church, the Church has the authority to determine how it should be celebrated. Union with the Church in liturgical expression is most important. When that union is not present, a particular liturgical expression is schismatic, that is, broken away from the Church. The action is not what the Church does. "Baptizing" puppies and kittens, for example, involves a ritual act using water, but the Church baptizes only people. Because the liturgy is the action of the Church, Church authorities determine when an action is not truly the liturgy of the Church.

Write it down

What can you do to respond to God's presence when you worship?

Talk about it

In the West for centuries the Mass was celebrated in the Latin language, even after it was no longer the language of the people. After the Second Vatican Council, the Catholic Church returned to the early practice of celebrating the Mass in the language of the people. Why was this an important change?

> Liturgy can only really live, worship can only truly express joy, sorrow, hope, faith, and love if it is firmly rooted in the actual lives and experience of the people who are worshiping.
>
> **Ianthe Pratt**

Talk about it

1. What do you think makes a "good" worship service?

2. How would you improve the quality of the liturgy or worship service at your church? Why do you think these changes would be good?

The liturgy of the Church must be an instrument of the saving action of God in Christ Jesus. The liturgy must clearly anchor itself in "the Christ event." For example, the Church cannot decide to baptize with champagne instead of water. Not only is water a natural religious symbol, but water is also identified with Christ's work and command to baptize the people of all nations.

For the same reason, the Church cannot use pizza and soft drinks for youth Masses. Although these items are legitimate food and drink, they are not historically linked to Christ, who used bread and wine at the Last Supper.

In fact, Jesus used many natural symbols. These symbols already had powerful meaning, but they have taken on additional meaning because of Jesus. The use of water, oil, laying on of hands, bread and wine, all had religious meaning at the time of Jesus. But now these symbols connect us to Jesus; they express our faith. We could also say that nature symbols become history symbols, that is, connected with salvation history.

Jesus didn't invent new liturgical signs. He used the signs and symbols of nature and history that were around him and gave them new meaning. And the Church continues to use the signs and symbols Jesus used to express its faith and celebrate liturgy.

"Very truly I tell you, whoever believes has eternal life. I am the bread of life."

John 6:47–48

REVIEW

1. What is liturgy?

2. Who determines how the liturgy is celebrated?

3. What are some of the symbols used in Catholic liturgical celebrations?

LITURGICAL CALENDAR

Christian liturgical celebrations have been happening for a long time. Nearly two thousand years have passed since the death and resurrection of Jesus. Over the centuries, the Christian Churches have developed rather elaborate systems of liturgical celebration.

To help anchor their public worship in Christ, many Christian Churches follow a **liturgical calendar.** Typical annual calendars begin in January and end in December. Fiscal calendars used by bookkeepers and many businesses often begin on July 1 and end on June 30 of the following year. Then there's the school calendar, August or September to June, which helps people keep track of events and activities in the school year.

Each of these calendars has its purpose. They are expressions of linear time. They help us keep track of time and, in a sense, bring meaning to the passage of time. The liturgical year is another way of measuring time. The liturgical year anchors itself in two significant dates: Christmas and Easter. Of the two, the celebration of the resurrection is the high point of all the Church's celebrations. Although the liturgical calendar has changed and adapted over the centuries, the liturgical year in the Catholic Church continues to follow a basic format.

liturgical calendar
the calendar of the Church year, the annual commemoration and celebration of the main Christian mysteries

---

In her concern for our salvation, our loving mother the Church uses

the liturgical seasons to teach us through hymns, canticles,

and other forms of expression, of voice and ritual,

used by the Holy Spirit.

She shows us how grateful we should be for our blessings.

St. Charles Borromeo

Sunday

Sunday is the Lord's day, the first day of the week. Sunday is the most important day for the Church to gather for liturgy. The Lord's Supper is the center of the Church's celebration on Sunday. When we listen to the readings and participate in the Eucharist, we recall the suffering, death, resurrection, and glory of Jesus. We give thanks to God for the resurrection of Jesus, which gives us hope.

See the *Catechism of the Catholic Church,* #s 1166–1167.

1. Why does the Church gather to celebrate on Sunday?

2. Why is the Saturday evening Mass a Sunday celebration?

Advent

Advent
the four-week period of preparation for the celebration of the birth of our Lord, or Christmas

The Season of Advent begins the liturgical year. **Advent** is the four-week period of preparation for the celebration of the birth of our Lord, or **Christmas**. The word *advent* comes from the Latin word *adventus*, meaning "arrival." Advent is a time of quiet and joyful reflection on the mystery of the Son of God becoming one of us in Jesus, born of Mary.

Christmas

Christmas
the Church's celebration of the birth of Jesus, the celebration of the incarnation

Christmas celebrates the event of the Son of God entering into human history in Jesus. It is the feast of the incarnation of God's Word. *Incarnation* means "becoming real in the flesh." This feast is not the actual birthday of Jesus, since no one knows the exact date of Jesus' birth.

Although the feast of Christmas has a long tradition, it has not been observed as long as Easter has. As the Christian Church grew, believers needed to counter the worship of the Roman Sun-god. This feast of the Sun-god was celebrated in relation to the winter solstice (December 21), when it appeared to the unscientific mind that the sun was dying. December 25 became the focal point of the celebration because it was clear by then that the sun was rising again.

Then do this
Research the way Epiphany is celebrated in Mexico or in a European country. Share your research with the class.

The Christians began their own celebration, the glorious celebration of Jesus, the Son of God, as the true light that has shown upon the world for its salvation. The play on words is obvious in English. The Christmas Season lasts a few weeks and includes the celebration of the Holy Family (Jesus, Mary, and Joseph), the Epiphany (manifestation to the nations of Jesus as Savior), and the Baptism of Jesus (the beginning of his ministry).

Ordinary Time

Ordinary Time
the time during the liturgical year that focuses on discipleship with Jesus

The weeks between the Christmas Season and the Season of Lent are the beginning of **Ordinary Time.** The use of "ordinary" here doesn't mean uneventful, as if nothing important were happening or that God takes a rest during these weeks! The word *ordinary* merely means the absence of a major liturgical season. It's an in-between time and gives the Church the opportunity to reflect prayerfully on its ordinary walk of discipleship and path of ongoing conversion. During this time the Church focuses on Jesus' teaching, miracles, and journey to Jerusalem.

Lent

Lent
the liturgical season for deepening the Christian's identification with the life, death, and resurrection of Christ; a time of repentance in preparation for Easter

Easter
the celebration of the resurrection of Jesus

The Season of **Lent** begins some forty days before Easter with the distribution of ashes on Ash Wednesday. The ashes are part of a solemn celebration which calls people to repentance from sin in preparation for the Triduum and the joy of **Easter,** when we celebrate the resurrection of Jesus. This is a time of penance and sacrifice, a time to deal with the reality of sin in one's life and in the world. It is especially a time to identify more with Jesus by deepening our conversion.

Originally in the history of the Church, this season—imitating the time Jesus spent in the desert—was the time those seeking to become Christians intensified their prayer as they prepared for the Sacraments of Christian Initiation. The entire community of the faithful joined them, entering into the mystery of death to selfishness and sin in order to rise with Christ.

Triduum and Easter

The Easter celebration begins with the **Triduum** (or Three Sacred Days). Beginning with a special Mass of the Lord's Supper on Holy Thursday evening, the Church celebrates the institution of the Eucharist by Jesus at the Last Supper. The washing of the feet at this Mass recalls the command of Jesus that we must serve one another in imitation of him. The liturgy also celebrates the beginnings of the priesthood.

On Good Friday, the Church solemnly commemorates the death of Jesus on the cross—Jesus' act of reconciliation for the salvation of the world. By tradition there is no Mass on this day. Instead, the beautiful service includes pertinent Scripture readings (culminating with the Passion from the Gospel according to John), prayers for many groups, veneration of the cross, and Communion.

The greatest celebration of the entire Church year is the Easter Vigil. During this lengthy celebration of Christ's resurrection, there is a lighting of the new fire, sung proclamation (the Exultet), several Scripture readings which proclaim in summary form God's work of salvation, and the blessing of water used for Baptism.

Those who have been preparing to enter the Christian faith participate in the Rite of Christian Initiation; they are baptized, confirmed, and, later in the Mass, share in the Eucharist for the first time. Baptized candidates are confirmed and receive the Eucharist. All present renew their baptismal promises and praise God for the life, death, and resurrection of Jesus, in whom fullness of light and life are to be found. Through the celebrations, the Church is reborn in union with Christ.

The Mass on Easter Sunday morning is a commemoration of the great Easter event celebrated at the Vigil. It's followed by the Easter Season. In the mind of the Church, the Vigil Mass celebrated the previous night and the Easter Sunday Mass are *the* celebration of Easter, which is then continued for several weeks.

Easter is a "floating feast." That is, the date for its celebration changes each year. What actually determines the exact date is the position of the moon. Easter is celebrated after the first full moon following the spring solstice. For the Jews, the feast of Passover is determined in a similar manner. For Christians, Jesus is our Passover, the one who leads us from the slavery of sin and death to new and eternal life.

The Easter Season is a time of festive joy which lasts for fifty days until Pentecost. Included is the Solemnity of the Ascension. Pentecost celebrates the fulfillment of God's plan of salvation in the generous outpouring of the Holy Spirit. The story is recounted at the beginning of the Acts of the Apostles.

Ordinary Time

Once the Season of Easter has concluded with the celebration of Pentecost, the Church returns to Ordinary Time. Ordinary Time after Easter extends twenty-five or more weeks and gives people time to deepen their spiritual life and to pray about what it means to be disciples of Christ.

Just before Advent begins once more, the Church celebrates on the last Sunday in Ordinary Time the Solemnity of Christ the King, acclaiming Jesus' kingdom as the measure of all things and all time.

Triduum

the Three Sacred Days; the time that begins with the Mass of the Lord's Supper on Holy Thursday, culminates with the Easter Vigil, and concludes with evening prayer on Easter

Then do this

1. Research the origins and meanings of some present-day Easter customs. Share your research in small groups.

2. Read the story of Pentecost in Acts 2:1–42. Then choose:
   - Draw a picture of one of the events that took place on Pentecost.
   - Write a news article for the *Jerusalem Herald* following the events of the first Pentecost.
   - Prepare the sermon you would give if you had been present with the disciples on Pentecost.

Then do this

Make a liturgical calendar to hang in the classroom or in your home.

Special days

During the course of every liturgical year, the Church celebrates special feasts in honor of saints, martyrs, and important events in the history and life of the Church. Perhaps you have seen a Church calendar which shows these special days.

Some of these feasts have been identified as **holy days of obligation**. If they are able, Catholics in the United States are obliged to attend Mass on these special occasions: the Solemnity of Mary (January 1), Ascension Day (forty days after Easter or the seventh Sunday after Easter), All Saints' Day (November 1), Christmas (December 25), the Assumption of Mary (August 15), and the Immaculate Conception of Mary (December 8).

holy days of obligation
special feast days of the Church on which Catholics are obliged to attend Mass

Special colors

In the Catholic Church the seasons on the liturgical calendar are marked with the wearing of special liturgical colors. There are four major colors: green, purple, white, and red.

The color green, which is used during Ordinary Time, symbolizes the life we have in Christ. The purple used during Advent symbolizes the struggle between light and darkness which culminates in the Light of God (Jesus) coming into the world. The color purple is used again, but perhaps in a different shade, during Lent when it symbolizes a spirit of penance for sin. White, of course, symbolizing the brilliant celebration of joy, is used during the Christmas and Easter Seasons. The color red is worn on Good Friday and on special occasions which focus on the work of the Holy Spirit or which celebrate martyrs—those who died for the faith.

Then do this
Visit the sacristy of a church or school chapel and have a staff member show you vestments of different colors.

Christmas is the day that holds all time together.
Alexander Smith

Easter, like all deep things, begins in mystery, and it ends, like all high things, in great courage.
Bliss Perry

REVIEW

1. How does a liturgical calendar differ from other calendars?
2. What are the major feasts and seasons in the Church's liturgical calendar?
3. What is the Triduum?
4. What are the holy days of obligation in the United States?
5. What are the liturgical colors used in the Catholic Church? Give an example of when each is used.

Gregorian chant

For many centuries the Church used a special liturgical music called *Gregorian chant*. While the chant is sometimes still used today, it is better suited for Latin than it is for English. The chant is named after Pope Gregory I, who was pope from 590 to 604 and who promoted this type of chant. One legend says that the pope sent missionaries out to gather new music and told them, "Why should the devil have all the good songs?"

Gregorian chant is also called *plainsong*, because it doesn't use harmony. The chant is sung in one voice and in a free rhythm; that is, it doesn't have a beat or meter or measures like most other music. It is often also sung without accompaniment by musical instruments, even the organ.

Gregorian chant uses a different staff and different notation than is used for other music. The staff has four lines and a clef which indicates where *fah* is on the scale. Most of the notes are square and without a stem. It takes some practice to learn to read chant, but many choirs have learned to do so and do it well. A cantor often introduces a song by singing the first line, and some chants can be learned and sung by the assembly.

This type of chant actually developed from Hebrew chants, and after the time of Pope Gregory, the chant that bears his name was modified considerably. There now exist approximately 3000 compositions of Gregorian chant. Certain chants were written for each Sunday of the liturgical year, such as for the entrance antiphon and the Communion verse. The words are in Latin.

While Gregorian chant is less common for many people today, it is still the music of the Catholic Church in the West. *The Documents of Vatican II*, while respecting other forms of sacred music, said:

> The Church acknowledges Gregorian chant as proper to the Roman liturgy: therefore, other things being equal, it should be given pride of place in liturgical services.

"Constitution on the Sacred Liturgy," #116.

Optional activities

1. Listen to a recording of Gregorian chant; several have been released in recent years. If a translation is available, read the translation before listening. While listening, put yourself into a prayerful mood.

2. Ask a liturgical musician to teach the class a simple chant or to teach the class how to read the notation of Gregorian chant.

SACRAMENTS

sacrament

a liturgical celebration of the Christian faithful which is a visible sign of their encounter with God in Christ

The **sacraments** of the Church are special forms of liturgical celebration. For the believer the sacraments are more than mere religious activities or events. From a Catholic point of view, they are special ways in which God encounters us. They are special ways in which the gift of God's life in Christ is shared with us through the Church.

To understand the meaning and importance of the sacraments of the Church, it's helpful to recognize the differences among signs, symbols, rituals, and sacraments.

Signs

Our daily life is full of signs. A sign is something which communicates a single meaning. That meaning has little to do with the thing itself. It can be changed. Think of the various signs around you. The sign on the corner means stop. So too do the flashing blue lights on the car behind you on the freeway! The red, white, and blue pole outside a place of business means that you can get your hair cut there. The exit sign above the door indicates the way out. Signs do not bring about what they point to or signify. A stop sign doesn't stop you.

Signs surround you! And their meanings can change. There was a time, for example, when blue flashing lights on a car meant nothing; now they mean "Stop, police!" A new law changed their meaning. Other signs—like the exit sign—change with the culture. In Mexico, a sign showing the way out of a building would say "*SALIDA*," not "EXIT." Whatever the sign, you don't look for a deeper meaning.

Then do this

Create a sign that gives a clear message about you.

Symbols

Your world is also full of symbols. Symbols are different from signs. They aren't limited to one meaning. They can mean different things at different times—and different things to different people. Some examples come to mind: the flag, a bouquet of flowers, a crucifix, a wedding ring.

Symbols speak to the heart. Symbols are richer than signs, and they are powerful. Signs communicate information. Symbols affect us. They put us in touch with our deep feelings. Symbols bring about what they point to or signify. A kiss doesn't just point to love, it realizes it and expresses it.

Talk about it

Do humans need signs and symbols to express their faith? Why?

Each sacrament is the personal saving act of the risen Christ himself,
but realized in the visible form of an official act of the Church.
Edward Schillebeeckx

Catholicism has always believed in the sacramentality of creation.
Andrew Greeley

Rituals

A ritual is a human activity which uses signs and especially symbols to communicate a sense of meaning. A marvelous example is the opening ceremony at the Olympics. Through the magnificent display of marching teams, flags, lights, songs, and, of course, the Olympic flame, runners, sportsmanship, friendship, unity, and physical excellence are celebrated.

But one doesn't have to turn to something so grand to find a ritual. The embrace of friends, the team's high-five after winning a championship, standing in silence for the singing of the national anthem—all of these and many more show how richly decorated our world is with ritual celebrations. Religious rituals use signs and symbols to communicate. They help us communicate our response to God's love.

Then do this

Make an outline of the Catholic Mass, paying attention to its four main parts: gathering, listening, thanking, and being sent. Give a report on how all the parts relate to each other.

Flannery O'Connor
An author and her symbols

Flannery O'Connor was born in 1925 in Georgia, where she lived most of her life. At the age of 25, she was diagnosed with lupus, a debilitating disease which had already claimed the life of her father. Flannery died in 1964, having spent over a decade in declining health.

But that isn't the whole story. Flannery O'Connor was one of the best writers of the twentieth century. She wrote essays, short stories, and novels that were widely read and discussed. Her stories and characters were often bizarre and violent, but Flannery understood humans.

Her writing was strong on symbols and addressed not only sin, but free will and redemption; she accurately portrayed the struggle between good and evil and the victory of the good. Flannery used religious imagery throughout her writing. She once wrote:

Flannery O'Connor was a Catholic who received Communion every day. The religious themes she wrote about came out of her religious tradition. To her, life was religious from beginning to end.

When I know what the laws of the flesh and the physical really are, then I will know what God is. We know them as we see them, not as God sees them. For me it is the virgin birth, the Incarnation, the resurrection which are the true laws of the flesh and the physical. Death, decay, destruction are the suspension of these laws. I am always astonished at the emphasis the Church puts on the body. It is not the soul she says that will rise but the body, glorified . . . flesh and spirit united in peace.

Optional activities

1. Read something written by Flannery O'Connor. Share your reactions with the class.

2. Look for a novel or mystery or book of science fiction that uses religious imagery and symbols. Read the book and write a book report that addresses the religious significance in the story.

The purpose of the sacraments

The reason we have sacraments is to make us holy, to put us in touch with God, and to build up the body of Christ. The sacraments assume that we have faith, an openness to the presence of God who works through Jesus Christ, the risen Lord, and through the Holy Spirit. With words and objects, the sacraments teach us. They nourish, strengthen, and give expression to our faith.

In celebrating the sacraments, the Church's faith comes before the faith of the individual. God is present as gift, not as the result of personal faith. When the Church celebrates the sacraments, it professes the faith received from the apostles. Liturgy, accordingly, is an essential part of the living Tradition of the Church.

See the *Catechism of the Catholic Church*, #s 1123–1124.

1. Is God present in the sacramental life of the Church when you are distracted or uncooperative?

2. What does your participation in the sacraments of the Church teach you?

3. How do the sacraments of the Church link the faith community to the teaching of the apostles?

Sacraments

A sacrament is an action by which God shows something that cannot be seen, but which is very real and is an encounter with God. A sacrament in a loose sense very uniquely uses symbols to help people enter into a personal encounter. In a loose sense, a sacrament is an effective symbolic activity for encounter. In its usual sense, it is effective symbolic activity for an encounter between God and humans. For example, a handshake or a hug is a *sacrament* of friendship. By means of what can be seen (the handshake, the hug) friendship (which cannot be seen) is expressed—and there is a sharing of oneself with another person. And it turns out that God is present even in a "sacrament" in the loose sense.

Admittedly, the word *sacrament* is usually heard only in relation to Church, but it is a profoundly human word. It's rooted in the depth of our human experience. Only humans can engage in sacramental activity in the sense of effective symbolic activity of encounter—not because some authority or law said so, but because of the very nature of what makes something sacramental. Something is sacramental in the loose sense when the thing used demonstrates a reality which cannot be seen but is very real—*and* where there is personal encounter, or a sharing of self.

When the Church speaks of its sacraments, it means more than the signs or symbols it uses in religious rituals. In all of the sacraments of the Church, God encounters us personally.

Of course, someone can take part in a sacramental celebration without realizing that this encounter is taking place—just as someone can give us a hug without our understanding that the person is offering the gift of friendship. We can certainly look and even be bored when a sacrament is being celebrated. The reason for the boredom, however, is not God, but our attitude or unwillingness to be touched by God.

Talk about it

1. Do you go to church to get something out of it or to participate?

2. If you participate, do you get more out of being there? Why?

THE SEVEN SACRAMENTS OF THE CATHOLIC CHURCH

The Catholic Church has officially identified seven religious rituals which it refers to as sacramental celebrations. These are often called *the seven sacraments*. They are:

Baptism

Confirmation

Eucharist

Penance (or Reconciliation)

Anointing of the Sick

Matrimony

Holy Orders

The Catholic Church teaches that these seven are the Church's official sacraments. We will study each of them in the next chapters. There is no official order of listing, but the Church does clarify the sacraments' relationship to one another in this way:

Then do this

Ask an adult Catholic to explain any one of the seven sacraments. Compare the person's understanding with what you learn in this course.

The Sacraments of Christian Initiation

Baptism

Confirmation

Eucharist

The Sacraments of Healing

Penance (Reconciliation) *celebrates God's forgiveness and our return to life in Christ.*

Anointing of the Sick *celebrates union with God despite illness and in death.*

The Sacraments of Christian Identity

Matrimony *celebrates God's presence in the unconditional love of a couple.*

Holy Orders *celebrates Christ's leadership in the community of faith.*

REVIEW

1. What is a sign? A symbol? A ritual?

2. What is a sacrament?

3. What are the three categories of sacraments in the Catholic Church? What sacraments are in each category?

THE ROLE OF THE SACRAMENTS

Then do this

1. Make a collage on one of the seven sacraments of the Catholic Church.

2. In your presentation on the collage, explain how we meet Christ in this sacrament.

3. Save your collage until the sacrament is discussed in more detail in a future chapter. Then add to it.

paschal mystery
Jesus' suffering, death, and resurrection

There are generations of Catholics in the United States who have grown up with a limited understanding of the sacraments: "outward signs instituted by Christ to give grace." Although this definition isn't erroneous, it doesn't express the full richness of our encounter with God in the sacraments.

Jesus used natural symbols to communicate with others. And like other Jews, he was formed in a religious culture for which certain symbols and actions carried deep meaning. In our brief study of Judaism, we saw a few of these symbols and actions: water, bread, wine, oil, and the laying on of hands.

Each sacrament is identified with Jesus' life and ministry. In each of the sacraments, we celebrate the **paschal mystery**, Jesus' suffering, death, and resurrection.

Jesus: the ultimate sacrament

There is an important relationship among God the Father, Jesus, the Church, and the seven sacraments. In an earlier chapter, you studied how God is not distant and disinterested; rather, God seeks to make himself known in human history through the things of the world. In that sense, all creation is a sacrament of God's loving presence.

God chose to enter into salvation history in Jesus. Jesus is not just a sign of God or a symbol of God's presence. As understood in the Christian Tradition, Jesus is God living among us. For that reason, theologians speak of Jesus as the ultimate sacrament of God's presence. In other words, in Jesus, we meet God. In Jesus, God encounters us, embraces our world. In our encounter with Jesus, we encounter God.

And the Church is the sacrament of Christ in the world. It is the way Christ works in the world today, through the Holy Spirit. The Church is a living, breathing, reality because the Church is the body of Christ. Baptized believers always belong to Jesus in some way. They have heard the good news—who Jesus is. They believe him and seek to follow him. And the Church is made up of these real people. They and the risen Lord are united.

In a very profound sense, the Church is the arms, legs, eyes, and mouth of Jesus, the risen Lord. In our actions, we continue his ministry and mission of salvation in the world. That's why and how we are the Church; the Church is us! The Spirit is poured out in abundance by Jesus so that all believers, regardless of gender, social status, or abilities can share in their glorious identity as sons and daughters of God.

Write it down

When do you encounter Jesus?

> *In the sacraments nature participates in the process of salvation.*
> *Bread and wine, water and light, and all the great elements of*
> *nature become the bearers of spiritual meaning and saving power.*
> *Natural and spiritual powers are*
> *united—reunited—in the sacrament.*
>
> **Paul Tillich**

Sacramentals

The seven sacraments of the Catholic Church are really important. They form the backbone of Christian life for Catholics. The Church also uses other less central things to express faith and keep us in touch with God. These "things" are sometimes called **sacramentals** and include blessings, special objects, and ritual actions and prayers. Here's an incomplete list:

- Blessings for people and of objects
- The Sign of the Cross
- Holy water
- Crucifixes and crosses
- Statues, pictures, and images
- Medals of Christ or a saint
- Body gestures like genuflecting, bowing, standing, kneeling
- Incense and candles
- The rosary
- The Advent wreath
- The Christmas crèche

Sacramentals don't replace sacraments, nor are they anywhere near as important. They are usually associated with private devotions, rather than community worship. If they are seen as a magical means to obtain God's favor, to in a sense bribe God, they are being misused. Sacramentals and private devotions are used correctly if they help us grow in faith and lead us to the worship, sacraments, and good work of the Church. Sacramentals and devotions need to reflect a wholesome relationship with God and must respect our human dignity.

sacramental
sacred signs—blessings, special objects, and ritual actions and prayers

Then do this
Tour your school, church, or home.

1. Make a list of all the sacramentals you identify there.
2. Next to the name of each item, explain what that sacramental is saying.

Your name, O God, like your praise,
reaches to the ends of the earth.
Psalm 48:10

REVIEW

1. What is the paschal mystery?
2. Who or what is the ultimate sacrament?
3. What is a sacramental?

CONCLUSION

For the believer it truly is not we who live, but Christ who lives in us. We are walking sacraments, individually and as a faith community. In us God's saving and redeeming love is at work, even in our homes, on the playing fields, and in our classrooms. Christian is who we are. We are the sacrament of Jesus, the risen Lord! Consider the following story:

Called to give

This story has been told in a variety of ways with different characters. Whether or not the story is factually true is not important.

A little girl was dying. Her six-year-old brother had previously recovered from the same disease. The doctor told the boy that only a transfusion of his blood would save his sister's life. "Are you willing to give her your blood?" the doctor asked.

The boy's eyes showed his fear, but after a brief time he said, "All right, Doctor. I'll do it."

After the transfusion the boy asked the doctor, "When do I die?" That was when the doctor realized why the child had been fearful—he had thought that by giving his blood he would give his life to his sister.

Optional activities

1. If you were the sister in the story, how would you react when you found out that your brother had been willing to give up his life for you? Taking the part of the sister, write a letter to your brother.

2. Write a very short story about what it means to truly live as a Christian.

Just as Jesus blessed the people with the Holy Spirit, so too does the Church. Just as Jesus nourished us with the Bread of Life, so does the Church. Just as Jesus forgave sins, so too must the Church be an instrument of reconciliation and peace in the world.

Just as Jesus was the fulfillment of God's unconditional love, so too do married couples in a special way commit themselves to this kind of love. Just as Jesus was the shepherd of his people, so too are ordained ministers in the Church. Just as Jesus conquered death, so too does the Church celebrate this same triumph when someone is in danger of death or suffering a serious illness.

In each and every sacrament of the Church, God gives us his very life. We meet God in Jesus Christ. Sacraments are our encounter with God in the person of Jesus, who brings us saving love and grace.

Christian, recognize your dignity.

St. Leo the Great

Then do this

Design a prayer service to be used with the class or at home.

Words you should know

Advent	**Ordinary Time**
Christmas	**paschal mystery**
creed	**pope**
diocese	**Reformation**
Easter	**sacrament**
holy days of obligation	**sacramental**
Lent	**Tradition**
liturgical calendar	**Triduum**
liturgy	

CHAPTER 10

The SACRAMENTS of CHRISTIAN INITIATION

The Word of the Lord

Jesus came and said to them, "Go therefore and make disciples of all nations, baptising them in the name of the Father and of the Son and of the Holy Spirit. . . ."

FROM THE GOSPEL ACCORDING TO MATTHEW, SEE 28:16–20.

CHAPTER OVERVIEW

• *Becoming a Christian*

• *Christian initiation*

• *The experience of initiation*

• *Baptism*

• *Confirmation*

• *Eucharist*

• *Parts of the Mass*

Make a joyful noise to the LORD,
all the earth.

Let Us Pray

Worship the Lord with gladness;
come into his presence with singing.
Know that the LORD is God.
It is he that made us, and we are his;
we are his people, and the sheep of his pasture.
Enter his gates with thanksgiving,
and his courts with praise.
Give thanks to him, bless his name.
For the LORD is good;
his steadfast love endures forever,
and his faithfulness to all generations.

PSALM 100

BECOMING A CHRISTIAN

In the last chapter, we talked about sacraments. We said that Catholics believe that God meets us in the sacraments, that sacraments are more than just celebrations or ceremonies. Catholics believe that God's creative and saving love is present in the sacraments. Through them, the Church is an instrument of God's love. Through them, God meets us and brings about our salvation.

The sacraments of the Church celebrate our Christian identity within a community of faith. They celebrate what God is doing for us as we search for happiness and fullness of life. The sacraments are faith responses to the active, living presence of God. They are all related to being Christian.

If someone were to ask you, "How does someone become a Christian?" what would your answer be? By being baptized? By making a personal commitment to Christ? By following the Lord's commands? In a sense, all of these are true, and it's important to recognize that Christians are made, not born. That is to say, you don't become a Christian simply by being born into a Christian environment. Life in Christ is not inherited. It calls for a personal response to God's love.

Conversion to following Jesus doesn't happen automatically; it takes time. First God touches your heart. Your faith community (Church family) shares its faith with you. Then you make the decision to respond. But becoming a Christian is not a one-time decision or action, with no further decisions or actions.

As Catholics, we believe that becoming a Christian is a process with lifelong consequences. We talk about being "initiated" into Christ. And there's more to that than just being baptized.

Talk about it

How *does* someone become a Christian?

Then do this

Invite someone who doesn't belong to any Church to attend Mass with you. Talk about the experience with the person. Then, in class, share the questions and reactions of the person (no names necessary).

Catechumenate

In the Catholic tradition adults who become Christians travel through a series of stages. This period of preparation for the Sacraments of Christian Initiation is known as the **catechumenate**. The Church provides for a gradual initiation into the Christian faith through various rites. The rituals for this process of conversion are known as the **Rite of Christian Initiation of Adults**.

This journey of conversion and initiation can be rapid or slow. The following elements are always present: the proclamation of the word, acceptance of the gospel's call to conversion, a profession of faith, Baptism, Confirmation, and the Eucharist.

See the *Catechism of the Catholic Church,* #s 1229–1230, 1232.

1. What is an initiation? What is a rite?

2. Does your parish community welcome new Christians through the catechumenate? If so, who is involved in the process?

3. Why does conversion take time?

4. Why are each of the noted elements necessary?

catechumenate
the time of preparation for an unbaptized person seeking identity with Christ and membership in the Church

Rite of Christian Initiation of Adults
the ceremonies marking the conversion of and initiation process for new members of the Church

Dorothy Day
Conversion and action

When Dorothy Day died in 1980, the *New York Times* described her as the most influential person in the history of American Catholicism. But that isn't how Dorothy started out. Born in 1897 in Brooklyn, Dorothy grew up in Oakland, CA, and Chicago. After two years of college in Illinois, Dorothy and her family moved to New York, where she went to work at a Socialist newspaper.

Soon Dorothy began writing for a Communist paper. Over the next few years, in addition to working for the Communist cause, Dorothy campaigned for the right to vote for women and against the First World War. Her personal life was less certain; she married, divorced, and then had a child outside of marriage.

Her daughter Tamara became the turning point in Dorothy's life. Around the time of her pregnancy, Dorothy met some dedicated Catholics who were trying to provide for the material and spiritual needs of some of the poorest people in one of the boroughs of New York City. With their help Dorothy took a long, hard look at her life and began the process of conversion. She and her daughter were baptized.

Less than a year after Dorothy's Baptism, the world changed when the stock market crashed. Unemployment spread rapidly, and millions of people faced dire poverty and even homelessness. Dorothy did what she could to assist those in need around her. Then in 1932 she met a very unusual man, Peter Maurin. Peter recognized Dorothy's talent and compassion and encouraged her to join him in publishing a small newspaper that would acquaint people with the Catholic Church's social justice teachings. Thus began *The Catholic Worker*, a newspaper that sold for one cent.

But Dorothy believed in practicing what she preached. In 1935 she began a house of hospitality in New York City. There people were provided with food, clothing, and shelter, and the assistance they needed to get back on their feet. Because the Depression was still battering the economy, houses of hospitality soon opened in many other cities. By the time World War II began, there were six communal farms and forty houses.

Dorothy's strong pacifism reemerged and continued through the Korean War and the Vietnam War. She also supported the cause of migrant workers who demonstrated for unionization. Through all the long years of Dorothy's ministry to those who were poor and oppressed, Catholic Worker houses continued to spread. Today there are about 130 Catholic Worker communities. Members of these groups provide for those in need and protest injustice, war, and violence wherever they find them.

Optional activities

1. Watch the video *Entertaining Angels: The Dorothy Day Story*. Discuss the signs of Dorothy's conversion, as portrayed in the video.

2. Call and arrange to visit a Catholic Worker house of hospitality at mealtime. Bring along some food to share, and join in the conversation.

Pretend you want to become a Christian. And imagine you haven't been raised around Christians. You haven't heard the gospel. If you looked in "slow motion" at becoming a Christian, you would see this:

The work of the Spirit

God's Spirit has been at work in your life inviting you since the moment of your conception. You were made in God's image. He has given you the gift of faith. That means that God wants you to be open to his love. Your hunger for God's love gradually causes you to search for God and his gift of salvation.

The work of the Church

You hear the good news of God's love in Jesus. You see the happiness of people who believe in Jesus, the risen Lord, those who have found fullness of life (salvation). The Church proclaims the gospel. And through the gospel, God unites you with the community of believers—those who have heard the good news and seek in the best way they can to live it. The Church invites you to "come and see" for yourself. You say "yes." You attend Church services and perhaps even some special sessions where people talk about their Christian faith.

Then do this
Interview someone who has become a Catholic through the Rite of Christian Initiation of Adults. Ask the person to explain the process to you and to share how he or she felt about the process. Report to the class.

Every story of conversion is the story of a blessed defeat.

C.S. Lewis

Personal faith

The truth of the gospel touches your heart. The community of believers attracts you. This is because the Spirit of God is already at work in your heart—the same Spirit who is at work in the hearts of the members of the community of faith.

The more you open your heart to this good news about Jesus, the more peace you experience. You begin to realize that this Jesus truly does lead you to life! He puts you in touch with "the God who saves," who makes you whole! Hearing what God does and promises you in Jesus, you come to believe, to give your heart to God. You too want to center your life on God and share in the faith of the community. (This part of the process of becoming Christian may take some time.)

The Church celebrates

Gradually, you show that you believe and that you are ready to join this community of believers. Inspired by the Spirit of God and attracted by the witness of the people, you want to "join the Church." The Church then celebrates what has been developing in your life: a relationship with Jesus Christ and his community of disciples. The community celebrates your new-found faith, assuring you of what truly has happened in your life. You profess your faith and are initiated into a saving relationship with Christ in his community of believers.

The Church does this by means of a single ritual which has three distinct, but not separate, parts—or moments of celebration. All three parts are necessary for the complete celebration of your Christian identity and your belonging to Christ and the Christian community.

- A bath of conversion (Baptism)
- A laying on of hands and an anointing with oil (Confirmation)
- A fellowship meal (Eucharist)

Talk about it
What in the Christian community attracts you and motivates you to be more Christian?

Whenever we penetrate to the heart of things,
we always find a mystery.
Life and all that goes with it is unfathomable. . . .
Knowledge of life is recognition of the mysterious.
Albert Schweitzer

I would rather live in a world where my life
is surrounded by mystery
than live in a world so small
that my mind could comprehend it.
Henry Emerson Fosdick

Life in Christ

From this time on, you continue to join the community for further Christian growth and regular participation in the Eucharist. You put your faith into practice. You live in a way that gives witness to the salvation you have received from God in Christ by the work of the Spirit.

Write it down

How are you "becoming a Christian"?

Your journey of faith has brought you to a relationship with Christ through his community of believers, the Church. What was originally just a vague feeling of God's presence (the work of the Spirit) has blossomed into a personal relationship. Your path of conversion isn't finished though—total conversion to God's ways is a lifelong process, a lifelong response to God's love.

You can see what it means to become a Christian. The process you just studied is the norm or model for understanding all aspects of Christian initiation. Even if you were baptized as an infant or have celebrated Confirmation at a later time, this process is the guiding light for understanding what these sacraments mean.

Becoming a Christian is more than celebrating a ritual. It's more than "good behavior." Becoming a Christian means living in the mystery of God, Father, Son, and Holy Spirit. It means sharing life with a community of faith. God's Spirit fills that community. That community celebrates God's blessings with a grateful heart and unites itself with the sacrifice of Jesus' gift of himself to his heavenly Father.

REVIEW

1. What is the Rite of Christian Initiation of Adults?

2. What is conversion?

3. What is the work of the Spirit?

4. What is the work of the Church?

5. Which three sacraments are necessary for full Christian initiation?

CHRISTIAN INITIATION

The Sacraments of Christian Initiation—life in Christ—begin with **Baptism** when the Spirit of God unites you to the community of faith. You then celebrate the Sacraments of Confirmation and Eucharist. The Eucharist is the sacramental completion of your initiation along your journey of faith.

The Catholic Church calls Baptism, Confirmation, and Eucharist the Sacraments of Christian Initiation. It teaches that these sacraments cannot be understood as separate celebrations; they must be seen in relationship to one another. Even when these sacraments are celebrated individually at different times during a person's faith journey, preparation for each of them needs to take note of their relationship to each other.

Baptism
the Sacrament of Initiation that makes us children of God and members of the Church and that takes away all sin, original and personal

Sacraments of Initiation

The unity of the Sacraments of Christian Initiation must be maintained. The Sacrament of **Confirmation** completes the grace of Baptism. The Sacrament of Confirmation binds those who are baptized to the Church and strengthens them with the Holy Spirit in a special way. They become witnesses of Christ, with the responsibility to share the faith by word and action and to defend it.

See the *Catechism of the Catholic Church*, #1285.

1. Why should the Sacraments of Christian Initiation be viewed together?

2. How can a teenager witness to his or her faith?

Confirmation
the Sacrament of Initiation that celebrates the work of the Holy Spirit who completes and seals our Baptism and leads us to the Eucharist

THE EXPERIENCE OF INITIATION

The Sacrament of Baptism must be understood in the context of initiation. If you have ever been initiated into a group, you know that forms of initiation carry far different meanings. The Church's celebration of *Christian* initiation is a specific form of an experience which is common in our culture. When you hear the word *initiation*, you may think of having to do something very awkward or embarrassing—like running around in strange clothes! Initiation need not be awkward or embarrassing, and Christian initiation isn't!

Usually the following things are true of initiations:
• The person qualifies to be a member of the group.
• There is some form of preparation through which the person learns about what is happening.
• There is a rite of some kind.
• As a result of the rite, the person becomes identified with the group.
• As a member of the group, the person relates to others in a new way.
• The person shares responsibility for the work or mission of the group.

Talk about it

1. Other than sacraments, what initiation rites are part of our culture?

2. Other than sacraments, have you ever been through an initiation ceremony? What happened? What difference did it make in your life?

3. What do other initiation ceremonies have in common with the Sacraments of Initiation? How do they differ from the sacraments?

We make our decisions, and then our decisions turn around and make us.
F.W. Boreham

Let's take a look at how these things are part of Christian initiation:

Qualifying and Readiness

A person qualifies for a relationship with Christ simply because he or she is a person. It has nothing to do with intelligence, looks, money, social status, or even moral excellence. What qualifies a person for Christian initiation is the fact that he or she is a person created in the image and likeness of God. Everyone qualifies just by being a person, but the Church makes sure that there is evidence of faith present, an openness to what God is doing.

The Church doesn't baptize people without preparing them (or, in the case of infants, preparing their parents). People need to be able to relate to what they're doing, what Baptism is, what is being celebrated. This period of preparation aims at helping the person relate to what is celebrated—the gift of God's saving love. The Catholic Church has always insisted that it's fine to baptize even infant children of Christian parents, because these infants can relate very well to the absolutely unconditional gift of God's saving love in Christ. Salvation is an absolutely free gift offered to them even before they know it.

Sacramental celebration

Christian initiation is celebrated in three closely related rituals—Baptism, Confirmation, and Eucharist. Often just the Rite of Baptism may be celebrated in the case of infants and small children, but something is missing in the life of the Christian if the other two rites are not eventually celebrated. Much like a beautiful piece of music which has different parts, the three parts of Christian initiation form a single unit.

Identity

Through Baptism, the person begins a journey of faith in union with Jesus Christ. The person's identity becomes that of a Christian, a living reflection of Christ—the person becomes united with Christ. From the moment of Baptism, the question is not whether one is a Christian, but how well one lives as a Christian. Baptism makes the baptized person a member of Christ's body, the Church, and an ambassador for Christ—one through whom Christ Jesus brings God's saving love to the world.

Ministry of service

The baptized person shares in the work of the Church, which is the privilege of sharing God's gift of unconditional love. This love is expressed in many ways, most of all in daily life at school, in the home, on the recreation field, or in the place of business. It is expressed too in the ministries of the Church.

Then do this

Ask a number of parents who have young children why they presented their children for Baptism. What are their expectations of this sacrament? Write an essay in response.

Then do this

Make a poster that shows the relationship between Baptism, Confirmation, and Eucharist.

Then do this

Borrow a Baptism ritual book from your parish. Study the Rite of Baptism and make a brief presentation on it.

REVIEW

1. What happens in Baptism?

2. What does Confirmation complete? To what does it lead us?

3. What qualifies a person for Christian initiation?

Pierre Toussaint
A ministry of service

Pierre Toussaint was born a slave in 1766 on an island off Haiti. His master, Jean Bérard du Pithon, saw to it that Pierre was baptized a Catholic and learned to read and write. In 1787, because of unrest on the island, Pierre's master moved with his family and slaves to New York City.

Once in New York, Pierre moved out of domestic service and became an apprentice to a hairdresser. Pierre became well known for his creative and beautiful hairstyles and was employed by many wealthy people. Unexpectedly, Jean Bérard died while on a trip back to Haiti. Because of Bérard's death and the loss of much of his wealth in the unrest of his home island, his widow, Marie, was left destitute. Pierre then took it on himself to support his master's widow. Twenty years later, before her death, Marie freed Pierre.

While still a slave, Pierre worked hard to help refugees who flooded to New York from his native island. After he himself was freed, Pierre purchased the freedom of many slaves from the island, including that of Juliette Noël, who became his wife. Together, they opened their home to black children who had been orphaned; they eventually raised funds for an orphanage. Pierre provided money and medical care for former slaves and former slave owners alike.

Pierre helped a servant in Baltimore, Fanny Montpensier, begin a religious community for black women—the Oblate Sisters of Providence. Pierre attended daily Mass and was known far and wide for his charity and joyfulness. He died in 1853. The process to have Pierre Toussaint named a saint is well under way.

Optional activities

1. Research another black saint. Write a report or give a presentation to the class on the person.

2. Find out what is happening in Haiti today, including the role of the Church there. Present your findings to the class.

3. Read up on black Catholics in this country; see, for example, the Internet and publications from the United States Catholic Conference. Summarize your research.

BAPTISM

Baptism is the first step in Christian initiation, which is completed in Confirmation and Eucharist. Baptism is the Church's celebration of God's relationship to you and your relationship to God and the Church. Baptism is about God guiding you to a community of faith where God's saving love continues to embrace you.

In Baptism, we become children of God and members of the Church. We share in God's own life—grace. All sins—original sin and, for those who have reached the age of reason, personal sin—are forgiven. We share in the common priesthood of all believers; that is, we share in Christ's mission as priest, prophet, and king.

God's gift of life in Christ celebrated in Baptism is a recognition of God's unconditional gift of love and salvation. Through a relationship with Christ, you are promised ultimate happiness and eternal life. The gift has no strings attached to it.

At the same time, the Christian life isn't automatic or magic. Although baptized, you can still be an "unbeliever." The parish record of your Baptism may confirm the fact that you have been baptized, but it doesn't record your claimed faith. The offered gift requires a grateful response which is put into action by the way you live.

Talk about it

1. Why does the Church baptize people?

2. What does Baptism really mean?

The signs and symbols of Baptism

- Water—Water is the natural symbol for life and cleansing. It is also the salvation history of death to sin and birth to Christ. (Water is an essential element of the sacrament.)

- Words—The minister says, "I baptize you in the name of the Father, and of the Son, and of the Holy Spirit." (This is the second essential element of the sacrament.)

- Oil (of catechumens)—The presence of the Holy Spirit makes us slippery to the grasp of sin and strong in our faith.

- Oil (chrism)—The baptized person is anointed, sharing in the priestly, prophetic, and kingly ministry of Christ, the "Anointed One."

- White garment—Freed from sin, we have become a "new" creation in Christ.

- Lighted candle—The baptized person shares in the Light who is Christ (symbolized by the Easter candle) and is charged to be a light for others on their way to God.

REVIEW

1. What kind of response does Baptism require?

2. What are the two essential elements of the Sacrament of Baptism?

3. What are the other signs and symbols of Baptism? What is the reason for each?

CONFIRMATION

Remember, we said that Christian initiation is made up of three sacraments, three celebrations, even if they are separated in time:

- A bath of conversion (Baptism)
- An imposition of hands and an anointing with oil (Confirmation)
- A fellowship meal (Eucharist)

These moments of celebration need to happen in the context of faith. Without faith, they don't mean anything. Faith comes from the Holy Spirit at work in your heart. This happens long before you are even aware of it.

Baptism celebrates the gift of the Spirit in your life as God's child. After Baptism the work of the Spirit continues, uniting you with the community of faith. This is what Confirmation celebrates. The Spirit, in fact, is the driving force behind all of the celebrations of Christian initiation. The Spirit leads you to unity with others in Christ. This is especially true when the community gathers for Eucharist.

In the early Church a person's Christian initiation was celebrated as a single ceremony at the Easter Vigil, the night-long watch before the sunrise celebration of Christ's resurrection. As the Christian community grew in numbers, this changed. It had always been important for the bishop to be there for Christian initiation because the bishop stood for the whole Church—and the baptized person was seen as united not just with the local community, but with the entire Church.

In the Church in the West, with so many members and so many initiations, the bishop couldn't be at the Easter Vigil everywhere at once. So people waited for the bishop to get to them. Thus there arose a separation in time of a week or so between the celebration of Baptism and the anointing by the bishop that we now understand to be Confirmation. It was necessary to celebrate Confirmation before sharing in the Eucharist.

As the Christian community grew even more, this anointing was celebrated even later. Over the centuries, most Christians were baptized as babies and later completed their initiation, usually at age twelve. The order of Baptism–Confirmation–Eucharist was the usual form of celebration in the Catholic Church in the West until 1910.

In 1910, for reasons that had nothing to do with the unity of the Sacraments of Christian Initiation, Pope Pius X decreed that children could receive Communion at the age of discretion, that is, when they could relate to right and wrong and understand what they were doing (usually about the age of seven to nine). So children started making their "First Communion" around second grade, and Confirmation was left for later. This created a situation in which Confirmation had to be explained in itself, separated from Christian initiation. As we'll see, these explanations aren't fully adequate.

Then do this

If your family has photos of relatives who lived in the early years of the twentieth century, look through the photos for pictures of First Communions or Confirmations. Try to judge the age of the person at the time. If possible, talk to older family members about the individuals.

The signs and symbols of Confirmation

The symbols the bishop uses for Confirmation are significant:

- The **anointing with oil** signifies the life-giving power of the Spirit.
- The **laying on of hands** signifies the sharing of the Spirit with this person.
- **Words**—The person being confirmed makes a profession of faith. The bishop prays for those being confirmed and then anoints them on the forehead, saying, "Be sealed with the Gift of the Holy Spirit."

Talk about it

1. When is the symbol of the laying on of hands used in our culture? In our religion?

2. What does the laying on of hands mean in Confirmation?

The role of the bishop

The bishop is the main minister of all three Sacraments of Christian Initiation. Priests and deacons share in his ministry. In the Catholic Church, the bishop is a sacrament of our unity; he is a successor of the apostles. Where the bishop is present, the Church is present.

The bishop's sacramental ministry is a sign of the life and ministry of the whole Church. The person who is initiated is integrated into that worldwide Church and its ministry, not just into the local parish community. For that reason, except for the Easter Vigil, the bishop usually comes to each parish for the celebration of the Sacrament of Confirmation.

1. When did your bishop last come to your parish? For what did he come?

2. In addition to presiding at the Sacrament of Confirmation, what does your bishop do?

God's Grandeur

The world is charged with the grandeur of God.
　It will flame out, like shining from shook foil;
　It gathers to a greatness, like the ooze of oil
Crushed. Why do men then now not reck his rod?
Generations have trod, have trod, have trod;
　And all is seared with trade; bleared, smeared with toil;
　And wears man's smudge and shares man's smell: the soil
Is bare now, nor can foot feel, being shod.
And for all this, nature is never spent;
　There lives the dearest freshness deep down things;
And though the last lights off the black West went
　Oh, morning, at the brown brink eastward, springs—
Because the Holy Ghost over the bent
　World broods with warm breast and with ah! bright wings.

Gerard Manley Hopkins

Optional activities

1. Illustrate this poem, and share your illustration with the class.

2. Write a poem of your own on the work of the Holy Spirit.

3. Page through a hymnal for songs that refer to the Holy Spirit. Share these with the class and lead a discussion on how the Spirit is portrayed in each hymn.

Approaches to Confirmation

Over the centuries, "What goes on in Confirmation?" became a key question. Various explanations were given at different times in history. Any explanation, separate from Christian initiation, is inadequate, however. Here are some of the understandings that developed, accompanied by some comments:

"The person gets the Holy Spirit in Confirmation."

This view seems to say that the Spirit was not given in Baptism—which is not true. The Holy Spirit *is* given in Baptism. The Spirit is also given in each of the other sacraments of the Church, and the Spirit is active outside the sacraments as well. The Sacrament of Confirmation has no special hold on the Spirit. Some parents believe that their child's life as a maturing person will be guided by the Spirit only if the child is confirmed. Confirmation doesn't start the process or give the gift of the Spirit for the first or last time—the Spirit is already with you and has been since the moment of your conception!

"Confirmation wakes up the Spirit given in Baptism."

The Spirit of God doesn't sleep! God is always creative and active in your life and in the world through the Holy Spirit. Surely, the Church doesn't need to wake up God!

"Confirmation gives the person more of the Spirit."

All the Church's sacraments celebrate the mystery of God's presence by the **indwelling** of the Holy Spirit, but we cannot cause God's presence to be added to. You cannot get *more* of the Spirit. You can become more aware of and affected by the Spirit acting in a special effective way in the sacrament.

indwelling
the presence of an inner activating or guiding force or spirit or power

"Confirmation makes us soldiers of Christ."

In other words, the Spirit prompts you to give witness to your Christian faith. But isn't it true that the Spirit prompts Christians of any age to give witness to who they are in Jesus Christ? Christian witness is a responsibility that began with your Baptism! It is not true that this responsibility is a result of being confirmed, since the responsibility was yours from Baptism on.

"Confirmation celebrates maturity in Christian faith."

As you mature, you look for signs that you are welcomed by the adult community. In our society, experiences like dating and getting a driver's license are such signs. These experiences have their place. Confirmation, though, really is not primarily a "coming of age" experience or a commitment-making event to mark a person's passage into adulthood.

Besides, the sacraments, including Confirmation, are not mainly *our* actions. They are God's actions, or, better said, God is the main one at work in the sacraments. This doesn't take us off the hook in terms of action, however. The sure sign that you have claimed your faith, accepted your life in Christ, is the witness of your life of service and ministry to others. There are hundreds of service opportunities in any community of faith, and those "confirmed in the faith" recognize their responsibility to be doers as well as believers!

Then do this
Ask ten people of different ages to explain what Confirmation is about. Record their answers and summarize them for the class. Discuss the areas represented by the answers.

> *E*very time we say "I believe in the Holy Spirit," we mean
> that we believe there is a living God able and willing
> to enter human personality and change it.
>
> **J.B. Phillips**

Gifts of the Spirit

The most important gift of the Holy Spirit, the source of all holiness, is grace, our sharing in God's life. God's saving presence in our lives is also shown in other gifts of the Spirit. These gifts bring us into contact with God's work of salvation. They help us work together for the good of others and for the growth of the Church.

The Spirit of God is active in all the sacraments of the Church. Through the Spirit, we also receive other graces or **charisms**. Some of these charisms or gifts are unusual (such as miracles), while others are quite ordinary. The gifts of the Spirit, however, are not given just to an individual; they must be used in love for the good of the Church.

See the *Catechism of the Catholic Church*, #2003.

1. What signs of the Spirit's presence can you see in those around you? How do you know that the Spirit is with *you*?

2. What are the seven gifts of the Holy Spirit (see the *Catechism* #1831)? What does each one mean?

charism
a special gift of service

Write it down
What is your special *charism*—the special gift from God that enables you to help people?

Confirmation and initiation

None of the previously stated understandings of Confirmation is fully satisfactory. The reason they are all inadequate is that Confirmation cannot stand alone. You cannot answer the question "What's happening in Confirmation?" if you think of Confirmation separate from the whole experience of Christian initiation. Christian initiation is our concern here because Christian initiation is *initiation into Christ*. The question "What's happening in Christian initiation?" is actually, "What does it mean to be a Christian?"

So a good understanding of Confirmation includes these important points:

• God is the primary one at work in the sacrament.

• The rite of anointing with oil and laying on of hands is very important within *the whole* of Christian initiation.

• The work of the Spirit closely connects one's personal Christian identity, given in Baptism, to the identity of Christ's community, the Church.

• The ritual role of the bishop is the ministry of unity.

• Conversion and maturity in the Christian life are open-ended.

If you keep these points in mind, you can better understand the role of the Holy Spirit in your life. The Spirit is not a thing to be controlled. Rather, the Spirit is God's presence within us (individually) and among us (as community). Therefore, you cannot measure readiness for Confirmation by knowledge of your religion, by perfect moral behavior, by the completion of service projects, or by a desire for welcome by the community. At any age, you are ready for the presence of the Holy Spirit. You are ready for a life in Christ.

Confirmation celebrates the work of the Spirit in your life. The Spirit unites you as a baptized person to the Church, where your Christian life is nurtured. Christianity is a communal faith. The Spirit unites you with that community and continues to breathe life into you. Without this work of the Spirit, the Church is without a soul, without life.

Talk about it

How does God's Holy Spirit make its presence known in your life?

Confirmation is the sacrament of the common priesthood of the laity.

Gerald Vann OP

Signs of the Spirit

Here are some ways that the Holy Spirit is at work in your life:

- The Spirit makes you sure of God's presence with you. The Spirit makes known to your heart that God loves you always and forever.

- God's Spirit is involved in the ongoing creation of you. The Spirit always leads you toward goodness and keeps you close to God.

- The Spirit unites you in a deep way with all people. After all, it is the same Spirit who works in everyone.

- The Spirit makes known to your heart that you are unique, one of a kind, loved by God, and that in a unique way, through you, God's love is given to the world.

- The Spirit lets you know that God is always with you. God is at work in you at all times and everywhere. You are never alone.

Write it down

What are the signs seen by others that tell them that the Holy Spirit is present in your life?

REVIEW

1. Why did Confirmation become a separate sacramental celebration in the Church in the West?

2. What are the signs and symbols of Confirmation? What does each signify?

3. Other than Christian initiation, what approaches to Confirmation have occurred over the centuries?

4. What is a charism?

5. What concepts does a good understanding of Confirmation include?

EUCHARIST

First Communion

the first reception of the Eucharist, which should properly be celebrated as the completion of Christian initiation

Eucharist

the sacrament of Jesus' presence under the form of bread and wine; also, the Mass

Most Catholics in the United States today are "cradle Catholics"—that is, they were baptized Catholic when they were babies. That means that they were initiated according to the pattern of Christian initiation that followed the decision of Pope Pius X in 1910. They were baptized as infants and made their **First Communion** in about the second grade. They were then confirmed years later—if they were confirmed at all.

The Eucharist is not just a sacrament you start receiving at some certain time. The **Eucharist** is a sacramental celebration in which you are brought by the Spirit into communion with what God the Father is doing in Jesus Christ, the risen Lord.

The celebration of the Eucharist is more than a remembrance. Catholics believe that at Mass we take part in the action of Jesus at the Last Supper and his later crucifixion, an action that continues today. The risen Lord is present at our meal.

At a natural human level, we see that at the Last Supper, Jesus gathered with his apostles at a meal much like many other meals he had shared with them. In retrospect, however, we recognize that what Jesus did at this last meal was a prophetic statement about the significance of his life. His breaking of the sacred Bread and sharing in the Cup of Salvation that evening were actions which pointed to the breaking of his body and the spilling of his blood—the sacrifice of his life—that would take place the next day on the cross.

Sharing bread

Alone, deep in thought, God searched for the way by which he could be among his people. They were not yet ready, he thought, for him to make himself completely and totally known to them. He needed a sign, an action, some way of helping them understand that he was indeed with them. And then it came—with a flash of heavenly light that startled even his closest advisors. Sharing. That's what it would be. If his people could be taught to share, then they would know that he shared his love with them and that he was with them. But what was it that they were to share? . . .

God looked down on his people once again. There they were, his people, and they did not know that he loved them. . . . That was it!!! Of course!!! They could share bread. They could share bread and still have plenty for themselves. . . . They could share bread and not lose it. . . . They could share bread and be together when they did. They could be happy and *not hungry. They could be strength for one another. And so God made known to them through their leaders that they should share their bread with one another.*

And the people did as they were told—they shared their bread. And from that day on they knew that God was with them.

Joseph J. Juknialis, *Winter Dreams and other such friendly dragons.*

Optional activities

1. Bring different kinds of bread to share with the class (check for food allergies). Lead a discussion on the reasons why bread is important to the Jewish people and important to Christians.

2. Find another story about bread to share with the class. Discuss the story and relate it to this section of the chapter.

Participation in the Eucharist

When we are at Mass, we should not act like strangers or silently look on, as if we were at a play. We should learn to understand the rites and prayers and actively participate. We should be conscious of what we are doing at Mass and should participate with devotion. At Mass we should let God's word teach us. We should be nourished by Holy Communion. Along with the priest who offers Christ's Body and Blood, we should offer ourselves as living sacrifices of praise. Day by day we should draw closer to God and to each other.

See *The Documents of Vatican II*, "Constitution on the Sacred Liturgy," #48.

1. What does it mean to participate in the Mass?
2. Why does it matter if you participate or not?
3. What can you do to participate more fully at Mass?

Roots of the Eucharist

The Eucharist, the Mass, has important historical and religious roots. What Jesus did at the Last Supper has been continued by Christians in some fashion ever since. The meal Jesus took part in at the Last Supper was rooted in his religious faith. In Jesus' day, meals were times for the celebration of God's loving care. In the cultural setting of Jesus' time, we can identify common elements of a meal that had deeper meaning for people of faith.

The people prepared for their meal.

It wasn't just the hunger of their bodies that brought people to the table; it was also the hunger of their hearts—to know God's love in their lives.

Those who gathered for the meal saw themselves as God's people.

They were a nation, a chosen people of faith. They shared a common identity and history of salvation through which God had become known and had given them a promising future.

The central food and drink at the Jewish meal were bread and wine.

At Passover time, the unleavened bread or matzo reminded the Jewish people of the Exodus when God delivered the Hebrews from slavery in Egypt. The wine always brought back memories and mixed emotions: the joy of being favored by God and the suffering that sometimes came with being faithful to God's way.

Talk about it
What is the relationship of the Mass to the Last Supper?

> *"Take, eat; this is my body."*
>
> **Matthew 26:26**

The ritual sharing of the bread at the beginning of the meal was important.

This action expressed in simple fashion the meaning and significance of the meal. The bread was blessed: "Blessed are you, Lord our God, for the gift of bread; it will be strength for our life." The bread then was shared. This action of eating the shared bread in silence was a form of communion. Through this action, those who ate the bread showed their commitment to become more truly the people of God. The people knew that when they were truly God's people, God would surely reign. The sharing of the bread was thus a sign of the approaching reign of God.

According to Scripture, when Jesus blessed, broke, and shared the bread at the Last Supper, he identified the bread and the bread-breaking rite with himself. "This is my body which will be given up for you." In other words, those who eat with Jesus become united with him and are part of the kingdom that God brought about in him! Those who eat the Bread of the Eucharist commit themselves to becoming more faithful people of God.

The most important part of the Jewish meal was the "Thanksgiving Prayer."

The Thanksgiving Prayer was said when the wine was blessed at the end of the meal. Beginning with the invitation to "Lift up your hearts," the head of the household led a prayer of praise and thanksgiving to God—first for the gift of creation, next for the promised land, then for the events of salvation history, and finally for the approaching reign of God on earth.

At the end of this prayer, the cup of wine was shared in silence. Through this action, those who drank of the cup again committed themselves to becoming more truly the people of God. God would surely reign. The sharing of the wine also was thus a sign of the approaching reign of God.

According to Scripture, when Jesus blessed and shared the cup of wine at the Last Supper, he identified the wine and the cup-sharing with himself. "This is the cup of my blood, the blood of the new and everlasting covenant. It will be shed for you and for all so that sins may be forgiven. Do this in memory of me."

The kingdom of God is really present, and our sharing of the Eucharist is an effective symbol of Jesus' presence and of the reign of God which will come in its fullness at the end of time. The Catholic Church recognizes the Real Presence of Jesus, the risen Lord, in the assembly, in the priest, in the entire Eucharistic liturgy: in the word and especially in the consecrated Bread and Wine. Jesus, the risen Lord, is not just present or remembered by sign; he is *really* present! The Eucharist is the sacramental Real Presence of Christ. The Bread and Wine still look and taste like bread and wine, but we believe— open our hearts to—the reality that Jesus, the risen Lord, is truly present.

Talk about it

1. Why do you think Jesus used bread and wine for the Eucharist?

2. In what way are bread and wine still important signs today? Explain.

The Eucharist is the Church at her best.

Gabriel Moran

Every Eucharist proclaims the beginning of the time of God's salvation.

J. Jeremias

The Jewish meal was a time of nourishment.

There was more to consume than bread and wine! The body was nourished at the meal, certainly, but more importantly, a fellowship was created. The people became a community with a common mission and purpose. The commitment made in the eating of the bread and the sharing of the wine made a difference in the lives of the participants. What they celebrated was expected to be a part of their lives after they left the table and went back to the daily responsibilities of life. This understanding continues in the lives of practicing Jews today.

So it is with Christians. Communion is not a matter of private encounter for an injection of grace. Communion is a commitment to God. It is a commitment to live as Jesus did in every possible way. Communion is very serious business. It should make a difference in the way we live!

Then do this

Choose one prayer from the Mass and answer these questions:

1. What type of prayer is it—blessing/adoration, thanksgiving, praise, intercession, petition?

2. Why do you like this prayer?

> *Holy Communion is the shortest and safest way to heaven.*
>
> **Pope Pius X**

REVIEW

1. What is the Eucharist?

2. What is the historical background of our Eucharistic celebration?

3. What are the ways in which Jesus is really present in the Eucharistic celebration?

Jacques Maritain
Seeing and believing

Jacques Maritain was born in France in 1882. In 1906 he and his wife became Catholics. Jacques was a professor of philosophy who taught at Princeton University during the 1940s and 1950s. For three years during the 1940s, he was the ambassador of France to the Vatican. Over fifty books came from the hand of Maritain before he died in 1973. The following story is told of him:

Writer Tim Unsworth recalls coming upon Maritain one morning in the 1950s in a small church on the tip of Long Island. It was the time when [the Mass was in Latin and] Catholics carried missals to Mass and frantically thumbed pages and flipped ribbons, seeking to stay abreast of the celebrant. Unsworth was one such Catholic. Maritain, on the other hand, sat quietly, his arm over the pew, absorbing the graces of the Mass. After Mass, Unsworth asked Maritain why he didn't use a missal. "Oh," he said, "I have most of that memorized. I just look at him and he looks at me."

John Deedy, *A Book of Catholic Anecdotes*.

Optional activities

1. Discuss: What do you think of Maritain's comment on his participation in the Eucharist? Do you think his response would have been different after the Second Vatican Council when the Mass was in English? Why? How would you respond if you were asked about your participation at Mass today? Why?

2. Interview someone old enough to have experienced the Mass before the Second Vatican Council. Ask the person to share how he or she participated then and how that compares with or contrasts with how he or she participates today. Share the interview and your reactions with the class.

PARTS OF THE MASS

In the celebration of the Mass, Catholics see themselves as taking part in the same thanksgiving meal and sacrifice that Jesus celebrated at the Last Supper. The elements of the Passover meal are still identifiable in the Mass, along with their deep religious significance—fulfilled in Jesus. At Eucharist, there is real encounter with Jesus, the risen Lord.

The basic structure of the Mass

The Mass contains four major parts:

- The gathering of the people (Introductory Rites)
- Listening to God's word (Liturgy of the Word)
- Giving God thanks (Liturgy of the Eucharist)
- Being sent to love and serve (Concluding Rite)

The Introductory Rites

In the Introductory Rites, we gather as God's people.

At Mass, we gather as Church, believers who are also sinners. So, in the Introductory Rites, we acknowledge our sinfulness and thank God for his mercy: "Lord, have mercy!"

The Liturgy of the Word

We experience the presence of Jesus in the Liturgy of the Word.

The Scriptures are God's word. At Mass, when we hear the Scripture readings proclaimed, we are hearing God's word. The word of God is always powerful, always creative. In the readings, God encounters us personally and in the community of faith. Through the proclaimed word, God forms a people, a Church. God's word calls us to shape our lives in accord with it. God's word truly becomes part of us if we listen with attentive, searching hearts.

The first reading is from the Old Testament, except, for example, during the Easter Season when it is from the Acts of the Apostles. The second reading is from one of the New Testament letters or, infrequently, from the Book of Revelation. And, of course, the third reading is from one of the Gospels. The proclamation of the gospel has the central place in the Liturgy of the Word. The gospel is the good news of God's love in Jesus, God's Word incarnated. The other Scripture readings selected by the Church lead up to and help us understand the gospel.

As we listen to the Scripture readings, we prepare our hearts for a grateful response to what God has done for us in Jesus Christ. The homily—or sermon—"breaks open" the word of God for us so that we can see God's saving love at work in our lives and in the world around us. The homily is a call to awareness which inspires us and motivates us to live our faith. The proper response to an effective homily is "Praise God!"

Talk about it

1. What were the readings about last Sunday?

2. What was said in the homily?

3. How could you apply the message of last Sunday's Liturgy of the Word to your life today?

Roots in the synagogue

At the time of Jesus, the Jewish people gathered in the local prayer house, or synagogue, to pray and to receive instruction in God's word. This devotional practice is the historical base for the part of the Mass called the *Liturgy of the Word*. A typical synagogue service at the time of Jesus included:

- Preparation time—singing of hymns and recitation of the psalms

- Holy reminder—the chanting of the phrase, "Remember, Israel, there is but one Lord, your God. You shall love him with your whole heart, your whole mind, and your whole strength."

- Scripture—usually taken from one of the first five books of the Bible (the Law) or the Prophets

- Teaching—an instruction which applied the word of God to daily life

- Praise—the people joining in a common verse of praise: "Holy, holy, holy Lord God of hosts! Heaven and earth are full of your glory! Hosanna in the highest! Blessed is he who comes in the name of the Lord! Hosanna in the highest!

- Prayers—a prayer leader leading the faithful in asking God to help them in their needs

- Psalms—the time of prayer ending with either reciting or singing psalms

Then do this

Make a floor plan for a new church. Consider these questions and be prepared to explain your plan to the class.

1. Where should you locate the baptismal font? Why?

2. What about the pews, altar, lectern, cross, candles, presider's chair, tabernacle? Why are you placing each item as you have?

The Liturgy of the Eucharist

With attentive hearts and the gift of self, we ritually prepare our gifts.

Our gifts and our offering of ourselves are prepared so that we can unite ourselves with Christ in his gift of himself for us. We ask God to accept our sacrifice "for the praise and glory of his name, for our good, and the good of his Church."

Jesus used bread and wine at the Last Supper, so our gifts of food at Mass are bread and wine.

These gifts are blessed with short prayers very similar to the prayers used in the Jewish tradition in blessings of the gifts of bread and wine.

Our meal "conversation" is a prayer, a long prayer which has its roots in the Thanksgiving Prayer of the ancient Jewish community.

We put into words what we celebrate. We lift up our hearts to the Lord. Then the priest prays the Eucharistic Prayer, our thanksgiving prayer. During this prayer addressed to God the Father, the community enters into the action of Jesus at the Last Supper and on the cross.

In this beautiful prayer, the priest leads the community in praising God for the gift of salvation in Jesus. We pray for our leaders and other members of the Church that all may be one and that Jesus the Christ will bring us to union with our heavenly Father.

As our prayer continues, we ask that we might be one with Jesus in his compassion, his caring for all people, his ministry of love. The priest calls on the Holy Spirit to bless and transform our simple gifts of bread and wine into the Body and Blood of Christ. While repeating the words of Jesus at the Last Supper, the priest consecrates the bread and the wine. Through the power of the Holy Spirit, the bread and wine become the very gift of Jesus himself, given for us; his Body and Blood are really present in the sacrament:

> *"Take this, all of you, and eat it:*
> *this is my body which will be given up for you. . . .*
> *Take this, all of you, and drink from it:*
> *this is the cup of my blood,*
> *the blood of the new and everlasting covenant. . . ."*

Calling to mind the death and resurrection of Jesus, we offer a memorial acclamation. As the priest continues, we ask God to accept our sacrifice, and we pray for those who have died and for ourselves. The Eucharistic Prayer ends in praise: "Through him, with him, in him, all glory and honor are yours, almighty Father, for ever and ever!" We respond with a grateful "Amen"—the Great Amen!

The Eucharistic Prayer is the prayer of the whole Church, so it's not an activity we watch as we would a ball game. The Eucharist both expresses the faith of the believing community and creates faith within us. God the Father calls us to Eucharist and, through Jesus, forms us into Eucharist, that is, forms us into a grateful people.

Then do this

1. Using a missalette or a parish prayer book, individually look up the Eucharistic Prayers (there should be at least four). Compare the prayers. What is common to all of them? What is different?

2. Discuss in class what you have found.

Gratitude is the heart's memory.

French proverb

We enter into Communion.

We prepare for Communion by praying the Lord's Prayer. We ask for the coming of God's kingdom. We wish each other Christ's peace. Then we go to the altar for Communion. Receiving Communion is not just a religious ritual. It's an act of faith. The "Amen" spoken at Communion is a confession of belief in Jesus' Real Presence in the consecrated Bread and Wine, and it is an affirmation of the presence of Jesus in the Church, his body.

More happens here than the private encounter with Jesus in the Blessed Sacrament. The "Amen" spoken here as we receive Communion is our pledge to enter into the work of Jesus—to be a people whose body is broken and whose blood is spilled for others. The community becomes one with the saving Lord Jesus, who is really present in the Eucharist.

The Concluding Rite

After Communion, we are dismissed, sent out to live our faith.

A few announcements may be made, and then the people are blessed and sent home. Mass is not just "over"—we are sent to put into action what we have celebrated.

Write it down

1. How many times have you received Communion in your life?
2. How many of those times were you aware of the faith statement you were making by your participation in this sacrament?
3. How does your past behavior challenge you to change or deepen your approach to Communion?

Write it down

What role do you personally have in "saving" the world in the name of Christ?

REVIEW

1. What are the four major parts of the Mass?

2. From which sections of the Bible are each of the Sunday readings taken?

3. What is the name of the great thanksgiving prayer of the Mass?

CONCLUSION

John at the Last Supper

It was when they got to the lamb that John knew something was up. He got that "prophet feeling" again. While Jesus seemed to be mentioning it in passing, John was positive he was telling them something in that parabolic way he had.

Jesus was reminding them of the importance of repentance when he digressed on the Day of Atonement. It was only a momentary thing about the scapegoat but that was when the gut wrench struck him. John looked questioningly at Jesus, who seemed to sense his anguish. . . .

Jesus ate some of the lamb along with the others. The "prophet feeling" in John was overwhelming. There was something he was trying to remember, just on the edge of his consciousness, something having to do with the lamb and the goat that was erupting to the surface.

Jesus held up the bread.

"Take and eat," he said. "This is my body."

"That's it!" John almost screamed out loud. Suddenly it all made sense. The strangeness of Jesus, the unusual discourse, that undeniable "prophet feeling" tearing at his innards begging to know if this would be for good or ill.

What he was trying to remember boiled to the surface. It was a fable he had heard a long time ago. It was about a lamb that was invited to a banquet only to discover that he was the meal.
John Aurelio, *Myth Man: A Storyteller's Jesus.*

Optional activities

1. Read the Last Supper discourse in the Gospel according to John, chapters 13–17. In class talk about the reading.

2. Write your own story of the Last Supper. In small groups, share your stories.

The Eucharist is "the source and summit of the Christian life"
("Constitution on the Church," #11).
Catechism of the Catholic Church, #1324.

At Eucharist, we become one with each other and with the source of our salvation. We become one with Jesus and his life and ministry. In a very real sense, the Eucharist is an end that is a beginning. It is an end because it completes our "path of conversion"; we become one with Jesus and his community of believers.

The Eucharist is also a beginning—because it nourishes us on our "path of conversion," which is a lifelong path. After "First Communion," we return again and again to the table of the Lord to be strengthened by the Bread of Life and Cup of Salvation until we share in the eternal life promised by Jesus.

The Eucharist, the Mass, is the central celebration of our Catholic faith. A particular Mass may or may not be enjoyable, filled with interesting activity, or set in a well-designed environment. Nevertheless, in every Eucharist, the same reality is present. In every Eucharist, we open our hearts and our lives to the saving love of God in Jesus.

In every Eucharist we recognize that Jesus, the risen Lord, is truly present in the worshiping community—in one another, in the presider, in the Sacred Scripture, and, above all, in the consecrated Bread and Wine. In every Eucharist, God calls us through Jesus to become exactly what we share in: the Body and Blood of Christ.

The Eucharist is far more than a religious service during which you receive Communion. The Mass is a faith activity of the people of God. Eucharist is what you do as well as what you receive. In the fullest sense of the word, Eucharist is *the* sacrament of the Church. It reveals who we are as Church, and in its celebration we become more deeply and really Church.

From beginning to end, the Eucharist is a single moment in which the faith life of the Church comes into focus. What happens in this special moment when the Church gathers around the table of the Lord is a reflection of the saving activity of God in the world.

There is nothing magic in any of this. And there's little gained by just "going to Mass." A Mass that is just attended is merely that: attended. It isn't what you "get out of" Mass that shows your maturity and appreciation of the gift that is offered to you. What you "give to it" shows that. Your behavior will not change God, but it will let God change you.

Write it down

Review the brief personal biography you wrote in chapter 1. Note any references to the following and add further thoughts on the questions.

1. How significant were your celebrations of the Sacraments of Initiation?

2. How have the Sacraments of Initiation shaped you?

Talk about it

1. How do you live out the meaning of your Baptism and Confirmation?

2. How do you live out the Eucharist?

Words you should know

Baptism	Eucharist
catechumenate	First Communion
charism	indwelling
Confirmation	Rite of Christian Initiation of Adults

CHAPTER 11

The SACRAMENTS of RECONCILIATON and HEALING

CHAPTER OVERVIEW

- *Awareness of sin*

- *Naming sin*

- *God's reconciling love made known in Jesus*

- *The Church is a reconciling people*

- *The Church's Sacrament of Penance*

- *Anointing of the Sick*

The Word of the Lord

Jesus said, ". . . Go your way, and from now on do not sin again."

FROM THE GOSPEL ACCORDING TO JOHN, SEE 8:3–11.

Are any among you sick? They should call for the elders of the church and have them pray over them, anointing them with oil in the name of the Lord.

FROM THE LETTER OF JAMES, SEE 5:14–15.

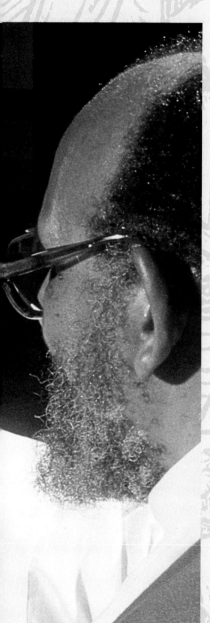

I acknowledged my sin to you,
   and I did not hide my iniquity;

Let Us Pray

I said, "I will confess my transgressions
      to the Lord,"
   and you forgave the guilt of my sin.
Therefore let all who are faithful
   offer prayer to you;
at a time of distress, the rush of mighty waters
   shall not reach them.
You are a hiding place for me;
   you preserve me from trouble;
   you surround me with glad cries of deliverance.
I will instruct you and teach you the way
      you should go;
   I will counsel you with my eye upon you.

PSALM 32:5–8

Awareness of Sin

In the previous chapter, you studied in some detail the exciting reality of belonging to Christ and his Church. Through the Sacraments of Baptism–Confirmation–Eucharist, you have entered on a lifelong journey of faith that leads you to genuine happiness and eventually to eternal life. Your union with Jesus Christ is an essential part of that journey as you grow into full stature as a son or daughter of God.

What wonderful dignity you have as a Christian! What a privilege it is to share the unconditional love of God in Christ through your relationships with other people! In union with Jesus Christ, you grow to your full human dignity. You grow to be all you are called to be. You also discover all that you are not supposed to be. As you die to selfishness and sin in union with Jesus Christ, the risen Lord, you rise to life with him.

Alas! There's that ugly word *sin*. What is sin? What does it mean to do something sinful? How do we know what is or is not sin? Some actions which some people used to consider sinful may not be named sin today. This or that sin may no longer be mentioned during the homily at church. We all seem to share the confusion.

Our culture, especially our media and our ads, steers us away from seeing any behavior as wrong, let alone sinful. We tend to look at selfishness and personal evil as merely the result of a bad home environment. Somehow we've lost the idea that we're responsible for what we do or don't do. Unfortunately right and wrong are judged more and more in our society by how an individual person "feels" about things.

Yet sin is part of the reality of your life. When you knowingly and freely choose to go against your **conscience** (where you hear the "voice" of the Spirit), you sin. You sin by refusing God's invitation to holiness and wholeness of life. So sin is an act against God—and against yourself. It is also an act against other people, in fact, against the world—it contributes to unhealthy and sinful relationships. That's because sin is like poison; it's toxic; it spreads and destroys.

So what is sin? **Sin** is an unloving choice and the unloving actions that come from the unloving choice. And it is rooted in an unloving heart. You are responsible for your choices and your actions and your refusals to act as you should act.

God calls you into relationship. When you refuse that call, you choose to cut yourself off from the source of life. When you refuse, you choose to be apart from love—and apart from love you die, especially spiritually. Sin is always a turning away from God, from other people, from ourselves, and from the world. Sin is about **alienation**—being alone. And we do it to ourselves.

Scripture's view of sin

It's helpful to look at how sin is viewed in Scripture. The writers of the Old Testament used several Hebrew words to describe sin, but the one they used most frequently was *hatta't*, which means "to miss the mark." Just as an arrow may fall short of its intended target when the archer doesn't aim high enough, the sinner falls short of the call of God.

When the Israelites sinned against God, they knew they were not just acting in a manner forbidden by some law. They knew that they were falling short in their relationship with God. They were not on center; they were missing the mark.

conscience

the gift from God that helps us know the difference between right and wrong and to choose what is right; the obligation we experience to do good and avoid evil

sin

an unloving choice and the unloving actions that come from the unloving choice; the choice to disobey God, to turn away from God, other people, ourselves, and the world

alienation

the sense of being alone, unconnected to others

The New Testament frequently uses the Greek word *harmartia* to describe sin. *Harmartia* means "alienation," "separation." The Gospels picture people struggling with sin, being alienated or separated from God and from each other.

The ministry of Jesus was about bringing people together—people and God, people and each other, people and themselves. Through Jesus, we can experience God's forgiveness for our alienation, our sin. Jesus made it possible for us to return to union with God, thus restoring us to his grace and friendship.

In light of the Old and New Testaments, sin is any action which is the opposite of the good God intends for you. It's an action made in revolt against what you know you should do. The cause of sin is not bad home environment or society's pressure. The cause of sin is choosing to do what you know is not right—and choosing to not do what you know is right.

But sin is not simple, and neither are you. If you feel confused about sin, it might be because you're confused about yourself. Who, where, is your true self? Can you be honest there? It's hard to face the truth of sin. We don't want to look at sin in ourselves.

Sin, unfortunately, is very real. If we miss the mark of responding to God's relationship of love, our sin is obvious. Christians should have a "no tolerance" policy regarding sin. We may want to make excuses for our sins, but there is no reason to be confused about what is sinful.

Jesus helps us deal with the reality of sin. Jesus calls us to be true to our relationship with God, with other people—and to be true to our best self. That's the person we really want to be. We don't want to be alienated from love, and sin has no place in life-giving relationships.

The good news is not about condemnation. Jesus' whole life was about God's saving love. True to the gospel, the Church faithfully announces God's forgiveness of sins, God's **mercy**. God is loving and compassionate, always calling us back, always calling us to a full, rich, and beautiful life.

God calls us to a covenant love relationship. We are blessed to share that love with others. Even when we sin and turn from our relationship of covenant love, Jesus assures you that God's love is steadfast and that God is always ready to forgive, ready to bring us back home, to bring us to the fullness of redemption.

Then do this
Share a story of a time when you were forgiven or when you forgave someone (avoid mentioning sins or names of others). How did you feel?

mercy
compassionate forgiveness

Then do this
Make a poster incorporating magazine photos and articles on areas of the world that are in need of peace and reconciliation. Discuss the poster with the class.

W*hoever falls from God's right hand is caught in his left.*
Edwin Markham

REVIEW

1. What is conscience?

2. What is sin?

3. How is sin presented in the Old Testament? In the New Testament?

4. What is God's response to those who ask forgiveness?

What is failure?

A troubled man paid a visit to his rabbi. A wise and good old rabbi, as all rabbis try to be. "Rabbi," said he, wringing his hands, "I am a failure. More than half the time I do not succeed in doing what I must do."

"Oh?" said the rabbi.

"Please say something wise, rabbi," said the man.

After much pondering, the rabbi spoke as follows: "Ah, my son, I give you this wisdom: Go and look on page 930 of The New York Times Almanac *for the year 1970, and you will find peace of mind maybe."*

"Ah," said the man, and he went away and did that thing.

Now this is what he found: The listing of the lifetime batting averages of all the greatest baseball players. Ty Cobb, the greatest slugger of them all, had a life-time average of only .367. Even Babe Ruth didn't do so good.

So the man went back to the rabbi and said in a questioning tone: "Ty Cobb—.367—that's it?"

"Right," said the rabbi. "Ty Cobb—.367. He got a hit once out of every three times at bat. He didn't even bat .500—so what can you expect already?"

"Ah," said the man, who thought he was a wretched failure because only half the time he did not succeed at what he must do.

Robert Fulghum, *All I Really Need to Know I Learned in Kindergarten.*

Optional activities

1. Find another story that addresses the human tendency to fail, or to sin. Share the story with the class and lead a discussion on it.

2. Write and illustrate a story of your own for young children on the human tendency to fail, or to sin. Include your resolution—what you believe about sin and about forgiveness.

NAMING SIN

Sin hasn't disappeared. Even the wonders of modern technology haven't freed us from self-centeredness and personally chosen evil. Despite the obviousness of sin, we are often reluctant to deal with sin in ourselves and in our society. No, sin hasn't disappeared—but we'd like to *pretend* that it doesn't really exist.

sinning mortally

having an attitude or acting in a way which involves a serious matter and which a person does with full knowledge and with full freedom

sinning venially

having a wrong attitude or acting in a way which involves either a less serious matter done with full knowledge and full freedom, or a serious matter done with less than full knowledge and/or less than full freedom

Experts in human behavior have challenged some traditional notions of sin. There was a time, for example, when the very word *sin* brought to mind some *thing* a person did which someone in authority identified as sin. Phrases like "Is it a sin to . . . ?" or "That's a sin!" reflect this perspective. Sins were sometimes judged by how "big" or serious the action was. Simplified measurements on the seriousness of sin found their way into our vocabulary.

Two terms commonly used in the Catholic Church to describe sin are *mortal* and *venial*. These concepts do not mean that there are simply big and little sins. They are attempts to describe degrees of sinfulness. These terms—*mortal* and *venial*—include some very important differences. **Mortal sin** describes an attitude or action which is a serious matter in itself and which a person does with full knowledge and with full freedom. **Venial sin** describes either a less serious matter done with full knowledge and full freedom, or a serious matter done with less than full knowledge and/or less than full freedom.

In the definitions for mortal and venial sins, we see three important areas of concern or conditions:

- the seriousness of the matter
- the amount of knowledge regarding rightness or wrongness of the action
- the degree of freedom in making a decision

So the simple definitions aren't really simple at all. That's why there isn't a long list of things that are automatically serious mortal sins. When the Church talks about "serious matter," it is saying that some actions can be considered objectively sinful. That is, they are the kind of behavior that must be avoided because they are contrary to the gospel, contrary to human dignity. The Church has a long tradition which has identified many actions as serious matters—the killing of another person, the telling of gravely harmful lies, and so on.

The most obvious mortal sin is murder; the word *murder* implies killing another person while having sufficient knowledge and freedom. When those conditions are not all present, we even use different words, such as *involuntary manslaughter*, *killing in self-defense*, and *justifiable homicide*.

Whatever the degree of seriousness, it is still true that when we sin, we are off the mark in our relationships with God and others. Mortal sins get their name because they are deadly; we cut ourselves off from our relationship with God when we sin mortally. Such sins are also often deadly in terms of our relationships with other people. These are the destroyed relationships.

Venial sins weaken relationships, but they don't destroy them. These lesser sins do, however, interfere with our ability to do what is right and may lead to the decision to commit a greater sin. Just because something isn't mortally sinful doesn't mean that we can or should just put up with it. Sin should have *no* place of welcome in the life of a Christian.

Talk about it

1. How would you explain sin to a fourth-grader?

2. What is the difference between a mortal sin and a venial sin? Give examples.

3. Why are the three conditions listed important in determining the seriousness of a sin?

Kinds of sin

Then do this
Scan the letters of the New Testament to find another list of sins. Compare and contrast the list you find with Galatians 5:19–21.

There are many kinds of sins. In the Bible, we can read several lists of sins. For example, in the Letter to the Galatians (5:19–21), Paul names many sins: fornication, impurity, licentiousness, idolatry, sorcery, enmity, strife, jealousy, anger, selfishness, dissension, factions, envy, drunkenness, carousing, and the like. Paul warns us that people who do these things will not inherit the kingdom of God.

One way to categorize sins is to look at what they are directed toward. Another way is to look at the virtues they are in opposition to. Sins can also be categorized according to the Ten Commandments. And they can be classified according to whether they relate to God, neighbor, or oneself. Some sins relate to the spirit, while some relate to the body. Sins can exist in thought, word, deed, or omission. However we may want to list or identify sins, the root of all sin is in the heart of people, in their free will.

See the *Catechism of the Catholic Church*, #s 1852–1853.

1. What do you think is the difference between *sin* and *sins*?

2. What do you think this means: "the root of all sin is in the heart"?

3. What is a change of heart?

4. Can a change of heart keep a person from sinning? Explain.

The Ten Commandments

Loving God

1. I am the Lord your God. You shall not have strange gods before me.

2. You shall not take the name of the Lord your God in vain.

3. Remember to keep holy the Lord's day.

Loving our neighbor

4. Honor your father and your mother.

5. You shall not kill.

6. You shall not commit adultery.

7. You shall not steal.

8. You shall not bear false witness against your neighbor.

9. You shall not covet your neighbor's wife.

10. You shall not covet your neighbor's goods.

1. How do the first three commandments help us express our love for God?

2. How do the rest of the commandments ensure that we will love our neighbor?

3. What else is necessary to love God and love our neighbor, as Jesus asks us to do?

Actions, omissions, and the heart

Because it requires your knowledge and your free choice, sin is very real and very personal. Sin is not a thing you do or commit somewhere out there, disconnected from your self. It's a wrong act or omission that shows what's in your "heart." Sin is about hurt or broken relationships—a lack of wholeness with God, self, others, and the world. It is a falling short of our Christian identity and responsibility. As a result, no one "gets by" with sin—neither very serious sin, of which you are capable, nor less serious sin.

If you treat sin as a thing separate from your true self, you'll find an excuse for it and never take full responsibility for your actions. You'll find yourself saying, "It's only human to sin"—implying that sinning is something you have to do because you are human. Since God created you human, wouldn't that mean your sin is God's fault? That is not the case. Unfortunately we humans do sin, but we weren't created to sin! There is no honest excuse for *any* form of sin. In your heart-of-hearts you know what is right and what is wrong.

God calls us to be faithful to the beauty and goodness for which we were created. God calls us to good, moral living—a giving of ourselves in loving relationships, where we come face to face with God. Whenever we respond to that call, we are living in a relationship of love with God. We find life in love. We find ourselves. We live in grace.

Write it down

1. Are there any broken relationships in your life?

2. What can you do to help heal them?

Punishment due to sin

There are two consequences of sin. If we do not repent when we commit a serious sin, that sin removes us from communion with God and thus from eternal life with God. This loss of heaven is called the "eternal punishment" due to sin. Every sin, mortal or venial, also brings with it "temporal punishment," consequences which must be lived with here and now. These two punishments are not God's vengeance. They are the natural consequences of our sins.

Even when sin has been forgiven and communion with God has been restored (the eternal punishment of sin has been removed), temporal punishment stays; that is, the person still lives with the consequences of his or her sinful choices. We must accept responsibility for our sins and do what is necessary to correct the consequences of our sin. We do this by choosing to live rightly.

See the *Catechism of the Catholic Church,* #s 1472–1473.

1. What does it mean to say that every sin carries with it its own punishment? Give some examples.

2. Who inflicts the punishment due to sin, God or the person? Explain.

3. Describe how people live with the temporal consequences of their sins, even when those sins are forgiven. Is this fair? Explain.

REVIEW

1. What are the conditions necessary for mortal sin?

2. What is venial sin?

3. What do the Ten Commandments ask us to do?

4. In addition to doing a wrong thing, how else can a person sin?

5. How is sin punished?

God's reconciling love made known in Jesus

In Jesus we meet God, who embraces us in the midst of our sinfulness with an unconditional love. Just look at the ministry of Jesus: He welcomed sinners; he even went out of his way to be with them. He forgave them and called them to better living. And how did he do that? Jesus touched the sinner; he filled empty hearts; he healed the broken hearts of those who searched for saving relationships. And that would be all of us.

Jesus didn't set out to "fix" every little thing that was wrong. But he did show compassion and love to every sinner who came his way. He helped each person he met to come to life, to recognize his or her dignity as a son or daughter of God to which he restored them. And he redeems all humans from sin.

An encounter with Jesus is an encounter with love that "takes away sin." The unconditional love of Jesus enables the lost sinner to come home. And all sinners, great and small, are lost—lost in a misdirected and dead-ended search for the kind of life and happiness that can be found only in God.

Jesus is God's Word in the flesh and in human history. Because of Jesus, we know that we are indeed created in the image and likeness of God and are called to live in that community of love which is God. A single word summarizes the ministry of Jesus: *reconciliation*. Understanding this word is important if we are to capture the significance of God's love made known to us in Jesus. The word *reconciliation* has four parts:

- (the prefix) *re-* means "again"
- (the preposition) *-con-* means "with"
- (the noun) *-cilia-* means "little hair" (like an eyelash)
- (the suffix) *-tion* means "state" or "condition"

The literal meaning of reconciliation is "the condition of seeing eye to eye again." In the context of this book, it means seeing eye to eye again with God—that is true reconciliation.

In Jesus, God has **reconciled** the world in the most beautiful and wonderful way. In Jesus, God literally looks us in the eye with unconditional love. In Jesus, God speaks the truth of who we are—in ourselves and in our relationships with one another, our world, and God. Jesus is God's good news. In Jesus, God does something of absolute importance for us—God saves us from our sins; God saves us from our separation from ourselves, from God, and from other people.

In Jesus, God touches us—and thus salvation can happen. Seeing Jesus, we come to believe in God's love. We open our hearts and lives to a way of living that reflects God's continuing work of saving and bringing life to the world.

God meets us in Jesus where it counts most: in our need for a saving relationship of love that leaves us free and makes us whole. Only unconditional love is not self-serving or manipulative. The love God has for us is love that has our best interest at heart.

Then do this
In small groups search the Gospels for stories in which Jesus forgives sins. Choose one of the stories and act it out. Then discuss the story with the class.

reconcile
to restore to friendship or harmony

Talk about it
1. What does it mean to be reconciled to another person? To God? To the Church?
2. How can something like recycling be a form of reconciliation?

. . . through [Jesus] God was pleased to reconcile to himself all things. . . .

Colossians 1:20

THE CHURCH IS A RECONCILING PEOPLE

God has become one with us in Jesus. Because of Jesus we can speak with confidence about who God is and what our relationship to God is. Jesus is our face-to-face encounter with God. Without the unconditional gift of the incarnation, reconciliation (seeing eye to eye with God) would be at best guesswork for us.

Because of Jesus, we know that we are reconciled to God, that in God we truly do find fullness of life. Jesus, the "sacrament" of the Father, makes visible and tangible our relationship with God.

As a community of sinners, the Church knows that salvation comes from God. Salvation and the forgiveness of sin cannot come from what *we* do. It is God who, in Jesus, makes us whole and calls us to fullness of life. The Church is those people who have heard the good news of Jesus, believe him, and seek to follow him in the service of others. This is the way the Church is a reconciling people. As a reconciling people, we have accepted the grace or gift of Jesus among us and do our best to live in him—in that way reconciling ourselves and others with God.

In the Sacraments of Christian Initiation, the Church celebrates a new Christian's relationship with God, with others, and with all creation. The new Christian is reconciled with God and united to the Church community in the unconditional love of Jesus, who is our risen Lord. This really is a new way of living. As Paul said, ". . . it is no longer I who live, but it is Christ who lives in me" (Galatians 2:20). The Christian is a visible manifestation—a sacrament—of Christ.

Talk about it

1. How do you feel when a friend ignores you for a while and then acts as if nothing had happened? Do you need to understand and forgive when this happens? Why?

2. If you have ever broken off a friendship and wanted to repair the brokenness, what did you say to show you were sorry? What did you do to make up for what you had done?

Jesus, the Church, and forgiveness

While Jesus lived on earth, he forgave sins. He also showed what forgiveness could do. Sinners who had been alienated or excluded from the community were brought back to the community when Jesus forgave their sins. Jesus gave a great sign of this return to the community when he welcomed sinners at the table; this action spoke to all of God's forgiveness and of the restoration of sinners to the people of God.

When Jesus gave his disciples the power to forgive sins, he also gave them the authority to bring sinners back into relationship with the Church. Jesus' words to Simon Peter address this task, "I will give you the keys of the kingdom of heaven, and whatever you bind on earth will be bound in heaven, and whatever you loose on earth will be loosed in heaven." Reconciliation with the Church is inseparable from reconciliation with God.

See the *Catechism of the Catholic Church*, #s 1443–1445.

1. How does sin affect the life of the Christian community? The life of a town or city? The life of the world?

2. How does forgiveness restore unity and peace?

3. Is the forgiveness of sins merely a matter between the sinner and God? Can the role of the Church be ignored when it comes to the forgiveness of sins? Explain.

Instruments of reconciliation

We have been reconciled by God in Jesus; therefore, we have the privilege and the responsibility of helping bring about reconciliation in the world. We are to minister to the world in the name of Jesus; we are to be one with him—to be God's love in the world. In this sense, *Church* is a verb rather than a noun. It's how we live and love.

When the Church touches the world, there is reconciliation. As a member of the Church, you are the hands, feet, eyes, and mouth, the heart of Jesus. You are the way Jesus continues his saving work. As a disciple of Christ, you are in the business of reconciliation, bringing the world of people, things, and even systems of self-serving power into the light of Christ's love. As a Christian, you are a reconciled person, a person who *must* reconcile.

The ministry of Jesus is always about relationships. He formed a community which was to be characterized by his unconditional love. So love resides in our very identity as Christians. When we love unconditionally, we are most truly who we are created to be: images of God. When we love unconditionally, we are most in union with God, one another, and our true selves.

The kind of love we see in Jesus is often opposed. At times, people selfishly prefer separation and alienation from God and from other people, especially if this helps them feel powerful and in control. By their natures, domination and control are in opposition to love. Various factors work in favor of domination and control and keep reconciliation from happening: ignorance, fear, prejudice, and sin.

But, because of Jesus, we know for sure that love wins in the conflict with domination and control. In a very true sense, when we open our hearts to salvation, we are reconciled. And the more whole each of us becomes, the more others become whole. We are witnesses that God is always present in the world, working for reconciliation and wholeness of life.

Talk about it

1. Who in the Church is responsible for the ministry of reconciliation?

2. Why are reconciliation and peace-making a special part of the Church's mission?

3. Make a list of the ways you see people in your parish or faith community being ministers of reconciliation.

Then do this

Work in small groups to write a story or put on a short skit showing how a student in your school can be a minister of reconciliation.

. . . perhaps if the Church can be seen as a forgiving and reconciling community, it will be possible to persuade people of the need for penitence.

James D. Crichton

REVIEW

1. What was Jesus' response to sinners?

2. What is reconciliation?

3. What is the relationship between the Church and reconciliation?

Paco, come home

In a small town in Spain, a man named Jorge had a bitter argument with his young son Paco. The next day Jorge discovered that Paco's bed was empty—he had run away from home.

Overcome with remorse, Jorge searched his soul and realized that his son was more important to him than anything else. He wanted to start over. Jorge went to a well-known store in the center of town and posted a large sign that read, "Paco, come home. I love you. Meet me here tomorrow morning."

The next morning Jorge went to the store, where he found no less than seven young boys named Paco who had also run away from home. They were all answering the call for love, each hoping it was his dad inviting him home with open arms.

Alan Cohen in *A 3rd Serving of Chicken Soup for the Soul*.

Optional activities

1. Read the story of the prodigal son, Luke 15:11–32. In discussion, compare the parable with the story of Paco. Then share modern-day stories of real-life reconciliations that remind you of the parable or the story of Paco.

2. Write or locate another story with the theme of reconciliation. Share the story with the class.

3. Find out something about the British poet Francis Thompson (1859–1907); the Internet has several useful Web-sites. Read his poem, "The Hound of Heaven." Share Thompson's sad story and some of the poem with the class and lead a follow-up discussion.

There's no point in burying a hatchet if you're going to erect a marker on the site.
Sidney Harris

Nothing graces the human soul so much as mercy.
St. Ambrose

A sacrament with a history

The way the Church has celebrated reconciliation has changed over the centuries. In the early centuries of the Church, baptized Christians who committed very serious sins (for example, idolatry, murder, and adultery) were required to submit to tough discipline. These **penitents** had to do public penance, often for years, before they were reconciled. People were permitted to join the order of penitents only rarely, and once in their lifetime.

When seventh-century Irish monks were evangelizing Europe, they introduced "private" penance. This form of reconciliation did not require long public penances. From then on, the sacrament became more and more a private celebration between a penitent and a priest. With this practice, repetition became possible, and this led to the regular celebration of the sacrament. The forgiveness of mortal sins and venial sins now took place in the same kind of sacramental celebration. In general, this is the form of the sacrament still practiced today.

See the *Catechism of the Catholic Church*, #1447.

1. How did the celebration of the Sacrament of Penance change during the twentieth century?
2. Why do you think a communal rite with individual confessions and absolution is an appropriate way to celebrate this sacrament?

penitent
one who repents of sin, seeks forgiveness, and does penance

THE CHURCH'S SACRAMENT OF PENANCE

Penance, Reconciliation
the sacrament that celebrates God's forgiveness of sin through the Church

By understanding how God sees us—even when we are selfish and sinful—we can understand how the Church ministers God's mercy in the Sacrament of **Penance**. When we "go to confession," we take a good look at what we've done or failed to do, how we have hurt people and stunted our own growth as good humans and Christians. We take responsibility for our morally wrong choices. We decide how we will do reparation for our sins. We ask God for forgiveness and thank him for his forgiveness and his mercy—for healing us.

So, in the Sacrament of Penance, we experience reconciliation, the return to a right relationship with God and with those we have harmed. This is why the Sacrament of Penance is frequently called the Sacrament of **Reconciliation**. It is the celebration of the wonderful mercy of God, a return to the kind of life for which we were created.

Nothing in this . . . world bears the impress of the Son of God so surely as forgiveness.

Alice Carey

These are the words of **absolution** or forgiveness which the priest speaks as part of the sacrament:

> God the Father of mercies,
>
> through the death and resurrection of his Son
>
> has reconciled the world to himself
>
> and sent the Holy Spirit among us
>
> for the forgiveness of sins;
>
> through the ministry of the Church
>
> may God give you pardon and peace,
>
> and I absolve you from your sins
>
> in the name of the Father, and of the Son, ✠
>
> and of the Holy Spirit.

absolution
words that announce the forgiveness of sins

These words of absolution make a clear statement regarding the action of the sacrament. What the priest does in this sacrament is rooted in what the Church itself does in the name of Jesus.

In the Sacrament of Reconciliation, we celebrate the wonder of God's mercy and healing love. In this sacrament, the Church, through the ministry of the priest, makes real for us the unconditional and forgiving love of God. Sinners that we confess ourselves to be, we are assured that God, whose love has always been there, is very much present and holds us in a relationship of love. In this sacrament, we experience God's gift of reconciliation.

Talk about it
What does it mean to accept responsibility for our sins?

If God and the sinner are reconciled, then the sinner and the Church are also reconciled. This reconciliation is important because sin harms the communion of relationships that is the Church. All broken relationships—with God, self, and others—are restored to life in the celebration of this healing sacrament. In the Sacrament of Reconciliation, the words of absolution spoken by the priest announce and clearly bring about the reality of what is being celebrated: You are forgiven.

Using the sacrament well

The Catholic Church encourages its members to celebrate the Sacrament of Reconciliation regularly. Reaction to this encouragement is often hesitation. "Why do I have to confess my sins to a priest? If I'm sorry for them and 'talk it out' with God, isn't that enough? Can't I tell God I'm sorry for what I've done? Wouldn't it be better to go to the person I've hurt and ask that person's forgiveness?"

There's a great deal of truth in those questions. Absolutely, you should talk it out with God—tell God you're sorry. And you certainly ought to ask forgiveness from the person you have hurt. The celebration of the Sacrament of Penance presumes these things—that you *are* sorry for your sins and that you either have or *do* intend to reconcile with people you have harmed or hurt.

The priest personally doesn't have a need to hear your sins or anyone else's, in the sense of just fulfilling his psychological needs! On the other hand, as the representative of Christ and of the Church, the priest has an obligation to be there for you. You, like all humans, need the assurance and clear bringing about of forgiveness. The priest has the awesome responsibility to tell you and effectively symbolize the fact that, when you are sorry, God indeed forgives your every sin and that the Church welcomes you back into the community if your sinful actions had separated you from God and the community.

Write it down
When I'm forgiven, I feel . . . because . . . .

1. Why is the regular celebration of the Sacrament of Reconciliation an important part of Catholic spirituality?

2. Why is the regular celebration of this sacrament good for you?

Then do this

Work in small groups to choose appropriate readings and songs for a communal celebration of Reconciliation. Share your results with the class and discuss as needed.

This sacrament is an opportunity to make things right with God and other people. It's a celebration of repentance, forgiveness, and mercy. It's as if Jesus were lifting up your sin-saddened face to look you in the eye and tell you that you are forgiven. You are freed from the burden of your sins and restored to a right relationship with God.

The Sacrament of Reconciliation can be celebrated in three different ways. The first of these is individual private confession. This form provides the opportunity for reconciliation for the individual sinner—by name, as it were. Another form is the communal celebration of the sacrament with individual confession and reception of penance and absolution.

A third form, called *general absolution*, is permitted by the Church in very exceptional circumstances when the other forms are not possible. In this third form, the priest gives a penance and absolution to an entire congregation, without individual confession.

REVIEW

1. What is another name for the Sacrament of Penance?

2. What happens in the Sacrament of Penance?

3. What do the words of absolution tell us?

4. What are the three ways of celebrating the Sacrament of Penance?

Elements of the sacrament

Here are the "steps" of the Sacrament of Reconciliation. Each step is connected in some way to the others.

1. Examine your conscience.

Readings from Scripture can help you reflect and "measure" yourself against the love God has for you. From Scripture, you also have the Ten Commandments. The Commandments and the moral teaching of the Church help you examine your consciences. Within your heart, you know where you have missed the mark, where you have fallen short—when you have sinned.

You may select a passage from Scripture to share with the priest or he might share one with you. It is God's word that calls us to repentance and brings us salvation.

The Holy Spirit moves you to look at your life and evaluate how you have lived: Am I honest? Am I faithful? Am I loving? Do I care about others? What needs to change? What keeps me from changing? How will I change? What must I do to live like Jesus? Quite often the list of sins any one of us could make for ourselves is actually a list of symptoms that point to a deeper sin.

2. Be sorry for your sins.

An honest examination of conscience will always lead you to name the things you've done that are wrong or things you've not done that you should have done. These things have alienated you from God, from your true self, and from others. When you look at what your choices have caused, you feel sorrow. This sorrow is more than regret for having broken a rule or law. It's the sorrow of knowing you have broken a relationship of love.

Then do this

Work in small groups to write an examination of conscience appropriate for young people. Share the results with the class, and create a combined examination of conscience from all the groups. Have copies made for each class member.

Conscience is the perfect interpreter of life.
Karl Barth

Conscience

Conscience is the heart of the person. Conscience helps us make the decision to do good and avoid evil. And it helps us decide whether the choices we have made already are good or evil. When we listen to our conscience, we can hear God speaking. By using our conscience, we recognize the morality of an act that we are planning to do, are in the process of doing, or have already done. In everything we do, we must always do what we know is just and right. It is important to be in touch with our inner self in order to hear and follow our conscience. This is especially true because we are often distracted from reflecting on our lives.

See the *Catechism of the Catholic Church*, #s 1777–1779.

1. Why does the Church describe conscience as the "heart of the person"?

2. What is the difference between a peaceful conscience and a guilty conscience?

3. What are some ways in which our lifestyle keeps us from listening to our conscience?

4. What can we do about that?

3. Confess your sins.

You need to admit verbally the things you've done that have hurt others, yourself, and your relationship with God. Most of us like to think we're perfect. But we're not. We sin—and we are responsible for our sins. Admitting our sins takes maturity and courage.

The experience of confessing one's sin is particularly powerful in the Sacrament of Penance. It's much harder to confess the real sins in your life than it is to vaguely admit that "I am a sinner." The naming of sins allows you to "put your finger" on those attitudes or actions which keep you from being the kind of person you are called to be. Jesus taught that the "truth will make you free." Nowhere is this more powerfully true than in the Sacrament of Penance.

When confessing sins to a priest, remember that the priest is a sinner too. He has the same need for the sacrament as you do! The priest isn't interested in ridiculing you or making you air your dirty laundry, as it were. If the priest asks you any questions, it's only to help you clarify things for yourself.

Remember too that the priest is bound by what is called the "**seal of the sacrament**" or the "seal of confession." He can never reveal to anyone—not to the bishop or the pope, not to your parents or the police—what you reveal to him in this sacrament. He can't even talk about it privately with you at a later date unless you tell him that he has your permission to do so. The seal is sacred!

4. Receive absolution.

After hearing your confession, the priest will ask you to make an act of contrition, that is, to say a prayer asking for forgiveness. Whether you use a memorized prayer or a spontaneous one, you express your sorrow for your sins. The priest then pronounces the words of absolution. To demonstrate the imparting of God's peace and forgiveness, he may lay his hands on your head as he says these words.

The words of absolution aren't magic. They're not a big eraser that clears your sins from a slate, only to be marked up again in the weeks to come. Rather, with the words of absolution, the Church addresses the sinner in the name of Christ, who brings God's forgiveness.

---

seal of the sacrament
the seal of confession, whereby the priest is solemnly obligated to never reveal anything he has heard in the Sacrament of Penance

Talk about it

1. Why do we hesitate to admit our failings and sins?

2. Why do you think the Catholic Church forbids the revealing of anything said to a priest in the Sacrament of Reconciliation?

An Act of Contrition

O my God, I am sorry for my sins.
In choosing to sin, and failing to do good,
I have sinned against you and against your Church.
I firmly intend, with the help of your Son,
to do penance and to sin no more. Amen.

Optional activities

1. Write your own act of contrition.

2. Talk with a young child about being sorry. Share some highlights of the conversation with the class.

5. Do your penance.

Just before he speaks the words of absolution, the priest will give you a penance to do (in a communal celebration, this may take place in the large gathering, with everyone receiving the same penance). In the "old days," this was almost always a certain number of Hail Marys and Our Fathers—or the recitation of the Rosary, if the sins were grave. This type of penance unfortunately left people with the idea that the mere saying of prayers made up for their sins, no matter how harmful those sins were.

Today, you will probably be given a penance that helps you change and live more like Jesus. You will probably be asked to do something to heal the hurt your sin has caused — because *healing* is what this sacrament is all about. Examples of penances include an act of kindness, a donation to charity, and concrete help for those who are poor.

Ideally, the penance given should relate to the sins confessed. Penance is a way of moving toward reestablishing broken relationships. The celebration of the Sacrament of Reconciliation is not complete until the penance is completed.

Talk about it

Imagine you are a priest hearing confessions. What kind of penances would you give to people to help them grow spiritually?

Place for the sacrament

Technically, the Sacrament of Penance may be celebrated in any place where a priest and the person confessing can find time and space. Normally, however, this sacrament is celebrated in a special place constructed in the church building for this purpose. This place, called the *Reconciliation chapel* or *Reconciliation room* or *confessional*, should be somewhat spacious and comfortable. The full rite of the sacrament calls for time for prayer, the sharing of Scripture, and some words of spiritual encouragement. The celebration should not be just the confession of sins and the reception of a penance and absolution.

Since reconciliation is celebrated as a personal encounter with God, the preference of the Church is face-to-face encounter between priest and penitent.

At the same time, according to Church law, the layout of the Reconciliation chapel must also allow the penitent to celebrate the sacrament anonymously—behind a screen. In other words, the penitent has the choice of whether or not to be known to the priest. The celebration of the sacrament over the telephone or the Internet, however, is not permitted! These would not be sufficiently personal encounters.

1. Where is the Reconciliation chapel in your church? What does it look like?

2. What are the advantages of face-to-face Reconciliation?

3. Why do you think confession over the telephone or the Internet is not permitted?

REVIEW

1. What are the steps in preparing for and celebrating the Sacrament of Reconciliation?

2. To what does the seal of the sacrament refer?

3. What does an Act of Contrition express?

4. What is a penance?

ANOINTING OF THE SICK

In the first part of this chapter, you studied the alienation from God, from oneself, and from others that we call *sin*. There is another kind of alienation which is part of the human condition. It's the alienation—or seeming alienation—of death. The death of another confronts us with the reality of our own mortality, the fact that our life in this world lasts only so long.

In a classroom setting, it's easy to talk about death. It's just an idea. It's something that happens to *other* people, older people. For young people, death is only a far-off idea. It isn't real. Even when you face the death of a family member or a classmate or friend, it's still *someone else's death*. These experiences make you more aware of the reality of death, but it still isn't *your* death.

For those who face their own death, for those experiencing serious illness or injury, the question of death isn't a classroom question; it's a life question. The heart cries out: "Is this all there is to life?" The answer? "No! This is not all there is to life! There is more! There is eternal life!"

Death forces upon us the question of "the end" and draws all of life into doubt. It is this fear of nothingness that tears at the human heart. For that reason, serious illness and death is not just news. Without a religious faith of some sort, they are *bad* news.

Suffering and serious illness have always been among those things that trouble the human spirit. Christians experience pain and death just as all other people do. But our faith in a risen Savior helps us face suffering with courage and face death with hope.

We *know* from Jesus' life, death, and resurrection that sickness and death have meaning. They have meaning because of the fullness of life promised us by Christ who fully embraced and conquered death—and enjoys the fullness of life with God! That's why we sing "Alleluia!" There's nothing to fear and everything to celebrate.

Then do this

1. Make a collage on one of the following themes and explain it to the class.
   - The signs of death and resurrection in nature
   - How our society deals with (or avoids) the reality of death
2. Write a poem about the Christian meaning of death.

> *In the last analysis, it is our conception of death which decides our answers to all the questions that life puts to us.*
>
> Dag Hammarskjöld

Christian death

Death for the Christian has a positive meaning because of Christ. Through death, we gain union with Christ, the risen Lord. We have already died with Christ through Baptism, in order to live a new life of grace. The Christian who dies in Christ's grace completes in a physical way this dying with Christ. He or she then completes the incorporation into Christ. When we die, God calls us to himself. The death of a Christian, in imitation of Christ, is raised into an act of obedience and love toward God the Father.

See the *Catechism of the Catholic Church*, #s 1010–1011.

1. Why is the Christian view of death so positive?

2. In Baptism, how do we "die with Christ"?

3. In physical death, how do we "die with Christ"?

4. What can Christians do to prepare for death?

St. Maximilian Kolbe
One who laid down his life for another

Raymond Kolbe was born in 1894 in southern Poland when the area was occupied by Russia. As a young man he became a Franciscan and took the name *Maximilian*. He had an aptitude for science and studied math, physics, and astronomy. At one point Maximilian designed a spacecraft and even applied for a patent on the design—long before space travel was foreseeable.

As a priest Maximilian taught Church history in Cracow and began a new monastery near Warsaw. In time over 700 priests and brothers lived there. The group built and ran a hospital, a fire department, a radio station, and a press devoted to religious books. From 1930 to 1936, Maximilian worked as a missionary in Japan. But he suffered from TB and returned home because of ill health.

In 1939 the Nazis invaded Poland, and Maximilian was arrested for the first time. He was released, but arrested again in 1941. This time he was sent to the notorious concentration camp, Auschwitz. One survivor of the camp, whose parents died there, later wrote the following of Father Kolbe:

Kolbe found me. He was like an angel to me, holding me, wiping away my tears. He gave me back my faith. He dispensed love and nothing but love. . . He gave away so much of his meager rations to others that it was a miracle he could live.

Later in the year a prisoner from Maximilian's section escaped, and the group faced the established reprisal. Ten men were randomly chosen to die by starvation. One of the ten chosen was a Polish soldier named Franciszek Gajowniczek. This man cried out in anguish that he would never see his wife and children again.

Never one to fear death, Maximilian stepped forward and volunteered to take the soldier's place. His offer was accepted, and, locked into a small, windowless cell in the barracks' basement, he led the men in prayer and song as they died, one by one. Even the guards exclaimed, "We never saw anything like it before!" Nearly two weeks later, four men were still alive, but only Maximilian was conscious. The four, Maximilian last, were killed with a lethal injection of carbolic acid. It was August 14, 1941.

In 1971 Maximilian Kolbe was proclaimed "Blessed" at a ceremony in Rome; Franciszek Gajowniczek was there to witness the event. Gajowniczek was still alive in 1982 when Maximilian was named a saint of the Catholic Church, and he lived for many more years, thanks to a man who lived and died for others.

Optional activities

1. Read the story of Maximilian Kolbe in *The Book of Virtues*, "The Volunteer at Auschwitz," in the section on "Faith." Share a summary with the class.

2. Write and perform a play on the life of Maximilian Kolbe.

3. Share with the class the story of someone you have known who faced death with courage and hope.

Understanding suffering and death

It's very important to know that sickness and death are not "punishments for sin." Sometimes it *seems* like they are. The human mind likes to look at everything in terms of causes: Why did this happen?

When we are seriously ill, or when a terrible accident happens, or when there is a death in the family, we need to make sense out of it. The more sudden these things are, the more we want to know *why* they happened. Since life and death are such mysteries, we automatically see the hand of God in them.

Illness, death, and natural catastrophes result from the laws of nature. Our hearts cry out: "Why?" We want to know why because we long for the ultimate fullness of life, we want human existence to be more than just X number of years, however long or short.

In our culture, we aren't realistic about sickness and disease. We expect science and technology to have all the answers, all the cures. We have pills for everything—or so it seems. Sickness and disease are seen as disruptions to our schedules. They are inconveniences that we want to remove so that we can get on with life.

It's certainly true that science and technology are enabling us to live longer, healthier lives. But we live with a false sense of reality. We think that we can defeat illness and death by the work of our own hands, and we think that we should do that—at all cost. We see no value in suffering and illness. We assume that we need to go to all lengths to avoid pain. We are deceived into thinking that we can even conquer death.

It's very good that, to some extent, we can control pain and limit suffering. It would be wrong to choose pain, just as it is wrong to cause pain needlessly. But we can't deny the reality of pain, nor the reality of illness, nor the reality of suffering—all because we want to deny the reality of death.

Talk about it

1. Do sickness and suffering have any meaning? If so, what is it?

2. Should they be avoided at all costs? Why or why not?

3. How do you feel when you are around someone who is seriously ill or dying?

4. How does our culture deal with the reality of death?

Then do this

Research the Hospice movement and prepare a presentation to give to the class.

In suffering, the deliverance consists in our being allowed to put the matter out of our own hands into God's hands.

Dietrich Bonhoeffer

REVIEW

1. Are sickness and death punishments for sin? Explain.

2. What is the Christian view of suffering?

3. What is the Christian view of death?

The importance of faith

Our Christian faith gives us a further perspective on serious illness and death. Our faith tells us that in themselves illness and death cannot rob us of our human value and dignity.

We are sons and daughters of God, now and forever. Neither suffering nor death should be sought—but, in the eyes of faith, suffering and death *can be made redemptive.* They can have value when seen from the perspective of faith in God. God has the ultimate answer to our lives. God alone is the source of all life and ultimate happiness.

In Jesus, God became one of us, sharing in the human condition. It's crucial to us that Jesus himself suffered and died. As evidenced in the Gospel stories, he feared the moment of his own death and wished the suffering were not going to happen. Like all humans he wanted to escape it. Yet he entrusted his entire life into the hands of God. Jesus embraced the human condition; he didn't hide from it or run from it, not even from suffering and death.

The cross which loomed before Jesus raised the questions that all human suffering and serious illness raise: What is the ultimate meaning of life? Is this all there is? Jesus fully embraced the mystery and entered into death. But God the Father raised him from death and gave him a new and full life!

Jesus' resurrection from the dead is the hinge of all history and the hinge of our personal faith as we too face the reality of death. Jesus doesn't lead us away from that reality, but *through* it—to eternal life! Our eternal life in God is a promise and a gift!

Talk about it
How does a Christian face death?

In the Sacraments of Christian Initiation, the Church celebrated who you are in God's eyes: a son or daughter of God, a brother or sister in Christ, who is destined to *eternal* life. Those sacraments were more than religious ceremonies; they were personal encounters with God in Christ Jesus. They were an occasion of promise to you—that when God creates human life, it is forever! The human condition of serious illness and death appears to say that isn't so: Were we born only to die, to return to the stuff of the earth or the cosmic dust of the universe? Were we believers initiated into Christ and his community of faith only to enjoy its fruits for a certain number of years? No!

As in the Sacraments of Christian Initiation, so in the Sacrament of the **Anointing of the Sick**—God encounters us. In this sacrament, God assures the sick or dying person that he or she belongs to God and that God's love is forever.

There is nothing magic about this sacrament; it's not the automatic assurance of healing and health. But it is the prayer for healing and the promise of eternal life—and through it the Lord Jesus greatly strengthens our faith. The celebration of this sacrament assures the person who is sick or dying that, despite appearances, there is nothing to fear. Sickness, serious illness, and even death do not separate us from ourselves or from God.

Anointing of the Sick
the sacrament for those who are sick or dying, the anointing with oil and prayers for physical and spiritual healing

And death shall have no dominion.
Dylan Thomas

Celebrating the sacrament

The Sacrament of the Anointing of the Sick is not just for those who are near death. Persons who suffer from sickness or from old age and begin to be in danger of death are encouraged to receive this sacrament. A sick person who recovers after being anointed can receive the sacrament again if he or she suffers another serious illness. Likewise, if during the same illness, the person becomes more seriously ill or if an elderly person becomes more frail, he or she may receive the sacrament again. Someone who is going to have a serious operation may also be anointed.

See the *Catechism of the Catholic Church,* #s 1514–1515.

1. Why does the Catholic Church not permit the anointing of those who have already died?

2. Can you describe a situation that would call for the celebration of the Anointing of the Sick?

3. Is the Anointing of the Sick necessary for entrance into eternal life?

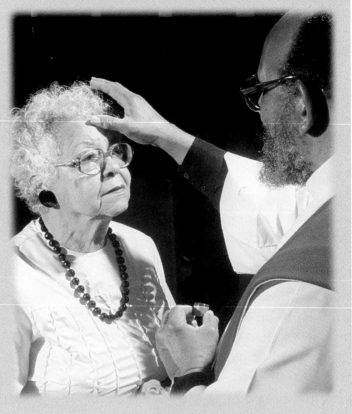

The encounter with God in the Sacrament of the Anointing of the Sick is for the spiritual benefit and welfare of people. They are strengthened in faith as they are touched by the ministry of the Church. They are given courage in Christ to embrace the mystery of death, courage to place their lives in the hands of God.

In a quite literal sense, the Church stands at the side of the seriously ill or dying person, assuring the person of God's blessing and favor, reminding him or her that death does not have the final say in life. In Jesus' death and resurrection, those who are sick and dying are promised eternal life. In union with Jesus, they are encouraged to embrace that mystery and let God lead them to new life.

Christians should fight against all forms of sickness and do what is reasonably necessary to preserve good health. At the same time, those who are seriously sick and dying show by the witness of their faith that our lives, though limited in this life, are eternal.

Those who are seriously ill need the special help of God's grace, lest they be broken in spirit or weakened in their faith. Through the Sacrament of the Anointing of the Sick, Christ himself meets those who are sick and dying, strengthening them in that situation when the very gift and meaning of life are brought into question.

Talk about it

1. When a person is seriously ill, what does he or she really need?

2. What can you do for someone who is seriously ill?

Jesus did not come to explain away suffering or remove it.
He came to fill it with his presence.
Paul Claudel

The celebration of the Anointing of the Sick

The Sacrament of the Anointing of the Sick is celebrated by a reading from Scripture, the laying on of hands by the priest, prayers, and the anointing with blessed oil. As he anoints the forehead and palms, the priest says,

> Through this holy anointing
> may the Lord in his love and mercy help you
> with the grace of the Holy Spirit.
>
> May the Lord who frees you from sin
> save you and raise you up.

The sick or dying person responds, "Amen," to each part of the prayer, opening his or her heart in faith to an encounter with the risen Lord who promises life everlasting. Thus, by this sacrament, the person is strengthened against doubt and against anxiety in the face of death. Accordingly, the sick or dying person is able to not only bear suffering bravely, but may also be able to resist the illness. A return to physical health sometimes follows the reception of this sacrament.

The Church insists that great care be taken to see that the members of the faithful whose health is seriously impaired by sickness or old age receive this sacrament. At the same time, the Anointing of the Sick should not be celebrated unless true need exists. The determination of when a person's health is seriously impaired is a pastoral judgment.

It's clear that the faithful are not to wait until the sick person's last breath before asking that a priest celebrate this sacrament. The primary purpose of the sacrament is to pray for healing and to strengthen the person who is ill and perhaps has a shaken faith. The sacrament also helps a person prepare for death.

The Eucharist is the primary sacrament for a dying person; it is spiritual food for the final journey into God's kingdom. This reception of the Eucharist is called **viaticum**, meaning "to take with one on the way"—food for the journey.

The priest is the proper minister of the Anointing of the Sick. Since this is a sacrament of the Church, it is most appropriate that as many of the community as possible gather for its celebration. When a person celebrates this sacrament at home or in the hospital or a care center, family and friends should be encouraged to be present.

This sacrament also takes place within Mass when the need arises or on a regular basis. The priest is a sign of the concern of the whole assembly for those who are suffering or near death. What the priest does in sacrament, the community does with and for those who are sick through their ministries of love and care.

Talk about it

What are some of the ways anointing with oil is used today?

Then do this

From your parish borrow a book that has the rite for the Anointing of the Sick. Report to the class on how the Church celebrates this sacrament.

viaticum

"food for the journey"; the Eucharist received by one who is dying

Talk about it

Why does the Catholic Church celebrate a funeral Mass for someone who has died?

REVIEW

1. How can suffering and death be redemptive?

2. What does the Sacrament of the Anointing of the Sick celebrate?

3. How is the Sacrament of the Anointing of the Sick celebrated?

4. What is viaticum?

CONCLUSION

As has been noted, forgiveness, mercy, and compassion are not just qualities of God. They would mean little if they weren't part of human living. The Sacraments of Reconciliation and Healing—Penance and the Anointing of the Sick—celebrate what God does for us, but God's forgiveness, mercy, compassion, and healing also challenge us to live these qualities in our relationships with others. Begin your reflection on how you might do that by reading the following story.

Grandmother's Table

Once upon a time a widow came to live with her son, daughter-in-law, and granddaughter. The woman was very old and feeble. Every day her eyes got worse and her hearing failed even more. Sometimes when the old woman was eating with the family at the dining room table, her hand would tremble and food would spill off her fork or spoon onto the table. When her shaky hand accidentally knocked her glass of milk over, her son and daughter-in-law had had enough. They were tired of watching her make a mess of her food and tired of cleaning up spills in the middle of a meal.

So they set up a little table in a corner of the kitchen and told the old woman that she would have to eat there from then on. And so she did, crying through each meal as the family ignored her. Usually her son and daughter-in-law spoke to her only in anger at the end of the meal when they had to clean up after her.

One day the little granddaughter was busily playing with her dolls and blocks when her father stopped to watch. He asked the girl what she was doing. Matter-of-factly, she replied, "I'm building a little table for my dolls. I'm putting them in the corner to eat supper, just like I'll do with you when I get big."

Both of the little girl's parents were shocked and dismayed. What had they done? That evening they led the old grandmother back to the dining room table, and there she ate as long as she was able. And from then on, no one complained when there were spills.

The Brothers Grimm, adapted.

Optional activities

1. Choose another fairy tale that relates to one of the themes of this chapter, and write a modern-day version. Share your story with the class. Alternative: write the story as a skit, and with classmates, act it out.

2. Interview five people about how they practice mercy and compassion in their lives. Write an essay on their answers, adding your reflections.

In every relationship in life, we are called to imitate the forgiveness, mercy, compassion, and healing of God. Within our families, first of all, we can be persons of peace rather than the cause of conflict. Being an adolescent isn't easy. Parents often want teenagers to act like adults, but they don't want to give them the privileges of adults. Of course, they know that it takes practice to "act like an adult," but adolescents may want to skip over that part and jump right into the privileges part. The problem is that without the practice, responsibility isn't learned.

So conflict may be frequent. When that happens, anger and shouting may become the normal language in family life. Then each hurt seems to lead to another hurt, until relationships are severely damaged and families are wrenched apart. No one wants that to happen, and no one feels good when it does.

On the other hand, often truly terrible things happen in a family, things that are not the fault of the young person. A child or teen can certainly be sinned against by other family members who act in immoral and destructive ways. No one needs to put up with such treatment, and help ought to be sought to change the situation or to remove the young person who is being abused.

No matter who is at fault when a family is torn apart, each person is called to do what he or she can to reconcile with family members. It takes real maturity to forgive and to live in peace. It takes maturity and courage and faith to show compassion to someone who has hurt rather than nurtured. But this is exactly what a Christian is called to do:

> As God's chosen ones, holy and beloved, clothe yourselves with compassion, kindness, humility, meekness, and patience. Bear with one another and, if anyone has a complaint against another, forgive each other; just as the Lord has forgiven you, so you also must forgive.
>
> — Colossians 3:12–13

This advice applies to our friendships and broken friendships as well as to our families. All of us recognize the feeling of being torn up, of having something eat away at us, when we are not at peace with someone. It's not healthy for humans to be "at war" with each other; it stunts our growth as persons and contributes to our unhappiness, and it interferes with our relationship with God.

The themes of reconciliation and healing that run through this chapter really speak to what it means to be human—truly and happily human. Jesus certainly knew what he was doing when he challenged us to forgive: "Forgive us our trespasses as we forgive those who trespass against us." "Peace be with you."

Write it down

Write a letter to Jesus asking for forgiveness and healing. Be specific about the areas in your life that need forgiveness and healing. (This will not be shared.)

Words you should know

absolution	Penance, Reconciliation	sin
alienation	penitent	sinning mortally
Anointing of the Sick	reconcile	sinning venially
conscience	seal of the sacrament	viaticum
mercy		

CHAPTER 12

The SACRAMENTS of CHRISTIAN LIFE

CHAPTER OVERVIEW

- *Christian life*

- *Holy Orders*

- *Single life choices*

- *Matrimony*

The Word of the Lord

[Jesus] appointed twelve whom he also named apostles, to be with him, and to be sent out to proclaim the message, and to have authority to cast out demons.

FROM THE GOSPEL ACCORDING TO MARK, SEE 3:13–19.

" '. . . a man shall leave his father and mother and be joined to his wife, and the two shall become one flesh.' So they are no longer two but one flesh. Therefore, what God has joined together, let no one separate."

FROM THE GOSPEL ACCORDING TO MARK, SEE 10:2–9.

It is good to give thanks to the LORD,
to sing praises to your name, O Most High;

Let Us Pray

to declare your steadfast love in the morning,
and your faithfulness by night,
to the music of the lute and the harp,
to the melody of the lyre.
For you, O LORD, have made me glad by your work;
at the works of your hands I sing for joy.
How great are your works, O LORD!
Your thoughts are very deep! . . .
The righteous flourish like the palm tree,
and grow like a cedar in Lebanon.
They are planted in the house of the LORD;
they flourish in the courts of our God.

PSALM 92:1–5, 12–13

CHRISTIAN LIFE

The Catholic Church celebrates seven sacraments, each of which relates to the others. As you learned in an earlier chapter, for example, the Sacraments of Christian Initiation have a unique interrelationship. They establish and celebrate a person's identity with Christ and his community of faith. The previous chapter explored how the Sacraments of Healing restore people to spiritual, and sometimes physical, health.

This chapter explores the remaining two sacraments of the Church—Holy Orders and Matrimony—the Sacraments of Christian Life. Each of these sacraments celebrates an essential aspect of the Church's life, especially in terms of service, and each is related to the Sacraments of Christian Initiation. This chapter also explores other vocations that are not celebrated with a sacrament: single life, consecrated life, and consecrated community life.

Talk about it

Why is service to others the main responsibility of all those who are baptized?

I am blessed

The following reflection is said to have been written by an unknown Confederate soldier. Its wisdom speaks to all of us as we try to live our Christian vocation with our unique gifts and talents.

I asked God for strength, that I might achieve.
I was made weak, that I might learn humbly to obey. . . .
I asked for health, that I might do great things.
I was given infirmity, that I might do better things. . . .
I asked for riches, that I might be happy.
I was given poverty, that I might be wise . . . .
I asked for power, that I might have the praise of [others].
I was given weakness, that I might feel the need of God . . . .
I asked for all things, that I might enjoy life.
I was given life, that I might enjoy all things . . . .
I got nothing I asked for—but everything I had hoped for.
Almost despite myself, my unspoken prayers were answered.
I am, among men, most richly blessed!

Optional activities

1. Add to the above reflection: I asked for . . . I was given . . . .

2. Find the story of someone who did great things despite difficulties. Share the story with the class, and lead a discussion on the lesson learned.

3. Find a Scripture verse to accompany each of the two-line statements.

REVIEW

1. What are the Sacraments of Christian Life?

2. What other vocations are there?

HOLY ORDERS

Church is God's work. We can see in the Bible how believers came together because of God's presence in their hearts and lives. God's actions pave the way for people to become a people of faith. It's because of God's action that the Church is a concrete historical reality. The "making of the Church" continues to this very day. And we are a part of that! We are part of God's continuing action of salvation in the world!

This is what Catholics celebrate in the Sacraments of Christian Initiation. Our life in Christ started in Baptism and is strengthened by the Spirit in Confirmation and nourished by the Eucharist. The Sacraments of Initiation unite us in the life and mission of the Church. All initiated members of the Church minister in the name of Jesus by the witness of our lives and by the activities to which we give our time and talent.

Church means being faithful. Church means sharing responsibility. We share the responsibility for the ministry of the Church. We have the privilege of living the good news of God's salvation and loving presence. We are all called to be signs of God's kingdom. We are all responsible, but we have different responsibilities.

Regardless of our position in the Church, we need to be united in shared responsibility and in faithfulness to the Word made flesh. Jesus is the historical "founder" or source of Christian life. That's why the Church must always be guided by the life and teachings of Jesus.

To really be a part of the Christian Church requires more than a personal relationship with the risen Lord Jesus. We need to be a part of the community of faith he established. The sacraments are an important part of that participation; they celebrate and bring about in our lives God's saving work.

Write it down

How do you help "make the Church"; that is, how are you part of God's continuing action of salvation in the world?

Talk about it

1. When you think about being a member of the Church, what do you think about?

2. As an individual, what does it mean to be guided by the life and teachings of Jesus? As a member of the Christian community?

Priesthood of the faithful

The ordained priesthood and the priesthood of the faithful are interconnected, even though they differ in an essential way, more than in degree. Both express a sharing in the priesthood of Christ. The ordained priest oversees the people in the parish; in the person of Christ he presides at the Eucharist and offers this sacrifice to God in the name of the people.

The people, joined in Baptism to the priesthood of Christ, participate in the offering of the Eucharist. The people also exercise their priesthood by participating in the sacraments, by prayer and thanksgiving, by the witness of their holy lives, and by self-sacrifice and works of charity.

The Documents of Vatican II, "Dogmatic Constitution on the Church," #10.

1. How do an ordained priest and the rest of the people of the Church share the same responsibility to give witness with their Christian life? How do their responsibilities differ?

2. What does it mean to be a "living sacrifice of praise"?

3. How is the Eucharist (the Mass) an action of both the ministerial (ordained) priesthood and the priesthood of the faithful? Who celebrates the Mass? Who presides at the Mass?

The apostolic Church

Jesus' life was witnessed in time and place by the first apostles. These men were selected by Jesus to carry out his mission in the world. For that reason, one of the Church's primary characteristics is that it is apostolic. The word *apostolic* is from a Greek word which literally means "sent." When the Church speaks of itself as **apostolic**, it means that it is founded on the apostles, those who were sent. It is apostolic in three important ways.

- First, the Church is apostolic in the sense that it is built on the foundation of the apostles and, therefore, like them, is sent on mission by Jesus. The Church shares in his authority. The Church's mission is that of Jesus, who made known the unconditional love of God for his people and proclaimed God's kingdom to all.
- Second, the Church is apostolic also in the sense that it is rooted in the teaching of the apostles. The Spirit guides the Church to faithfully hand on this teaching.
- Third, the Church is apostolic because it carries on the ministry of the apostles who were chosen by Jesus to lead and care for his community. These apostles and their successors (the bishops, in union with the pope and assisted by the priests and deacons) have continued the mission of Christ. Through the apostles the Church at any point in time is the *same* Church as the community which is historically identified with Jesus himself.

As with the first apostles, men are chosen from among the faithful to serve them as successors of the apostles. Historically speaking, there has been development in how the successors of the apostles have exercised their ministry. In the early Church some men were overseers, others presiders, and still others servers. Later these somewhat vague divisions came to be identified with the different ministries of bishops, priests, and deacons.

This division of roles was probably modeled on the structure in the Jewish community. There is evidence in the Judaism of the first century of positions of oversight, governance, and service. In the Jewish faith tradition, individuals were often given their positions in a ceremony that included prayer and the laying on of hands. Clearly this is the origin of the **ordination** rite by which individuals become deacons, priests, and bishops. These are the three orders which account for the name of the sacrament in the Catholic Church: **Holy Orders**.

apostolic
founded on the apostles

Talk about it

1. Have you ever attended an ordination? If so, share your impressions with the class.
2. What is the reason for ordination?
3. From your observation, what do you see as the differences among the three orders of the Catholic Church?

ordination
the rite by which a man becomes a deacon, priest, or bishop

Holy Orders
the sacrament by which a man is ordained as a deacon, priest, or bishop

The role of the apostles

All the events during the time of Jesus' suffering, death, and resurrection involve each of the apostles—especially Peter—in the building of a new age. This new era in human history began on Easter. The apostles were eyewitnesses of the risen Christ; therefore, they are the foundation stones of the Church. The faith of the first community of believers is based on the witness of very specific people known to the early Christians and, in the case of most, still living among them. While they were not the only witnesses to Jesus' resurrection, Peter and the other apostles are the primary witnesses.

See the *Catechism of the Catholic Church*, #642.

1. Why is an eyewitness to the life, death, and resurrection of Jesus important to the Christian community?
2. Identify a successor of the apostles in your own faith community.

The hierarchy

Together, bishops, priests, and deacons are called the **hierarchy** in the Catholic Church. Commonly, however, the word refers to the bishops, including those bishops with special roles and titles: the pope, cardinals, archbishops. *Hierarchy* literally means "priest ruled," but don't let the word deceive you. It isn't spelled *higher*-archy! Bishops don't rule their part of the Church like CEOs (chief executive officers) of major corporations who have no real connection with the CEOs of other companies. They don't set rules and regulations independent of the other bishops.

Bishops are members of the **college of bishops**, with the pope at their head. They represent Christ, who is the head of the Church, which is his body. Christ leads everyone in the Church, including the hierarchy. Although members of the hierarchy have sometimes misused their position, that position is not supposed to be about power and domination. Jesus expected an attitude and practice of service from those who minister in his name.

Bishops, priests, and deacons are not more holy than the other members of the Church, nor are they more talented or intelligent. At the same time, through ordination, they do share in the pastoral leadership of the Church. They are sacraments of Christ who is the head of his family of faith.

In the Catholic Church, this leadership "office," or work, is a sacrament. Jesus continues to lead the Church in and through its bishops, priests, and deacons. These leaders are called to proclaim the gospel, foster the growth of the Christian community, and minister to others through service.

hierarchy
clergy; commonly understood, the bishops of the Catholic Church, including the pope, cardinals, and archbishops

college of bishops
the bishops of the Catholic Church with the pope at their head

Then do this
Find out the role of an ordained minister (bishop, pastor, deacon) in another Christian denomination. Compare your findings with ordained ministry in the Catholic Church.

> *In Jesus the service of God and the service of the least of the brethren were one.*
> **Dietrich Bonhoeffer**

St. John Bosco
Youth ministry priest

John Bosco was born in northwest Italy in 1815. His father died when he was a toddler, and his illiterate mother took on the task of preparing him for the sacraments and teaching him the basics of her religion. John, in turn, taught the catechism to other youngsters in his poor neighborhood. John's mother was also anti-clerical (it was just past or at the time of Napoleon, Marx, and Darwin), so she wasn't happy when John decided to become a priest.

Even during his years of study, John gathered young people from poor areas to help them learn the basics of the faith and to prepare them for a newly industrialized society. Once a priest, Don Bosco provided a refuge in Turin for abandoned boys (his mother came to help) and served as a chaplain for a refuge for girls. He became well-known for the education, social activities, and prayer experiences he organized for young people. The work he did with young people is today called *youth ministry*.

Within about fifteen years time, Don Bosco and his helpers were providing a home for up to 800 orphaned or abandoned boys at a time. John started workshops in which the boys learned trades: shoemaking, tailoring, book binding, printing, and iron working. Often the number of boys involved in the programs were double the number he housed.

When a cholera epidemic came to Turin, the boys carried those who were sick to hospitals and took the bodies of those who had died to mortuaries. None of the boys came down with cholera because John made sure they washed their hands frequently with vinegar. Many people thought the reason was that Don Bosco was a miracle worker.

One of the many books Don Bosco wrote was on youth formation, and this particular book had 118 editions during his life. John was the subject of a press review in 1884, and in the same year a participant in a major exhibit on book making at an industrial trade show. But throughout his many endeavors, John's attention went first to his ministry among young people, especially those who were poor. John died in 1888 and was canonized a saint in 1934.

Optional activities

1. Look up the life of another saint who was a priest. Write a paper or present your research to the class.

2. Investigate the youth ministry programs in your area, both Catholic and Protestant (and Jewish and Muslim). Compile your findings and draw conclusions.

REVIEW

1. What are the two kinds of priesthood?

2. What does it mean to say that the Church is apostolic?

3. What does the Sacrament of Holy Orders celebrate?

4. What are the three orders?

5. Who are the hierarchy?

Roles and responsibilities

As has been noted, in the Catholic Church today, the primary leaders are its bishops, priests, and deacons. Serving the people of God, these individuals are responsible for preaching the gospel of Jesus and making sure that the Christian community is united and cared for.

Bishop

The **bishop** of a diocese has three main functions: teaching, preaching, and sanctifying (especially through the sacraments).

- The bishop is the chief shepherd, or overseer, of the Christian faithful entrusted to his care. He proclaims the gospel and serves as the main teacher of Scripture and Tradition in the diocese.
- The bishop is also the primary decision maker in his diocese.
- And, in the very person of the bishop, the community is assured, sacramentally speaking, of the presence of Jesus as head of his Church. The bishop is the main presider at all the sacraments in his diocese, although he is assisted by the priests and sometimes by deacons in this large task.

The bishop is sometimes referred to as the *Ordinary* of his diocese. He and the members of his diocese are a full expression of the Catholic Church at the local level. In other words, the bishop and his faithful are not just a portion of a larger reality called the Catholic Church. Rather, the full reality of the Catholic Church exists in the bishop and the members of his diocese.

Only a bishop can ordain other bishops, that is, share his apostolic office with others. However, a bishop never acts on his own when it comes to ordaining other bishops. This is always a function exercised for the whole Church and in union with the pope.

bishop
a successor of the apostles, usually the head of a diocese

Priest

A **priest** is a man ordained by a bishop to the order of presbyter (the work of presider). He works with his bishop in proclaiming the gospel and fostering Christian community. The Catholic Church holds that only men can be ordained to the priesthood—as well as to the orders of deacon and bishop.

Most priests work in parishes. They preside at the Eucharist and the other sacraments. Priests preach, teach, counsel, pray with parishioners, lead, administer, coordinate, supervise, collaborate, and console. In the typical parish, it's easy to see the servant nature of the work of the priest.

priest
ordained man who presides at the sacraments and ministers to people in the name of the Church

Then do this

1. Try to find out what your parish priest does in a typical week.

2. Share your list of activities with someone who has collected the same information from a priest in another parish.

3. As a class, determine a common list of work done by priests in parishes. Put a star by each activity that affects young people directly. Put a check by those activities that affect young people indirectly.

> *Be sure that you first preach by the way you live.*
> **St. Charles Borromeo**

Deacon

deacon
first order of the ordained; does works of charity and may preside at Baptisms and marriages

There are two kinds of **deacons**.

- The first kind is the *transitional deacon*. These men are on the way to being ordained priests, so they are first ordained deacons, that is, they receive the first order.
- A *permanent deacon* does not intend to become a priest, but rather intends to remain a deacon.

The deacon is not a mini-priest or "Father's helper" around the parish; he has his own ministry. The deacon is himself a sacrament of service, a living reminder that the Church exists for others.

Although he may perform some of the same sacramental functions as a priest, the deacon's primary ministry is clearly one of service, especially care for those who are poor. The sacraments a deacon can preside at are Baptism and Matrimony (though he doesn't preside at a wedding Mass). A deacon can also conduct a funeral, though not a funeral Mass. In most dioceses, a deacon may also preach. The more a deacon is known for—and promotes—service of others, the more faithful he is to his unique calling in the Church.

Married men may become permanent deacons. While some permanent deacons hold full-time jobs in the Church, the majority work full- or part-time in other occupations and devote whatever time they can to their ministry as deacons.

Archbishop

archbishop
a bishop who is usually the leader of an archdiocese (a prominent or large diocese)

In terms of the Sacrament of Holy Orders, an **archbishop** is equal with any other bishop. By Church law, however, an archbishop is one who is given more oversight authority. For example, in addition to his own archdiocese, an archbishop may serve as spokesperson for the bishops of the other dioceses in his region, which might include the other dioceses in a given state. Some other archbishops hold administration positions in the Church, often in Rome.

Monsignor

monsignor
an honorary title given to some priests

Monsignor is an honorary title given to some priests. In terms of the Sacrament of Holy Orders, a priest so named remains equal to any other priest. The title *Monsignor* adds nothing to the priesthood. The title is usually given to a priest in gratitude for faithful work as a priest.

Cardinal

cardinal
a bishop who is eligible to elect the pope

Then do this
Find out who the cardinals in your country are. What archdiocese does each one serve? How many Catholics are there in each of those archdioceses?

Many people believe that the **cardinals** of the Church are so called because of the red cassocks they wear at liturgy and some formal events. This is probably not true, however. Rather, the name most likely comes from the Latin word *cardo*, which means "hinge" and refers to important positions of administration in the Church.

Cardinals originated somewhat early in the Church with ordained men who were associated with basilicas and parishes in the city of Rome. According to Church law today, cardinals ordinarily are named from among the world's bishops. One of the most important functions of cardinals is to elect a new pope after a pope has died or resigned (this latter is rare). The title of cardinal is retained after the cardinal passes the age limit for those who elect the pope.

Religious order priests

In the history of the Church, certain individuals have formed religious communities or "orders." Such groups are committed to living gospel values in community. Members of these **religious orders** make solemn **vows**, or promises before God, to witness to the virtues of poverty, chastity, and obedience. That is, for the sake of gospel witness, they vow to personally own nothing, to not marry, and to place themselves at the service of the Church according to the rule or "order" which governs their particular group.

Members of religious orders usually refer to one another by the title of *Brother* or *Sister*. Some of the men in religious communities are ordained to the priesthood in order to serve the community or the Church at large. Within their communities, these men may be referred to as *Father*, as priests are often addressed.

religious order
a group of men or women who make vows and live in a community governed by an approved rule

vows
solemn promises to God

Then do this
Find out which, if any, religious communities of priests work in your (arch)diocese. If possible, research one of these groups and report to the class.

Diocesan priests

Obviously, not all priests belong to religious orders. Those who don't are diocesan priests. Diocesan priests are responsible to their bishop rather than to a religious community superior. They do not make the vows that members of religious communities make. They do promise obedience and respect to their bishop, and, in the Latin Rite, promise to be celibate and to not marry. There are exceptions to the **celibacy** rule in the Catholic Church in the West, such as when a married Episcopalian priest becomes a Catholic and is ordained for ministry in the Catholic Church.

celibacy
the Church discipline requiring most priests of the Catholic Church in the West to not marry

Celibacy

In the Catholic Church in the West, most ordained ministers are celibate (excluding married permanent deacons) and intend to stay celibate "for the sake of the kingdom of God." They are called to **consecrate** themselves wholeheartedly to God and to God's work. Celibacy is a sign of their new life of service. When it is accepted with a joyous heart, celibacy proclaims the kingdom of God.

consecrate
to make holy or to dedicate

See the *Catechism of the Catholic Church*, #1579.

1. What is celibacy? What does it mean to be celibate?

2. Is celibacy a denial or rejection of sexuality? Explain your answer.

3. What is chastity? How is celibacy different from chastity? Who is called to be chaste? To be celibate?

REVIEW

1. What are the three functions of a bishop?

2. What is a priest?

3. What are the two kinds of deacons?

4. What are some of the other titles given to some priests and some bishops?

5. In addition to diocesan priests, what other kind of priests are there?

6. What does celibacy mean?

The leadership of the pope

We read in the Gospels that Jesus chose twelve men as his apostles, special disciples. The Twelve were to become the leaders in the community of Jesus' followers. From among the twelve apostles, Jesus selected Simon Peter for the position of headship. He was the first among equals in exercising the authority of the apostles. Peter wasn't a holier or more moral person than the others. He wasn't better than the others in any way; in fact, he was very impulsive. But Peter loved Jesus and believed in him with all his heart.

Down through the centuries, many men have followed Peter as the leader of the Church. However, due to changing times and the differing situation of the Church, the role of this person has changed significantly from the time of Peter.

In the Catholic Church, this leader is known today as the *pope*. That word comes from the Italian word *papa*, which of course means "father"—an affectionate title the bishop of Rome has enjoyed for centuries. The word **papacy** comes from the same word and refers to the office of the pope—also called the *Petrine office* (after Peter).

papacy
the office of the pope

Throughout the centuries, many popes have been humble servants of the Church, and some have been severely persecuted. A few popes have been corrupt and, like kings, have tried to reign triumphantly over the Church and over large territories of land. Other popes have been great defenders of Church teaching. Still other popes have seen a need for change in the Church and in the world around them, and have become world leaders.

Volumes have been written about the evolution of the papacy. In your own lifetime, you will likely see further developments in this leadership office as the pope seeks to preserve unity in the local Churches, or dioceses, and strives for greater unity with other Christian Churches.

Most popes have lived in Rome because, for centuries, Rome was the center of the Roman Empire. The pope is a bishop like any other bishop in the Catholic Church (actually an archbishop); he is the bishop of the diocese of Rome. This means that the pope has a diocese just as the bishop of the diocese in which you live does.

What makes the pope unique is that the bishop of the diocese of Rome is the head on earth of the Catholic Church. He appoints bishops to dioceses throughout the world and oversees the governing of the Catholic Church by means of his teaching authority, by means of canon (Church) law, and through a variety of administrative offices called the *curia*. Since the pope is also the head of the **Vatican** (a nation itself, with its own yellow and white flag), the pope is recognized as a world political leader.

Vatican
the tiny, sovereign nation in which the pope lives, located within Rome

Talk about it

1. Who is the present pope?
2. How long has he been pope?
3. What was his name before he became pope?
4. Where is he from?
5. What is he known for?

The strength of the Church is her unity. . . .
Archbishop Alban Goodier

And you, O Church, are a most excellent assembly . . .
whose assistance comes from God.
St. John Damascene

Pope Leo XIII
The pope of social justice

Vincenzo Gioacchino Pecci was born in Italy in 1810; he was pope from 1878 until his death in 1903. He was a contemporary of John Bosco, and the pope for the last ten years of John's life. Like Don Bosco, Pope Leo XIII was interested in the people who were flooding the cities because of the industrial revolution and who ended up living lives of dire poverty there, often alienated from the Church.

Pope Leo is best known for his letter to the worldwide Church on social justice, the first major Church document on the subject. Entitled *Rerum Novarum* (On the Condition of Workers), the letter was published in 1891. In the letter, Leo outlined the rights and responsibilities of the family and of private property, both of which were often threatened by the state. He took a strong stand for the right of workers to just wages and the right of workers to unionize. Leo challenged the state to protect laborers from exploitation and other injustices.

This document inspired Catholics over the following decades to be active in labor unions and in politics. Interestingly, Pope Leo was uncomfortable with democracy, especially in its American form. But the Catholic Church in North America took to Leo's social justice teachings with gusto and remains dedicated to the principles of justice to this day.

Optional activities

1. Look up the life of another saint who was a pope. Write a paper or present your research to the class.
2. Research the state of unions in your area and present your findings to the class.
3. Locate another Church document on a justice issue and read part of it. Summarize your reading in an essay.
4. In small groups, brainstorm other justice issues. Then find out what the Catholic Church teaches on one of the issues.

Keep God's word in this way: let it enter your very being,
let it take possession of your desires
and your whole way of life.
St. Bernard of Clairvaux

The office of the pope

Like Peter and the other apostles, the pope and the bishops of the world are inter-related and united as a single apostolic college or permanent assembly. Peter was named by Jesus as the "rock" of the Church. To Peter was given the keys of his Church, and Jesus named him the shepherd of the flock that is the Church.

The pastoral office of binding and loosing given to Peter and the other apostles united with him is foundational to the Church. The Catholic Church sees this office continuing today in the bishops under the leadership or primacy of the pope. The pope is bishop of Rome and Peter's successor. Because he is the Vicar of Christ and pastor of the whole Church, the pope has the responsibility of authority over the whole Church. The bishops together exercise this same universal authority, though only with the pope's agreement.

See the *Catechism of the Catholic Church*, #s 880–883.

1. What is the primary service or ministry of the pope in the Catholic Church?
2. How many popes can you identify? What have been the outstanding qualities of their ministry?
3. How do other Christian Churches see the role of the pope?
4. Can the way the pope exercises his leadership change? Explain.

Infallibility

infallibility
the quality of teaching without error under certain circumstances, held by the pope and the bishops in union with the pope

Regardless of the personality and accomplishments of an individual pope, the person in this office serves the Catholic Church as its unifier and truth-keeper. The pope speaks **infallibly**, that is, without error, when he intends to and uses the authority of his office in union with the faith of the Church to make a statement on a matter of faith or morals. The bishops in union with the pope can also teach infallibly under the same conditions. Such pronouncements, however, are very rare, since there is not often a pressing need for such a statement.

This doesn't mean that *everything* the pope says is infallibly true. But it also doesn't mean that, unless the pope speaks infallibly, his teaching should be ignored by the believing community. Leadership in the Church doesn't have to be exercised only in extraordinary ways. Most often it is exercised in ordinary ways: homilies, instructions, pronouncements, letters, speeches, and so on. When you see the pope speaking on television, you most likely see him in the ordinary exercise of his authority.

If members of the Church take their faith seriously, they will seek guidance from those in leadership in the Church to help them understand better how to apply the gospel to their lives. They will listen attentively and seriously to the **magisterium**, or teaching authority of the Catholic Church.

magisterium
the teaching authority of the Catholic Church

All the bishops of the world share in the teaching authority of the Church. In fact, all the members of the hierarchy exercise this authority in some form or another—usually by preaching and teaching. Many bishops (and groups of bishops called *episcopal conferences*) publish pastoral letters to help guide members of the Church in understanding the gospel and its application to a particular situation.

When the bishop of Rome, the pope, publishes a letter for the entire Church, this letter is called an **encyclical**. In modern times, popes have frequently used this means of teaching and have issued special letters on a variety of subjects related to the Church or to the wider world. Pope John Paul II, for example, has left the Church with many encyclicals which have addressed a variety of topics.

The main thing about the teaching authority of the Catholic Church is keeping the unity of the faith. The Catholic Church affirms that the beliefs and the believers should be unified. This is not the same as conformity (everyone acting and thinking alike in everything); in fact, the Catholic Church can and does experience a great degree of diversity throughout the world.

To help maintain unity within diversity, the bishops of the world work together in a special way called **collegiality**. The pope himself is the head of this "college" or union of bishops. On very special occasions, this body of the world's bishops comes together to discuss important Church issues or teachings. These gatherings are called **ecumenical councils**. The last one, the Second Vatican Council, was held between 1962 and 1965.

Other less universal gatherings of bishops, called **synods**, often are convened to explore a specific issue for the Church. Sometimes a synod of bishops is composed of bishops from a particular part of the world (for example, Latin America) and is held to discuss a topic of concern for the Church in that part of the world.

Leadership in the Church takes many forms. For most people, the leadership they experience takes two forms. The teaching of the hierarchy helps them understand why the Church takes the stands it does; it also helps people form their consciences and make good moral decisions. The other leadership comes from those who lead by example. That can be anyone in the Church who inspires others to live as Jesus did. This is the leadership of discipleship to which every Christian is called.

encyclical
a letter by the pope to the worldwide Church

collegiality
the working together of the bishops of the Church to lead and unify the members of the Church

ecumenical council
a gathering of the world's bishops to discuss important Church issues or teachings

synod
a gathering of a group of bishops, usually from a particular part of the world, to discuss an issue

---

Mother and Teacher of all nations—such is the Catholic Church in the mind of her founder, Jesus Christ.
Pope John XXIII, *Mother and Teacher*, #1.

The whole company of the faithful, who have an anointing by the Spirit, cannot err in faith.
"The Constitution on the Church," #12.

Talk about it

1. Consider an issue and decide how decisions on that issue could best be made. Who should be involved in the discussion? In the decision? How should the decision be explained to the people?

2. How are decisions made in the Christian community?

REVIEW

1. What is the role of the pope?
2. Where does the pope live?
3. What does infallibility mean?
4. What is the magisterium?
5. What is an encyclical?
6. What is an ecumenical council? What does it do?

SINGLE LIFE CHOICES

Talk about it
What are the vocation options for single people?

Christian discipleship isn't meant to be lived by only a few committed people. As we have seen earlier, all who are identified with Christ through the Sacraments of Initiation are called to discipleship with Jesus. All of us are called to a life of learning, conversion, and service. Once initiated in Baptism, Confirmation, and Eucharist, the question is not whether a person is a disciple of Jesus; the question is how *good* of a disciple the person is!

There is still a tendency today to identify discipleship with priests, brothers, and sisters. Ask a classmate or a neighbor what kind of person he or she thinks of as a disciple of Jesus. People often will name the local priest, the sisters in the school or at the hospital, or perhaps the brother who taught them in high school. They see true discipleship modeled only by those who have committed themselves to live gospel values in the priesthood or **religious life**.

religious life
the vocation of vowed persons who usually live in community

Within the Catholic tradition—and some other Christians traditions as well—certain individuals have indeed made the commitment to witness to their discipleship in extraordinary ways. Some of these people have made either an individual, formal dedication of their lives to God and the work of the Church or have made such a commitment in the context of a community.

A question of love

Every human wants to love and be loved. When we talk about being mature, we think of selflessness and commitment to other people; we talk about a love that isn't self-centered. Certainly this kind of love is different from the self-absorbed feeling of "falling in love" and different from infatuation with another person. "Love" is dead-ended if it is self-serving.

Fulfillment in life comes with the free and conscious choice to give oneself to others, to be there for another person. For most people, that mature choice to love unselfishly leads to a commitment to another person in marriage. Marriage is a special way for a Christian to live out his or her commitment to Christ in an exclusive love relationship with a person of the other gender.

In addition to Holy Orders and Matrimony, there are other ways Christians can express their commitment to Christ, even though these ways are not celebrated as sacraments. This section of the chapter takes a brief look at three of those ways to live Christian discipleship in a wholesome and life-giving way. These are single life, consecrated life, and consecrated community life.

Single life

Let's take a look at the first of these three ways. There's a stage in everyone's life when they are single—that is, not married. In our culture, we almost expect everyone to marry, and we look a bit suspiciously at those who are well into the "marrying age," but have not made such a commitment. We joke about people who *finally* "tie the knot," as if marriage were the only natural and fulfilling way for people to live.

The **single life** can be defined simply as not being married, and, certainly, not everyone is called to marriage. But single life can also be more. It can be a way in which people freely and consciously chose to work for the welfare of others and witness to the commitment of Christ to his Church.

It's a fact of life that because of hardships like death and divorce, many people re-enter the single life. For those who are raising children alone, the single life is really the parenting life. Their responsibilities, emotional and financial, can be almost overwhelming, and there is little time to even think of themselves. With the assistance of family, friends, and the Church community, most single parents succeed in bringing up their children well and in seeing themselves as valuable persons in the lives of many.

Those people who find themselves no longer married, like those who have never married, don't necessarily think of their lives as tragic. Many single people find that the single life is right for them at this time or for life. For them, it's a vocation; that is, they feel called to this way of life. They may find that they are free to express their love for others in a variety of appropriate and fulfilling ways. For some, the single life is truly a vocation from God which helps them express a lifelong desire to be of service to others with generosity and presence.

The Church welcomes this kind of witness to the vocation of the single life, whether it is for a short time (before or after a marriage) or on a permanent basis. On occasion, individuals who have embraced the single life as their vocation become known to others as committed, dedicated Christians.

single life
not being married; the vocation from God of living unmarried and celibate, chosen in order to be of service to others

Talk about it

1. Identify some single people who are living their Christian vocation well. Discuss the impact of their witness.

2. Explore how the Church can support and assist single parents.

*T*he vocation of every man and woman is to serve other people.

Leo Tolstoy

REVIEW

1. To what does the term *religious life* refer?
2. As a vocation, what is single life?
3. Who has a vocation to the single life?

Jean Donovan
Single lay missionary

Jean Donovan was an unlikely martyr. She grew up in a wealthy family and received an excellent education. At age twenty-four, with a master's degree in economics, she became an executive in a Cleveland accounting firm.

But Jean, single and having fun spending her money, wasn't quite satisfied with how her life was going. When Jean had lived in Ireland as an exchange student, she had met a priest who had worked in Peru as a missionary. Now she began to consider mission work for herself. She felt called by God.

At that time the Cleveland diocese sponsored a mission team in El Salvador. So Jean prepared to join the team by taking a study program at Maryknoll (a mission community) and studying Spanish in Guatemala. In 1979 Jean headed for El Salvador to work with Sister Dorothy Kazel, who was also from the Cleveland diocese. And there she met Archbishop Oscar Romero, the champion of the people who were poor and being oppressed by the military at that time.

A year after Jean's arrival in the country, Archbishop Romero was assassinated as he celebrated Mass in a hospital chapel. Though fearful of the strained situation that was pitting the Church against the government, Jean continued her missionary work. The team of which she was a part provided food and medicine for countless people. They led the people in prayer and taught them about the faith. They buried those killed by the death squads.

On December 2, 1980, Jean and Sister Dorothy went to the airport to pick up two Maryknoll Sisters returning from the United States—Sisters Ita Ford and Maura Clarke. On their way back from the airport, the four women disappeared. Two days later their bodies were found in a shallow grave fifteen miles from the airport. They had been raped and shot.

While the soldiers who were directly involved in the killings served a few years in prison, those who ordered the deaths were never punished. Jean and the three women religious have not been forgotten; they, along with Archbishop Romero and many others, are

honored as martyrs in El Salvador. Jean lived her life to the fullest, courageously answering the call by God that took her to another country and even death for the sake of the people she served.

Optional activities

1. Look up the life of a saint who was a single lay person. Write a paper or present your research to the class.

2. Watch a video on the life of Jean Donovan, such as "Roses in December." NBC also produced a movie on her entitled "Choices of the Heart." At least one play has been written about Jean. Write a reflection after your viewing.

3. Research what your diocese is doing in terms of missionary work. Find out who is involved—priests, religious, lay people. Share your findings with the class.

4. Contact a diocesan office or a religious community connected with work in the missions, and ask for literature. Share the materials with the class.

Consecrated life

Some individuals in the Christian community deliberately consecrate themselves to being disciples of Christ. The word *consecrate* means "to make holy with" or to "set apart." These people don't claim to be holier or better disciples; all are called to be holy. Through the Church, these individuals commit their entire lives to God. The Church provides a special ceremony for this unique profession and publicly accepts the vows, or promises, of these persons.

Before making such a serious profession, they go through a period of preparation. Beginners in religious communities are sometimes called *novices* or beginners. They make their commitment in stages, first with temporary and then with permanent vows. Traditionally these individuals make three vows:

Then do this
Interview five Catholics and ask them to explain their understanding of the role of women and men religious in the Church. Report back to the class.

Poverty

Popularly, this vow is understood as the promise to own nothing. A better way to explain the vow of **poverty** is to see it as the promise to live simply without clinging to material possessions. Persons who vow poverty attempt to place God and the needs of those they serve before their own needs and wishes. They try not to let things possess them and distract them from their trust in God.

Poverty is not seen as an end in itself, but as a way to listen more deeply and freely to the Holy Spirit at work in the Church and all humankind. Often consecrated persons experience in their practice of poverty a call to care for those who are poor. They try to help those who have no choice about being poor to experience the depth of God's love.

poverty
the religious vow to place God and the needs of those served before the individual's own needs and wishes

Chastity

The vow of **chastity** is the most misunderstood of the three vows. To be chaste is to live out the gift of sexuality according to one's vocation and state in life—single or married. For single people, that means not marrying and not engaging in sexual activity. Those who make a vow of chastity do so for the sake of God's kingdom. God and the needs of his people are the entire focus of their love.

Those who consecrate themselves to God and the work of the Church do not repress or deny their human sexuality. Such denial leads to real psychological and relational problems! Consecrated persons remain sexual beings, but redirect their need for intimacy toward their relationship with God and their ministry for others. They don't merely give up engaging in acts which lead to procreation; rather, they share in God's creative love in a unique manner. Chastity is more than the absence of sex. It's putting one's entire being at the service of love for God and others.

chastity
the religious vow to live chastely in the unmarried state

Obedience

Unfortunately, obedience is commonly understood as giving a blind "yes" to the demands of those in authority. Because of our sense of personal freedom, we yearn for independence and self-determination. As a result, we may balk at obedience. Many people even consider obedience to be dehumanizing.

More properly understood, the vow of **obedience** involves the effort to become more like Christ—those who make this vow freely choose to try to always do God's will. Consecrated persons commit themselves to grow according to God's will in a community led by legitimate superiors with a certain mission in the Church.

obedience
the religious vow to freely choose to try to always do God's will

Why do this?

Write it down

Those who respond to a vocation to the religious life take vows of poverty, chastity, and obedience. Every Christian's life should be characterized by these three virtues. How can you live the virtues of poverty, chastity, and obedience?

To understand the life of the consecrated person and his or her commitment to live a life characterized by the gospel values of poverty, chastity, and obedience, we must return to a central question: What motivates people to make this kind of dedication?

The first motivation for people to consecrate their lives to God and the work of the Church is God's love. The vows are not a request that God take over their lives; rather the vows express the belief that God has already taken hold of their hearts in a relationship of love. Because of this love, these people seek to give of themselves to the service of others in real and practical ways. In other words, living the vows is far different from taking an oath of office or making promises to behave in a certain way. The vows are life-deep, but that can be understood only with faith.

All of us are embraced by God's love. Consecrated persons don't claim a special knowledge of God, or greater holiness. They do witness to God's love in their lives—a love that is intense and very focused. The central focus for consecrated persons is not a particular work or service, but the free gift of themselves in love to God. Their witness is a sign to everyone that selfish ways of measuring happiness and success are not God's way. Consecrated persons help all of us keep the love of God in our minds and hearts.

Write it down

What would attract you to the religious life?

Not everyone is called to the consecrated life, but everyone is called to union with God. The consecrated life is a witness to our ultimate destiny. In that sense, consecrated persons share in the prophetic work of the Church. They do not *foretell* the Church's future as a clairvoyant would, but they *tell forth* the unfolding mystery of God's plan of salvation for humankind. Consecrated persons make visible in their lives the dedication that the saving grace of God makes possible for everyone.

We are born subjects, and to obey God is perfect liberty.

Seneca

Dedication and witness

The consecrated life is one way to experience a fuller dedication to God, a dedication rooted in our Baptism. Inspired by the Holy Spirit, consecrated people commit themselves to follow Christ more nearly and to give themselves to the God they love above all else. They try to live in love as they serve God's kingdom. By their lives, they witness to the glory of the world to come.

See the *Catechism of the Catholic Church*, #916.

1. What makes someone in the religious life different from you?

2. How do people in religious life give witness to the "glory of the world to come"?

St. Philippine Duchesne
Doing one's best

Rose-Philippine Duchesne was born in France in 1769 as the country was approaching its famous Revolution. As a teenager she joined a religious community of Visitation Sisters, but she returned home during the Revolution because of the anti-Church atmosphere of the time. During the years that followed, Philippine cared for people who were sick or in prison and taught many children.

Catholicism was reinstated as the established Church in France in 1801. Rose-Philippine returned to the Visitation Convent in a failed attempt to reestablish the community. Eventually Philippine and four other women joined the Society of the Sacred Heart, another religious community.

After many years of waiting and preparing, Philippine and four other sisters went to Louisiana as missionaries in 1818. They traveled up the Mississippi to St. Louis and were given a log cabin in St. Charles, on the Missouri River. There the women opened a school for the children of poor families. Luckily for Rose-Philippine, most of the families were bilingual—French and English, because she now faced the cold fact that learning another language was very difficult for her.

Philippine faced other disappointments as well. Many of the Native Americans of the area were hostile, many of the settlers, both men and women, drank to excess, and slavery was common. A year later the community moved closer to St. Louis, where Philippine began to accept new members into the community. The sisters continued their work among the settlers.

In time Rose-Philippine and four others set out for Sugar Creek in Kansas to work among the Potawatomi. Again, Philippine was faced with a language she couldn't master. But she could pray, and so she became known to the Potawatomi as "the woman who prays." She was also known as the "St. Francis of the Society of the Sacred Heart." Rose-Philippine died at St. Charles in 1852 and was named a saint in 1988.

Optional activities

1. Look up the life of another saint who was a man or woman religious. Write a paper or present your research to the class.

2. Find out more about St. Philippine Duchesne. Write a paper or prepare a presentation for the class.

3. Research the missionaries who worked in your part of the country when it was first settled by Europeans. Write a paper or prepare a presentation for the class.

4. Find out something about a person who seemed to fail or had great difficulty in an area, but who made a success of his or her life in spite of the difficulties and failures. Share the person's story with the class.

Consecrated community life

Talk about it

1. Why do some people like to see priests, brothers, and sisters dressed in a religious habit or other identifiable clothing?

2. Why do some religious choose not to wear distinctive garb?

Then do this

Research the history and charism of one religious community. Prepare a presentation for the class.

In terms of numbers, relatively few people make an individual consecration through the Church to God and the work of the Church. Because they are so few in number, they don't attract much attention. The consecrated people we normally encounter belong to special groups of consecrated individuals—religious orders or communities of religious. We normally identify them as priests, brothers, and sisters. (Remember, not all priests are members of religious orders. The Sacrament of Holy Orders—bishop, priest, deacon—preceded religious orders.)

These are people who have made vows in a specific community recognized by the Church. Sometimes these individuals wear a habit, or religious clothing, that identifies them with a particular religious order. Many others simply wear a certain type of cross or another identifying item.

There are scores of religious communities throughout the world. Some of the more widely known in the United States are the Benedictines, Marianists, Christian Brothers, Jesuits, Dominicans, Franciscans, Sisters of the Holy Names, Maryknoll, Notre Dame Sisters, Sisters of Providence, Immaculate Heart of Mary Sisters, Sisters of St. Joseph, and the Mercy Sisters.

Each of these groups has a unique history. Some religious communities were founded by bishops; others by lay people. Some were founded by members of other religious communities. For example, Mother Teresa left the Sisters of Loretto to work with the poorest of the poor. She then began a new community, the Missionaries of Charity.

Whatever their origin, these groups are home to people who profess to live the vows of poverty, chastity, and obedience within the structure of the group and under the rule (organizing philosophy and manner of living) followed by that community.

This rule is approved by Church authorities. It presents practical ways the religious order will witness to its charism in the service of others. A *charism* is the unique way in which the Holy Spirit works in the community, giving it a unique focus on ministry and service. For instance, the charism of the Sisters of the Visitation is hospitality, and they take their inspiration from the story of Mary and Elizabeth, when Elizabeth welcomed Mary into her home.

Even with a particular charism, however, not every member of a given community will be involved in the same work. The charism is not a specific job assignment but an opportunity to witness to the work of the Spirit in a special way in whatever work each member does.

Some orders have the special charism of the cloistered life—that is, they live in a rather secluded situation, separated from the normal course of the work-a-day world, in order to have more time and opportunity for contemplation and other prayer.

> *Witnessing is removing the various barriers of our self-love to allow Christ, living within us, to show himself to our neighbors.*
>
> **Paul Frost**

These contemplative communities support themselves with a variety of projects that generally can be done within the monastery and in the time available outside of the time spent in community and private worship and prayer. Other religious and lay people are usually welcome to join the contemplatives for prayer and even for work at times.

Priests, brothers, and sisters don't choose their life in order to provide a cheap labor force in the Church. Far more important is who they *are* as witnesses to the Christian life and the destiny we share—union with God in the new creation. So religious are a catalyst to the conscience of the world. They challenge all of us to make our own the mission of the Church. That mission is to proclaim the good news of the kingdom and to help others know Jesus and follow him. Men and women religious lead us in a search for a God whose love is boundless.

Talk about it
How does a member of a religious community live?

Then do this
Interview a priest, deacon, or man or woman religious about his or her vocation. Share the interview with the class.

> *The primary declaration of Christianity is not "This do!"*
> *but "This happened!"*
> **Evelyn Underhill**

REVIEW

1. To what does the term *consecrated life* refer?

2. What three vows do most men and women religious make?

3. What does each vow mean?

4. What is consecrated community life?

5. What does *charism* mean in relation to consecrated community life?

MATRIMONY

The vocation still to be studied is that of marriage. In the Catholic Church this vocation is celebrated with the Sacrament of Matrimony. As with Holy Orders, an important dimension of the Sacrament of Matrimony is service to others—spouse and children first, then the wider community.

Marriage in the Church

When a couple approaches a Catholic priest or deacon or another pastoral worker for marriage preparation, the conversation usually begins with the question, "Will you marry us?" The couple wants something more than "just a wedding." They want to be married "in the Church." They want God's blessing and the blessing of the Church community on their new life together.

If either of the two people is a baptized Catholic, they can be married in the Catholic Church. Before the marriage takes place, there is a time of preparation, of learning together what a marriage should be. The priest or other parish staff member guides the couple in this preparation for marriage, which includes various facets of Christian marriage: its faith dimension, communication skills, management of finances, sexuality, and family issues.

Actually, the couple's preparation for marriage began long before they knocked on the parish door. Their experience of life, and especially their experience of the marriage between their own parents, have already shaped their understanding of marriage. The preparer will advise the couple that, in the Western Church, the couple are the ministers of the Sacrament of **Matrimony** for one another; they marry one another. In the Eastern Rite, the priest is considered the minister of the sacrament.

In the United States, clergy have the legal authority to witness marriages. This authority is granted by the state in which the priest, deacon, or minister lives. In contrast, in many countries, the couple has to go first to the court system (a judge or justice of the peace) to be married legally and then to their faith community for a religious ceremony or celebration.

However, a minister or priest or deacon, in conscience, can witness a marriage only if that marriage seems to be a true Christian marriage. Do the man and woman who want to marry understand what marriage is? Do they realize that a wedding happens in an hour or so—and a marriage is a lifelong commitment of love and faithfulness? Are they capable of and willing to live up to that commitment?

It's certainly true that the atmosphere of a church building helps make a lovely wedding celebration, but, in the Catholic Church, marriage is a sacrament and the main concern of the priest or deacon is helping the couple appreciate that fact. He wants them to really understand what it means to be married "in the Church."

Success in marriage is more than finding the right person;

it is a matter of being the right person.

Rabbi B.R. Brickner

The Sacrament of Marriage

A couple marrying in the Catholic Church may not be fully aware of why their love relationship is sacramental. They even may have the expectation that by some sacred pronouncement the priest or deacon changes their relationship into a sacred reality. So what exactly does marriage as a sacrament mean? *Sacrament*, as discussed earlier, is a personal encounter with God.

At the level of rights and civil law, marriage celebrated as a sacrament is no different than the marriage of any other couple. From the point of view of the government, marriage is an arrangement which establishes certain rights and gives certain legal privileges and responsibilities. Marriage is simply marriage—and there's a license or certificate to prove it.

The Catholic Church, however, sees the bond between baptized believers as far more than a legal bond. It's even more than the sharing of the same values. True Christian marriage has three major characteristics:

- The permanent commitment to each other by the couple
- The couple's true and free gift of self to one another; unconditional love
- The community of love and life they share; the ability to procreate

When a couple is united in a sacramental marriage, their love is the very "place" where the couple most experience God's saving love. Marriage is the way a couple live out their baptismal identity. Together they are Christ for each other and for others; their unselfish love transforms them and helps them reach out to others.

As celebrated in the Catholic Church in the West, the couple themselves are both the ministers and the receivers of the Sacrament of Marriage. They minister God's unconditional love to one another and they receive the benefits of their love. They give and accept one another's consent to a shared and committed life.

With a sacramental marriage, the couple enter into a new dimension in their relationship with the Church. Marriage is their unique vocation from God to live in a very practical way their Christian identity. For that reason, the Church's preference is that Catholics who marry not only have been baptized, but also have been confirmed and actively share in the Eucharist.

True Christian marriage is shown by the permanent commitment to each other by the couple, their true and free gift of self to one another and to the community in which they share. The Church recognizes the handiwork of God in a true Christian marriage.

Then do this

Make a poster that shows the ideals of Christian marriage. Explain your poster to the class.

Then do this

Interview a couple married in the Catholic Church and report to the class.

1. Ask them to explain the relationship they experience between the Sacraments of Initiation and the Sacrament of Matrimony.

2. Ask them how their marriage has changed over the years.

The vocation of marriage

Marriage has been created by God, who has given marriage its own proper laws. The vocation of marriage is written in the very nature of men and women—in the very way God created them. Marriage isn't just a human institution, even though it has been expressed in different ways in different cultures over the centuries. Marriage has common and permanent characteristics, and its dignity and greatness is evident in varying degrees in all cultures.

See the *Catechism of the Catholic Church*, #1603.

1. How are men and women created for one another?

2. What are some of the ways the institution of marriage is viewed differently in different countries?

3. How can marriage look different but share common characteristics?

Wherever committed, faithful, and life-giving love is present in a marriage, the Christian couple's very way of life together is recognized by the Church as a sacrament. It's important to remember that in the Sacrament of Marriage, the Church celebrates what *God* is doing—God encounters his people in and through the unconditional, committed love of the couple.

The marriage of a Christian couple is a covenant by which the man and the woman establish a partnership of love for life. The couple commit themselves to each other by means of a covenant, a partnership for the whole of life. This covenant involves an interpersonal relationship which is total; that is, it involves the couple's spiritual, emotional, and physical joining—the gift of the whole person to the other. Because of God's presence in their love, the two are able to give themselves to one another on a day-by-day basis.

Talk about it

What does it mean to be married "in the Catholic Church"?

Write it down

Write an essay explaining why marriage is a sacrament in the Catholic Church.

Cesar Chavez
Husband, father, activist

Cesar Chavez was born in Arizona in 1927. His parents, second generation immigrants from Mexico, owned a small farm at the time Cesar was born. But the Depression hit the family hard, and they lost their farm. At this point the family set out for California to do migrant farm work. As a result, Cesar attended over sixty-five schools.

Eventually Cesar's father became a union organizer in San Jose, setting a model that Cesar was to follow. After a time in the navy, Cesar returned to California to work with the existing unions. In 1958 he formed a new union, the National Farm Workers Association (*La Huegla*) and led a five-year strike against California wineries. Ten years later Cesar organized a nation-wide boycott of California table grapes. After two years the growers agreed to bargain with the National Farm Workers Association.

Cesar was also a family man. He and his wife Helen were the parents of eight children. They knew that their children and the children of migrant workers deserved a better life than they had had as children. At the time Cesar began his work, migrant workers were poorly paid for doing back-breaking work for long hours in the hot sun. Medical care was rare, housing was a disgrace, and schooling was minimal. Even children had to work in the fields so that their families would have enough money to survive.

Cesar's leadership in strikes and boycotts and a documentary called *The Harvest of Shame* alerted the country to the unjust conditions suffered by those who put food on the nation's tables. By the time Cesar died in 1993, the situation faced by most migrant workers had improved significantly.

Optional activities

1. Look up the life of a saint who was married. Write a paper or present your research to the class.

2. Research the migrant worker situation in the United States during the twentieth century. Write a report or give a presentation to the class.

3. Find out the condition of migrant workers today. Present your findings to the class.

4. Read more about Cesar Chavez, and write a summary of what you read.

REVIEW

1. What does the Sacrament of Matrimony celebrate?

2. What are the three major characteristics of Christian marriage?

3. Why is marriage a vocation?

Marital equality

There's a lot of talk these days about the equality of men and women—and that's good. Our culture, however, still tends to think of women in secondary roles—and that's not good. In its understanding of marriage, the Catholic Church has been a force which has worked against this unequal treatment.

The example of Jesus, first of all, has challenged people to recognize the equality of women and men. His disciples included both men and women who heard the very same message and set out to live it. Paul later wrote to the Galatians, "There is no longer Jew or Greek, there is no longer slave or free, there is no longer male and female; for all of you are one in Christ Jesus" (Galatians 3:28). Even the author of the Letter to the Ephesians recognized this fundamental equality in Christ. This letter is rather well known, but part of it is very much misunderstood:

Be subject to one another out of reverence for Christ.

Wives, be subject to your husbands as you are to the Lord. For the husband is head of the wife just as Christ is the head of the church, the body of which he is the Savior. Just as the church is subject to Christ, so also wives ought to be, in everything, to their husbands.

Husbands, love your wives, just as Christ himself loved the church and gave himself up for her, in order to make her holy by cleansing her with the washing of water by his word, so as to present the church to himself in splendor, without a spot or wrinkle or anything of the kind—yes, so that she may be holy and without blemish. In the same way, husbands should love their wives as they do their own bodies. He who loves his wife loves himself. For no one ever hates his own body, but he nourishes and tenderly cares for it, just as Christ does for the church, because we are members of his body. "For this reason a man will leave his father and mother and be joined to his wife, and the two will become one flesh." This is a great mystery, and I am applying it to Christ and his church. Each of you, however, should love his wife as himself, and a wife should respect her husband.

— Ephesians 5:21–33

To be able to find joy in another's joy, that is the secret of happiness.

George Bernanos

These were bold words for the time! In that day it was common for a man to treat his wife as a piece of property which was given to him on the day of marriage. Does that tradition continue today—even if in a subtle form—when fathers "give away" their daughters on their wedding day? Doesn't it make more sense when the parents present or accompany their daughter to the altar to enter into the Sacrament of Matrimony and the groom is presented or accompanied in similar fashion?

When scholars apply their study tools to this passage from the Letter to the Ephesians, they discover that the author was using a typical Jewish form of literary parallelism. In other words, he says the same thing twice, but by using different words each time. This is one example of how good Scripture study keeps the reader from jumping to conclusions. What this reading comes down to is that men and women are equals in marriage and both are intimately involved in reflecting Christ's unity with the Church.

As a minister of the Church, the priest or deacon can witness only this kind of sacramental love. When a couple asks to be married "in the Church," the priest or deacon wants to be sure that they are committed to this kind of life together and are capable of living in this way. Their consent, or exchange of vows, proclaims the truth of their relationship in a community of faith.

Permanent commitment

Sacramental Christian marriage calls for maturity and a conscious act of the will. It's more than a sexual attraction or an emotional feeling; it's more than a need for companionship. It's a deliberate choice to give one's *self* to one's companion for life. And this choice is not made just on the occasion of one's wedding. Because marriage is a relationship, and relationships by their nature mature and grow, this decision to marry must be made constantly, daily. True love is a choice, not a feeling.

A marriage involving a baptized Christian is presumed to be sacramental. As such, "What God has joined together, let no one separate." The reality of true Christian marriage cannot be "undone" by any human person or human institution.

This is what the Church means by the **indissolubility** of marriage. It's also why you hear that the Church doesn't believe in **divorce**. Truly, what God has put together in marriage cannot be taken apart by human decisions. Technically, divorce is a legal decision which determines rights and obligations. It is the ending of a legal bond, but in the eyes of the Church it does not end the sacramental reality.

Sometimes you may hear that a legally divorced person has received an annulment (the technical term is **declaration of nullity**) so that he or she can marry again in the Catholic Church. An annulment is an official declaration by the Church that, although a couple may have tried to enter into a truly sacramental marriage, they were not able to achieve that reality. They "attempted" a sacramental marriage but were not able to bring it about. It was not there; it was *nullus* (a Latin word that means "nothing" or "not at all").

Write it down

1. What do you believe about marriage and parenting?

2. What qualities in yourself would help you be a good marriage partner? A good parent?

Talk about it

1. What would a family be like without authority?

2. What would a town or city be like without authority?

3. What would a Church be

indissolubility
cannot be "undone" by any human person or human institution

divorce
a judicial declaration dissolving a marriage; the ending of a marriage in the eyes of civil law

declaration of nullity
formal Church recognition that a sacramental marriage did not exist

Applied to marriage, this means that after careful consideration the Church has officially determined that the sacramental reality of marriage was not reflected in the marriage. The granting of a declaration of nullity isn't a moral judgment on the dignity or value of the two people involved.

In granting a declaration of nullity, the Church hasn't "wiped out" a marriage and by some human decision countermanded God's action. Nor does it mean that children born of such a marriage are illegitimate and without proper family identity and social rights—those persons requesting an annulment must first obtain a legal divorce. The declaration of nullity is a statement that the sacramental bond which was presumed to be there did not exist.

The Catholic Church believes that the intimate partnership of life and love in marriage has been established by God. Married love is one of the ways we learn about God. That's why marriage is often referred to as a covenant, a self-giving, a personal encounter between God and humankind through the love of the couple. With the eyes of faith—eyes that are open to "read" God's presence in the world—marriage, therefore, is more than a decision shared by two people. God himself is present in true married love.

Then do this

Talk about the process with someone who has received a declaration of nullity. Share with the class the process and the learning that can take place through the process.

Talk about it

How is God present in true married love?

A *happy marriage is the union of two good forgivers.*
Robert Quillen

REVIEW

1. Are men and women equal in marriage? Why?

2. What is the difference between a divorce and a declaration of nullity?

Marriage and children

God uses the love of the couple to assure the continuation of the human race and to create a community of love and shared life. The benefits of that community enrich society and, in a sense, the entire human race. For that reason the Catholic Church doesn't recognize so-called same-sex, or homosexual marriages. Because these couples are not capable of procreation as the result of shared sexual encounter, their unions cannot be true marriages, not even if legislation or court decisions make them legal.

By its very nature marriage and married love is ordered to the procreation and education of children. This means that there is something in the very purpose of married love that tends toward the procreation of children and all that is necessary for their growth and development. A married couple doesn't just produce offspring. Their children are beautiful expressions of their total love for one another and their responsibility to "stay with" the love they have expressed. For that reason the Church has always insisted that sexual intercourse is an act that is proper only to marriage.

As you saw early in this book, sexuality is a beautiful gift from God. But, like all functions of the human body, it must, for Christians, be governed by a sense of morality which is guided by the gospel and a well-formed conscience. As soon as someone reaches the age of puberty, he or she is physically capable of having sex, but it takes years to connect with the power of true sexuality.

The goal is a true and lasting gift of self which is always open to the partner and open to the gift of life. Puberty signals a physical readiness for sex, but it takes maturity to reach the truly loving and lasting relationship that sex properly expresses. Sex without permanent commitment is not worthy of the human person. It's an abuse of self as well as an abuse of others. Sex outside of marriage isn't the truth; it doesn't communicate the full truth of a lasting, committed, and responsible love.

Indeed children are the supreme gift of marriage and greatly contribute to the happiness of parents—usually. The creation stories in the Book of Genesis tell us that it isn't good that people should be alone. From the beginning God made people male and female—wishing to associate them in a special way with his own creative work. Men and women are meant for each other, not just physically, but relationally as well. God blessed man and woman and said to them, "Be fruitful and multiply" (Genesis 1:28).

The Christian community has always recognized the unique nature of marriage involving a baptized Christian. A Christian marriage covenant reflects God's covenant with his people established in Jesus. In marriage God encounters us with a covenant of love and fidelity, just as he encountered the Jewish people in Old Testament times. Through the love of the couple, Christ, who has united himself to the Church, now encounters Christian spouses through the Sacrament of Marriage.

Authentic married love is caught up in God's love. In this manner the spouses are led to God and are helped and strengthened in their role as fathers and mothers. Spouses are consecrated for their responsibilities by God's saving love and grace given in the Sacrament of Matrimony.

> *Concern for the child, even before birth, from the very moment of conception and then throughout the years of infancy and youth, is the primary test of the relationship of one human being to another.*
>
> **Pope John Paul II**

Keeping love true, free, and open to life

The Catholic Church realizes that marriage is a challenging vocation today. Married people are often hindered by situations which challenge and even threaten their love. Sometimes they find it difficult to be open to each other. When this happens, it can be hard to preserve faithful love and intimacy. But when the intimacy of married life is broken, faithfulness itself is often weakened and the children also suffer.

Married couples must be honest about their partnership needs and must communicate those needs to their spouse. In very practical ways they must face whatever threatens their marriage and work together on solutions to their problems. They need to reach out for help before it's too late. Trained marriage counselors, for example, can help people understand themselves, their partner, and their marriage. Unfortunately, too many couples turn to a counselor only after their difficulties have gotten way out of hand and the relationship has been seriously damaged.

As the giver of life, God has entrusted to married men and women the noble mission of transmitting and safeguarding life. God is the creator; married men and women are co-creators in a most intimate and awesome way. In procreation, married couples act in union with God, the source of all life and salvation. Accordingly, couples must always respect their human dignity when they share in God's creative, life-giving love.

Abortion and infanticide

Life must be protected with the greatest of care from the moment of conception, from that very moment when the father's sperm penetrates the mother's egg and a person is created. For that reason abortion and infanticide are abominable crimes not only against faith, but also against humanity. **Abortion** is the destruction of human life (a person) in the womb by chemical or mechanical means.

Infanticide is the taking of the life of a child. Infanticide, unfortunately, is still a common practice in several countries today. In the United States this immoral practice is prohibited by law. A decision by the United States Supreme Court, however, has made legal the destruction of human life within the mother's womb. This law may protect doctors and women from being punished for performing or having abortions, but it doesn't make the action morally right.

It's very important to understand this distinction between law and morality. The law of the land is not necessarily the law of a well-formed conscience. People in the United States tend to pride themselves on their ability to go their own way and make their own decisions. Hence, the right to abortion is championed by "pro-choice" groups who believe that the woman has the right to control the functions of her body (including pregnancy). Pope John Paul II called this mentality part of a "culture of death."

The Supreme Court's decision to allow abortions has been challenged by people of many faiths. Although the abortion issue is fundamentally a human rights issue—the rights of unborn persons—and not just a matter of Catholic opinion, the Catholic Church has taken the lead in defending the rights of the unborn. A nation-wide right-to-life movement continues to lobby lawmakers for the protection of *all* human life, "from the womb to the tomb."

The Catholic Church sees this protest as an integral part of its consistent ethic of life. It insists that we cannot be selective about what kind of human life we want to protect. Life is life. And all human life ultimately finds its creation and destiny in God.

abortion
the destruction of human life in the womb by chemical or mechanical means

infanticide
the taking of the life of a child

Then do this
Research one of the following groups and share your research with the class.

1. The pro-life group in your area

2. Birthright

3. Project Rachel

Artificial birth control

Related to a consistent life ethic is the matter of artificial birth control. Humans' sexuality and reproduction wondrously surpass the abilities of other forms of life. As we saw earlier, men and women never just have sex. The sexual act is always a reflection of the gift of self. (Even in the sexual violence of rape, a man is expressing himself or herself as an angry, anti-women person.) Sexual intercourse must be a true expression of a couple's open and free gift of one's best self to the other.

In other words, according to Catholic Church teaching, nothing mechanical or chemical should come between the act of intercourse and its natural end. Of course, many chemicals, pills, and mechanical means (diaphragms, condoms) are on the market. Some of these make it possible to artificially "control" conception, while others prevent a fertilized egg from embedding in a woman's uterus (an early abortion). Just because artificial means of birth control are readily available doesn't mean that it is moral to use them. Just because something is possible doesn't mean it is moral.

Some of these methods are advertised as ways to make sexual relations "safe." We all want to be safe from danger, but this is a very curious and misleading use of the word "safe." Safe from what danger? Is human life a threat and a danger? In a strange twist of words, it appears that artificial birth control makes people "safe" from the very thing that blesses their dignity as humans: the generous and open expression of love, and especially the gift of life that comes from the act of genuine love-making.

Objectively speaking, the Catholic Church considers the use of artificial birth control morally wrong because it frustrates God's plan for marriage. The Church recommends the use of natural family planning methods when a couple is not in a position to provide for a child or another child. This is a moral issue that all couples need to address—whether or not they are members of the Catholic Church. Couples must seriously consider the wisdom of the Church's teaching and form their consciences according to it as they discuss when to begin having children and how to space them.

Marriage and family

Marriage and the family that results from its expression of unconditional love are the building blocks of society. For that reason most people recognize the need to regulate marriage with license requirements and records. Marriage is never just a decision between a man and a woman; their relationship affects society.

The Christian faith Tradition has consistently valued the family, in whatever shape it takes. Some families consist of parents and children. Others include only one parent and child or children. When there are no children or the children are raised and on their own, the couple themselves are a family.

Whatever the case, the family is the school for human development and enrichment. Family isn't just an address where certain people happen to live. Family is a network of relationships in and through which people receive their identity and give it expression. And family is the domestic Church!

If it's to really work, members of a family must respect each other and communicate openly and honestly. The building of family life is a collaborative effort; each member must contribute to the family. When one member is selfish, the strength of the entire family is weakened. The active presence of a loving father and a loving mother is best for a family. And children are important too—you are a contributing member of the family! Your sharing in the family—and your attitude have their effect!

Write it down

1. How do you contribute to your family?

2. What more could you do with and for your family?

Children have more need of models than of critics.

Joseph Joubet

After the gift of life, the greatest gifts parents can offer their children are love and education. These are not mechanical responsibilities like painting the house or mowing the lawn. These are the fundamental responsibilities of personal relationships.

Ideally, the love that is experienced in the family affirms people in their uniqueness and frees them to be their true selves. It's the kind of love that needs to be "tough" when family members need direction, correction, and challenge to their ways of acting and thinking. Respect, trust, and open communication are needed to make love a living reality!

The education of children in the family is of equal importance. The exercise of this responsibility involves more than the need to get the children off to school. What happens at school during a few hours each day can only supplement the basic education that is taking place in the family.

Education is more than the giving of information with comprehension tested on an exam. The accumulation of information is a minor, but important, part of education. The information you learn in school helps you find your place in the world; it helps you be your true self.

Life is larger than any classroom—life itself is the great classroom. Outside the classroom and school environment you continue to learn about life—usually without knowing it. You're picking up more than the mannerisms which may or may not be part of your family. You are developing your values and your way of relating to the world around you. It's the duty of parents and teachers to guide you with prudent advice and love-filled direction.

What you learn in your family you will carry with you for the rest of your life: intellectually, emotionally, and spiritually. You, in turn, in your own vocation—as a married person or a single person or a priest, brother, or sister—will reach out and mold and shape the people around you in the relationships you create.

Talk about it

1. What are the responsibilities of parents?

2. What is "tough love"? When is it needed?

3. What are the qualities of a good parent?

Write it down

What kind of a parent do you hope to be?

REVIEW

1. What does the Church ask of married couples regarding children?

2. What is abortion? What is infanticide? Why are they wrong?

3. What is a consistent ethic of life?

4. To what does the term *artificial birth control* refer? According to the Church, why is it wrong?

CONCLUSION

The family is the place where different generations come together. It's the place where people help each other grow wiser. The family harmonizes the rights of individuals with the demands of wider social life.

Families together weave the fabric of society. When they are strong, society is strong. When they are weak, society is weak. Therefore, everyone with influence in a family and in the larger community has a responsibility to foster good marriages and families. This is especially true for Christians who claim special insight into family life; we are called to promote families as communities of life and unconditional love so that the very presence of God is experienced there.

All vocations begin with the family. No matter what life choice you make, you will be influenced by the family in which you were raised. That's what God had in mind. But all families can be stronger and more loving, and that's your task now and in the future. Everything depends on how well you do.

> *Love is the key to the meaning of life.*
> **Thomas Merton**

Talk about it

1. Why does the Catholic Church need committed bishops, priests, and deacons?

2. Why does the Catholic Church need committed men and women religious?

3. Why does the Catholic Church need committed lay people?

Before I die

Have you ever thought about the things you would like to do before you die? What are your dreams? What achievements would you like to look back on? Consider the following items and list as many responses as you can think of. In each set, choose two of your items and write down your reason for including each. When this course is over, you might like to keep the list somewhere special and refer to it every few months. Check off each accomplishment.

1. I would like to visit these places . . .
2. I want to learn more about the people of . . .
3. I want to read . . .
4. I would like to meet . . .
5. I want to try these occupations . . .
6. For sheer enjoyment, I would like to . . .
7. I would like to own . . .
8. I want to accomplish . . .
9. I want to be known for . . .
10. I would like to help the world . . .

Words you should know

abortion	consecrate	infallibility	priest
apostolic	deacon	infanticide	religious life
archbishop	declaration of nullity	magisterium	religious order
bishop	divorce	Matrimony	single life
cardinal	ecumenical council	monsignor	synod
celibacy	encyclical	obedience	Vatican
chastity	hierarchy	ordination	vows
college of bishops	Holy Orders	papacy	
collegiality	indissolubility	poverty	

CHAPTER 13

DISCIPLESHIP

CHAPTER OVERVIEW

- *The call to discipleship*

- *Call to sainthood*

- *The perfect saint: Mary*

- *Virtues*

The Word of the Lord

Therefore, my beloved, . . . work out your own salvation with fear and trembling; for it is God who is a work in you, enabling you both to will and to work for his good pleasure.

FROM THE LETTER TO THE PHILIPPIANS, SEE 2:12–18.

Praise the LORD!
Praise the LORD, O my soul!

Let Us Pray

I will praise the LORD as long as I live;
I will sing praises to my God all my life long. . . .
Happy are those whose help is the God of Jacob,
whose hope is in the LORD their God,
who made heaven and earth,
the sea, and all that is in them;
who keeps faith forever;
who executes justice for the oppressed;
who gives food to the hungry.
The LORD sets the prisoners free;
the LORD opens the eyes of the blind.
The LORD lifts up those who are bowed down;
the LORD loves the righteous.
The LORD watches over the strangers;
he upholds the orphan and the widow,
but the way of the wicked he brings to ruin.
The LORD will reign forever,
your God, O Zion, for all generations.
Praise the LORD!

PSALM 146:1–2, 5–10

THE CALL TO DISCIPLESHIP

The first several chapters of this book reminded you of how special you are to God—that you are loved dearly and empowered by the Holy Spirit to be a sign of God's kingdom. The story of your life is the story of your response to God's love. In the Sacraments of Christian Initiation—Baptism–Confirmation–Eucharist—the Catholic Church celebrated your call to **discipleship** in Jesus Christ. As a member of a community of faith, you have grown and matured as you have learned to follow him.

Christian discipleship is an experience of life made possible by a personal encounter with Jesus. As a disciple of Jesus Christ, you are a learner, but the teaching you've received from your earliest years is more than shared information. You have "learned" who Jesus is for you; you have learned to follow his way. You have received a very special invitation. And you truly have good news to share with others—the good news of God's love. You have found the source of your wholeness and happiness.

Jesus called his first followers to a change of heart. And he called them to take responsibility for being signs of the reign of God. They were to be the seed of that community which would continue proclaiming God's kingdom through the centuries.

As Jesus called the first disciples amid their everyday occupations, so he calls people in every age to be partners with him in bringing life and wholeness to the world—in the home, in the workplace, and, yes, in the classroom and on the play field—wherever people go.

To a great extent, Western societies are founded on a Christian value system. You were most likely born and raised in a family for whom Jesus and his way were accepted as given facts. You probably learned your prayers and received your first understanding of God from your parents and other family members. Your parents enrolled you in religious education classes or sent you to a Catholic school. Over the years, you have learned a great deal about Jesus. Hopefully you have developed a personal relationship with Jesus—and have become his disciple. Hopefully you have claimed your faith.

You've been called to discipleship. Discipleship with Jesus is born, not out of a search for knowledge, but out of the need for life. And Jesus doesn't wait for you to reach a certain level of maturity or wholeness before he calls you. He calls you where you are—in your imperfection and neediness. He comes to you, calls you, and gives you the faith, the strength, the desire, and the courage to follow him.

discipleship
being a learner; for Christians, the vocation of following Jesus

Write it down
Each day that you spend on this chapter, reading or discussing, write down your experiences and your reflections. Try to identify the challenges and joys of discipleship in your life.

Then do this
Interview a person whose Christian example you admire. Ask the person to tell you about the challenges and joys of being a Christian. Write a reflection after the interview.

Whoever heeds instruction is on the path to life. . . .
Proverbs 10:17a

Living as a disciple of Jesus

The way Jesus has touched your life truly does make a difference—both to you and to those whom you meet. Your personal encounter with Jesus blesses you with a wholeness which affects the way you live. As a disciple, you know the challenge of trying to live in a Christian way.

It isn't always easy to seek God's reign, nor is it always clear how you are to live a Christian life in the world. Learning from Jesus and his community of believers, you seek a true sense of self in being a son or a daughter of God.

Just as the people of Israel followed God, who led them through the desert toward the promised land, so every disciple must follow Jesus toward life in God. This isn't just a matter of learning *about* Christianity and obediently accepting the rules and regulations of your Church community. It's mainly about staying close to Jesus, sharing his life and his destiny and sharing his free and loving obedience to the will of his heavenly Father.

Following Christ is the foundation of Christian morality and conscientious decision making. As you seek to grow in your ability to make good decisions, the Holy Spirit will guide you, especially through your community of faith.

As disciples of Jesus today, we live in a world in which many things compete for our allegiance. We often experience conflicts of interest as well as conflict within ourselves. The battle to be faithful to one's true self is often lonely and scary, but Jesus succeeded—and so can we! He remains with us in his Holy Spirit to help us.

Then do this

The text mentions the importance of our families in helping us be disciples of Jesus. Together reflect on your experiences.

1. Make a list of the ten most important characteristics of a Christian parent. Give a reason for each characteristic.

2. In small groups discuss your lists and compare your reasons.

A true Christian may be almost defined as one who has a ruling sense of God's presence within him [or her].

John Henry Newman

Discipleship as invitation

God wants people to share in the life of God. So God gathers us around his Son. The Church is this gathering; it is the seed of God's kingdom on earth. Christ is at the heart of this gathering. Through words and signs that point to the reign of God and by sending out his followers, Jesus calls all people to gather around him. *Everyone* is called to God's kingdom.

The kingdom was announced first to the Israelites, but it is for all people. We enter it when we accept Jesus' good news of salvation. Those who are poor and lowly, that is, those who have accepted it with humble hearts, belong to the kingdom of God. Sinners though we be, all are invited into the kingdom of God.

See the *Catechism of the Catholic Church*, #s 541–545.

1. When did you first become aware that you were invited to be part of God's kingdom?

2. How is the Church a sign of the kingdom of God on earth?

3. Why does a person have to be humble and recognize his or her neediness to enter into the kingdom of God?

4. What do you need to do to enter more fully into God's kingdom?

Prayers of St. Ignatius of Loyola

Receive, Lord, all my liberty,
my memory, my understanding,
  and my whole will.
You have given me all that I have,
  all that I am,
and I surrender all to your divine
  will, that you dispose of me.
Give me only your love and
  your grace.
With this I am rich enough, and
  have no more to ask.

Dearest Lord, teach me to be
  generous.
Teach me to serve you as you
  deserve,
to give and not to count the cost,
to fight and not to head the wounds,
to labor and not to seek to rest,
to give of myself and not to ask for reward,
except the reward of knowing that I am doing your will.

Optional activities

1. Write your own prayer along the lines of these two.

2. Find a prayer written by a saint. Lead the class in prayer, using the saint's prayer as your beginning.

3. Find out something about the life of St. Ignatius of Loyola. Write a paper or prepare a class presentation on his life.

*One can never pay in gratitude; one can only pay "in kind"
somewhere else in life. . . .*

Anne Morrow Lindbergh

REVIEW

1. What is a disciple?

2. What does a disciple of Jesus do?

3. What is the foundation of Christian morality and conscientious decision making?

Where discipleship leads

Jesus' call to you is to seek after God even if those around you are not involved actively at the moment in the same search for fullness of life. If you are faithful to your calling as a disciple of Jesus, you find yourself in conflict with people who choose a direction in life that takes them away from God. To follow Jesus involves some tension; it isn't always easy.

Walking with Jesus, you learn that you don't create or achieve your goals by your own effort alone. God is always sharing the gift of grace with you—God's own life and help. As a true disciple of Jesus, you must live not just to make your life better or more comfortable, but to be welcomed into the fullness of God's kingdom. Right now you may catch only an occasional glimpse of what lies before you, but in Jesus you see where the path of discipleship leads—to true life.

The Church believes that Christ, who died and was raised for the sake of all people, can show humankind the way to its proper destiny. The Church also believes that the key, the center, and the purpose of the whole of history is to be found in its Lord and Master, and that beneath all that changes there is much that is unchanging, much that has its foundation in Christ, who is the same yesterday, today, and forever!

When Jesus calls you to follow him as a disciple, he doesn't promise an easy life. There is no ready-made blueprint. You do, however, know that Jesus leads to fullness of life. Your life's purpose is found in Jesus. During his ministry, Jesus risked reputation and acceptance. He also risked his life that you may live.

He demanded that the way to God be free from obstacles like personal gain, monetary profit, or comfortable religious practices. He insisted that the way to God is found in prayer—an openness of mind and an eagerness of heart to know God and do his will. With Jesus, you will have opportunities every day to know and to do God's will. Every day you will have opportunities to give witness to your faith.

Although few Christians today face physical **martyrdom**—giving one's life for one's faith—all Christians are called to live what they believe. All Christians should be like Christ—at home, in school, at work, at play. In the end, that's what Christian discipleship is—being like Christ.

martyrdom
giving one's life for one's faith

Martyrdom

Martyrs give the highest witness to the faith; they are witnesses to the death. Martyrs gives witness to Christ by offering their lives as testimony to the Christian faith. The Church has very carefully collected and maintained the records of those who have given their lives in witness to the faith. These "acts of the martyrs" form "the archives of truth written in letters of blood."
See the *Catechism of the Catholic Church*, #s 2473–2474.

1. How is the Church "built on the blood of martyrs"? What does that mean?

2. How are all Christians called to be witnesses to Christ? What does that mean?

Write it down

What religious symbol is especially meaningful to you? What are the reasons for this?

Talk about it

1. What are the challenges of being a Christian disciple? What are the joys?

2. Why does the world need dedicated Christian disciples?

3. Even today in some parts of the world, young people are sometimes persecuted for being Christian. How would you respond if you were denied a job, laughed at, or jailed because you were a Christian?

Then do this

Make a poster using newspaper and magazine clippings; show situations in which Christians are called to witness to their faith. Explain your poster to the class.

The disciple's mind and heart must be given over to the way of the Master. The disciple tries to not become sidetracked in pursing the way of God. Being a disciple of Jesus means that sometimes you will be in situations where you need to point out to others—even people in your own family, peer group, or local community—obstacles which block their way to God.

Discipleship with Jesus Christ can be risky. The way of Jesus is the way of the cross. To be a disciple of Jesus is to embrace that same cross and to know that you too share in its promise. The heaviest cross we carry is the need to be true to ourselves before God.

As Christians we live under the sign of the cross. Throughout the centuries the cross or crucifix has been a sign that those whose homes or places of worship it marks are disciples of Jesus. You make the Sign of the Cross with holy water as you enter a church, and you recall your Baptism into Christ. You begin and end your prayers with the Sign of the Cross. The cross or crucifix is placed on the burial casket of the Christian—a powerful sign that the cross is the way to life forever with the risen Lord.

There is a power in the cross; when you bear it, you follow in union with the Crucified One. Paradoxically, the cross leads to life.

> *We, the Christian community, assemble to celebrate the memory of the martyrs with ritual solemnity because we want to be inspired to follow their example, share in their merits, and be helped by their prayers.*
>
> **St. Augustine**

The martyrs of Uganda
Courageous to the end

In the late nineteen century, many European Christian Churches sent missionaries to Africa. One Catholic missionary group, the White Fathers (the color of their robes) established a mission in Uganda. Mwanga, the son of the king, attended the mission school, but he was an indifferent student given to pleasure-seeking.

When the king died in 1884, eighteen-year-old Mwanga became king. His poor education embarrassed him when he found that the Christians in the court could read and write. Feeling threatened by the Europeans moving into the area, Mwanga was easily convinced by his advisors to rid the country of Christian leaders.

Mwanga's search for pleasure led him to abuse alcohol, to use mood-altering plants, and to indulge in homosexual practices with young men in his court. Some of the pages and their leaders were Christian and refused Mwanga's advances, as they were instructed to do by the missionaries. The Catholics in the group included Charles Lwanga, Joseph Mkasa, Denis Sebuggwawo, Mwafu, and Kizito (who was only thirteen).

In 1886 the Christians in the court were put to death, some of them by being slowly roasted over a fire. Many were stacked on a pyre and set afire. One of the executioners commented: "There was not a sigh, not even an angry word. All we heard was a soft murmur on their lips. They prayed until they died." Other influential Christians in the country were also killed. But then an internal rebellion prevented Mwanga from completing his plan to kill all the Christian and Muslim leaders in the country.

Twenty-two Catholics honored under the title "The Martyrs of Uganda" were declared saints in 1964. A shrine in their country is built in the shape of a pyre, and their story is carved on the doors of the church. The first time a pope visited Africa was 1969; during the visit Pope Paul VI made a pilgrimage to this shrine.

Optional activities

1. Find out more about the martyrs of Uganda. Share the information with the class.

2. Research the Catholic Church in Africa, perhaps by contacting a missionary group that works there. Share your findings with the class.

3. Read the story of a martyr, and write a reflection on the story.

Courage is almost a contradiction in terms. It means a strong desire to live taking the form of a readiness to die.

G. K. Chesterton

REVIEW

1. What kind of life can a disciple of Jesus expect to have?

2. What is martyrdom?

CALL TO SAINTHOOD

In an earlier chapter, you learned about the importance of the Catholic Church's liturgical calendar. That calendar revolves around two major feasts—Easter and Christmas. The Church's liturgical calendar spans 365 days, just like the normal annual calendar, but the "year" spreads over those days in a different manner. In addition to the major feasts and Sundays of the year, there is another part to the liturgical year, called the *sanctoral calendar*.

If you look at a typical Catholic calendar, you will notice that a specific Christian event or person is noted on many of the dates. For example, the calendar box for August 4 reads "St. John Vianney;" October 4 reads "St. Francis of Assisi," and October 15 reads St. Teresa of Avila. These are days the Catholic Church sets aside to prayerfully reflect on the Christian witness of holy men and women whose lives the Catholic Church has determined to be worthy of canonization. These are the canonized **saints** of the Church.

Canonization

Remember learning earlier about the word *canon*? It was a word used in connection with the books of the Bible being guides of faith. It's what we measure our lives by.

In addition to Scripture, there are men and women from our Christian history whose lives have become recognized by the Church as a measure for our walk of discipleship and who are now with God. These are the **canonized** saints of the Catholic Church. The Church offers them to us with the assurance that the imitation of their lives will lead us to God.

In simple words, the Church "names someone a saint." The Church recognizes or affirms that God's presence has been uniquely and wonderfully shown—for our benefit—in the lives of these people.

We are called to be saints. Every Christian is called to follow the way of Jesus and show God's love to others; that's what holiness is. Have you ever thought of yourself as a saint?

A saint isn't someone who runs around all day with his or her hands folded in prayer. Despite the pictures you have seen, a saint doesn't attract attention with a heavenly glow around his or her head. Saints don't float through crowds with their feet six inches off the ground.

There's a more realistic way to look at saints. The saints were ordinary people who by the grace of God lived lives of great faith and Christian witness. They came from all walks of life. Some were married; some were priests and religious. Some were rich; some were poor. Some were young; some were old. Some were politically powerful; others were not. Some were athletically talented; others not. Quite a mix!

---

saint

a person of heroic virtue; a person who by the grace of God lived a life of great faith and Christian witness

Write it down

Where did you get your image of a saint? Is it true-to-life? Explain.

canonize

to officially name someone a saint

Write it down

Do *you* want to become a saint? Why?

Everyone cannot become a genius,

but the path of holiness is open to all.

St. Maximilian Kolbe

If you were to study the lives of the saints, you would find that each of them has his or her own life story. Each was born, lived, and died. The saints shared in the human condition, but they followed in the way of Jesus and united themselves with his passion, death, and resurrection. They did this to such an extent that the Church considers them outstanding examples of Christian discipleship for the rest of us.

Not all of the saints are included in the Church's liturgical calendar; many truly holy people are no longer remembered on earth. Chances are you won't be remembered by the universal Church as a saint either. But sainthood isn't about getting your name in a box on a calendar. It's about coming to fullness of life in God.

All of us must strive for excellence in Christian living—for personal sainthood. In fact, this is the call of the Spirit already at work in your life. The saints didn't set out to gain recognition. The saints were people who lived their lives to the full—while struggling often against selfishness and sin—as God's saving love drew them into union with God.

There have been millions of genuine saints in the history of the Christian faith. Perhaps only a couple thousand or so of these people are remembered, but God doesn't forget. All these holy people share eternal life with God. They have been given the gift of full life in union with Christ, the risen Lord. Where they have gone, we hope to follow.

Then do this

Study the life of one saint (many biographies are available on the Internet). In a report to the class, share the saint's story and explain how the saint might live if he or she were living physically on earth today. With what issues might the person be concerned?

Canonizing saints

When the Catholic Church canonizes some Christians, it solemnly proclaims their great virtue and acknowledges that they lived faithful to the grace of God. By doing so, the Church recognizes the power of the Spirit at work in the holiness of the Church and helps believers continue to hope because of the example and **intercession** of these saints. The saints have always been a very important source of renewal in the Catholic Church, especially in times of great difficulty.

See the *Catechism of the Catholic Church*, #828.

1. Who is your favorite saint? Why?

2. Do you know anyone you would "propose" for canonization by the Church? Who is the person? Why would you propose the person for canonization?

3. How do the saints help you in your personal journey of faith?

intercession
prayer asking on behalf of another

Write it down

1. Are there any saints whose life stories have influenced you? Who are they?

2. How have these saints' stories helped you find direction in life?

REVIEW

1. What is a saint?

2. What is a canonized saint?

3. What does it mean to intercede for another?

The communion of saints

communion of saints
all the faithful, living and dead—on earth and in heaven—united by the saving love of God

In the Creed we proclaim our belief in the **communion of saints**. This sense of communion is fundamental to our understanding of being a community of faith, a Church. God's grace and saving love unite the faithful in a single family, in a single communion. God's grace and saving love make us holy, make us saints. Do you realize that you belong to this communion of saints? Yes, this communion includes all the faithful: the living and the dead—the few who have been canonized saints by the Church and all the dead whose faith is known to God alone.

Even in our imperfection and sinfulness, God seeks to unite us in the communion of saints. Even though it is our personal responsibility to grow in holiness, no one makes himself or herself perfect in this life. We all die imperfect—needing to be saved, to be made whole, by the grace of God. We who die in God's grace and friendship, but are still imperfect, are indeed assured of our eternal salvation. The Catholic Church teaches that to the extent necessary after death, we undergo purification, so that we can achieve the holiness necessary to enter the joy of **heaven**.

heaven
the life after death in which people experience God's life and love forever

purgatory
the state of purification for those who have died

The Church gives the name **purgatory** to this state of final purification. In this state of being, God makes us perfect, uniting us in the communion of saints. No one knows what purgatory is like or how long this state of being-made-perfect lasts. We have to be careful about describing purgatory as a *place* where people suffer. It's a state of being, not a place.

Those who are outside the communion of saints for all eternity are those who are in a state of being called **hell**. Our God of love doesn't condemn people to hell; they get what they themselves have chosen in life. No one wakes up one day to suddenly find themselves there; hell doesn't come as a surprise. If any persons are in hell, it is because they have consciously and freely chosen to alienate themselves from God and his goodness during the course of their lives. Their hell began on earth and continues for all eternity.

hell
the state of eternal separation from God

As wild as our imaginations may run about what hell is like, the chief punishment of hell is eternal separation from God. It is in God alone that we find the life and happiness for which God created us and for which our hearts long. That's why telling someone to "Go to hell!" is such a curse—and a very unchristian thing to say. How can a disciple of Jesus wish someone to be separated forever from the saving love of God?

You need not fear that you may automatically or blindly go to hell for committing sin. But you are still responsible for your actions. God calls you to a constant conversion of life which moves you away from sin. No one is predestined to go to hell—in fact, quite the opposite is true! But if you constantly refuse God's call—choosing self over others and trashing the goodness of creation—then you choose your own alienation, your own hell. Those who persist to the end in their rejection of God get what they freely choose: the eternal punishment of hell.

More things are wrought by prayer
Than this world dreams of.

Alfred, Lord Tennyson

The intercession of the saints

Many people have a special devotion to the saints, and often to one or two saints in particular. There may be personal reasons for this. Perhaps they were named after a saint. Perhaps they have chosen a particular saint as a patron at the time of Confirmation. Perhaps there is something about the life or profession of a particular saint that is especially inspiring.

Because we believe that these holy men and women now live fully with God, we Christians can ask for their *intercession*, that is, their help, in nudging us to become better disciples of Jesus. When we pray to the saints, we don't pray in the same way we pray to God. When we ask for a saint's help, or intercession, we actually are asking them to intercede with God for us. We join our prayers to God with the prayers of the saints to God for us.

Your destiny as a disciple of Jesus is to be a saint. You are called to be one with Jesus, who leads you to eternal life. The path to that union is not separate from your personal life history. The path to sainthood always leads through your life now to life forever in the fullness of God's kingdom. In following that path, don't look for the extraordinary; rather, find God in the ordinary life you live. Whether you are at school, at home, at play, or at work, you tread on holy ground—where saints gather!

Talk about it

1. What does it mean to belong to the communion of saints?

2. How can praying for the intercession of the saints help you?

3. What is the purpose of purgatory? Why does it make sense?

4. How does a person choose hell?

Write it down

1. What do you need to do to remain a faithful disciple of Christ?

2. How can you make the following practices more a part of your life?
   • personal prayer
   • communal prayer
   • Scripture reading

> For you are a people holy to the LORD your God,
> the LORD your God has chosen you out of all peoples on earth
> to be his people, his treasured possession.
>
> **Deuteronomy 7:6**

Sharing the stories of the saints

During her childhood Dorothy Day lived in a poor neighborhood of Chicago, and it was there she first met Catholics. Years later she reflected on that experience; in the following she wrote about one of those Catholics and her influence on Dorothy.

The Harrington family also lived in that block of tenements, and there were nine children, the eldest a little girl of twelve. She was a hard-working little girl, and naturally I had the greatest admiration for her on account of the rigorous life she led... Often [Mary] was so tired that we just stretched out on the long back porch, open to the sky. We lay there, gazing up at the only beauty the city had to offer us, and we talked and dreamed.

I don't remember what we talked about, but I do remember one occasion when she told me of the life of some saint. I don't remember which one, nor can I remember any of the incidents of it. I can only remember the feeling of lofty enthusiasm I had, how my heart seemed almost bursting with desire to take part in such high endeavor. One verse of the Psalms often comes to mind: "Enlarge Thou my heart, O Lord, that Thou mayest enter in." This was one of those occasions when my small heart was enlarged. I could feel it swelling with love and gratitude to such a good God for such a friendship as Mary's, for conversation such as hers, and I was filled with lofty ambitions to be a saint, a natural striving, a thrilling recognition of the possibilities of spiritual adventure.

Optional activities

1. Debate: The ambition to be a saint is a natural striving.
2. List ten saints with whom you are familiar along with the quality for which each is famous or a quality of the person that is meaningful to you.

Then do this

Interview people in different ways of life on how they live out their Christian vocation. Summarize the interviews and share the summary with the class.

> *I am trying to learn to recall my soul... and lift my heart to the Blessed Mother and the saints, since my occupations are the lowly and humble ones, as were theirs.*
>
> **Dorothy Day**

REVIEW

1. What is the communion of saints?
2. What is heaven? Purgatory? Hell?
3. What is the destiny of a disciple of Jesus?

THE PERFECT SAINT: MARY

During its long history, the Catholic Church has offered the people of the Church an example of the true disciple: the mother of Jesus. In this woman from the village of Nazareth in northern Israel, we find the perfect example of a person who was open to God's will and was willing to let God work through her, to be an instrument of God's salvation.

Even after two thousand years, we still don't know very much about the historical Mary. Much of what people believe about Mary has come to us through the devotional life of the Church. You have seen statutes and many pictures of Mary. Perhaps you have watched movies of the life of Jesus, which, of course, begin with his conception and birth; the stories begin with Mary's response to God.

Every once in a while throughout history, people have claimed that Mary appeared to them and gave them special messages for the welfare of all God's people. These experiences are very personal. Even if they involve more than one individual, they are what the Church considers to be **private revelation.** That means that even when the claims are true, they are not essential for your Christian faith.

Scripture and God's self-revelation in Jesus are **public revelation;** that is, they are part of open, public human experience, directly available to everyone. There was nothing secretive or selective about God's revelation. Its focus was not special knowledge or messages. That revelation, moreover, culminated in the gift of God's very self to us in Jesus.

The Catholic Church is very cautious about **apparitions.** After lengthy investigation and healthy skepticism, the Church may declare that it is permissible for members of the Church to be "followers" of a particular devotion to Mary.

It does not say that anyone *has to* believe in or follow the personal, private experience of any other believer. Christians believe that Jesus is the source of our salvation and that discipleship with him will lead us to salvation and the fullness of life. Any devotion to Mary ought to assist us on this path, not lead us into another path.

Then do this

Draw a picture of the way you imagine Mary. Share your drawing with the class.

private revelation

personal messages from God

public revelation

Scripture and God's self-revelation in Jesus

apparition

visions or appearances of Jesus, Mary, or a saint claimed to be seen by an individual or a small group

In honor of Mary

At the annunciation scene in the Gospel according to Luke, Mary says this: ". . . all generations will call me blessed" (1:48). These words are reflected in the constant tradition of the Christian community in giving Mary, the mother of Jesus, a very special place of honor. The Church's devotion to Mary is an important part of Christian spirituality. From early in the Church's history, Mary has been honored as the Mother of God.

The Catholic Church's devotion to Mary is not adoration and worship, which are properly given only to the Trinity: Father, Son, and Holy Spirit. But proper devotion to Mary can help us adore and praise God. The feasts of Mary and other forms of prayer directed

to her, the Rosary, for example, are expressions of this devotion. When we reflect on the life of Mary, we see in her an example of the Church's "pilgrimage of faith" and the goal of that journey.

See the *Catechism of the Catholic Church*, #s 971–972.

1. How is Mary the icon or reflection of Jesus for the Church?

2. What is the Rosary? How can this prayer strengthen your Christian life?

3. What part of Mary's life do you find most inspiring?

Devotion to Mary and the saints

Devotion to Mary, the mother of Jesus, or to any other saint, can be given a three-fold test:

- Does the person honored in this devotion reflect the nature and qualities of God, as revealed in the Old and New Testaments?
- Do this person and this devotion lead us to a more Christ-like life?
- Do this person and this devotion unite us more closely with the rest of the Church?

If a devotional practice fails one of these points, it should be avoided. Alleged appearances of Mary aren't authentic, for example, if they frighten people or if they tell us that God is ready to unleash his anger and vengeance on a sinful world. We know that God the Father didn't send Jesus to destroy, but to offer forgiveness and reconciliation. A proper devotion to Mary is rooted in her humanity, in the down-to-earth quality of her life and her willingness as a daughter of God to open her life and heart to God.

Talk about it

With what devotions to Mary are you familiar?

Marian devotion must be attentive to the cries of the poor.

Mary T. Malone

An ancient Marian hymn

The following hymn is sung in the Greek Church on the Fifth Sunday of Lent. Its author is unknown, but it has been referred to as the most beautiful and profound ancient Marian hymn in all of Christian literature.

> *Hail, O space of the spaceless God;*
> *hail, O gate of the sublime mystery.*
> *Hail, O message unsure to men without faith;*
> *hail, O glory most certain to those who believe.*
> *Hail, O sacred chariot of the One above the Cherubim;*
> *hail, perfect dwelling of the One above the Seraphim.*
> *Hail, O you who reconciled opposites;*
> *hail, O you who combined maidenhood and motherhood.*
> *Hail, O you through whom transgression was erased;*
> *hail, O you through whom Paradise was opened.*
> *Hail, O key to the kingdom of Christ;*
> *hail, O hope for the ages of bliss.*
>
> *Hail, O Bride and Maiden ever-pure.*

Optional activities

1. Search a parish hymnal for songs honoring Mary. If possible, obtain a recording of each to play in class. Talk about the message of the hymn.

2. Ask ten people to share with you their favorite title for Mary. In class combine the lists to create a litany honoring Mary. Make copies of the litany and pray it together and privately.

Qualities of Mary

Here are some important factors about Mary's life which should inspire your own spiritual journey as a disciple of Jesus.

Mary's humanness

Mary was born like any one of us. She wasn't a mythical goddess or female divinity. Her parents traditionally are identified as Joachim and Anna. According to the Catholic Church, what is unique about her conception is that she was not conceived with original sin like the rest of humanity. And, from the very first moment of her existence, Mary was free from the effects of original sin, namely concupiscence or any tug toward selfishness and sin.

The Catholic Church teaches this in the doctrine of the **immaculate conception**. Actually this teaching of the Church says more about Jesus than it does about Mary: When Jesus was conceived in the womb of Mary, she had already been prepared by God's grace to be a worthy "vessel" of the Son of God. Mary is truly "full of grace." She was never separated or alienated from God by selfishness and sin. Mary was redeemed from the moment of her conception.

immaculate conception
Mary's conception free from original sin, redeemed from the moment of her conception

Her ordinariness

Mary grew up in the little village of Nazareth. A Jewish maiden, she carried out the typical tasks of a Jewish woman. She knew her prayers, and, without a doubt, she celebrated the Passover and other Jewish feasts. Like many others in her faith tradition, she longed for the coming of the messiah and the salvation of God's people. She knew her history and the meaning of daily work and of suffering.

Perhaps her family arranged her marriage to Joseph, one of the village carpenters. This engaged couple was most likely only in their mid- or late teens, the marrying age at the time.

Her trust in God

Just when her fondest dreams were beginning to unfold, Mary was asked by God to be the mother of the Savior. Luke's Gospel pictures an encounter with Gabriel, an angel messenger from God. This maiden said "Yes" to God and allowed the Word of God to become incarnate in her womb.

The Church celebrates this event as the **annunciation**—that moment when the Word of God came to live not just *with* us, but as one *of* us. Mary trusted that God would use her, a simple small-town maiden, to bring about his plan of salvation.

annunciation
the visit to Mary by an angel, who told her that she was to be the mother of the Savior

Her constant faithfulness

While little is known about the life of Mary, we certainly know that she gave birth to Jesus and reared him in the Jewish faith. On occasion, she appears in the Gospel stories, but never as an equal partner with Jesus in the salvation of the world. She remains always in the background, pointing others to her son. She is a faithful mother, still there in the end when her crucified son hangs on the cross. When even his chosen twelve abandoned him, Mary remained at his side.

Her sharing in the faith community

Mary was present among the disciples when the Holy Spirit came upon them on Pentecost Sunday. She was part of the early Church, the assembly of the Lord chosen to give witness to the world of its new and full life in Jesus, her risen Son.

Her ultimate destiny

The Catholic Church teaches that, at the end of her life, Mary was assumed into heaven, body and soul (spirit), where she now shares in the gift of resurrected life with her son, Jesus. Where she has gone, we hope to follow. Our hope is based on the promise of resurrected life made to all who die in Christ.

Honoring Mary

All Christians should hold Mary, the mother of Jesus, in special esteem, giving her a special place of honor. This doesn't mean that Christians have to approach God through her. Because of the life, death, and resurrection of Jesus, Christians have free and direct access to God in the most intimate and trusting way. Mary, however, should not and cannot be removed from the history of salvation. She is the mother of Jesus.

And since Jesus was the Son of God, she is also the Mother of God.

Every statement about Mary made by the Church is actually a statement about the uniqueness and the wonder of God's redeeming love made known in Jesus, her son. We don't have to approach God through Mary, but we cannot understand Jesus without meeting and coming to know his mother.

The more we relate to Mary as a real human who has a real human history and who lived a real life in real time and place, the more we come into contact with the mystery of God's love. She is the perfect disciple—an open instrument for God to use in bringing about the kingdom. As the perfect disciple, Mary also is God's special gift to you as you too seek to become a follower of Jesus, her son.

REVIEW

1. Who is the perfect saint?

2. What is the difference between private revelation and public revelation?

3. What does the term *immaculate conception* mean?

4. How is Mary honored in the Church?

CONCLUSION

Mary and all the saints are great examples of living the **virtues**. As disciples of Jesus, we are all called to follow their example. Perhaps the best way to end this course is to look briefly at the main virtues practiced by disciples of Jesus. Virtues are good attitudes that develop into habits of goodness; they help us make good decisions and do what is right.

The first group of virtues are already familiar to you; these are the **theological virtues** of faith, hope, and love. These virtues are gifts from God that help us relate to him. **Faith** as a virtue helps us believe in God and in all that he has revealed to us. **Hope** helps us trust in God and in the salvation he has promised us. It also helps us trust that God is with us and will give us all we need to come to him. **Love** is the virtue that helps us love God and others unselfishly.

It's obvious from the definition of love that God doesn't want us to live lives of virtue for his sake alone; virtues help us be better persons. As a result we are happier with ourselves and we relate to others in more loving ways. The four main virtues that help us put our love for others into practice, while developing the qualities that help us grow personally, are the **cardinal or moral virtues**. These virtues are temperance, prudence, justice, and fortitude.

The virtue of temperance isn't always easy to appreciate—neither by adults nor by teens. **Temperance** means moderation in all things. That means not overeating, not dieting to the point of illness, not getting drunk, not using illegal drugs, not letting sex rule us, not becoming workaholics, not seeking thrills at the expense of safety, and so on. Lots of NOTs!

What temperance teaches us is that going overboard isn't the best way to become the best persons we can be. Moderation helps us control ourselves and our appetites. When we do this, we are "in control"; that is, our bodies and our desires aren't controlling us. As a result, we are much more likely to avoid the horrors of addiction, which devastates so many lives and relationships.

Then do this

Read 1 Corinthians 13, Paul's essay on love. Write a personal reflection on the reading and share it with a good friend.

---

virtue
good attitudes and habits that help us make good decisions and do what is right

theological virtues
gifts from God that help us relate to him; the virtues of faith, hope, and love

faith
the virtue that helps us believe in God and in all that he has revealed to us

hope
the virtue that helps us trust in God and in the salvation he has promised us

love
the virtue that helps us love God and others unselfishly

cardinal or moral virtues
the virtues that help us put our love for others into practice, while developing the qualities that help us grow personally

temperance
the virtue that helps us be moderate in all things

The next moral virtue is **prudence**, another word often unappreciated. Prudence is tact in what we say and good judgment in what we do. When we come away from an encounter with another person shaking our head at how stupid we've been, we can be pretty sure we said or did something that wasn't prudent, that wasn't wise or that we did not say or do something that would have been prudent or wise. Imprudent words and actions or failures to speak or act always hurt someone—including ourselves. The prudent person is usually at peace—within and with others.

Justice is the virtue by which we give God and others what is their due. When we are just, we treat everyone fairly and work to make sure the structures in our society are just. Many of the people highlighted in the last chapter worked for justice in their society, but justice always began with those people themselves. The area of justice also includes how we relate to our environment. The great gift of creation requires our respect and care.

Finally, the virtue of **fortitude** gives us the courage, the strength, to do what is right. Knowing the right thing to do isn't enough; we have to carry through. That's where fortitude comes into play. It isn't easy to do what is right when surrounded by pressures to do otherwise—to take the easy way out, to put pleasure before responsibility. But the gift of courage helps us surmount every obstacle and walk forward as true disciples of Jesus.

So there we have it—God is a loving Father who gives us all the gifts we need to be happy, all we need to be saved. Christian life is truly a gift and a blessing.

Write it down

1. How are you a co-creator with God?

2. How do you show respect for all creation? How do you fail to show respect for all creation?

Then do this

Choose one:

1. Make a list of service organizations in your area.

2. Search the newspaper for examples of people involved in service to others.

REVIEW

1. What are the theological virtues?

2. What does each theological virtue mean?

3. What are the cardinal or moral virtues?

4. What does each cardinal virtue mean?

The fruit of the Spirit

. . . the fruit of the Spirit is love, joy, peace, patience, kindness, generosity, faithfulness, gentleness, and self-control. There is no law against such things. . . If we live by the Spirit, let us also be guided by the Spirit. Let us not become conceited, competing against one another, envying one another. . . .

So let us not grow weary in doing what is right, for we will reap at harvest time, if we do not give up. So then, whenever we have an opportunity, let us work for the good of all, and especially for those of the family of faith.

Galatians 5:22–23, 25–26; 6:9–10

Optional activities

1. Discuss: What resolutions for future action are suggested by this reading?

2. Find another Scripture passage to summarize this course for you. Share the reading with the class and tell them why you chose it.

Then do this

Find a story in *The Book of Virtues* or *The Moral Compass* (both edited by William J. Bennett) or a similar book on one of the virtues discussed here. Share the story with the class and lead a discussion on the story and the virtue.

Words you should know

annunciation	heaven	private revelation
apparition	hell	prudence
canonize	hope	public revelation
cardinal or moral virtues	immaculate conception	purgatory
communion of saints	intercession	saint
discipleship	justice	temperance
faith	love	theological virtues
fortitude	martyrdom	virtue

APPENDIX

THE APOSTLES' CREED

I believe in God, the Father Almighty,
  creator of heaven and earth.
I believe in Jesus Christ, his only Son, our Lord.
He was conceived by the power of the Holy Spirit
  and born of the Virgin Mary.
He suffered under Pontius Pilate,
  was crucified, died, and was buried.
He descended to the dead.
On the third day, he rose again.
He ascended into heaven,
  and is seated at the right hand of God the Father.
He will come again to judge the living and the dead.
I believe in the Holy Spirit,
  the holy catholic Church,
  the communion of saints,
  the forgiveness of sins,
  the resurrection of the body,
  and life everlasting. Amen.

THE LORD'S PRAYER

Our Father, who art in heaven,
hallowed be thy name.
Thy kingdom come;
thy will be done on earth as it is in heaven.
Give us this day our daily bread
and forgives us our trespasses
as we forgive those who trespass against us.
And lead us not into temptation,
but deliver us from evil. Amen.

HAIL MARY

Hail, Mary, full of grace!
The Lord is with you.
Blessed are you among women
and blessed is the fruit of your womb, Jesus.
Holy Mary, Mother of God,
pray for us sinners,
now and at the hour of our death. Amen.

GLORY TO GOD (DOXOLOGY)

Glory to the Father, and to the Son, and to the Holy Spirit:
as it was in the beginning, is now, and will be forever.
Amen.

THE NICENE CREED

We believe in one God,
  the Father, the Almighty,
  maker of heaven and earth,
  of all that is, seen and unseen.
We believe in one Lord, Jesus Christ,
  the only Son of God,
  eternally begotten of the Father,
  God from God, Light from Light,
  true God from true God,
  begotten, not made, one in Being with the Father.
Through him all things were made.
For us men and for our salvation
  he came down from heaven:
by the power of the Holy Spirit
  he was born of the Virgin Mary,
  and became man.
For our sake he was crucified under Pontius Pilate;
he suffered, died and was buried.
On the third day he rose again
  in fulfillment of the Scriptures;
he ascended into heaven
  and is seated at the right hand of the Father.
He will come again in glory to judge the living and the dead,
  and his kingdom will have no end.
We believe in the Holy Spirit, the Lord, the giver of life,
  who proceeds from the Father and the Son.
With the Father and the Son he is worshiped and glorified.
He has spoken through the Prophets.
We believe in one holy catholic and apostolic Church.
We acknowledge one baptism for the forgiveness of sins.
We look for the resurrection of the dead
  and the life of the world to come. Amen.

BLESSING BEFORE MEALS

Bless us, O Lord, and these your gifts
which we are about to receive from your goodness.
Through Christ our Lord. Amen.

THANKSGIVING AFTER MEALS

We give you thanks, almighty God,
for these and all your blessings,
through Christ Our Lord. Amen.
May the souls of the faithful departed,
through the mercy of God, rest in peace. Amen.

HAIL, HOLY QUEEN

Hail, Holy Queen, Mother of mercy,
hail, our life, our sweetness, and our hope.
To you we cry, the children of Eve,
to you do we send up our sighs,
mourning and weeping in this land of exile.
Turn, then, most gracious advocate,
your eyes of mercy toward us;
lead us home at last,
and show us the blessed fruit of your womb, Jesus.
O clement, O loving, O sweet Virgin Mary.
Pray for us, O holy Mother of God,
that we may be made worthy of the promises of Christ.

THE MEMORARE

Remember, most loving Virgin Mary,
never was it heard
that anyone who turned to you for help
was left unaided.
Inspired by this confidence,
though burdened by my sins,
I run to your protection
for you are my mother.
Mother of the Word of God,
do not despise my words of pleading
but be merciful and hear my prayer.

— St. Bernard

THE MAGNIFICAT

My soul proclaims the greatness of the Lord,
my spirit rejoices in God my Savior;
for he has looked with favor on his lowly servant.
From this day all generations will call me blessed:
the Almighty had done great things for me,
and holy is his Name.
He has mercy on those who fear him
in every generation.
He has shown the strength of his arm,
he has scattered the proud in their conceit.
He has cast down the mighty from their thrones,
and has lifted up the lowly.
He has filled the hungry with good things,
and the rich he has sent away empty.
He has come to the help of his servant Israel
for he has remembered his promise of mercy,
the promise he made to our fathers,
to Abraham and his children forever.

— Luke 1:46–55

CONFITEOR

I confess to almighty God,
and to you, my brothers and sisters,
that I have sinned through my own fault
in my thoughts and in my words,
in what I have done,
and in what I have failed to do;
and I ask blessed Mary, ever virgin,
all the angels and saints,
and you, my bothers and sisters,
to pray for me to the Lord our God.

THE TEN COMMANDMENTS

1. I am the Lord your God. You shall not have strange gods before me.
2. You shall not take the name of the Lord your God in vain.
3. Remember to keep holy the Lord's day.
4. Honor your father and your mother.
5. You shall not kill.
6. You shall not commit adultery.
7. You shall not steal.
8. You shall not bear false witness against your neighbor.
9. You shall not covet your neighbor's wife.
10. You shall not covet your neighbor's goods.

THE BEATITUDES

Blessed are the poor in spirit,
   for theirs is the kingdom of heaven.
Blessed are those who mourn,
   for they will be comforted.
Blessed are the meek,
   for they will inherit the earth.
Blessed are those who hunger and thirst for righteousness,
   for they will be filled.
Blessed are the merciful,
   for they will be shown mercy.
Blessed are the clean of heart,
   for they will see God.
Blessed are the peacemakers,
   for they will be called children of God.
Blessed are those who are persecuted for righteousness' sake,
   for theirs is the kingdom of heaven.

— Matthew 5:3–10

SPIRITUAL WORKS OF MERCY

Teach the ignorant.
Counsel the doubtful.
Comfort the sorrowful.
Bear wrongs patiently.
Forgive injuries.
Warn the sinner.
Pray for the living and the dead.

CORPORAL WORKS OF MERCY

Feed the hungry.
Give drink to the thirsty.
Shelter the homeless.
Clothe the naked.
Visit the sick.
Visit the imprisoned.
Bury the dead.

PRAYER TO THE HOLY SPIRIT

Come, Holy Sprit, fill the hearts of your faithful.
And kindle in them the fire of your love.
Send forth your Spirit and they shall be created.
And you shall renew the face of the earth.
Let us pray:
Lord, by the light of the Holy Spirit
you have taught the hearts of your faithful.
In the same Spirit,
help us choose what is right
and always rejoice in your consolation.
We ask this through Christ Our Lord. Amen.

GLORIA

Glory to God in the highest,
   and peace to his people on earth.
Lord God, heavenly King,
almighty God and Father,
   we worship you, we give you thanks,
   we praise you for your glory.
Lord Jesus Christ, only Son of the Father,
Lord God, Lamb of God,
you take away the sins of the world:
   have mercy on us;
you are seated at the right hand of the Father:
   receive our prayer.
For you alone are the Holy One,
   you alone are the Lord,
   you alone are the Most High,
      Jesus Christ,
      with the Holy Spirit,
      in the glory of God the Father. Amen.

ACT OF CONTRITION

My God,
I am sorry for my sins with all my heart.
In choosing to do wrong
and failing to do good,
I have sinned against you
whom I should love above all things.
I firmly intend, with your help,
to do penance,
to sin no more,
and to avoid whatever leads me to sin.
Our Savior Jesus Christ
suffered and died for us.
In his name, my God, have mercy.

SERENITY PRAYER

God, grant me the peace
to accept the things I cannot change,
the courage to change the things I can,
and the wisdom to know the difference.

MYSTERIES OF THE ROSARY

Joyful Mysteries (Mondays and Thursdays)
   The Annunciation
   The Visitation
   The Nativity
   The Presentation
   The Finding of the Jesus in the Temple

Sorrowful Mysteries (Tuesday at and Fridays)
   The Agony in the Garden
   The Scouring at the Pillar
   The Crowning with Thorns
   Jesus Carries His Cross
   The Crucifixion

Glorious Mysteries (Sundays, Wednesdays, and Saturdays)
   The Resurrection of Jesus
   The Ascension of Jesus
   The Descent of the Holy Spirit
   The Assumption of Mary
   The Coronation of Mary

STATIONS OF THE CROSS

1. Jesus is condemned to death.
2. Jesus carries his cross.
3. Jesus falls the first time.
4. Jesus meets his mother.
5. Simon helps Jesus carry his cross.
6. Veronica wipes the face of Jesus.
7. Jesus falls the second time.
8. Jesus speaks to the women of Jerusalem.
9. Jesus falls the third time.
10. Jesus is stripped of his garments.
11. Jesus is nailed to the cross.
12. Jesus dies on the cross.
13. Jesus is taken down from the cross.
14. Jesus is laid in the tomb.

PRAYER OF ST. FRANCIS

Lord, make me an instrument of your peace.
Where there is hatred, let me sow love;
where there is injury, pardon;
where there is doubt, faith;
where there despair, hope;
where there is darkness, light;
where there is sadness, joy.
Lord, grant that I may not so much
seek to be consoled as to console;
to be understood as to understand;
to be loved as to love.
For it is in giving that we receive,
in pardoning that we are pardoned,
and in dying that we are born to eternal life.

LAWS OF THE CHURCH

You shall attend Mass on Sundays and holy days
  of obligation and rest from servile labor.
You shall confess your sins at least once a year if there is
  serious sin.
You shall receive the Sacrament of the Eucharist at least
  during the Easter Season.
You shall observe the days of fasting and abstinence
  established by the Church.
You shall help to provide for the needs of the Church.

FAST, ABSTINENCE, AND DAYS OF PENANCE

All Christians, by the nature of their lives, are obliged to live in a spirit of penance whereby their exterior act of prayer, self-denial, and charity bear witness to the inner values of their faith.

Fasting is the limitation to one full meal and two lighter meals in the course of a day, with no food in between meals. In the United States the obligation to fast binds those from eighteen years of age to the beginning of the sixtieth year.

Abstinence generally refers to refraining from eating meat on certain days. The obligation to abstain from meat binds Catholics from the age of fourteen throughout life.

Ash Wednesday and Good Friday are days of fast and abstinence. All the Fridays of Lent are days of abstinence. All the Fridays of the year and the entire Season of Lent are days of penance. Works of penance include voluntary abstinence, fasting, prayer, works of charity, and other acts of self-denial.

The Eucharistic fast requires that a person fast from food and drink for one hour before receiving Communion. This does not include water and medicine. The fast for those who are elderly or sick is fifteen minutes.

The substantial observance of these laws is a grave obligation. That is, anyone who neglects all forms of penance or deliberately shows contempt for the Church's penitential discipline may be guilty of serious sin. Occasional failure to observe penitential regulations is not seriously sinful. Proportionately grave circum-stances—sickness, dietary needs, social obligation—excuse a person from the obligations to fast and abstain, but not from seeking out other forms of penance.

GLOSSARY

abortion—the destruction of human life in the womb by chemical or mechanical means

absolution—words that announce the forgiveness of sins

abstinence—the choice not to engage in intercourse outside of the situation intended by God, namely, marriage

Acts of the Apostles—book in the New Testament which tells the story of the early Church

Advent—the four-week period of preparation for the celebration of the birth of our Lord, or Christmas

alienation—the sense of being alone, unconnected to others

alms—donations for those who are poor

anawim—people who were completely without resources or social status

annunciation—the visit to Mary by an angel, who told her that she was to be the mother of the Savior

anointing—the pouring of oil over a person to signify a special role or identity

Anointing of the Sick—the sacrament for those who are sick or dying, the anointing with oil and prayers for physical and spiritual healing

Apiru—an ancient wandering class of people, possibly the ancestors of the Hebrew people

apocalyptic—highly imaginative writing about a great conflict between good and evil, revealing hidden insights into the meaning of events by means of symbols and images

Apocrypha—books of the Old Testament that are part of Catholic Bibles, but not Protestant Bibles; all of these were written in Greek rather than Hebrew

apostle—literally, one who is sent; one of twelve men chosen by Jesus to be his closest followers and, after Jesus' death and resurrection, responsible for preaching the gospel and unifying the Christian community

apostolic—founded on the apostles

apparition—visions or appearances of Jesus, Mary, or a saint claimed to be seen by an individual or a small group

archbishop—a bishop who is usually the leader of an archdiocese (a prominent or large diocese)

atheist—someone who believes there is no God

Baptism—the Sacrament of Initiation that makes us children of God and members of the Church and that takes away all sin, original and personal

Bible—the written story of what God has done in human history and particularly over that span of several thousand years we call "salvation history"

biography—an historical account of a person's life

bishop—a successor of the apostles, usually the head of a diocese

blasphemy—the act of showing contempt or grave irreverence toward God

canon—books of the Bible kept by the community as normative for the faith development of the people of God

canonize—to officially name someone a saint

cardinal—a bishop who is eligible to elect the pope

cardinal or **moral virtues**—the virtues that help us put our love for others into practice, while developing the qualities that help us grow personally

catechumenate—the time of preparation for an unbaptized person seeking identity with Christ and membership in the Church

celibacy—the Church discipline requiring most priests of the Catholic Church in the West to not marry

charism—a special gift of service

chastity—the religious vow to live chastely in the unmarried state; the virtue that helps you control your sexual powers and use them in proper and morally right ways

chosen people—a people favored by God; the Hebrews or Jews

Christian Scriptures—the New Testament of the Bible

Christmas—the Church's celebration of the birth of Jesus, the celebration of the incarnation

Church—the community of Jesus' followers who have heard the good news, believe it, and seek to follow it

circumcision—Jewish rite of inclusion for males, involving the cutting of the foreskin on the penis

claimed faith—faith that has been made one's own through a process of conversion

college of bishops—the bishops of the Catholic Church with the pope at their head

collegiality—the working together of the bishops of the Church to lead and unify the members of the Church

communion of saints—all the faithful, living and dead—on earth and in heaven—united by the saving love of God

Confirmation—the Sacrament of Initiation that celebrates the work of the Holy Spirit who completes and seals our Baptism and leads us to the Eucharist

conscience—the gift from God that helps us know the difference between right and wrong and to choose what is right; the obligation we experience to do good and avoid evil

consecrate—to make holy or to dedicate

consecration—act of making or declaring someone or something holy or sacred

conversion—(1) the lifelong process of developing a relationship with God; (2) the radical and significant change from one faith tradition to another

covenant—a commitment of individual persons or groups to one another; a solemn, unconditional agreement or promise between God and people

creed—a statement of the main things we believe about God and his relationship to us

culture—the beliefs, social forms, and material traits of a group

cyclic time—the experience of time passing in circles, with events repeating themselves in some fashion

Day of Atonement, Yom Kippur—the Jewish day of fasting and corporate confession of sins

deacon—first order of the ordained; does works of charity and may preside at Baptisms and marriages

declaration of nullity—formal Church recognition that a sacramental marriage did not exist

denomination—a subset of a religion, a group within a major religion

diocese—a group of parishes headed by a bishop

disciple—one who learns from and follows another

discipleship—being a learner; for Christians, the vocation of following Jesus

divorce—a judicial declaration dissolving a marriage; the ending of a marriage in the eyes of civil law

dogma—an official, essential teaching of a Church or other group

doxology—prayer or hymn of praise to God, such as the "Glory to the Father"

Easter—the celebration of the resurrection of Jesus

ecumenical council—a gathering of the world's bishops to discuss important Church issues or teachings

editing—the process of making additions, corrections, and deletions to a manuscript

encyclical—a letter by the pope to the worldwide Church

environment—the world around a person; where a person lives and the social, economic, and political atmosphere in the family, neighborhood, school, and Church

epistle—a New Testament letter

Eucharist—the sacrament of Jesus' presence under the form of bread and wine; also, the Mass

evangelist—one who tells the good news; a Gospel writer

evangelization—the process of sharing the good news of Jesus and the reign of God

Exodus—the Hebrews' escape from slavery in Egypt, through the Sea of Reeds, into the desert of the Sinai peninsula

experienced religion—religion that is experienced through interaction with people who have faith and who practice (or don't practice) their religion

faith—(1) belief in someone or something and trust in a person or in God; (2) openness to salvation; trust in someone, especially God; a firm belief; an expression of loyalty; a system of beliefs; a set of principles; a belief in something real that can't be proved; (3) the virtue that helps us believe in God and in all that he has revealed to us

faith tradition—the beliefs and practices of a particular religion

Feast of Tabernacles—the Jewish fall harvest celebration commemorating the time of travel in the wilderness between Egypt and the promised land

First Communion—the first reception of the Eucharist, which should properly be celebrated as the completion of Christian initiation

fortitude—the virtue that gives us the courage, the strength, to do what is right

freedom—liberation from restraint or the power of another, within reasonable bounds

friendship—a relationship based on mutual acceptance and love

frontier mentality—rugged individualism; the expectation that we stand alone and do for ourselves

gender—what "sex" a person is, male or female

genetic—relating to or determined by the origin or development of something; related to the traits carried in genes

genital—having to do with the sexual or reproductive organs

Gentiles—non-Jews, *goyim*; those without the light of true faith

gospel—the good news of Jesus

grace—God's life and love in us; God's help to do what is right

Hanakkah—the Jewish feast commemorating the rededication of the temple in 164 B.C.

heaven—the life after death in which people experience God's life and love forever

Hebrew Scriptures—those books of the Bible held sacred by the Jews; includes most of the Old Testament

Hebrews—ancestors of today's Jewish people

hell—the state of eternal separation from God

hierarchy—clergy; commonly understood, the bishops of the Catholic Church, including the pope, cardinals, and archbishops

high places—places of worship situated on hill tops or mountain tops

holiness—the state of being the whole person God created one to be

Holocaust—the systematic, bureaucratic annihilation of six million Jews by the Nazi regime and their collaborators during World War II

holy days of obligation—special feast days of the Church on which Catholics are obliged to attend Mass

Holy Orders—the sacrament by which a man is ordained as a deacon, priest, or bishop

homily—a reflection rooted in one or more Scripture readings proclaimed at a given liturgy

hope—the virtue that helps us trust in God and in the salvation he has promised us

hypocrisy—the act of pretending to be what one is not or to believe what one doesn't really believe

idolatry—an act or attitude in which a person gives to a thing the power of salvation, the power to bring ultimate happiness and fulfillment; the worship of false gods or of images

immaculate conception—Mary's conception free from original sin, redeemed from moment of her conception

incarnation—the act of God becoming a human in Jesus

indissolubility—cannot be "undone" by any human person or human institution

indwelling—the presence of an inner activating or guiding force or spirit or power

infallibility—the quality of teaching without error under certain circumstances, held by the pope and the bishops in union with the pope

infancy narrative—a story which explains the divine origin and greatness of Jesus, even from the moment of his conception and birth

infanticide—the taking of the life of a child

inspired, inspiration—God's influence in Scripture, working through human authors and their powers and abilities to reveal religious truth

intercession—prayer asking on behalf of another

intimacy—the state of being in a close, personal relationship

Israel—the twelve tribes, named for sons and grandsons of Jacob; eventually, the united kingdom, and later the northern kingdom

Judeo-Christian—the tradition based on the religious concepts and experiences of Jewish and Christian peoples

judge—a charismatic leader raised up by God to unify the Hebrew tribes during times of crisis

justice—the virtue through which we give God and others what is their due

kairos time—the experience of time as an invitation to respond; time where meaning and purpose are discovered

kosher—ritually proper food or the preparation of food according to Jewish law

laying on of hands—action of conferring God's blessing on someone chosen for a special task or identity

Lent—the liturgical season for deepening the Christian's identification with the life, death, and resurrection of Christ; a time of repentance in preparation for Easter

Levites—usually non-priests who assisted at the temple

life questions—questions that go much deeper than everyday questions, that tug at the heart

linear time—the experience of time as progressing, moving forward

literal truth—what is said or written exactly as said or written

literary form—kind or type of literature, such as poetry, history, and letter

liturgical calendar—the calendar of the Church year, the annual commemoration and celebration of the main Christian mysteries

liturgy—the structured rites or ceremonies of worship; the Church in worship (such as sacramental celebrations); the "work" of the community of faith

love—the virtue that helps us love God and others unselfishly

magisterium—the teaching authority of the Catholic Church

martyrdom—giving one's life for one's faith

Matrimony—the sacrament by which a man and a woman vow faithfulness to each other in marriage

mercy—compassionate forgiveness

messiah—the anointed one who ushers in the time of salvation, the Christ

miracle—an event that can't be explained naturally; a marvel that shows God at work

missionary—one sent on a task, such as taking the good news of Jesus to others, especially those in another area

monarchy—rule by a single person

monsignor—an honorary title given to some priests

mosque—community place of prayer for Islamic men

myth—a traditional story that explains something about a worldview or a belief or practice; a story about the gods or God

nature religions—religious expressions that see nature as a visible extension of the spirit world

neediness—the state of being in want of something

normative—the standard for something, canonical

obedience—the religious vow to freely choose to try to always do God's will

Ordinary Time—the time during the liturgical year that focuses on discipleship with Jesus

ordination—the rite by which a man becomes a deacon, priest, or bishop

papacy—the office of the pope

parable—a story which teaches a lesson

parousia—the return of Jesus in glory at the end of time

paschal mystery—Jesus' suffering, death, and resurrection

Passover—the eight-day Jewish festival commemorating the Exodus, the night the Hebrews in Egypt were spared the death of the firstborn sons and gained their freedom from slavery

patriarch—founding father

Paul—a Christian convert after Jesus' resurrection who eventually became known as the *apostle to the Gentiles* (non-Jews)

Penance, Reconciliation—the sacrament that celebrates God's forgiveness of sin through the Church

penitent—one who repents of sin, seeks forgiveness, and does penance

Pentecost—the Jewish spring harvest feast commemorating the gift of the Torah

Pharisees—Jewish laymen who practiced exact observance of the Law

pope—the bishop of the diocese of Rome and the head of the entire Catholic Church

poverty—the religious vow to place God and the needs of those served before the individual's own needs and wishes

practiced religion—religion that a person lives with a certain degree of commitment

prayer—turning the mind and heart to God

priest—ordained man who presides at the sacraments and ministers to people in the name of the Church

priests—in Judaism, men who offered sacrifices in the temple and performed other religious rites

private revelation—personal messages from God

prophet—a person who speaks for God; one who speaks forth God's call to repentance and reform

prudence—the virtue that helps us use good judgment in what we say and do

public revelation—Scripture and God's self-revelation in Jesus

purgatory—the state of purification for those who have died

rabbi—in Judaism, a teacher; at the time of Jesus, especially from among the scribes

reconcile—to restore to friendship or harmony

Reformation—the sixteenth century religious protest movement that resulted in a split in the Catholic Church in the West and the formation of several Protestant Churches

religion—an organized group of worshipers who share beliefs, religious practices, and a moral code

religious life—the vocation of vowed persons who usually live in community

religious order—a group of men or women who make vows and live in a community governed by an approved rule

responsibility—accountability, reliability, trustworthiness

reveal—to make known as true, to open, to establish a relationship based on trust

revelation—God's sharing of himself with humanity

reverent—respectful, holding in awe

Rite of Christian Initiation of Adults—the ceremonies marking the conversion of and initiation process for new members of the Church

rites and rituals—special ways of praying and of expressing faith, directly in words, and symbolically through signs

ritual—action or actions repeated in a particular manner on similar occasions by a person or group

Sabbath or Shabbat—the Jewish day of rest, prayer, reflection, and study (sunset on Friday to sunset on Saturday)

sacrament—a liturgical celebration of the Christian faithful which is a visible sign of their encounter with God in Christ

sacramental—sacred signs—blessings, special objects, and ritual actions and prayers

sacred—holy, comes from God, set apart for God

sacred time—God's time

sacrifice—an offering of something, usually to God, to be made holy

Sadducees—a group of priests and their followers in Judaism known for their reliance on the Pentateuch alone

saint—a person of heroic virtue; a person who by the grace of God lived a life of great faith and Christian witness

salvation—being made whole by God, made right with God; saved from the power of sin and everlasting death

salvation history—the concept that history—the passage of time and events—is the very place where God makes himself known for our well-being

scribes—the recorders of Scripture, often called on to instruct others in applying Scripture to daily life

seal of the sacrament—the seal of confession, whereby the priest is solemnly obligated to never reveal anything he has heard in the Sacrament of Penance

searching faith—the stage in which people seek their own ideas and try to form their own convictions regarding their understanding of God and of religion and the practice of religion

sexual orientation—a person's direction or sexual attraction toward others: toward members of the other gender or members of the same gender

sexuality—one's way of relating to others as a male or a female person

sin—an unloving choice and the unloving actions that come from the unloving choice; the choice to disobey God, to turn away from God, other people, ourselves, and the world

single life—not being married; the vocation from God of living unmarried and celibate, chosen in order to be of service to others

sinning mortally—having an attitude or acting in a way which involves a serious matter and which a person does with full knowledge and with full freedom

sinning venially—having a wrong attitude or acting in a way which involves either a less serious matter done with full knowledge and full freedom, or a serious matter done with less than full knowledge and/or less than full freedom

social justice—right relationships among people and the preservation of human dignity

spiritual truth—the religious meaning of a text in Scripture

spoken tradition—stories and teachings of a group passed on by word of mouth

synagogue—Jewish house of prayer in which the Torah is read and where people pray and are instructed in their faith

synod—a gathering of a group of bishops, usually from a particular part of the world, to discuss an issue

Synoptic Gospels—the three most similar Gospels: Matthew, Mark, and Luke

temperance—the virtue that helps us be moderate in all things

temple—the central place of sacrifice and worship for the Jewish people, located in Jerusalem

testament—a statement of the truth about someone or something, especially concerning God's actions as written in Scripture

theocracy—rule by God

theological virtues—gifts from God that help us relate to him; the virtues of faith, hope, and love

Torah—the Law, the first five books of the Bible: Genesis, Exodus, Leviticus, Numbers, and Deuteronomy; also called the *Pentateuch*

Tradition—the truth that people have discovered as the result of the revelation of God

Triduum—the Three Sacred Days; the time that begins with the Mass of the Lord's Supper on Holy Thursday, culminates with the Easter Vigil, and concludes with evening prayer on Easter

ultimate source—that from which we come: God

unchurched—people who have no association with the practice of organized religion

Vatican—the tiny, sovereign nation in which the pope lives, located within Rome

viaticum—"food for the journey"; the Eucharist received by one who is dying

virtue—good attitudes and habits that help us make good decisions and do what is right

vows—solemn promises to God

worship—the response of adoration and praise we humans make to God, who has taken the first step to love us

written tradition—stories and teachings of a group passed on in written form

YHWH—the Hebrew "name" (vowels were not written) for God; "I AM" as in "I AM HERE" or "I AM WHO I AM."

INDEX

Bolded numbers indicate page where word is defined.

A

abortion, 313
Abraham and Sarah, 83–84
absolution, 271–272
abstinence, 30
Act of Contrition, 274
Acts of the Apostles, 4, 188, 196–198, 253
Advent, 220
Alexander the Great, 97
alienation, 260, 268, 276
alms, 149
anawim, 146, 166
anointing, 135, 237, 242, 243
Anointing of the Sick, Sacrament of the, 227, 276–279, 280–283
annunciation, 333
Antonio, Sister, 101
Apiru, 76–100, 133, 146, 150
apocalyptic, 198
Aprocrypha, 122
apostle, 4, 156
apostles, 8, 167, 175, 178, 182, 288
Apostles' Creed, 57, 212
apostolic, 205, 288
apparition, 331
Arab–Israeli conflict, 102–103
archbishop, 292
archdiocese, 292
atheist, 13
awareness of sin, 260–261

B

Baptism
  as taking part in Christ's life, 41, 189, 207, 276, 324
  meaning of, 239, 242, 276, 287
  of Jesus, 165, 220
  Sacrament of, 227, 234, 237, 239, 242, 287, 324
  signs and symbols of, 242
Baptist, 213
Beatitudes, 166
becoming a Christian, 234–251
being saved, 38, 40–49
Bernardin, Joseph Cardinal, 64
Bible (see also Old Testament; New Testament; Gospels), 112, 113
  and the canon, 125, 181
  and God's revelation, 106–127, 176–201
  and sin, 260–261, 264
  and truth, 117–118
  as God's word, 253
  as salvation history, 106–127, 176–201
  authorship of, 114–116, 181–189
  books of, 121–127, 181–201
  division of, 113–186
    Old Testament, 121–127
    New Testament, 176–201
  inspiration of, 116
  message of, 118, 182, 186–187
  purpose of, 115–181
biography, 190
bishop, bishops, 175, 243, 244, 289, 291
blasphemy, 137

Bosco, St. John, 290
breaking bread together, 250

C

Cabrini, St. Frances (Mother), 33
call to sainthood, 326–330
canon (Church) law, 294
canonize, 326
cardinal, 292
cardinal (moral) virtues, 335
catecumenate, 234
"Catholic Bible"—"Protestant Bible," 122
Catholic Church (see Church; Sacraments)
Catholic–Lutheran *Joint Declaration on Justification by Faith, 1998*, 43
Catholic Worker, The, 236
celibacy, 293
charism, 246, 304
chastity, 30, 293, 301
Chevez, Cesar, 308
chosen people, 77, 131, 141, 149, 150, 154, 160, 162, 174, 189, 249
Christ, 172 (see Jesus Christ)
Christian, a sacrament of Christ, 267
Christian communities, 182, 197, 204–205
Christian initiation, 239–251
Christian life, 286–317, 336
Christian Scriptures, 120 (see Bible; New Testament)
Christian unity, 206, 213–214
Christian view of suffering and death, 276–281
Christianity
  and Judaism, 130, 150, 154, 198, 204
  the history of, 76–103
  the key question of, 38
  the purpose of, 53
Christmas, 220
Church, the, 161
  and abortion, right to life, 313
  and anointing of the sick, 276–283
  and celibacy, 293
  and Christian initiation, 232–257
  and discipleship, 323
  and forgiveness of sin, 261, 267–268, 270–275
  and hierarchy, 289–297
  and Jesus Christ as center of history, 323
  and marriage, 28, 130, 227, 306–315
  and Mary, 54, 164, 195, 331–334
  and prayer, 60, 68–71, 143
  and purgatory, 328
  and reconciliation, 267–268, 270–275
  and religious communities, 304
  and Scripture, 118, 204
  and sex/sexuality, 28–29
  and sin, 262–263
  and the gospel, 158, 204, 236
  and the Holy Spirit, 163, 173, 178, 188, 196, 197, 201, 211, 215, 216, 226, 228
  and Tradition, 118, 204–231
  and worship, 59–60, 133–134, 140, 156, 198, 216–218

as apostolic, 175, 205, 210, 288
as Christ in the world, 228
as community of believers, 237, 238, 328
as community of faith, 287
as missionary, 197
characteristics (marks of), 205
fragmentation of, 212–215
mission/purpose of, 13, 197, 220, 236
nature and meaning of, 174, 204–205, 208
renewal of, 206
the early Church, 201, 204–205, 334
unity of, 214
work of, 216, 236
circumcision, 136
claimed faith, 62–63, 159, 161, 242
clergy, 289
college of bishops, 289
collegiality, 297
Commandment of Jesus, 166
Communion, Holy, 243, 248, 251, 255
communion of saints, 328–334
compassion, 281–283
confession, 270–275
Confirmation, Sacrament of, 207, 227, 234, 237, 239, 240, 243–247, 287, 329
conscience, 260, 273
consecrate, 293, 301
consecrated life, 301–305
consecration, 136
conversion, 62, 63, 161, 234–238, 328
covenant, 78, 87–88, 109, 130–132, 136, 140, 143, 161, 205, 308, 310–312
Covenant House, 26
created in God's image, 19, 24, 38, 47, 161
creed, 56–57, 212
cross of Jesus and our cross, 324
crucifixion, 162, 169–170, 248
culture, 16, 122, 154
cyclic time, 79

D

David, King, 90, 124, 164
Day, Dorothy, 235, 330
Day of Atonement (Yom Kippur), 145, 256
deacon, 292
Dead Sea Scrolls, 122
death, 162, 276, 278–281
death narrative, in Gospels, 190
Decalogue (Ten Commandments), 87–88, 132
declaration of nullity, 310–311
denomination, 62
diocese, 208, 291, 292
disciple, 157, 167, 172–173, 178, 320–336
discipleship, 178–210, 232–251, 252–282, 298, 320–336
Disciples of Christ, 213
divorce, 310
Documents of Vatican II, 13, 66, 112, 116, 131, 155, 214, 223, 249, 256, 287, 297

dogma, 56
Dome of the Rock, 102
Donovan, Jean, 300
doxology, 68
Duchesne, St. Philippine, 303

E

early Church, 182, 197, 204–205
Easter, 220–221
Easter Vigil, 221, 243–244
ecclesia, 204–205
ecumenical council, 206, 297
ecumenism, 206, 213–214
editing, 113
encyclical, 297
environment, 20
environmental responsibility, 20–22
Epiphany, 220
epistle, 182
Essenes, 122
eternal life, 157, 170–171, 178–179, 276, 279, 329
Eucharist, Sacrament of the, 189, 201, 207, 227, 234, 237, 240, 243, 248–257, 287
  Real Presence, 250–251, 254
  roots of, 249–251
Eucharistic Prayer, 254
evangelist, 155
evangelization, 2–13
examination of conscience, 273
Exile, the, 94–95, 124
Exodus, the, 85, 86–88, 132, 144, 249
experienced religion, 58

F

faith, 8, 10–11, 13, 16–35, 48, 50–55, 56–73, 74–105, 106–151, 152–175, 175–201, 235, 237, 279–280, 333, 335
faith tradition, 76, 118, 132, 154, 204–231
false gods, 5, 6, 8, 34, 38, 40, 56, 94, 149
First Communion, 243, 248
Fitzgerald, F. Scott, 49
forgiveness, 270–275, 281–283
  (see also God; Jesus Christ)
fortitude, 336
Francis of Assisi, St., 72
free will, 24, 28, 161
freedom, 19, 24–25, 26, 38
friendship, 45, 283
frontier mentality, 43
fruit of the Spirit, 337

G

gender, 27
genetic, 19
genital, 28
Gentiles, 4, 11, 149, 157, 196, 198
gifts of the Spirit, 246
God
  and forgiveness, mercy, 261, 266
  and revelation, 108–127, 130–151
  and sin, 260–263, 266
  and social justice, 133
  and the gift of faith, 48, 73, 235
  at work in our hearts, 38, 41, 73, 237, 302

in the image of, 19, 24, 38, 47, 118, 161, 240, 266
is known to us through Jesus, 6–7, 10, 16, 34, 41–42, 45, 53–54, 105, 112, 130, 154, 157, 160–169, 178, 186, 190, 205, 228, 234, 236–237, 240, 257, 260, 266
is love, 6, 7, 16, 41–42, 45, 47–48, 77, 78, 109, 110, 112, 118, 130, 131, 154, 160–169, 170, 190, 235, 240, 257, 260, 266, 305, 320, 336
is one, 77, 140, 150
is the Holy One, 139
Israelites' experience of, 108–109, 114, 130–151, 155
our relationship with, 7, 9, 16, 19, 41, 52, 58, 60, 63, 65, 67–69, 73, 108–109, 110, 117, 128–151, 160–162, 209, 212, 226, 260–261, 263–65, 267, 301, 336
speaks through creation, 135, 160
speaks through history, 74–105, 130, 160, 181
speaks through Scripture, 108–127, 130, 201
Good Friday, 190, 221
"good news," (the gospel), 7–8, 16, 34, 42, 154–158, 160–162, 178–201, 208–209, 236, 320
gospel, 4, 7–8, 10, 16, 34, 42, 154–162, 178–201, 204, 208–209, 253, 320
and Gospels, 186–195
Gospels, 186–195
John, 189
Luke, 188
Mark, 187
Matthew, 187
Synoptic, 187, 188, 189
types of literature in, 190–195
grace, 10, 19, 36–49, 110, 173, 231, 242, 246, 265, 276, 323, 328
gratitude, 133, 140, 142, 250, 254
Greek and Roman rule, over the Jews, 97–99
Greek language, and the New Testament, 97
Gregorian chant, 223

H

hagiography, 191
Hanakkah, 145
happiness, 38, 40, 42, 46, 73, 159
healing miracles of Jesus, 192–193
heaven, 44, 162, 171, 265, 328
Hebrew Scriptures, 96, 106–120, 121–127
Hebrews, 76–100, 106–151
hell, 328
hierarchy, 289–297
history narrative, in the Gospels, 190–191
holiness, 47, 183, 326, 328
Holocaust, the, 100, 105
Holy Communion, 243, 249, 251, 255
holy days of obligation, 222
Holy Family, 220
Holy of Holies, 102–103
Holy Orders, Sacrament of, 227, 287–288, 289–297
Holy Scripture (see Bible; Old Testament; New Testament)
Holy Spirit, 10, 41, 162–164, 171, 173, 178, 188, 195–197, 207, 211, 215–216, 226, 228, 236–239, 242–247, 273, 301, 304, 320–321, 334, 336

Holy Thursday, 221
homily, 201, 253
homosexuality, 29, 312
hope, 335
humanity,
called to relationship, 19
created in God's image, 19
created to love, 162
humanity of Jesus, 165–171, 188, 279
hypocrisy, 137, 167

I

identity, 14–35, 240
idolatry, 56, 149
Ignatius of Loyola, St., 322
immaculate conception, 333
image of God, 19, 24, 47, 161, 240, 266
incarnation, 54, 155, 164, 220
indwelling, 245
indissolubility, 310
infallibility, 296–297
infancy narrative, in Gospels, 195
infant Baptism, 240
infanticide, 313
initiation, 234, 239–240, 246
inspired, inspiration, 116
intellectual responsibility, 23
intercession, 327
intimacy, 29
Isaiah the prophet, 92–93
Islam, 102
Israel, 7, 90, 74–103, 110, 148, 167
Israelis and Palestinians, 102–103
Israelites (See also Hebrews; Jews)
and God, 109–111, 130–151, 260
and salvation history, 74–103, 105, 126, 130
and time, 82
history of, 83–100

J

Jerome, St., 119, 126
Jerusalem
center of Judaism, 135, 140, 144, 165, 195
fall of, 90, 124, 147, 148, 189
unification of, 102
Jesus Christ, 152–175
and discipleship (following Jesus), 10, 16, 42, 167, 210, 234–251, 260–261, 268, 298, 305, 318–336
and fullness of life, 34, 53, 157, 159, 188, 190, 234, 260, 320, 323, 331
and prayer, 60
and sin/forgiveness/reconciliation, 260, 261, 266, 267
and the apostles, 288, 294
and the Pharisees and Sadducees, 147–148, 158, 169
and the poor, 166
and the Roman rulers, 98, 169
as a Jew, 130, 154, 204, 333
as God's love, 16, 45, 53, 112, 130, 154, 160–163, 169–170, 190, 234, 236, 242, 257, 260–261, 266
as God's saving grace, 10, 41, 53, 130, 163–164, 169–170, 172, 178, 190, 193, 242, 257, 260–261, 266, 331
as God–with–us, 228, 279
as head of the Church, 289
as Messiah, 105, 172–174, 187, 188, 193, 201
as teacher, 194
as the Lamb of God, 86
as the New Adam, 165

as the risen Lord, 170–174, 178–179, 181, 226, 236, 248, 257, 267, 276, 281, 287, 324, 327
as the Savior, 154, 161, 188–189, 193, 333
as the turning point of history, 100, 154, 198, 323
as the Ultimate Sacrament, 228, 250
as the Word of God, 112, 118, 131, 253, 266, 333
ascension of, 171
baptism of, 165, 220
call of, 320, 323
commandment of, 166
death of, 162, 169, 190, 276, 279–280
humanity and divinity of, 155, 163–169, 279
life of, 164–169, 180, 276
miracles of, 167, 192–193
parables of, 194
Real Presence of, 251, 254–257
resurrection of, 162, 170–171, 276, 279–280
return of, 182
sayings of, 192
temptations of, 165
the revelation of God, 7, 10, 34, 41–42, 45, 54, 112, 154–155, 170, 178, 190, 205, 260, 266
the Son of God, 6, 54, 112, 154, 160–162, 164, 186, 193, 235
Jews, and God, 74–151
Jewish and Gentile Christians, 198
Jewish faith tradition, 74–151, 154, 204, 288
Jewish religious feasts, 144–145, 333
Jewish rites and rituals, 128–151
Jewish spirituality, and gratitude, 142, 250
John the Baptist, 165
John, the Gospel according to, 189
John Paul II, 104, 163, 213, 297, 312, 313
John XXIII, 206, 297
John 3:16, 160–162
Jordan River, 102
Joseph, foster-father of Jesus, 165
Joseph, son of Jacob and Rachel, 84
Judaism, 74–151
Judeo–Christian, 76, 130, 150
judge, 89
justice, 335

K

kairos time, 81
King David, 90, 124, 164
King Saul, 90
King Solomon, 90
kingdom of God (presence of God), 82, 166, 187, 194, 320, 321, 323, 329
Kingdoms of Israel and Judah, 94
kings, leaders of Israel, 89
Kino, Fr. Eusebio Francisco, 17
Kolbe, St. Maximilian, 277
kosher, 141

L

land, importance of, 89, 102–103
Last Supper, the (Lord's Supper), 219, 248–250, 252, 254
Law (Torah), 96, 115, 121, 123, 137, 145, 147–148, 169
lay people, 298–316
laying on of hands, 136, 237, 243
leadership in the Catholic Church, 289–297

Lent, 220
Leo XIII, Pope, 295
Letters of the New Testament, 182–185
Levites, 148
life in Christ, 238, 320–336
life questions, 52–53
linear time, 80
literal truth, 117
literary forms in the Bible 120, 190–195
liturgia, 216
liturgical calendar, 219–222
liturgical colors, 222
liturgy, 136, 201, 216–218, 223
Liturgy of the Eucharist, 254–255
Liturgy of the Word, 253
Lord's Prayer, 255
Lord's Supper, the (Last Supper), 219, 248–250, 252, 254
love (See God; Jesus Christ)
in family, 314–316
our love of God, 16, 41, 47, 131, 140, 264–265, 267, 271, 286–315, 320–336
our love of Jesus, 10, 16, 42, 167, 210, 260–261, 267, 286–316, 320–336
our love of others, 131, 133, 140, 264–265, 267, 271, 286–315
unconditional love, 41, 45, 109–110, 130, 166, 231, 260, 267–268
real love, 46, 298
virtue of, 45, 335
loving God and others, 264–265, 267–268, 271, 283, 286–315, 320–336
Luke, the Gospel according to, 188–189, 331, 333

M

MacKillop, Mary (Mother), 39
magisterium, 296–297
Mark, the Gospel according to, 187, 189
marks (characteristics) of the Church, 205
Marriage, Matrimony, 28, 130, 227, 298–299, 306–315
as a permanent commitment, 310–311
martyr, 180, 281
martyrdom, 323
martyrs of Uganda, 325
Mary, 54, 164, 195, 331–334
Mass, 201, 248–249, 252–257
parts of, 252–257
roots of, 253
Matthew, the Gospel according to, 187, 189
maturity, 22, 25, 31–32, 35
mercy, 261, 271, 281–283
Messiah, 96, 135, 144, 172–174, 187, 188, 195, 201, 333
miracle, 167
miracles of Jesus, 192–193
mission of the Church, 13, 158, 197
missionary, 4, 13, 17, 33, 197
monarchy, 90
monsignor, 292
moral (cardinal) virtues, 335–336
mortal sin, 262–263
Moses, 85–88, 132
mosque, 102
Mount Sinai, 87–88, 132
Muslims, 102
myth, 6

N

nature religions, 79
need for God, 7, 9, 16, 19, 24, 34, 40–42, 45–48, 73
neediness, **43**, 52, 156
needs, human, 43–47, 156
new Israel, 167
New Testament, 113, 176–201
  Acts of the Apostles, 196–198, 253
  and liturgy, 201, 253
  and sin, 261, 264
  and the disciples' experience of Jesus, 178–181
  Book of Revelation, 198–199, 253
  canon, 181
  formation of, 181
  Gospels, 186–195, 253
  Letters, 182–185, 253
Nicene Creed, 212
normative (canonical), **125**

O

obedience, **301**
O'Connor, Flannery, 225
office (responsibility of the pope), 296
oil (chrism), 242
oil of catechumens, 242
Old Testament, 113–114, 116–127, 186
  and Israel's experience of God, 108–110
  and revelation, 110–127
  books of, 121–124
  canon, 125
  formation of, 113–115, 125
Ordinary Time, 220–221
ordination, 288
original sin, 162, 239
Orthodox Church, 213

P

Palestine, 7, 88–99, 100–103
Palestinians and Israelis, 102–103
Palm Sunday, 190
papacy, **294–297**
parable, 166, **194**
parousia, **182**
paschal mystery, **228**
Passion of Christ, 190
passions, 31
Passover, 85–86, 136, **144**, 221, 249–250, 252, 333
patriarch, 83
Paul, St., 4–5, 11, 16, 158, 163, 179, 196–197, 264, 309
Paul VI, Pope, 10, 325
penance, 275
Penance, Sacrament of, 227, **270–275**
  elements (steps), 273–275
  history of, 270
penitent, 271
Pentateuch, 123
Pentecost, **144**, 173, 221, 334
personal relationship with Jesus Christ, 10, 16, 42, 167, 234–235, 237–239, 261, 320
personal responsibility, 24–26
Pesah (Passover), 144
Peter, St., 168, 179, 267, 288, 294, 296
Petrine office (papacy), 294–297
Pharisees, **147**, 158, 159
physical responsibility, 18–19
Pierre Toussaint, 241
poor, the, 142, 146, 150, 166
pope, **208**, 294–297

poverty, chastity, and obedience, 293, **301**
practiced religion, **59–60**
prayer, 56–57, 59–60, 67–71, 142–143, 145, 254–255, 323
  Eucharistic Prayer, 254
  Thanksgiving Prayer of Passover, 250
priest/priests, **148**, 270–272, 281, 287–291, 293
private revelation, **331**
prophet(s), **92–93**, 131, 133, 137, 140, 166, 205
Protestantism, 213
prudence, **336**
Psalms, 124
public revelation, **331**
purgatory, **328**

Q

Qumran, 122

R

rabbi, **148**
Real Presence of Jesus, in the Eucharist, 250, 254–255, 257
reconcile, **266**
reconciliation, 231, 266–268, 283
Reconciliation, Sacrament of, **270** (see Penance)
Reformation, 213
reign of God, 157, 167, 170, 171
relationship with Jesus, 10, 16, 42, 167, 210, 234–239, 261
relationships with others, 27–32, 45–46, 140, 261, 263–265, 267, 271, 283, 286–315
religion, 38, 53, **58–60**
  as part of life, 9
  experienced, 58
  practiced, 59
  purpose of, 53
religious communities, 301, 304–305
religious life, 298
religious order, **293**
religious practices of the Jews, 135–145
responding to God, 59, 301
responsibility, **16–35**
  and sin, 260–275
  as responding to life, 17
  environmental, 20–22
  intellectual, 23
  personal, 24–26
  physical, 18–19
  sexual, 27–31, 313–315
  social, 32–33
resurrection of Jesus, 157, 170, 171, 178, 179
reveal, **109**
revelation, **110**
  and Scripture, 106–129
  as God's gift of self, 108–112, 116
  private/public, **331**
Revelation, Book of, 198–199
reverent, **8**
right to life, 313
Rite of Christian Initiation, 221, 234
rites and rituals, **135–151**
ritual, **59**, 225
ritual cleanliness, 141
Roman Rule over the Jews, 98–99
Rosary, 229, 275, 331

S

Sabbath (*Shabbat*), 138–139
sacrament, **224**
sacramental, **229**

sacraments, 59, 128, 136, 207–208, 226–228, 232–283
Sacraments of Christian Initiation, 232–257, 267
  Baptism, 239–242
  Confirmation, 243–247
  Eucharist, 248–251
Sacraments of Christian Life, 284–317
  Holy Orders, 287–297
  Matrimony, 306–317
Sacraments of Reconciliation and Healing, 258–283
  Anointing of the Sick, 276–281
  Penance, 270–275
sacred, **47**
sacred places, 102
sacred time, **79**
sacrifice, **137**, 140, 249
Sadducees, **147**, 169
saint, **326**
sainthood, 326–336
  Mary, the perfect saint, 331–334
salvation, **40** (see God; Jesus Christ)
salvation history, 78, 74–103, 105, 110, 112, 114, 128–151, 152–175
Saul, King, 90
sayings of Jesus, 192
scribes, **148**, 169
Scripture (see also Bible)
  and God's revelation of himself, 106–127
  and liturgy, 201, 253
  and sin, 260–261, 264
  reading of, 201, 253
seal of the sacrament, **274**
searching faith, **61–62**
Second Vatican Council, 206, 214, 252, 297
self-awareness, 24, 27–28
self-image, 18–20
service, 210, 240
sex, 28–29, 314
  and marriage, 312
sexual orientation, **29**
sexual responsibility, 27–31, 314
sexuality, **27–31**
  and celibacy, 293
  and the vow of chastity, 301
Shabbat (Sabbath), **138–139**
Shavu'ot (Pentecost), 145
Sign of the Cross, 229, 324
signs and symbols, 135–136, 224
  of Baptism, 242
  of Confirmation, 244
signs of the Spirit, 247
sin, 193, **260–275**
single life, **299–305**
sinning mortally, 262–263
sinning venially, 262–263
Six Day War, 102
social justice, **133**, 295
social responsibility, 32–33
society, as a gift, 21
Solomon, King, 90
sorrow for sin, 273
spiritual truth, **117**
spoken tradition, **114**, 181
Stein, Edith (Saint Teresa Benedicta), 104
Stephen, St., 180, 191
suffering and death, 276, 278–281
Sukkot, 147
Sunday, 138–139, 219
synagogue, **96**, 182, 201, 253
synod, **297**
Synoptic Gospels, 187, **188**, 189

T

Taizé 215
Tatanka Yotanka (Sitting Bull), 146
tax collectors, of Israel, 149
teaching authority of the Church, 296–297
teenagers
  and homelessness, 26
  and needs, 45
  and sex, 28–31
temperance, **335**
temple, **95**, 99, 102–103, 140
temple worship, 140
temptations of Jesus, 165
Ten Commandments, 87–88, 132, 264, 273
testament, **114**
Thanksgiving Prayer, of Passover meal, 250
theocracy, **90**
theological virtues, **335**
time,
  and the Israelites, 82–83
  cyclic, 79
  kairos, 81–82
  linear, 80
  sacred, 79
Torah, **96**, 115, 121, 123, 137, 144, 148
Toussaint, Pierre, 241
tradition and Tradition, **204**
Tradition
  and Judaism, 74–151, 154, 204
  and the Catholic Church, 204–231
Triduum, 220–221
Trinity, 41, 57, 162–163, 197, 226, 238, 242, 331
Twelve, the, 294 (see disciples, apostles)
twelve tribes of Israel, 148, 167

U

ultimate source (God), **40**
ultimate sacrament (Jesus), 228
unchurched, 66
unconditional love, 41, 45, 109–110, 130, 166, 231, 240, 260, 267–268
unity of Christians, 213–214
unity of the faith, 297

V

Vatican, the, **294**
Vatican II, 206, 214, 251, 297
venial sin, **262–263**
viaticum, **281**
Vicar of Christ, 296
virtues, **335–336**
vocation, 284–317
vows, 293, 301

W

wholeness, 40, 53
  and holiness, 47
word of God (see Bible)
Word of God (see Jesus Christ)
worship, 59–60, 67–71, 128–151, 156, 202–231
written tradition, **114**, 181

X

Xavier, St. Francis, 17, 33

Y

YHWH, **139**
Yom Kippur, 145
youth ministry, 290